STUDIES IN GREEK AND ROMAN HISTORY

TO MY WIFE

Who never reads any of them

STUDIES IN
GREEK AND ROMAN
HISTORY

by E. BADIAN

M.A., LITT.D., D.PHIL.

BARNES & NOBLE · M · CM · LXVIII

PRINTED IN GREAT BRITAIN

Contents

Preface

THIS book was first planned by Sir Basil Blackwell to cheer me during a long and serious illness. I should like to record my gratitude to him both for the original idea and for persevering with it when my health was said to be improving. The selection—a task that should never be left entirely to the author—is based on a *prokrisis* by Mr P. A. Brunt, though the final choice, on criteria of both quality and accessibility, is my own. Mr Brunt has throughout helped me with his usual generosity, particularly during a time when I was unable to do much myself.

The articles and reviews have not undergone any major revision. Minor errors (where known to me) have been eliminated and some small changes have been made, particularly where I can no longer defend the views I originally advanced. References to recent literature have been added, where this seemed specially useful. Deletions and verbal changes have not been indicated; additions are in square brackets. The titles of journals are abbreviated—as they always ought to be, were it not for editors' whims —in accordance with the system used in *L'Année philologique*, with slight modifications to accord with common usage in this country. (These will cause no difficulties.)

My thanks are due to all the editors and publishers who have kindly consented to republication in this form, in some cases not long after the original appearance of the work concerned. I should also like to take this opportunity of thanking them for the patience and courtesy that they have invariably shown in their dealings with me.

Academic indebtedness has (I hope) been duly recorded in each instance. But I must here specially stress how much I (and many of my contemporaries) owe to the late Friedrich Münzer and to my teacher, Sir Ronald Syme, the pioneers and masters of prosopographic method; to Professor T. R. S. Broughton, who has made its proper application to the history of the Roman Republic possible; and to the late Maurice Holleaux, whose work on the relations of the Roman Republic with the East will never be improved, except in details to which he did not attend or through the discovery of evidence unknown to him.

I dare hardly hope that the way in which I have followed in the footsteps of these and other masters will not be considered altogether unworthy of them.

Finally, I am happy to acknowledge my great debt, both personal and academic, to Professor Eric Birley, *amicus certus in re incerta*. Without his encouragement, most of these studies would not have been written.

September 1963   E. B.

Notes on Roman Policy in Illyria
(230–201 B.C.)

THE history of the relations of the Roman Republic with the kings, tribes, and cities of Illyria cannot at present be written, as the evidence does not permit the construction of a coherent and comprehensive account. This, perhaps, is why scholars have often tended to neglect the subject,[1] and have thereby been led into serious errors in dealing with the history of Roman expansion and early imperial organization. It is the aim of this paper to set out what conclusions can be reached on some important aspects of the subject, and to indicate the way in which these conclusions may be related to the general study of Roman foreign policy during its most interesting period.

I

Holleaux has shown (on present evidence beyond refutation) that Rome had no Eastern policy or aspirations until she was drawn into the First Illyrian War.[2] It is at this point, therefore, that we must take up our study (with Rome the greatest power in the West, but as yet barely on the political horizon of the Hellenistic East) and consider the origins of that war which first turned Rome towards the Eastern Mediterranean.[3]

The Illyrian tribe of the Ardiaei, forced south by Celtic pressure, had rapidly conquered its neighbours and by 230 controlled an extensive empire east of the Adriatic. It was, however, far from being a civilized state, and the Greeks regarded it as a scourge. But Demetrius II of Macedon was skilful enough to turn the rise of this new power to his advantage: in 231 he obtained the Illyrian king Agron's help[4] against the Aetolians, who were then trying to force the Acarnanian city of Medeon to join their League. The Illyrians put 5000 men ashore from their *lembi*—swift little boats, which they used with equal success as pirate craft and as troop transports—and, marching inland, defeated the

Aetolian army besieging the town. The best soldiers in Greece, who had beaten off the Celtic invader, had succumbed to the new barbarian enemy. At this point Agron died and his wife Teuta, it seems, was made regent for his son Pinnes, who must have been a small child.[5] She or her advisers, encouraged by their recent success, embarked on what appears to have been no longer a raid, but a policy of southward expansion. In 230 a force was sent south on *lembi*, to all appearance bent on another of the usual raids on Peloponnese. But this time Scerdilaidas—a dynast about whom we shall have more to say later—was sent overland over the Aous pass to invade Epirus with 5000 men and meet the force disembarked from the boats. The latter had in the meantime put in at Phoenice (on the pretext of buying provisions) and, with the help of some Celtic mercenaries stationed there, had captured the city. The Epirot army, forced to send a detachment against Scerdilaidas, was defeated by the Illyrians and Northern Epirus occupied.[6] But not long after, an Achaeo-Aetolian relief force arrived at Helicranum (near Phoenice), summoned by the appeals of the Epirots. The Illyrians, marching out from Phoenice, in vain offered battle: the Greeks, in superior positions, thought they had no reason to risk defeat. Strategically this was no doubt sound; but politically it was unwise. The Illyrians arranged a truce with the Epirots and (probably on receiving the promise of an alliance) withdrew northward, to crush a rebellion by some tribes. Teuta must have thought the result of that short campaign highly satis-factory: Epirus and with it Acarnania (so far as it was not Aeto-lian) became allies of the Illyrians, after seeing that no Greek force had dared to meet them in the field. In addition, it seems, the Epirots had had to cede Atintania, the important territory round the Aous-Drynon gorges: its cession, laying Epirus open to inva-sion from the north, must have been a pledge for the promised alliance and then for the continued fidelity of the new allies.[7]

But it was this campaign which led to Roman intervention. Piracy had always been a legitimate pursuit among the Illyrians, and Italian shipping had not been exempt. But Rome, though the leader of the Italian Confederacy and (since the defeat of Carth-age) the greatest naval power, had not been willing to undertake the troublesome task of policing the seas for the benefit of her allies. And, having no Eastern ambitions, she had ignored the activities of the Illyrians. In 230 this attitude suddenly changed. While the Illyrians were occupying Northern Epirus, their *lembi* had intercepted many Italian traders crossing the Adriatic. This time the Senate decided to take the matter more seriously and sent C. and L. Coruncanius to the Queen-Regent. They found her besieging the Greek island-city of Issa, perhaps the only Adriatic island not under her control. She listened to their complaints and promised to guarantee the Romans—i.e. the Italians—immunity from all public action by her navy, but said that she could not prevent private acts of piracy—a recognized way of earning a livelihood. It seemed that the way to negotiation lay open, especially as no mention appears to have been made of an indemnity. But the envoys now delivered what was in effect a declaration of war. On their return journey one of them was murdered—by the Queen's orders, it was naturally said. If war had not previously been decided upon, it was now inevitable. For the first time Rome was involved in war east of the Adriatic.

The reasons for this sudden development have often been discussed. At one time it was fashionable to make the war part of a deep-laid Roman plan for expansion and regard it as the logical consequence of the defeat of the Western enemy. Holleaux showed such theories to be untenable and substituted for them his own account (reproducing that of Polybius) of a Senate unwillingly drawn into an unwelcome entanglement by a barbarian ruler behaving γυναικοθύμως καὶ ἀλογίστως.[8] Since then the 'imperialist' theory has at times been revived, but never with much success.[9] Holleaux has proved that for a generation after the Illyrian War nothing was further from the minds of the *Patres* than schemes for Eastern expansion; and this demonstration still stands, even if we have to reject many of his views on the war itself—as indeed we do.

The Roman decision to take action at that precise time is, on his thesis, left unexplained; and so, even more clearly, is the scale on which action was taken. The Roman case, which the Coruncanii had to present to Teuta, was very poor: if previously Rome might with good reason have complained of injuries inflicted on her allies by pirates, she now had to demand satisfaction for what was in fact a legitimate operation of war. If Italian blockade-runners carried cargoes to the enemy the Illyrian forces were then fighting (whether the war was one of aggression is irrelevant), the Illyrians can hardly be blamed for interfering. Italians, as we know, were given to blockade-running (then as now a profitable operation) under the protection of the Roman name; on one occasion they had almost precipitated a major war by their activities.[10] But that time there had been a peaceful settlement. This time there was not—through no fault of the Queen's, whose answer, as even Polybius' hostile account reveals, was as conciliatory as it could be. The insulting reply of the Roman envoy made it impossible.[11] It is clear enough from Polybius' narrative that the ambassadors, though not the Senate, had decided upon war.[12] And we have no reason to assume that, if they had returned unscathed and reported, war would not have broken out: they had been sent ἐπίσκεψιν ποιησόμενοι,[13] and we know from many second-century examples that the Senate usually accepted the recommendations of its commissioners.

What, then, had made the Coruncanii decide upon war, seeing that they had not had instructions to bring it about? To be able to answer this question we must first ask what precisely had been the purpose of their mission. There was no need for an ἐπίσκεψις on the Illyrian attacks on Italian shipping—the facts were plain and widely confirmed. Holleaux therefore rejects Polybius, in this one instance, and believes that the ambassadors were sent to demand satisfaction and exact guarantees.[14] On that hypothesis, as we have tried to point out, events become difficult to understand. But once we admit (only in a somewhat wider sènse) their task of ἐπίσκεψις, everything is much clearer. They were sent, above all, on a mission of investigation into a part of the world of which the Senate probably knew little. And their investigation convinced them that the state of affairs they found constituted a danger to Rome. It has been urged that this was because of the Illyrian kingdom's Macedonian connections. But this hypothesis is not needed; for the recent successes of that kingdom and the terrible impression they had made on the mind of Greece[15] must have made it appear much more formidable than it was later seen to be. Indeed, the scale of the Roman operation that followed is evidence that this was so: the forces finally sent out consisted of 20,000 infantry, 2000 cavalry, and 200 ships. This strong deployment has baffled scholars and cannot be explained by

Holleaux,[16] who thinks it due to Roman fear of Macedon, although (as he himself points out) there is no evidence for an anti-Macedonian policy on the part of Rome; and the later settlement of Illyria shows (cf. below) that fear of Macedon cannot have been one of the motives for the expedition. The simplest explanation is the best. The events in Epirus, reflected in numerous Italian reports about Illyrian strength, decided the Senate to send a mission of inquiry, but do no more. This mission convinced itself of the reality of the danger and, deciding that war would be necessary, used the *rerum repetitio* in that way (familiar to students of Roman history) which implied war. As it happened, one of the envoys was later killed. But the ἀληθεστάτη πρόφασις of the war lay deeper: it was the usual Roman fear of strong neighbours and (as so often) was based on a misapprehension.

At the beginning of the campaigning season of 229,[17] Teuta, having been warned of the Roman attack, took the only measures that offered any hope against it: she attempted to forestall it by seizing the landing places along the Illyrian coast which were not yet under her control—Epidamnus and Apollonia—as well as Corcyra, the key to the southern flank of her position and to the Epirot coast. Her troops all but succeeded in seizing Epidamnus and then sailed on to Corcyra, where they landed and laid siege to the city. An Achaeo-Aetolian fleet of ten cataphracts, coming to raise the siege, was intercepted by the Illyrians with the help of their Acarnanian allies and defeated off Paxos; Corcyra surrendered and received a garrison under the dynast of Pharus, the Greek Demetrius. The Illyrians now settled down to besiege Epidamnus.[18] At this point the Roman fleet under Cn. Fulvius Centumalus appeared off Corcyra. Demetrius, who had incurred Teuta's suspicion (perhaps because he had designs on the Illyrian throne), had communicated to the consul his willingness to surrender the island;[19] he kept his word, handed over Corcyra and the garrison, and henceforth helped the Romans against his suzerain. The rest was easy. At Apollonia the army under L. Postumius Albinus joined the fleet, and the city (like Corcyra before it) was received into the Roman *fides*. Next Epidamnus was relieved and similarly treated. Embassies from all over Illyria now met the victorious consuls, and no doubt diplomatic compliments were exchanged. Most important of all, the strong tribes of the Parthini in the north and the Atintanes in the south sent to offer their surrender, which was accepted. Next the island of Issa was relieved and also received *in fidem*, and some minor Ardiaean places along the coast north of Epidamnus were taken. Teuta entrenched herself at Rhizon, and the consuls, having put Demetrius in charge of the conquered Illyrian territory, returned to Epidamnus. One consul now left for Rome with the greater part of the forces (seen to be unnecessary), while the other stayed behind and in the following spring granted Teuta terms.[20]

It is the terms of this peace that we must next consider; for on this subject the gravest errors seem to have been committed by some modern scholars, with the effect that the history of an important period in Roman foreign policy has (I would urge) been constructed on imaginary foundations. According to the Polybian account, which most historians profess in the main to be following, Teuta agreed to pay tribute, gave up most of Illyria, and undertook never to send more than two ships (and those unarmed) south of Lissus. The 'tribute' was probably a war indemnity payable in instalments.[21] As for the rest, it is said that Polybius or his source did not know the extent of Illyrian territory, and that some important terms have been omitted. We must therefore next inquire what were the boundaries of the territories the Queen ceded; and the state of our evidence makes this question not at all easy to answer. The accepted theory is that the Illyrian kingdom lost all its possessions south of the parallel of Lissus, and that all these territories became a Roman protectorate.[22] We shall consider the latter statement first, as its falsity can (it seems) be demonstrated. Polybius' narrative mentions only the following as received into the *fides* ('friendship', etc., we may take to mean the same) of Rome: Corcyra, Apollonia, Epidamnus, the Parthini, the Atintanes, Issa. In addition, we are told that from Epidamnus the Romans προῆγον εἰς τοὺς εἴσω τόπους τῆς Ἰλλυρίδος, ἅμα καταστρεφόμενοι τοὺς Ἀρδιαίους, and that on its way from Epidamnus to Issa the fleet took πόλεις τινὰς Ἰλλυρίδας ἐν τῷ παράπλῳ κατὰ κράτος. Zippel rightly explains τοὺς εἴσω τόπους τῆς Ἰλλυρίδος as referring, not to the interior, but to the country north of Epidamnus;[23] and there is no mention of either conquest or voluntary surrender of any other tribe or city. In fact, Polybius, when recording the embassies that flocked to meet the

Romans, makes it clear that only the Parthini and Atintanes offered and were allowed to surrender *in fidem*.[24] The list of tribes and cities given by Holleaux[25] and generally accepted as forming the Roman 'protectorate' is therefore largely imaginary and the usual map of the protectorate entirely misleading. The protectorate consisted of the cities of Apollonia and Epidamnus and their territory, the islands of Corcyra and Issa, and the tribes of the Parthini and Atintanes. If there was more, we do not know it; but we have no reason to assume that there would be much,[26] and in any case it would not form a continuous strip of territory from Lissus to the mainland facing Corcyra. In addition, however, Demetrius of Pharus had become a client of Rome.

It is generally believed that the Illyrian dominions after 228 (i.e. the territory later under Demetrius' control) must have been north of Lissus, both because of the boundary at sea ('Fahrtgrenze') imposed by the Romans and because of their protectorate over the South.[27] But if we are right in denying the existence of a continuous protectorate, the 'Fahrtgrenze' alone does not justify any conclusion at all as to the 'Landesgrenze'.[28] What made the Illyrians dangerous (as Polybius tells us) was chiefly their navy; and with the latter kept well **north of** the Straits of Hydruntum that danger was gone—though it is to be noted, as bearing on any discussion of the causes of the war, that apparently nothing was done to safeguard Italian shipping in the Adriatic. On land, with the Parthini in the north and the Atintanes in the south barring its way, and a chain of Greek cities no doubt ready to report any signs of activity to Rome, the kingdom could never again aspire to be a great power. Thus we can take the territorial provisions of the treaty as they are implied by Polybius and expressed by Appian and need not assume that Rome detached from Illyria any more territory than had already surrendered to her; the remainder of the South remained dependent on the kingdom, though (especially in view of the 'Fahrtgrenze') this dependence would be difficult to maintain and in practice vary with the strength of the central government. But that was of the essence of barbarian kingdoms and would not be unwelcome to Rome. There is in fact some evidence (often ignored) suggesting that the regions concerned remained attached to the kingdom. Appian, when recording Demetrius' later anti-Roman activities, credits him with having

caused a Histrian war and an Atintanian revolt.[29] The Histrian
war (whatever we think of Demetrius' share in it) is historical (see
below); and the Atintanian revolt must come from the same
source and should probably be accepted. But in this case 'revolt'
cannot mean open warfare: in the circumstances of the time and
the position of the Atintanes (see below) it can only mean that
Demetrius, who is accused of having revolted against the Romans,
succeeded in again bringing them into some sort of dependence
on the Illyrian kingdom (i.e. himself). This he can hardly have
done, if the latter extended only as far as the 'Lissus line', as a
glance at the map will show. And though we may postulate a
series of unrecorded encroachments establishing a land connection, it is simpler to reject the Lissus frontier (itself a modern
postulate) and, returning to the sources, to believe that with the
exception of a few districts the Illyrian kingdom extended as far
south as the borders of Atintania.

As for the effect of the war on the positions of Teuta and Demetrius, this is a much more difficult question to answer with any
degree of certainty; for Polybius, our only good source hitherto, is
not interested in Illyrian internal affairs (he never mentions
Pinnes) and our other sources, though at times apparently well
informed, are unreliable. Polybius says that the Queen ceded
nearly all of Illyria and that Demetrius was left in charge of 'most
of the Illyrians'—but the former statement cannot be accurate as
it stands (for all the rest of our evidence shows that Demetrius
remained a vassal of the kingdom), and the latter refers to the
autumn of 229 and is not necessarily implied in the final settlement, where the Pharian is not mentioned. Dio-Zonaras makes
her resign her regency to Demetrius, but elsewhere reports that
she died. Appian says that Pinnes kept all his territories except
those ceded to Roman protection (of which he gives an incomplete list), while Demetrius was given a few places on precarious
tenure because of his untrustworthiness. But the latter statement is
an annalist's *ex post facto* invention and may be dismissed at once.
Scholars have tried to combine the evidence in various ways. De
Sanctis[30] gives Demetrius 'un piccolo dominio' consisting of Lissus
and Pharus—an impossible combination, as Holleaux points out,
and one based on no evidence. Holleaux himself suggests Pharus
and some places in the vicinity, but is wise enough not to insist.[31]

In any case, Demetrius soon supplanted the Queen as regent and married the King's mother Triteuta;[32] and it is perhaps most likely that this was arranged by the Romans in 228, Teuta agreeing to give up the regency and withdrawing to a δυναστεία, such as that of Demetrius had been (it was probably Rhizon, to which she had fled after her defeat in 229—cf. the parallel case of Demetrius and Pharus in 219). This would fit in with Polybius' facts (that she retained only ὀλίγους τόπους), and as his account is probably based on Postumius' own summary,[33] his facts must not be lightly rejected; while on Illyrian constitutional matters his knowledge is obviously as slight as his interest. Moreover, such an arrangement would be very welcome to the Romans, dispelling any fear of the Illyrian kingdom they may still have had and converting the latter, if not into a client state, at least into a state controlled by a client. It is probably thus that the Illyrian settlement was completed.[34]

We have now, as far as our sources will permit, determined the provisions and the immediate effects of the peace of 228. It remains to say a few words on the position of what we have called the Roman protectorate. That the states concerned were left free, i.e. without taxes, garrisons, or governors, is generally agreed.[35] And we need not consider the old idea that they 'counted as *dediticii* enjoying *libertas precaria*';[36] for it has been demolished by Heuss's researches.[37] In consequence, we need no longer assume that a city which (like Corcyra) seems to have been held in some regard by the Romans must have had a treaty,[38] when there is no evidence for any treaties with Illyrian states except for that with Pinnes. The cities and tribes concerned appear to have been left in the position of *amici* of Rome without any formal obligations, but tied to her by the *beneficium* of their liberation—an act which imposed on Rome the moral duty of maintaining their liberty and safeguarding their interests and on them that of showing their gratitude in every possible way. This position, with its legal freedom, must at first have seemed exceptionally favourable, when compared with the constant sacrifices to which Roman allies in Italy were committed; and indeed, it had first been bestowed upon a few specially favoured cities in Sicily.[39] In the case of the Parthini and Atintanes we may think it a mistake to have relied entirely on moral claims (if such was indeed the case); but in

B

view of what Polybius tells us, we cannot help suspecting that
Rome did not particularly care about these or any other Illyrian
tribes.[40] As for the Greek cities, the arrangement turned out
satisfactory for both sides,[41] and this was no doubt largely responsible for the later decision to extend the policy to Greece proper.
The Illyrian protectorate of 228, which we can now, if this presentation has been correct, see in its true shape, marks an important step in the substitution of extra-legal for legal forms of dependence as the favourite method of Roman diplomacy, i.e. in the
application of the idea of *clientela*—that nexus of moral obligations
between the weaker and the stronger (with the interpretation
ultimately in the hands of the latter) which was characteristic of
Roman life—in the sphere of foreign policy.[42] The freedom of the
Illyrian cities, itself descended from that of a few Sicilian cities,
leads directly to the Isthmian proclamation.[43]

This, then, was the result of the First Illyrian War. Roman arms
for the first time turned east and acquired for the Republic a
footing east of the Adriatic, and at the same time Roman diplomacy, following a precedent set some years before, worked out a
system of treating Greek cities which it was to follow, through
success and failure, during the period of imperial expansion. At
the same time (though we must beware of exaggerating the
importance of this) Rome for the first time established diplomatic
contact with the Greek homeland: for the victorious consul sent to
inform the Greeks of what he had done.[44]

II

Having dealt with the Illyrian danger, Rome for several years
shows no further interest in affairs east of the Adriatic. If modern
scholars believe that her friends there, 'though allowed free
self-government ... remained in entire dependence upon the
Republic',[45] this can certainly not have been the opinion of the
men and communities concerned. They must have regarded themselves as free, though in friendly relations with their powerful
neighbour, who had made no attempt to limit that freedom. The
Roman view, however, which at that time they could not have
known, was different again: those who had received from Rome
the signal *beneficium* of their freedom (and other benefits to boot)

were tied to her by bonds that nothing could dissolve, even though they were not those of a contract. The client's moral obligation did not lapse through the patron's additional *beneficium* of neglecting to press his claim. It is this misunderstanding of a peculiarly Roman category of social and political thought (a misunderstanding that was to persist well into the second century and was to have many grave consequences) which underlies the strange events leading to the Second Illyrian War.[46]

Demetrius of Pharus, whatever the extent of his private δυναστεία, succeeded (as we have seen) in taking charge of the Illyrian kingdom, and at first (if we may argue from silence) behaved with sufficient restraint not to attract the attention of his Roman friends or of his Greek enemies. But the continued absence of Roman interest led him to believe that the friendship of Rome was not enough to further his ambitions; and perhaps (as Polybius says) the Gallic invasion of Italy gave him a momentary impression of Roman weakness. Since the settlement of 228, the way to Illyrian southward expansion had been barred by friends of Rome; while eastward expansion, which might have been possible with Roman help or even encouragement, could not be considered in the face of Roman indifference. By helping the Romans against Teuta, he now found he had achieved his object of gaining control of the kingdom only at the cost of making it hardly worth controlling.[47] Left to himself, he could not hope to restore the power of Illyria. Thus he again turned to the Macedonian alliance, which the war and the death of his namesake of Macedon had broken up. At some time in the late twenties[48] he became the ally of Antigonus Doson, who could do with any help in his struggles for the hegemony in Greece and who was no doubt pleased to regain the alliance his predecessor had formed.[49] This was not an action that Rome would necessarily regard as directed against herself, for she was not at that time interested in Macedon; but the man for whom Demetrius won the battle of Sellasia[50] was deeply in his debt and had learnt the value of Illyrian support. Yet Demetrius continued to proceed cautiously: during 221 there is no record of any action by him. Nor does Rome seem to have given him any reason to believe that he was offending her. If he had ever doubted the genuineness of the freedom the Republic allowed its friends, he must now have been convinced of it.

So far we have had no difficulty in accounting for Demetrius' actions. But in 220, if we are to believe Polybius and the consensus of modern opinion, he suddenly went mad and by a series of outrageous acts of aggression against Rome (contrary to his determined, but cautious, policy in the preceding years) brought upon himself Roman intervention and inevitable defeat. It is this series of actions immediately preceding the Second Illyrian War that we must now consider in detail, in the hope of making it more intelligible than it appears in the pages of Polybius. If we succeed, we may also hope to solve some of the difficulties that have baffled scholars about the final settlement following the war.

According to Polybius[51] the danger of a conflict with Carthage had by then become serious and the Senate decided to secure the Roman position in Illyria, especially as Macedon was becoming dangerously strong: Demetrius at the time, contemptuous of Roman strength first because of the Gallic and then because of the Carthaginian danger, had just broken the treaty of 228 by sailing on a piratical expedition far beyond Lissus, and had then made armed attacks on cities in Illyria under Roman protection;[52] in this he had relied on the support of the Macedonian royal house. This short account is, as it stands, quite unacceptable, and Holleaux himself, though he does not question it, recognizes some of its weaknesses.[53] The reference to the Gallic War may be defended as giving us the date of Demetrius' first alliance with Doson, although we do not know of any association between the two before 222, and Doson is most likely to have wanted it in or after 224. As a reason for his final 'defection'[54] in 220 it will not do: if Demetrius knew anything about the Gallic War, he must have known its outcome; and if its beginning taught him to despise the Romans, its progress at any time after 225, and especially its end, must have taught him to respect them. As for the Carthaginian danger, we know that by the summer of 220 war was not by any means certain, and there cannot have been any idea (except in the mind of Hannibal) of how dangerous for Rome the war would turn out to be. If Demetrius was indeed relying on Carthage in his rebellion (and why should an Illyrian prince give much thought to the far West?),[55] he would surely have waited until the next campaigning season (as he had waited in 221) in order to see whether war really broke out. Nor can he, at that particular time, have placed much reliance on the royal house of Macedon, where the youth Philip had recently come to the throne and was facing extreme difficulties.[56] Thus Polybius' account of his motives is untenable. But we cannot even agree with the claim of modern historians that Demetrius was simply relying on that lack of interest in the Adriatic or that 'longanimity' towards his own actions which Rome had shown during the preceding years.[57] For he had not so far done anything that can be described as obviously anti-Roman and seems indeed to have cautiously avoided such actions; while now we find him in the same year attacking cities under Roman protection and ignoring a treaty only eight years old—enough to overstrain the 'longanimity' of any power; the sudden complete change cannot be explained without more positive motives. Yet, what is more, he had recently had a demonstration of Roman power and interest very near home—in 221, after their success in overruning Cisalpine Gaul, the Romans had secured its eastern flank in a victorious campaign against the Histrians. Demetrius could hardly ignore this.[58]

The Polybian account, as expounded by modern historians, requires us, then, to believe that Demetrius, having just observed the conquest of Cisalpine Gaul and Roman operations nearer his own borders in Histria; knowing Roman power as well as anyone east of the Adriatic by his own experience in the First Illyrian War; knowing that at the time Rome had no war on hand (for she had finished in the North and nothing irreparable had been done in the West), but might have a major one within a year or two (for Hannibal had already picked a quarrel with Saguntum); having moreover just heard of the death of his only powerful ally and the accession to the latter's throne of a boy of unknown ability and intentions—that Demetrius chose that precise moment, at which he knew he would stand alone against a great power that was both able and willing to deal with him, for a flagrant breach of a treaty with that power and a series of attacks upon her allies. In modern politics we should be very suspicious of an account accusing a small state of such behaviour at a time that could not have been better chosen as being unfavourable to itself and favourable to its powerful opponent. Yet the evidence in this case consists only in the account of Demetrius' enemy Polybius, based on that of the Senator Fabius. We have seen the failure of this account to explain Demetrius' motives (which it seems to do mainly *ex post facto* and without regard for contemporary probabilities); it is time to scrutinize its statements of fact.

That Demetrius, with the help of Scerdilaidas, sailed beyond Lissus and engaged in some raids in the Ionian and the Aegean (none of them directed against friends of Rome: Epidamnus, Apollonia, and Corcyra, it seems, were carefully avoided, though nearest to home)—that much we must accept; for Polybius in his Greek chapters gives details of their operations.[59] But whether (and for this we have only the word of Polybius, i.e. probably of Fabius)[60] that constituted a violation of the treaty of 228 is a different question. When giving the terms of the treaty,[61] Polybius makes the 'Fahrtgrenze' apply only to Teuta, i.e. (if she signed as Queen-Regent) at the most to the Illyrian kingdom. There is nothing to suggest that the Queen promised (what, as she herself had once said, no Illyrian ruler could hope to perform) that it would apply to every Illyrian in his private capacity. Demetrius' forces, however, were not those of the kingdom, but those of his private δυναστεία; we can see this by comparing their numbers with those under Scerdilaidas and by the very fact that the latter appears on the expedition as the equal of Demetrius.[62] Thus it is doubtful whether the raid did infringe the treaty of 228; and considering the Illyrians' care in avoiding the known friends of Rome, and the fact that Rome at the time had certainly shown no intention of making herself the general protecting power over all the Greeks, it seems very probable that the raiders, at any rate, did not think they were breaking the treaty. Demetrius probably did not see so very much difference between fighting Greeks on land at Sellasia and fighting them from the sea in the Aegean—if the former had not caused Rome any concern, why should the latter? At the most he might expect a rebuke (and an annalist, in building up the story, in fact made the Romans rebuke him first and take action against him only for contumacy);[63] but he had no reason to think that he, who had become Rome's friend by serving her so well only a few years ago and had since then been given no indication that he was not still thus considered, would provoke an immediate attack by Rome's full strength.

The other charge against him was that he was 'destroying and subduing the cities in Illyria subject to Rome'; and the annalist adds that he was doing so 'by abusing the friendship of Rome'.[64] It would be tempting to use this last statement as evidence for the view that Demetrius did not consider himself to be provoking Rome, but on the contrary thought of himself as Rome's watchdog (such as Massinissa and to some extent Eumenes were to be later). But we can only suggest that as a possibility; for the source is too bad to be used with any confidence. However, we have seen how unlikely the Fabio-Polybian picture of his suddenly storming one after another of the cities under Roman protection is made by the historical background. Here again, as in the case of the motives ascribed to him, we have evidence of later manufacture: the phrase τὰς ὑπὸ 'Ρωμαίους ταττομένας can hardly be contemporary (and certainly not contemporary Greek), as the cities and tribes concerned were not theoretically in the position of subjects at all (see above), while there had been no evidence during the preceding years that they were practically thus regarded. It was this war that was first to provide such evidence. As it happens, we can probably glimpse the foundations on which this charge was raised; for when Demetrius heard that the Romans were about to attack him (we are told), he put his own faction in power in all the cities.[65] The cities concerned are clearly places not yet under his influence; for in the others, though ἀντιπολιτευόμενοι might exist, his φίλοι would certainly be in charge of the government. Thus we see that what Demetrius had in fact done was to encourage the rise of parties favourable to himself (they may well have been the pro-Roman parties) in the territory of Rome's friends—i.e. among the Parthini and Atintanes[66]—and thus pursue his plan of strengthening his own power without attacking Rome. It is obvious that he had been doing this for some years and did not suddenly start in 220; for by the beginning of 219, at the latest, all was ready for the *coup d'état*. But it was only in 220 that the Romans suddenly decided to take notice and charged him with trying to subdue the cities by force—if indeed even the charge was in fact made.

In 220 (as we have seen, the moment most favourable to themselves and least so to Demetrius) the Romans suddenly decided to act. War with Carthage seemed to be at hand, and although they had as many friends in Illyria as they had at one time thought necessary, the most important of those friends had shown that he regarded himself as independent, even if not hostile to Rome. As Polybius implies, he had forgotten his station as a client.[67] But it would not do to have an independent power of some strength on one's eastern flank (the very fear that had brought on the war with Teuta), especially if war was to be waged in the West. It is said that, behind the 'middle power' of Demetrius, Rome feared the great power of Macedon, and it is likely that some far-sighted senators did see this danger. But, despite the statement of Polybius (perhaps again written *ex post facto*) and his modern followers,[68] it was again not a motive for action. For the settlement again shows that Macedon was not the danger against which protection was felt to be needed (see below), and the years following it confirm this view. Besides, if Rome had indeed thought ἀνθοῦσαν τὴν Μακεδόνων οἰκίαν under Doson (when she had taken no action), that can hardly have been her motive for action in 220–19, when his death seemed to have shaken the foundations of his work. The Romans considered only Demetrius and the effect of his example of independence.[69]

Having decided upon action, the Romans prepared to send an expedition and surprise Demetrius. If there was a declaration of war (and we are not told of one), it can only have been a last-minute formality.[70] Demetrius, however, was somehow warned of Roman plans and had some time to take counter-measures. He had seen the failure of Teuta's strategy; besides, there was now no hope of seizing the Greek cities on the coast, as she had tried to do. He thus decided on the opposite plan: he would, if necessary, give up most of his territory, adopting only delaying tactics, and concentrate on the defence of one or two strong places. He had seen the Romans in the field and knew that he could not meet them; but he may not have known their siege tactics (he may even have witnessed a slight reverse, when they attacked a township)[71] and, being a Greek ruling over Illyrians, he no doubt thought very highly of the strength of fortified places. He thus sent a strong force into Dimale—a town near the country of the Parthini and probably not far from Epidamnus[72]—and himself, with 6000 men specially selected from his own δυναστεία, took charge of Pharus. To give Dimale added protection, it seems, he entrusted the government in the cities of the Parthini to his supporters and removed the opposing faction.[73]

In the spring of 219 a Roman force (no doubt again a full consular army and a fleet) under the consuls L. Aemilius Paullus and M. Livius Salinator[74] crossed to Illyria, probably landing at Epidamnus, and at once proceeded to lay siege to Dimale. Roman siegecraft captured the place within a week, and all the other cities in the vicinity thereupon surrendered. With the Parthini again under Roman control, Demetrius' southern territories were cut off at a blow. Ignoring the rest of Illyria, the Romans now sailed straight for Pharus, which they took by a stratagem. Demetrius, giving up hope of further resistance, fled to Philip, who received him kindly. Pharus was razed, Demetrius' οἰκεῖοι removed for internment, and the war was over. Having regulated affairs, the Romans sailed home to celebrate a triumph.

The settlement, this time, was simple. Rome merely retained her old 'friends', and Pharus and Dimale, about which probably nothing was done, remained in the same position of 'freedom'.[75] The fate of Demetrius had taught them their lesson, and the Parthini had to submit to some penalty for their secession. Pinnes was left on his throne, though perhaps ordered to pay an indemnity.[76] There was no desire to increase Roman commitments in the East or to multiply client states. We need not therefore be surprised at Rome's failure to take any measures, aggressive or defensive, against Macedon, at a time when either would have been possible. Though the King of Macedon, only a few months before the arrival of the Roman troops, had visited the dynast Scerdilaidas and made a treaty of alliance with him,[77] there was no suspicion of Philip. It would have been quite easy to cut off Macedon from the coast by extending the protectorate to the area modern historians assign to it as early as 228, or perhaps even to station troops in the Greek cities of the coast. Nor were more active measures (such as support for the Aetolians) beyond the range of the possible, as Philip seemed to be doing rather badly in the Social War.[78] He could certainly not have helped his new ally Scerdilaidas, had the Romans chosen to attack him. But they ignored the dynast: he was not even called to account for that 'breach of the treaty of 228', which was alleged as a pretext for action against Demetrius—unless the very allegation is the work of later apologists. Yet Scerdilaidas, in 220 as 'guilty 'as his friend Demetrius and now the ally of the King of Macedon, was (it seems) next of kin and in succession to Pinnes.[79] On the Polybian (as on the 'imperialist') theory of Rome's motives in undertaking the war, her inactivity is inexplicable.[80] But once we recognize the true motive and its historical context, the settlement is its natural consequence: Rome had achieved precisely what she wanted.[81]

III

Having achieved what she wanted, Rome again withdrew from the scene. The Senate's main thought was to avoid provoking Philip, and the outbreak and alarming course of the Hannibalic War must have appeared to justify this policy; for the Republic did not want another enemy. This time, however, care was taken not to give the impression that Illyria had been completely forgotten: when Pinnes, perhaps encouraged by the series of Roman defeats, delayed paying an instalment of his indemnity, envoys were sent to collect either the money or hostages for it.[82]

Pinnes is not mentioned again and cannot have lived much longer. Scerdilaidas now becomes King (i.e. the most powerful dynast) of Illyria. He had at first remained faithful to his alliance with Philip and even assisted him in his campaign of 218;[83] but the campaign (as far as Scerdilaidas was concerned) was a failure[84] and Philip's resources were too strained to permit satisfactory payment for the Illyrian's services. The dynast, as he had done once before, decided to help himself. He began to collect his dues by piracy and finally went so far as to invade Macedonian territory and take a few towns in Pelagonia and Dassaretia.[85] It is sometimes thought that Rome must have encouraged these actions.[86] But this is contrary to the whole course of her policy from 219 down to the time when Philip forced her to take action against him. Thus she had done nothing to assist or even encourage the Aetolians, who were his most dangerous enemies, and she did nothing (except where her own interests demanded it) to help Scerdilaidas in the war he had provoked. The Illyrian, we know, did not need advice on how to collect his debts, and he may have thought (if he considered defeat at all) that Rome could not allow him to be completely defeated. But of direct encouragement by Rome there is no sign, and it would take good evidence to make such a view plausible to the student of Roman policy at this time.

Scerdilaidas' attack failed for a reason he had not foreseen: Philip, informed of Hannibal's victory at Lake Trasimene, patched up a peace with the Aetolians and (under the influence of Demetrius of Pharus) decided to turn all his energy towards the West.[87] Scerdilaidas was the first to feel the effect of his new policy: Philip at once drove him from the territory he had occupied and proceeded to conquer the greater part of southern Illyria,[88] posting himself firmly on the upper Genusus and Apsus and probably on the shores of Lake Lychnidus. The Romans did not interfere. This encouraged Philip to take more daring action: building a fleet of 100 *lembi*, he sailed into the Ionian Sea in the spring of 216, intending to land on the Illyrian coast. Polybius seems to imply that he was planning a surprise attack on Apollonia; and this is not impossible, as the capture of that city would have greatly improved his bargaining position in his negotiations with Hannibal. But in view of Roman inactivity during the following year it is likely that at the time his intention was thought to be nothing more than an attack on Scerdilaidas by sea—as perhaps it was. For if he completed the defeat of Scerdilaidas, he would obtain some bridgeheads on the coast outside Rome's sphere of influence, and he had some chance of doing this without Roman intervention: but for the panic, he might have succeeded. In the light of the events of 214 those of 216 were bound to be reinterpreted.

Scerdilaidas had thought the coming attack (of which he learnt in good time) directed against himself and hurriedly sent to Rome to ask for assistance: he knew from two wars that Rome would not permit a major power, potentially hostile, to establish itself on the Straits of Hydruntum. The Romans, alarmed by the Illyrian's envoys, but unwilling to commit themselves to war with Philip on the strength of his word, detached a squadron of ten ships from their fleet at Lilybaeum and sent it towards the danger area. The approach of this squadron caused a panic among Philip's fleet and he ingloriously abandoned his expedition.[89] But Rome took no further chances: in 215 the squadron detached to watch Philip was brought up to the strength of twenty-five and assigned to P. Valerius Flaccus, prefect under the praetor Laevinus, with the task of guarding the Calabrian coast; and after Philip's treaty with Hannibal became known, it was reinforced by another twenty-five (or thirty) ships and the praetor was asked to take personal charge of it.[90]

In 214 Philip, now Hannibal's ally, decided to take action against Rome. While Hannibal moved against Tarentum (also entrusted to Laevinus), he, with a fleet of 120 *lembi*, sailed into the Straits of Hydruntum and, having seized Oricum, laid siege to Apollonia. It was no doubt hoped that the double attack would overstrain the Roman defences; for Laevinus clearly could not efficiently guard both Illyria and Tarentum.[91] But the plan failed: Laevinus, at the time still in Italy, sent M. Livius to Tarentum and the city was saved. He himself, after envoys from Oricum had reported the capture of their city and stressed the danger to Rome's ally Apollonia and to Rome herself, set sail for Illyria, where he at once retook Oricum and relieved Apollonia. Philip was forced to burn his fleet and retreat overland.[92] The result of this campaign was to station a Roman fleet permanently in Illyrian waters: Laevinus wintered at Oricum and seems to have remained east of the Adriatic until his successor took over.[93]

Philip's course henceforth was clear: having no chance of seizing the coast, he must subdue the interior and, if possible, drive a wedge between the Roman allies in the South and Scerdilaidas, who was still fighting in the North. This course he pursued during the next two years. Though we have few details, we can to some extent see the result of his operations: he probably secured his position in Dassaretia and round Lake Lychnidus, subdued the Parthini (taking Dimale) and the Atintanes, and, in a brilliant dash across country, took Lissus and its citadel Acrolissus, thus gaining access to the sea and the allegiance of many of Scerdilaidas' subjects.[94] The Romans had now been cut off from Scerdilaidas, and his final defeat might seem only a matter of time; and if the Punic fleet showed any enterprise, the Roman allies on the coast would not resist for long.[95]

In the face of this danger the Romans, unwilling to send a large army to Illyria, succeeded in raising the Aetolians against Philip and entered into the famous alliance with them. Thus the war was transformed from a defensive war in Illyria into an offensive war throughout the Balkan Peninsula. Henceforth very little is said about Illyria and the centre of interest shifts to Greece.[96] It was only after the Aetolians had been forced into making peace that a strong Roman army again appeared in Illyria, detached the Parthini from Philip and attacked Dimale. But by now neither side wanted a continuation of the war: in 205 peace was made at Phoenice, and Philip abandoned the Parthini, Dimale and some smaller places, but was (it seems) permitted to retain the Atintanes.[97] Scerdilaidas had meanwhile been succeeded by Pleuratus (who is first mentioned in the Aetolian treaty) and the latter is included in the Peace. How much, if any, of his father's territory was returned to him is unknown. Probably Philip had already had to abandon his outlying conquests (like Lissus), but was allowed to retain those nearer home: if the Romans could not persuade him to give up Atintania, it is unlikely that they made him withdraw from Dassaretia.[98] Roman protection had not proved very effective, and we see the germs of what was to bear bitter fruit in the second century: Rome was coming to regard her 'friends', towards whom she had no treaty obligations, as having no claim to be considered where Rome's own interests were at stake. It was the first step towards regarding them as outposts in the Roman system of defence—holding potential enemies at a distance, but given up without hesitation, when strategy or diplomacy made it advisable. After 196 this view is fully developed.

Meanwhile this was not yet clearly discernible: Rome could claim to be in a difficult position and to have done her best. And in future Roman interests were bound to coincide with those of her Illyrian friends: Philip could not be permitted to make any further gains and, in particular, had to be kept at a safe distance from the coast, where the Romans now for the first time controlled a long and continuous strip of territory. Her Illyrian friends acted as buffers, but as indispensable ones. The Peace of Phoenice marks Rome's first attempt (since she became a great power) to establish a *modus vivendi* with a dangerous neighbour without having either reduced him to impotence or at least thrown him beyond the seas. It was done, as we have seen, by the interposition of buffer states; and in the second century Rome was to apply this new diplomacy to Antiochus. It was the accident (if we may call it such) of the failure of Rome's attempt to live at peace with other great powers that led to the need to subdue them and thus to the establishment of the Roman Empire as we know it. We must finally, therefore, try to see how the policy failed in the case of Philip—i.e. why the

Senate, genuinely eager to make peace in 205,[99] five years later forced another war upon both Philip and an unwilling Roman people.

Few subjects in the field of Roman history have been as much discussed as the origins of the Second Macedonian War.[100] Yet no satisfactory explanation has been given. We shall not discuss the various motives historians have assigned to Rome: they range from fear of a navy just defeated in the Aegean to fear of exclusion from Eastern markets; yet few of these hypotheses have satisfied even their authors. We shall only inquire into events in Illyria during the years concerned, and we hope to find at least a contributory motive for Roman action. Unfortunately our view of events during those years is obscured by the attempts of Roman annalists to find a legal and moral (as distinct from a merely political) justification for the war that followed; and it is undeniable that there has been a great deal of distortion and invention. But by careful scrutiny we can perhaps distinguish the outline of what happened.[101]

That Philip occupied some territory in Illyria after the Peace of Phoenice is clearly stated by Polybius and ought never to have been doubted.[102] We do not, however, know any details. But we may connect this statement with the annalistic account of attacks by Philip on Roman 'allies' in Greece. It has been pointed out that these attacks may well have taken place in Illyria and involved, i.a., Rome's Greek friends there: there were certainly no such attacks in Greece itself, and we know the annalistic tendency to make Rome at all times (but especially before the Second Macedonian War) the protectress of the Greeks.[103] This gives us a coherent picture of events. Philip had no doubt felt encouraged by the Roman attitude at Phoenice and had judged that Rome did not want to be involved in fighting in Illyria on behalf of her friends. He could not risk a major invasion: for he had just made peace in order to avoid large-scale fighting, and his main ambitions now lay in the East. But he probably thought that Rome would not act against smaller encroachments supported by diplomatic intrigue.

This put the Romans in a difficult position: they had made peace on fairly disadvantageous terms in order to be rid of the Macedonian war and live at peace with Philip. They did not want to start it again at the time of the decisive effort against Hannibal, merely because of slight Macedonian pressure on the frontiers of their friends. Yet it was clear that those friends could not be left exposed to Philip's new policy: their loyalty was not reliable under such a strain. Thus Rome seems at first to have sent an embassy to complain and investigate; it consisted of C. Terentius Varro (a distinguished consular), C. Mamilius Atellus (a praetorian), and M. Aurelius Cotta. When the embassy did not get satisfaction and saw the dangers of the situation among the allies, Cotta (it is said) stayed behind to organize resistance among them —and prevent defection. In spite of his efforts Philip must have made some progress: perhaps he even succeeded in detaching the Parthini (or at least part of that tribe) from the Roman friendship; for Polybius tells us that after the Second Macedonian War they (or part of them?) were assigned to the kingdom of Pleuratus, after having been under Philip's rule.[104] In any case, it seems, Rome's attempt to keep her friends loyal without defending them against attack or pressure was not wholly successful: Philip was again becoming a dangerous neighbour, probably without giving any just cause for military action, even if Rome had been willing to take it. The Senate, therefore, decided that its policy had failed; if events in Illyria were permitted to take their course, the loyalty of all the friends of Rome (perhaps even of the Greek cities on the coast) might falter and Philip might turn against Rome when it suited him. It was at this moment, with Rome free at last of her Carthaginian enemies, that envoys came from Attalus and the Rhodians, announcing that Philip was in serious trouble in the East and was unpopular among the Greeks, and that they would welcome the alliance of Rome.

APPENDIX

ROMAN AIMS IN 229–8

Holleaux's case that the Roman settlement was at least in part determined by fear of Macedon rests on two main foundations: the length of 'continuous coastal strip' and the extension of the protectorate over the Parthini and Atintanes. We hope to have shown that there is no authority in our sources for the coastal strip such as he considers it;

but Oricum provides a test case and deserves special comment. Holleaux makes it surrender to the Romans on the strength of Zon. ix 4 and Livy xxiv 40. But Zonaras' evidence, on a point like this, is useless; and the Livian passage (from Polybius?—thus Holleaux and others, with great probability) points the other way. For Livy, reporting the appeals of both Apollonia and Oricum to the Romans for help against Philip, makes the envoys of the former claim that it had been attacked 'quod deficere ab Romanis nollent'; while those of Oricum say that they are threatened 'ob nullam aliam causam nisi quod imminerent Italiae' and ask Laevinus to assist them 'ut … hostem haud dubium Romanis … arceret'. It seems clear that in these passages Apollonia is, while Oricum is not, thought of as an ally of Rome. This is fully confirmed by Polybius' account of operations in 229, which leaves no room for the establishment of a protectorate over Oricum: it is not mentioned either in what would be its proper place (the crossing of the fleet from Corcyra to Apollonia) or at any other stage of operations; and it was not received *in fidem* at the same time as the Parthini and Atintanes (cf. p. 77, above). Now, as it happens, we know that Polybius was aware of the strategic situation of Oricum (Pol. vii 14d) and is not likely to have omitted it from ignorance. Slight further confirmation may be sought in Philip's treaty with Hannibal (Pol. vii 19, 3): though the enumeration of the protectorate is not complete (Issa is omitted), Oricum was after all of much more importance to Philip than Issa (as his attack on it shows) and its omission is of some significance. It is thus reasonably clear that Oricum did not form part of the Roman protectorate after 228 (or even after 219—for our evidence still applies).

As for the Parthini and Atintanes, they must not be used as a basis for speculation about Rome's hidden motives: Holleaux himself has disposed of the more extravagant views (*Rome* 109 f.); but the criticism applies even to his own view (put more strongly by Carcopino 57) that Rome was guided by fear of, and hostility to, Macedon. There is no justification for speaking of a 'mainmise de Rome sur l'Atintania' (*Rome* 109): the Romans ignored Atintania and made no attempt to penetrate into the interior along the Aous. It was only when envoys from the Atintanes came and asked for Roman friendship (at a time when there can have been no military pressure on them) that the consul decided to grant them this favour. In this he may well have been influenced by their strategic situation: after Scerdilaidas' invasion of Epirus he must have been aware of the importance of the Aous-Drynon gorges (on which see Walbank 148 f.) as the invasion route from Illyria to the south. But there is nothing whatever to show that he thought of the Aous as the invasion route from Macedonia to the west, or that he even knew sufficient geography to do so. (Holleaux has to refer to Roman interest in the region in 209!) The Romans will have been under no illusions as to the difficulty of securing the fidelity of the Atintanes without control of Chaonia, the coastal strip on which their territory bordered. The fact that they made no attempt to gain control of it, although the Epirots had been the allies of Teuta, suggests that they did not care very much. As a result, the Atintanes soon came under Demetrius' influence (see p. 79 above).

There is thus no support whatever for the view that the Romans in 229–8 tried to take precautions against Macedon. I have offered a simpler alternative explanation of their policy in the text.

BIBLIOGRAPHY

Ancient authors are cited according to the Teubner text. The following modern works, referred to more than once in the footnotes, are quoted there under the author's name (and, if necessary, an abbreviated title):

Carcopino, J., *Points de Vue sur l'Impérialisme romain* (1934).

De Sanctis, G., *Storia dei Romani* (1916–17), vol. iii 1–2.

Fiehn, K., *RE*, Suppl.-Band v, coll. 978 f., s.v. 'Skerdilaidas'.

Fine, J. V. A., 'Macedon, Illyria, and Rome, 220–19', *JRS* 26 (1936) 24 f.

Fluss, M., *RE*, s.v. 'Teuta'.

Grueber, H. A. (ed.), *Coins of the Roman Republic in the British Museum*, 3 vols (1910).

Holleaux, M., *Rome, la Grèce et les Monarchies hellénistiques au IIIe Siècle av. J.-C.* (1921) (cited as *Rome*).

Holleaux, M., 'La politique romaine en Grèce et dans l'Orient hellénistique au IIIe siècle', *RPh* 50 (1926) 46 f., 194 f. [= *Études* iv (1952) 26 f.].

Holleaux, M., 'The Romans in Illyria', *CAH* vii 822 f.

Lenschau, T., *RE*, s.v. 'Pleuratos'.

May, J. M. F., 'Macedonia and Illyria (217–167 B.C.)', *JRS* 36 (1946) 48 f.

Münzer, F., *RE*, s.v. 'Livius', no. 33.

Petzold, K.-E., *Die Eröffnung des zweiten römisch-makedonischen Krieges* (1940).

Sherwin-White, A. N., *The Roman Citizenship* (1939).

Täubler, E., *Imperium Romanum* (1913), vol. i (all published).

Tarn, (Sir) W. W., 'The Greek Leagues and Macedonia', *CAH* vii 732 f.

Treves, P., 'Studi su Antigono Dosone', *Athenaeum* N.S. 12 (1934) 381 f.; N.S. 13 (1935) 22 f.

Vulić, N., 'Première guerre d'Illyrie', *Bulletin de l'Acad. des Lettres, Acad. Royale Serbe* i (1935) 231 f.; 238 f. also as: 'La première guerre illyrienne', *Eos* 32 (1929) 651 f.

Walbank, F. W., *Philip V of Macedon* (1940).

Walek, T., 'La politique romaine en Grèce et dans l'Orient hellénistique au IIIe siècle', *RPh* 49 (1925) 28 f.

Zippel, G., *Die römische Herrschaft in Illyrien bis auf Augustus* (1877).

[Since this article appeared, these matters have been thoroughly discussed by F. W. Walbank in his notes on the relevant passages of Polybius in vol. i of *A Historical Commentary on Polybius* (1957). The following works are also worth noting:

Oost, S. I., *Roman Policy in Epirus and Acarnania* (1954).

Walser, G., 'Die Ursachen des ersten römisch-illyrischen Krieges', *Historia* 2 (1954) 308 ff.]

ACKNOWLEDGMENT

The writer wishes to record his thanks to Professor Syme for listening to, and making valuable comments on, many of the ideas in this paper in their original form; and to him, to Mr. H. M. Last and to Mr. J. B. Ward Perkins, Director of the British School at Rome, for their help in getting the paper into publishable shape.

NOTES

1 Zippel's account is the only attempt to treat the subject as a whole; but, though still indispensable, it is now in many respects out of date.

2 *Rome, passim.*

3 Our main sources are Polybius (ii 2–12), Dio (fr. 49) and Zonaras (viii 19), and Appian (*Ill.* 7). For discussions of them, see especially Zippel 46 f.; Holleaux, *Rome* 98, n. 2; Vulić 235 f.; Fluss, coll. 1140 f. Zippel was inclined to prefer Dio to Polybius, and this unfortunately influenced De Sanctis (iii 1, 295 f.). Holleaux gives reasons for rejecting Dio and following Polybius. Appian, though his source seems to have been well informed on the Illyrian side, is full of annalistic inventions and has added his own confusions. Vulić's attempt to trace Appian and Dio to one common source is unconvincing. Dio derives from an annalistic account plus Polybius (or an account based on his); Appian may be ultimately based on the former. The importance of the war was recognized by Polybius (ii 2, 2: ἅπερ οὐ παρέργως, ἀλλὰ μετ' ἐπιστάσεως θεωρητέον τοῖς βουλομένοις ἀληθινῶς . . . συνθεάσασθαι . . . τὴν αὔξησιν καὶ κατασκευὴν τῆς Ῥωμαίων δυναστείας).

4 For the family tree of the royal house, as far as we can trace it, see Lenschau, coll. 237–8.

5 Polybius ignores Pinnes, probably because he can never have framed policy. The information comes from Dio and Appian and is confirmed by Livy (cf. n. 76).

6 Polybius (ii 4–15) describes all this as a series of accidents, making the Illyrians intent only on plunder. He often refuses to credit these barbarians with any ability for planning or using reason, where we can see from his facts that his judgment is mistaken (cf. nn. 18 and 53 below), and modern scholars have often been misled by this (e.g. Holleaux, *CAH* vii 830; Fluss, col. 1145). In this case, the dispatch of Scerdilaidas and the co-ordination between the two forces, as well as the treaty finally made, show the seriousness of the plan.

7 For Atintania, see Holleaux, *Rome* 110, n. 1 (with summary of earlier views and conclusive argumentation).

8 Holleaux, *Rome* 98 f., with references to earlier views; also *CAH* vii 831 f. Cf. Pol. ii 8, 12.

9 E.g. by Carcopino 50 f. Cf. also Walek's debate with Holleaux in *RPh* 1925–6.

10 Pol. i 83, 7 (Mercenary War in Africa). For a similar view of this case, see Walek 32 f. (not refuted by Holleaux). Holleaux's insistence, against the 'imperialist' theory, on the fact that 'l'occasion de châtier les Illyriens s'offrait depuis longtemps et chaque jour aux Romains' (*Rome* 98, n. 3) only throws into greater relief the weakness of his own explanation for the sudden change in attitude.

11 Holleaux again echoes Polybius' judgments instead of using his facts. Thus he describes Teuta's reply as 'd'une insolence calculée, qui rend vaine toute négotiation' and states that after Coruncanius' speech 'son orgueil de femme s'exaspère' (*Rome* 100–1). This phrase comes almost straight out of Polybius, and much Illyrian (and some Hellenistic) history has been obscured by such reflection of his prejudices.

12 We cannot regard this as based merely on an apologia for the Senate, as we know

that by the time the fleet got under way (the army was even later) the next campaigning season was well advanced. (See below.)

13 Pol. ii 8, 3. In view of their position Holleaux's insistence that 'les paroles prononcées par le légat [Pol. ii 8, 10–11] gardent un caractère privé' (*Rome* 101, n. 1) is pointless.

14 *Rome* 99.

15 Pol. ii 6, 7–8; cf. 12, 6.

16 Pol. ii 11, 1 and 7; *Rome* 102, n. 3. To the Romans Macedon was a distant kingdom (cf. Fine, 'The Problem of Macedonian Holdings', *TAPA* 63 (1932) 126 f.), causing no concern. The Illyrian peril, however, seems throughout Greece to have assumed the proportions of the earlier Gallic peril: 'οὐ μικρὰν οὐδὲ τὴν τυχοῦσαν κατάπληξιν καὶ φόβον' Polybius calls it; and the Romans cannot have been ignorant of this feeling, which was probably even shared by their Italian informants.

17 For the chronology, see Holleaux in *REG* 43 (1930) 243 f. [= *Études* iv (1952)9 f.]; though it is probably better to put the death of Demetrius a little later than he would do, and there is no need to think that it had anything to do with the Achaeo-Aetolian decision to send a force to Corcyra (rightly Vulić 232 f.).

18 The story is told graphically, but without any understanding for the Illyrian plan, in Pol. ii 9–10. To what extent the Polybian view has imposed itself upon modern scholars is shown by Holleaux's account (*Rome* 101; *CAH* vii 833), according to which the Illyrian operations of 229 are 'une expédition de piraterie plus ample et plus hardie que les précédentes' and are used as evidence that Teuta did not believe in a Roman invasion! For a more reasonable (but still over-complicated) view, see Treves (1934) 391. We cannot easily conceive of a plan that would have given Teuta as good a chance of forestalling the Roman invasion as the one she adopted might have done.

19 Treves (1934, 389–90) believes that Demetrius had first contacted the Coruncanii at Issa, since Polybius describes him, at the time of his final treason, as ἐν διαβολαῖς ὢν καὶ φοβούμενος τὴν Τεῦταν (ii 11, 4). But such a view is contrary to what Polybius actually says, since he makes the διαβολαί the cause and not the effect of Demetrius' contacting the Romans. It is much more probable that Demetrius (perhaps with the help of Pinnes' mother) was even at that time intriguing for the guardianship of the boy king, which he later obtained (cf. below).

20 Pol. ii 11–12. Cf. Zippel 50 f.; Holleaux, *CAH* vii 836 and map 14 (facing p. 825). On the Parthini, see Polaschek in *RE*, s.v. The Roman forces did not penetrate inland. On the questions of which consul returned to Italy in 229 and why only Fulvius triumphed (*Inscr. It.* xiii 1, 78–9 and 549–50) certainty cannot be attained. The tale that Issa surrendered to the Romans and that this was the cause, or one of the causes, of the war is unfortunately accepted by De Sanctis (like so much that comes from Dio), but Holleaux has shown that it may be dismissed (*Rome* 23, n. 6). That Issa received a *foedus aequum* is a pointless conjecture based on this and meant to explain the omission of the city in Philip's treaty with Hannibal; as Holleaux points out (*Rome* 106, n. 3), it fails to do so and ought never to have been considered.

21 This was pointed out by Beloch (*Griech. Gesch.* iv² 1, 666, n. 1); but the instalment payable in 217 is probably not part of this indemnity, but belongs to a new one imposed in 219: the Romans by this time never bore the cost of their victorious wars.

22 This 'protectorate' is described as 'about 120 miles in length and from 20 to 40 miles in width' (Walbank 12); cf. Zippel 53 f.; Holleaux, *Rome* 105 f. and *CAH* vii 836 and map 14; Treves (1934) 392; and others.

23 51. It is, for a Greek, the region 'inside Illyria proper'.

24 ii 11, 11: συμμιξάντων δὲ πρεσβευτῶν αὐτοῖς καὶ πλειόνων, ὧν οἱ παρὰ τῶν Παρθίνων ἧκον ἐπιτρέποντες τὰ καθ' αὑτούς, δεξάμενοι τούτους εἰς τὴν φιλίαν, παραπλησίως δὲ καὶ τοὺς παρὰ τῶν Ἀτιντάνων προσεληλυθότας, προῆγον. . . .

[25] *CAH* vii 836 and map 14; cf. also map by Fluss.

[26] The townships of the Ardiaeans north of Epidamnus taken by the Romans (see n. 23 and text) may have been assigned to the Parthini or to Demetrius' personal δυναστεία and thus remained within the protectorate. On Oricum, see Appendix.

[27] Thus Zippel 53 f.; De Sanctis iii 1, 302; Holleaux, *Rome* 105 and *CAH* vii 836; and others.

[28] For the terms, see Täubler 77, where the conclusion is stated as a matter of fact.

[29] *Ill.* 8.

[30] iii 1, 302 and n. 98.

[31] *Rome* 105; *CAH* vii 835. There is no evidence on the subject, and it hardly matters.

[32] Dio, fr. 53. His control over the kingdom is shown by events.

[33] See Fluss, coll. 1140–1.

[34] Zippel (55) believes that the Romans divided the regency between Teuta and Demetrius without destroying the unity of the kingdom; but this far-fetched hypothesis, far from combining our sources, is contrary to all of them. None of our sources says that Teuta continued to rule the Illyrian kingdom after the peace, while Dio states (and Polybius implies) that she did not.

[35] Holleaux, *Rome* 109. None of the various attempts to find formal marks of Roman domination has been convincing. On the ἄρχων ὁ ἐν Κερκύρᾳ (Pol. xxi 32, 6), see Zippel 94. Even if he is a Roman, he is only a wartime commander. On the Corcyraean coins with the legend ROMA (Grueber ii 196–7) no final conclusion has been reached; but the magistrate's initials show that they are coins struck by Corcyra on behalf (i.e. probably at the request) of Rome, and not coins struck by Rome at the Corcyraean mint. They were probably struck to pay Roman troops in the East.—On the victoriate coinage, see Mattingly, H., 'The first age of Roman coinage', *JRS* 35 (1945) 71; Milne, J. G., 'The problem of early Roman coinage', *JRS* 36 (1946) 91 and n. 1. The victoriate was not an official Roman coin, and there seems to be no good reason for doubting Pliny's statement that it was first struck in Illyria and thence introduced to Italy (*n.h.* xxxiii 3, 46). [Numismatists are still far from agreed about the date, though the late third century seems likely.]

[36] Holleaux, *CAH* vii 836; cf. *Rome* 106, n. 3 (with references to earlier views).

[37] *Die völkerrechtlichen Grundlagen der röm. Aussenpolitik in rep. Zeit* (*Klio*, Beih. 31 (1933)).

[38] Thus Zippel 89. *Libertas* is attested for Corcyra by App. *Ill.* 8; Strabo vii, fr. 8 (which must belong in this context); Pliny, *n.h.* iv 12, 52; for Apollonia by App. *Ill.* 8. That Issa had no treaty is made all but certain by Livy xlv 26, 13.

[39] The subject cannot be developed here [it has since been developed in my *Foreign Clientelae* (1958)], but a few indications may be given. Cic. 2 *Verr.* iii 13 gives the list of *ciuitates liberae* in Sicily in his day; their status, as we see from the Verrines, had deteriorated considerably. Segesta, about which we know most (though the case of Centuripa seems to have been similar), was always treated with special consideration on account of her *cognatio* with Rome, and it seems that she never revolted (*ibid.* v 83 and 125). There is no reason to think that her status was originally considered inferior to that of the Mamertine *foederati* (on which see Cic. 2 *Verr.* v 50 f.), or that she could not have had the burden of a treaty with formal commitments if she had preferred it. It can be shown that even in the second century friendship without a treaty was considered by the Greeks a status much preferable to a treaty not on equal terms.

[40] This is the inference from Polybius' account (see n. 24 above and text). Cf. Appendix.

[41] Cf. Holleaux, *CAH* vii 837.

[42] For the extra-legal nature of *clientela*, see Kaser, M., 'Gesch. d. Patronatsgewalt über Freigelassene', *ZRG.* 58 (1938) 88 f.; for the social and political importance of

the concept, Gelzer, M., *Die Nobilität d. röm. Republik* (1912). Sherwin-White rightly protests against Täubler's misuse of the term *clientela* for a treaty relationship (162); its elusiveness to legal analysis is of its essence in the foreign as in the domestic sphere.

[43] This is worth stressing because (as a consequence of the general lack of interest in Illyria) it is often forgotten, with the result that the development of Roman foreign policy is misunderstood. Thus, e.g., Sherwin-White writes (150): 'The practice of declaring a community to be "free" ... is one that Rome first learned from the Greeks'; and he describes the settlement of Greece as 'her first experiment'. Täubler (436), followed by many other historians, derives Flamininus' policy from that of Artaxerxes and Polyperchon.

[44] That this act of courtesy had no important consequences is shown by Holleaux (*Rome* 113 f.). Yet it was Rome's first diplomatic contact with the Greeks (Pol. ii 12, 4–8).—The failure to send envoys to Pella should not be made a sign of anti-Macedonian scheming (rightly Holleaux, l.c.): it would have been odd to send an embassy to announce to the King of Macedon that the scourge of Greece, his Illyrian ally, had been defeated, and it could only have been regarded as a public announcement of hostility. In the circumstances it is the *absence* of any interest in Macedon that shows Rome's peaceful intentions. If even the outline of our analysis is accepted, it should be clear that at no stage of the war did Rome show any fear of, hostility towards, or indeed interest in, Macedon; and the final step confirms this view.

[45] Holleaux, *CAH* vii 837.

[46] The sources are again Polybius (iii 16, 18–19), Appian (*Ill.* 8) and Dio (fr. 53)—Zonaras (viii 20, *fin.*). Polybius' is the only account of any value, though again there seems to be a good source somewhere at the back of Appian. Polybius, as we shall see, is not as good as on the First Illyrian War; his source is generally thought to be Fabius (and indeed, no one else can plausibly be suggested), who gave the official Roman version as shaped by later events; while Polybius' own bias against Demetrius made him unable to show any critical spirit.

[47] We cannot know much about conditions inside Illyria, but it is reasonable to suppose that the power of the King, who was only one dynast among many (cf. Pol. xxi 21, 3), had been seriously weakened by the events of 229–8. Though Demetrius was the King's guardian, strong dynasts (e.g. Scerdilaidas) were his equals and had to be conciliated; this was no doubt the price of their remaining quiet and allowing Demetrius to strengthen the hold of the central authority in the South, which he must have done before devoting his attention to the Parthini and Atintanes (see below). These two tribes will have occupied his attention for some time, as the *coup d'état* of 219 presupposes long preparation (see below).—Scerdilaidas in a similar position found the dynasts formidable (Pol. v 4, 3; cf. n. 79 below).

[48] Holleaux, *Rome* 131–2, puts this as early as 225, basing his view on Pol. iii 16, 2. Cf. below.

[49] On Doson's fear of Rome, see Holleaux, *Rome* 119 f. and *CAH* vii 839 f., and (with considerable exaggeration) Treves' paper in *Athenaeum*.

[50] Pol. ii 65, 4; 66, 5 f.; cf. Tarn's evaluation, 760–2. For the date of Sellasia I accept 222 (see Tarn 863–4, and—using new evidence—Treves (1935) 54 f., and Walbank 296, n. 5).

[51] iii 16.

[52] The perfects seem decisive for the chronology. (*Contra* Holleaux, *Rome* 134, n. 4.)

[53] *Rome* 133 f. He has to turn Demetrius practically into a madman (135).

[54] Holleaux, *Rome* 132.

[55] Holleaux's desperate attempts to motivate Demetrius' actions are well illustrated by the following (*CAH* vii 849): 'If, *as is probable* [my italics], the Pharian received

prompt advices regarding the news from Spain, he must have drawn favourable auguries from it.'

⁵⁶ The exact date of his accession is doubtful, but it was almost certainly some time during 221. On its effects see Pol. iv 3, 2 f.; 5, 3; 22, 5. By autumn 220, at the latest, the Social War had begun. (See Pol. iv 13, 6, and cf. Walbank 32.) Yet this is just the time when Demetrius is said to have made Roman action inevitable by attacking the Roman protectorate. That Demetrius did not receive any encouragement from Philip is shown by Fine ('Macedon').

⁵⁷ Thus Holleaux, *Rome* 134 f.; De Sanctis iii 1, 324.

⁵⁸ Livy (*per.* xx) and the Livian tradition. Appian (*Ill.* 8) accuses Demetrius of instigating this war—a further development of annalistic apologia. Holleaux (*Rome* 134, n. 1) recognizes the effect such an expedition must have had in 'recalling Demetrius to prudence' (i.e. making him aware of Roman power and interest) and for that reason alone rejects the campaign as apocryphal. But a Histrian campaign was a natural consequence of the Cisalpine campaigns (as we see in the second century) and we have no reason for rejecting its authenticity—it is Holleaux's premiss (Demetrius' rebellion) that must go.

⁵⁹ Pol. iv 16, 6 f. Note τὸ μὲν πρῶτον τῇ Πύλῳ προσμίξαντες (s. 7).

⁶⁰ Modern historians tend without question to quote the Polybian passages as conclusive; e.g. Zippel 54; Holleaux, *Rome* 105, n. 3.

⁶¹ ii 12, 3.

⁶² Pol. iv 16, 6 f. Note that in iii 16 (the version from Roman sources) all mention of Scerdilaidas is omitted.

⁶³ Dio, fr. 53 = Zon. viii 20, *fin.*

⁶⁴ Dio, l.c.

⁶⁵ Pol. iii 18, 1.

⁶⁶ See App. *Ill.* 8 for the latter, and cf. p. 79 above. There is no mention of 'attacks' on the Greek cities.

⁶⁷ He describes him as ἐπιλελησμένον τῶν προγεγονότων εἰς αὐτὸν εὐεργετημάτων ὑπὸ 'Ρωμαίων (iii 16, 2) and gives it as the Romans' intention to secure their position ἐπιτιμήσαντες καὶ κολάσαντες τὴν ἀχαριστίαν καὶ προπέτειαν τὴν Δημητρίου (*ibid.*, s. 4).

⁶⁸ Pol. iii 16, 4. Cf. Holleaux, *Rome* 136.

⁶⁹ Holleaux, *Rome* 136, paints a vivid picture of Roman fears, which must not be uncritically accepted.

⁷⁰ This is shown by Polybius' wording (iii 18, 1): ἅμα τῷ συνεῖναι τὴν ἐπιβολὴν τῶν 'Ρωμαίων.

⁷¹ Nutria (Pol. ii 11, 13).

⁷² On the situation of this town, see Zippel 56; Holleaux, *Rome* 135, n. 1. Holleaux is probably right in placing it inland, but wrong in putting it 'dans le pays des Parthini': though associated with them in our sources, it is named alongside of them (see especially Pol. vii 9, 13) and was probably just outside the tribal territory. Further than this we cannot go. We do not know when Dimale came into Demetrius' power: he may have held it ever since 229–8; he may have brought it under his control at any time after; or he may have seized it as a strong place—it was reputed impregnable (Pol. iii 18, 3)—to hold against the Roman attack. There is no evidence to enable us to decide.

⁷³ Pol. iii 18, 1. The cities, as we have tried to argue, must be those not yet under his control, and they were probably those of the Parthini: the Illyrians did not usually dwell in πόλεις (see Zippel 86 f. for the sources), but the Parthini are known to have had 'urbes' (Livy xliii 23, 6).

⁷⁴ Polybius consistently omits Livius, but Zonaras mentions him; and the story about his condemnation after the war is so well attested that it must be accepted (see Münzer. coll. 892 f.). In the circumstances we cannot discover what action is to be

attributed to each of them and whether Livius also triumphed. Why Polybius ignores him is a difficult question; but we have seen that on this war he is not a very good source. Münzer thinks he has done it on purpose in order to flatter the Aemilii Paulli. But, though Polybius is not above some 'interpreting' for such a purpose (cf. his treatment of the great L. Paullus' massacre in Epirus—Livy xlv 34; Plut. *Paull.* 29— which has even misled moderns into attributing the responsibility to the hero's political opponents), we should not lightly accuse him of deliberate falsification of facts. The latter may well be due to his source Fabius, as the Fabii were hostile to Livius (cf. Münzer, col. 895).

75 Polybius' account is rather sketchy: the Atintanes are not mentioned, but (with the Parthini again friends of Rome) they no doubt returned to their previous status; the Greek cities, it seems, were never deemed to have revolted. For the extent of the protectorate after 219, see (not quite accurately) Pol. vii 9, 13. Polybius' phrase τῆς λοιπῆς Ἰλλυρίδος ἐγκρατὴς γενόμενος (iii 19, 12) probably means that the Romans had the Illyrian king at their mercy.—De Sanctis (iii 1, 325, n. 150) rejects Polybius' statement that Pharus was razed. But as it was apparently taken by assault, there is no reason why it should not have been. It was probably resettled after. For Demetrius' οἰκεῖοι see Pol. vii 9, 14 (Philip's treaty with Hannibal).

76 App. *Ill.* 8, *fin.* Cf. Livy xxii 33, 5. The Parthini and Atintanes no doubt could not pay much and there was no one else from whom the cost of the war could be collected.

77 Pol. iv 29, 2 f. For the chronology, see Holleaux, *Rome* 142, n. 3. That Philip had no hostile intentions towards Rome is shown by Fine ('Macedon'); but those who make Roman fear of Macedon the main motive for the war cannot regard the Romans as believing this.

78 Cf. Walbank 42. 'The first round had gone to Aetolia', as Tarn puts it (766). This was by the autumn of 219, just when the Roman army was returning home ληγούσης τῆς θερείας (Pol. iii 19, 12).

79 On Scerdilaidas, see Fiehn. Zippel (59) thinks that the Romans made him guardian of Pinnes! This is rightly rejected by De Sanctis (iii 1, 325, n. 152). After 217 (see n. 76 and text above) Scerdilaidas appears as king. He had probably seized the guardianship after Demetrius' flight, and this was perhaps responsible for the ταραχὰς περὶ τοὺς κατὰ τὴν Ἰλλυρίδα πολιδυνάστας (Pol. v 4, 3), which prevented him from sending more than fifteen *lembi* to assist Philip before Cephallenia in 218 (wrongly put in 217 by Fiehn, col. 978). We do not know where Scerdilaidas' δυναστεία was, but it may have been round Scodra (cf. De Sanctis iii 1, 322) and Lissus. Scodra, which is not mentioned before, later appears as Genthius' capital (e.g. Livy xliv 31, 2), while Lissus, which in spite of its strategic importance we do not find connected with either Teuta or Demetrius, is also mentioned as a residence of Genthius (Pol. xxviii 8, 4; Livy xliv 30, 6; cf. May 53 f., for the parallel histories of the two cities). Neither city surrendered to Rome in time to receive favourable treatment (cf. Livy xlv 26, 13 f.). If these two cities were indeed the hereditary δυναστεία of the line of Scerdilaidas, this also furnishes an additional motive for Philip's attack on Lissus (Pol. viii 13–14; see p. 20 above).

80 Thus Holleaux (*Rome* 139 f.; *CAH* vii 851 f.) is inclined to blame the Romans for failing to carry out their purpose properly. On his (and Polybius') premises their action is indeed absurd.

81 Note that in Philip's alliance with Hannibal the Romans are called κύριοι of the places and tribes concerned (Pol. vii 9, 13).

82 Livy xxii 33, 5.

83 Pol. v 4, 3. This is duly stigmatized by Holleaux as another flagrant breach of the treaty of 228 (*CAH* vii 851–2), and as it comes so soon after the Roman campaign against Demetrius, he is at a loss to explain it. Surely it shows that neither the Romans

nor Scerdilaidas (nor, probably, Philip, who at the time was not yet planning to attack Rome) considered the dynast's action a breach of the treaty—any more than his joint operation with Demetrius had been.

[84] Scerdilaidas' contingent is not mentioned after the attack on Cephallenia, which had to be abandoned (Pol. v 4, 13).

[85] Pol. v 95, 1 f.; 101, 1 f.; 108, 1 f. His alliance with Philip had been brought about by the Aetolians' failure to pay him (Pol. iv 29, 5 f.).

[86] E.g. Holleaux, *Rome* 165 f.; *CAH* vii 854 f.; doubtfully De Sanctis iii 2, 398; Walbank 68. Holleaux's chief argument is the statement that Scerdilaidas would not have undertaken military action in the vicinity of the Roman protectorate without Roman permission!

[87] Pol. v 101, 6 f. Cf. Walbank 64 f.

[88] Pol. v 108, 8—not a satisfactory account. Cf. Zippel 60 f.; De Sanctis iii 2, 405 f.; Holleaux, *Rome* 167 f.; *CAH* vii 855; Walbank 68 f.

[89] On these events, see Pol. v 109–10. Cf. Holleaux, *Rome* 175 f.; *CAH* viii 117 f.; Walbank 69 f.—both perhaps too prone to accept Polybius' account, especially of Philip's intentions. It is unlikely that he hoped to occupy the whole Illyrian coast and cross to Italy, at a time when he was not yet the ally of Carthage.—That the Roman squadron ever entered Apollonia (thus Holleaux, *Rome* 179) is unlikely; it probably remained at Brundisium or even Tarentum and was the kernel of Laevinus' force (cf. below).

[90] Livy xxiii 32, 17; 38, 7 f. There is no reason to reject the substance of this annalistic account, though the wording (as so often) is probably that of Livy or an annalist. (E.g. 'primo quoque tempore in Macedoniam transmitteret' is belied by the facts.) Owing to a slip by Livy or a copyist the number of ships cannot be determined.

[91] Livy xxiv 20, 9 f.; 40. It is generally asserted (e.g. Holleaux, *Rome* 189, n. 1; Walbank 75, n. 4) that Philip's move is subsequent to Hannibal's. There is no authority for this in Livy (who says 'eadem aestate' and implies late summer for both); Philip's action, reasonable on the obvious hypothesis of concerted action with his ally against a very weak point of the Roman defensive system, is without this hypothesis turned into an act of reckless gambling. (Thus, e.g., Walbank 77. Walbank, who admits the principle of concerted action, is misled by his chronology into failing to see its application.)

[92] Livy ll. cc. (last note). It is likely that Laevinus only heard of the attack on Apollonia after crossing to Oricum.

[93] See Holleaux, *Rome* 193, n. 2.

[94] Pol. viii 13–14b (Lissus, Dassaretae, 'Hyscana'—i.e. Uscana, north of Lake Lychnidus); Livy xxix 12, 3 and 13 (Dimale, Parthini, Atintanes—for the latter, cf. xxvii 30, 13). The 'Ardiaeans' (Livy xxvii 30, 13) are those north of Epidamnus (cf. Pol. ii 11, 10; 12, 2). Zippel's view that Philip penetrated beyond the Naro is untenable and has found little support: we do not even know whether he took Scodra (cf. May 49 f.). On Lissus, see n. 79 above.

[95] Cf. Walbank 81 f., rightly refusing to believe that Philip was hoping to invade Italy.

[96] For the Aetolian treaty, see Livy xxvi 24 f. The war is discussed in all the standard works.

[97] Livy xxix 12.

[98] Livy, l.c. (Cf. xxvi 24, 9, where 'Thracum' can hardly be right.) Cf. May 49 f. On Pleuratus, see Lenschau, col. 237.

[99] This is shown by Holleaux, *Rome* 284 f., and *CAH* viii 136 f., although not all his arguments are sound.

[100] The most recent discussion is Petzold's; cf. also McDonald and Walbank, 'The

origins of the Second Macedonian War' (*JRS* 27 (1937) 280 f.), with references to earlier views. [Discussions continue to multiply, and there is no point in extending the bibliography. For a long treatment, incorporating most other work up to that point (but adding little), see B. Ferrua, *Le origini della II guerra macedonica*, Palermo, 1960.]

[101] Livy xxx 26, 2 f. and 42, 2 f., gives the annalistic account. Cf. Petzold's study (which must be used with caution). We shall confine our attention to what concerns Illyria.

[102] xviii 1, 14: Flamininus in 197 demands of Philip τοὺς κατὰ τὴν Ἰλλυρίδα τόπους παραδοῦναι Ῥωμαίοις, ὧν γέγονε κύριος μετὰ τὰς ἐν Ἠπείρῳ διαλύσεις; which Livy (xxxii 33, 3) translates: 'restituenda ... loca quae post pacem in Epiro factam occupasset'. This was challenged by Zippel, mainly on the ground that Philip could not have occupied Roman territory ('römisches Gebiet') without its being explicitly mentioned in our sources (73 f.); and he suggested that Polybius means 'the territories ... he had acquired after and in accordance with ['nach ... und gemäss'] the Peace ... ' (e.g. Atintania). This suggestion has been generally followed (e.g. Holleaux, *Rome* 278, n. 1; Walbank 103, n. 4; but not De Sanctis iii 2, 435, n. 2—unfortunately without discussion). Yet not only is it doubtful whether the Greek as cited can mean this: if we look at the context, it is at once clear that Zippel's interpretation cannot stand. Polybius (l.c.) continues: ὁμοίως δὲ καὶ Πτολεμαίῳ τὰς πόλεις ἀποκαταστῆσαι πάσας, ὃς παρήρηται μετὰ τόν Πτολεμαίου τοῦ Φιλοπάτορος θάνατον. The parallelism, already sufficiently obvious, is stressed by ὁμοίως; and as μετὰ τὸν ... θάνατον cannot mean anything but 'after (= since) the death of ... ', μετὰ τὰς ... διαλύσεις must mean 'after (= since) the peace ... '. There was no 'römisches Gebiet' in Illyria.

[This argument, which still seems to me conclusive, has been independently advanced by J. P. V. D. Balsdon, *CQ* N.S. 3 (1953) 163 f., and attacked by S. I. Oost, *CP* 54 (1959) 158 f. Cf. the discussion in *CP* 55 (1960) 182 f.]

[103] Cf. Petzold, *passim*. The account (Livy ll. cc., n. 101) is sometimes rejected (e.g. Holleaux, *Rome* 278, n. 1). But the names of the envoys are those of historical persons and (though in the state of our knowledge this is not decisive) nothing we know about those persons makes their participation in this mission impossible. Nor is Cotta, who is the hero of the story, the sort of figure around which legends are spun. The mission is accepted in the relevant biographies in *RE* (s.vv. 'Aurelius', no. 103; 'Mamilius', no. 5; 'Terentius', no. 83); Broughton (*MRR* i 313 and 315) is inclined to accept it as based on archival material. It is worth noting that 'ne socii ... ad regem deficerent' (Livy xxx 42, 5), besides giving us valuable information on Philip's methods, is a naïve admission of Roman motives quite unlike the tendentiousness of annalistic fiction, in which Rome appears as the unselfish champion of the wronged.

[104] Pol. xviii 47, 12. Zippel's attempt to query this (77 f.) is unconvincing.

Caepio and Norbanus

Notes on the Decade 100-90 B.C.

Fr. Muenzeri manibus

It is not customary to head articles with dedications; but so great is the debt that we all—and the author of this article in particular —owe to the author of *Römische Adelsparteien* and of countless invaluable entries in the *Real-Encyclopädie* that no lesser form of acknowledgment can do it justice. His method has since been applied, with masterly skill and important results, to various periods of Roman history. And although some recent work reveals the dangers and inadequacies of the method, where it is used with excessive confidence and insufficient safeguards, it is eminently suited to a period like the age of Marius, where there is sufficient other evidence to permit constant checking, yet not nearly enough to enable us to construct an intelligible account without effort. Much has been written about that age, which has naturally stood in the forefront of interest and enquiry; yet it is an obvious fact that, e.g., the first decade of the first century B.C. is as obscure in the standard accounts as any dark age in history. Ancient historians were, on the whole, chiefly interested in bloodshed and sedition; and until its very end this decade offers little of either. Thus Livy, amid the expanding scale and scope of his later books, devotes only one book to nearly the whole of it. And this has had its effect on the modern tradition. One of the greatest living historians of ancient Rome says that in the nineties 'the state came near to the felicity of those that have no history'[1]—yet this blissful period, unaccountably interrupted by the *lex Licinia Mucia*,[2] ends with the explosion of the Rutilius trial in internal and the Social War in external affairs. A beginning of serious study has recently been made by E. Gabba;[3] but there is room for more. The two great trials that mark the middle of the decade—that of the younger Q. Caepio and that of C. Norbanus—make an obvious starting-point. That they are linked, and that they are important in the political history of the period, is clear from the persons involved; yet the connection is not usually given due weight, and closer

34

investigation may shed light on the whole of this obscure period.

Q. Servilius Caepio the younger, who was defended by L. Crassus, the orator, in the latter's consulship (95 B.C.),[4] had been one of the chief enemies of Saturninus and was now accused of violence in opposing that tribune.[5] It seems that Saturninus, in his first tribunate, had been among the chief enemies of his father, Q. Caepio the elder.[6] For Caepio the elder, guilty of the defeat of Arausio, was accused of *maiestas* under the law passed by Saturninus in his first tribunate and went into exile after conviction. This by itself would not necessarily show Saturninus' hostility; but there is more. Cn. Mallius Maximus (*cos.* 105), who commanded in the battle, was impeached for his share in the defeat by Saturninus himself and also driven into exile.[7] It is clear that some connection exists between these two attempts to turn the fortune of war (in the same battle) into a criminal charge;[8] and it is clinched by the fact that the prosecutor of Mallius passed the law under which Caepio was convicted. It was perhaps the younger Caepio's turbulence, earlier in that fateful year of 103, which sealed his father's fate.[9]

Next, Norbanus. He, in his tribunate, was the prosecutor of the elder Caepio; and it is all but certain that he held office as a colleague of Saturninus in that same year.[10] M. Antonius, under whom he had been quaestor, defended him when he was now accused of *maiestas* for his high-handed treatment of some tribunician colleagues who intervened in Caepio's favour.[11] The date of his trial has been much discussed. An older view, which put it before the turn of the century,[12] is decisively refuted by Cicero's statement that Antonius was already *censorius* at the time of the trial[13]—a statement that we have no reason whatever for thinking erroneous. The trial is thus dated not before 96. On the other hand, 91 is too late: not only is it the dramatic date of the *de oratore*, in which the trial is anything but recent news, but the political events of that year offer no proper context for it. Most scholars rightly accept 95 or 94;[14] and though there is no irrefutable argument as between the two, we shall see that 95 (and perhaps fairly early in the year) is the most likely date. In any case, however, the two trials must be kept firmly connected: not only did they both deal, after a lapse of many years, with events that took place in the same year (103), but Norbanus was brought to trial for his behaviour in connection with the prosecution of the younger Caepio's father, while Caepio himself was tried for his behaviour towards Norbanus' associate. Moreover, Caepio was defended by the orator L. Crassus, while Norbanus was prosecuted by one of Crassus' foremost disciples, young P. Sulpicius Rufus.[15] Thus, as we know that Caepio was tried in 95, this at once appears the more likely date for Norbanus' trial as well.

A picture thus begins to emerge. To fill in the outlines we must go far back into the past. The Aurelii Cottae, obscure in the background, first draw our attention. Their association with the Metelli went back a long way; and M. Scaurus, the *princeps senatus* and practically head of the house of the Metelli, was the chief witness against Norbanus,[16] as he had been one of the chief supporters of the elder Caepio.[17]

The first Aurelius to reach the consulship, C. Cotta, held the office twice: once in 252 and again in 248 B.C. In both cases he was a colleague of P. Servilius Geminus, and in both cases one of the consuls of the following year was L. Caecilius Metellus (*cos.* 251 and 247).[18] It is admittedly dangerous to deduce political association from association or succession in office—an argument that has often been pressed too far in an attempt to supplement insufficiency of sources; but this precise repetition of both collegiality and succession within the space of four years is too striking to be conceivably accidental; and it only remains to add that Cotta and Geminus were first elected in the consulship (253) of a cousin of the latter, Cn. Servilius Caepio.[19] This distant association is too interesting to be ignored; though we can merely point it out. It is quite uncertain to what extent it continued during the succeeding century. But about the middle of the second century B.C. it again leaps into prominence in precisely the same form; and this time it is lasting and irrefutably attested. In the years 144–140 we find the following men as consuls:[20]

144—L. Aurelius Cotta;
143—Q. Caecilius Metellus Macedonicus;
142—L. Caecilius Metellus Calvus, brother of the preceding;
     Q. Fabius Maximus Servilianus;
141—Cn. Servilius Caepio, brother of the preceding;
140—Q. Servilius Caepio, brother of the two preceding.

Again we must beware of arguing from mere proximity; but again there is solid evidence. Q. Metellus Macedonicus, despite outstanding achievements, had suffered two *repulsae* before he at last secured election.[21] It was practically his last chance: three were considered final rejection.[22] The belated success suggests powerful support. The course of history might have been very different, if Cotta had not helped Macedonicus to that consulship which laid the foundations of the most glorious period in the history of the Metelli.[23] Nor was Metellus forgetful of the *beneficium*: when L. Cotta, a most unsatisfactory character,[24] was prosecuted, a little later, by Scipio Aemilianus, Metellus successfully defended him.[25] The connection of the two Metelli (Macedonicus and Calvus) and the two Servilii Caepiones is equally well attested: they united against their common *inimicus* Q. Pompeius in one of the *causes célèbres* of the period.[26] Perhaps it is worth adding—if only because there is no mention of it in *The Magistrates of the Roman Republic* —that in 133 Macedonicus and Cn. Caepio collaborated, probably with special *imperium*, in subduing a serious slave revolt in Italy.[27]

Aurelii Cottae, Caecilii Metelli, Servilii Caepiones—the connection now continues. A L. Cotta, probably the son of the *ueterator*, was consul in 119 with L. Metellus Delmaticus, the son of Calvus and nephew of Macedonicus.[28] It was the fateful year of the prosecution of C. Carbo and P. Decius and of the tribunate of C. Marius.[29] When the tribune turned against his benefactors, the Metelli, and proposed a revolutionary bill, Cotta joined his colleague in determined opposition to it.[30] The next L. Cotta appears as tribune in 103 and colleague of Saturninus and Norbanus, whom he opposed. Name and date suggest that he is a son of the *cos.* 119.[31] He is notorious as a bad orator;[32] but it is also worth noting that he was a friend of another interesting character, Q. Lutatius Catulus.[33] This man, known to us from Cicero's loving admiration, had the common and difficult task of restoring the fortunes of a fallen family;[34] in this endeavour he suffered three *repulsae*: the first when his brother-in-law, the ill-fated Q. Caepio, was elected (for 106), the next in Caepio's consulship, the third in the following year.[35] That was as much misfortune as a man was permitted, and in the following year we do not hear of his being a candidate.[36] Then comes a sudden change: in 103 he is elected, as colleague of Marius.[37] And the events of their consulship and later proconsulship show that Marius was throughout friendly and co-operative, even going to the length of refusing a separate triumph and celebrating a joint one with his colleague.[38] How does the brother-in-law of Caepio, *patronus senatus*[39] through his notorious jury-law[40] and example of oligarchic reaction and arrogance,[41] come to be promoted to previously unattainable office with the support of C. Marius, in the very year that saw his brother-in-law's final misfortune? Closer investigation suggests an answer. A few years before (probably just before 110)[42] Marius had temporarily achieved respectability of a sort by marrying a Julia, of the family of the Caesares—a lady descended from kings and gods, who was to be immortalized by the *laudatio* pronounced by her nephew.[43] The family, of ancient lineage, had—like so many others—lost the public eye and was at the time represented by energetic young men eager to restore its glories. In 103 the link, forged perhaps for an entirely different purpose, binds the *adfines* in revolutionary co-operation: either in that year or perhaps in 100 we find two Caesares serving on commissions connected with the schemes of Marius and Saturninus.[44] The date does not matter much for our purpose: the Caesares, who demonstrably supported those schemes by 100, will certainly have done so in 103, however the accident of epigraphic survival be dated. Of these two young men, however, one—the famous orator and wit C. Caesar Strabo—was the uterine brother of Q. Catulus.[45] Not much imagination is now needed to understand the sudden change in the latter's fortunes: during 103 he will have deserted the losing cause of his brother-in-law Caepio and, through his brother Caesar, attached himself to Marius, whose support at last brought him the consulship and martial glory. Another important marriage marks these unstable years: C. Caesar, the future dictator, was born—as everyone should now admit—in 100.[46] His father, the other of the two Caesares associated with Marius and Saturninus, must have married Aurelia (of the family of the Cottae)[47] in 102 or 101, i.e. at the very time when Marius was the friend of Catulus. The *volte-face* from the violence offered to Norbanus by L. Cotta in 103 is instructive: the example of Catulus showed that the friendship of Marius was worth cultivating; and the Caesares were willing intermediaries.

Marius, as we have seen, was generous.[48] Yet it did not help much in the long run. Catulus, seeing his glory eclipsed, in popular estimation, by that of his colleague, and seeing the fortunes of Marius less bright than before, began, with the eager help of Marius' enemies, to spread his own version of the Cimbric campaigns, extolling his own exploits and belittling his colleague's achievement.[49] No wonder that friendship turned to implacable hatred; on no one's death did Marius more emphatically insist, after his capture of Rome in 87, than on that of his ungrateful colleague, who had requited kindness with denigration.[50]

Catulus, then, is a further link between the Cottae and the Caepiones. Another link with the Metelli is provided by a successful *nouus homo*, P. Rutilius Rufus (*cos.* 105). This man's sister had married M. Aurelius Cotta, whose three sons were in due course to reach the consulate.[51] Rutilius himself was a special favourite of the Metelli: his praetorship is probably to be connected with the consulate of Metellus and Cotta in 119;[52] he suffered a *repulsa* for the consulship in 115, when a Metellus was campaigning together with him and was elected. Rutilius was defeated by M. Aemilius Scaurus.[53] The Metelli seem to have at once 'adopted' the victor, who was obviously destined for greatness: in the same year he became *princeps senatus* and soon married a Metella, perhaps a daughter of the Metellus who, as censor, had raised him to that dignity; and in due course he became the most honoured member of their *factio*.[54] But their protection of Rutilius continued, or at least was soon resumed; he went to Numidia as a legate of Numidicus and, at least after the latter's quarrel with Marius (if not before), became his chief lieutenant.[55] Marius remained his enemy and over a decade later was to be chiefly responsible for his conviction.[56] Finally Rutilius obtained the consulship for 105. There is little doubt that he was intended by the *factio* as the colleague of Catulus: the latter (we are told) was defeated by the *nouus homo* Cn. Mallius Maximus, not by Rutilius; and it is against Mallius that the spite of Q. Caepio (*cos.* 106) is concentrated,[57] even though Rutilius bore a similar stigma of *nouitas*.

As we have seen, the shade of the elder Q. Caepio dominates the trials of 95. Careful study of his political circle—which is that of the Metelli—is necessary if we are to understand them. Let us next look at his family. His wife is not known; it is just possible that she was a Metella.[58] His son, the younger Caepio (prosecuted in 95), married Livius Drusus' sister and gave his own sister (i.e. the daughter of the elder Caepio) in marriage to Drusus.[59] Drusus and Caepio were good friends as well as *adfines*: it was only a private quarrel that led to Caepio's desertion of his friends and emergence as Drusus' chief enemy in the latter's tribunate.[60] Drusus himself retained the support of the *factio*: Scaurus was to be his chief adviser.[61] It is again Rutilius who points and reinforces the connection—and enables us to date it back. His wife, famed (fortunately for the historian) for longevity, was a Livia— no doubt, as there is only one important family of Livii at the time, a sister of M. Livius Drusus (*cos.* 112) and therefore aunt of his son, the tribune of 91, and of his daughter, the wife of the younger Caepio.[62] Rutilius, it may be gathered from Cicero, supported the elder Caepio's jury-law—even if not to the extent of declaring himself the slave of the People, as a more unprincipled orator could do.[63] It now becomes clearer why it was the conviction of Rutilius in 92 that gave M. Drusus, his nephew, the final impetus towards working out his own projected reforms, with the help of M. Scaurus, himself threatened by Rutilius' enemies.[64] It has sometimes been maintained, after superficial enquiry, that Scaurus must have been hostile to Rutilius, as he had been in 116, before his close association with the Metelli and their *factio*.[65] That this is absurd for the nineties should now, at least, be clear.

It is regrettable that we have no precise evidence about the date, and little about the nature, of the quarrel between Drusus and Caepio—that quarrel which was to have such ·momentous consequences. Münzer[66] would put it as early as *c.* 103, when the elder Caepio's possessions would be up for auction. It is thus that he explains Pliny's statement that the cause of the estrangement was a ring. But this unsupported conjecture, however reasonable in itself, cannot stand in view of the impossibility of putting the quarrel so early; nor is the ring, even thus defined, a sufficient cause in itself. In Pliny[67] it is the cause of the Social War—which is silly, but does suggest a date not too remote from 91; and it is most unlikely either that the man defended by L. Crassus in 95 was then already 'nimis equestri ordini deditus' and hostile to the Senate,[68] or that personal enmity between Drusus and Caepio took a whole decade before it developed its political consequences.[69] We may take Pliny's word for the ring; but there must have been—perhaps pre-existing and activated by this incident—more serious causes of enmity between the two men, though we must certainly believe the testimony of our sources that private preceded political antagonism. As it happens, there is a very probable cause of such private enmity that we can recover. Strabo, in telling the story of the tainted gold of Delphi and Tolosa, informs us that the daughter of the elder Caepio led a shameful life.[70] Now this daughter was at one time, as we have seen, the wife of M. Drusus. It is a reasonable suggestion that Drusus, high-minded and priggish,[71] divorced her for adultery—an action that would naturally be resented by the high-spirited Caepio. For such resentment—unjust, but understandable—we have, as it happens, a precise parallel a generation later: when Pompey divorced Mucia, he stirred up a hornet's nest.[72] Here, at last, we have a proper explanation for Caepio's astonishing *volte-face*—especially, of course, if the *boni* approved Drusus' action.

And this may help us with the date. For that now depends on what we can deduce about the two marriages of Livia, the sister of Drusus.[73] She was married twice and had children by both her husbands: we hear of a Caepio and a Servilia, obviously the children of the younger Q. Caepio, and of a Porcius Cato (the later Uticensis) and a Porcia, the children—as we happen to be told explicitly—of a M. Porcius Cato, son of the child of Cato the Censor's old age, M. Cato Salonianus.[74] Thus, after being divorced by Caepio, Livia must have married Cato,[75] who died soon after (clearly before 91), leaving her and the children in the charge of her brother M. Drusus. It is interesting to observe that this Cato (or possibly—though we have no real reason for thinking so—his brother L. Cato) had been tribune in 99 and, with Q. Pompeius Rufus, had unsuccessfully proposed the recall from exile of Metellus Numidicus.[76] Pompeius, grandson (no doubt) of the *cos.* 141, whose *inimicitiae* with the Metelli had finally been happily resolved,[77] was later to be *cos.* 88 as colleague and *adfinis* of Sulla, whose daughter married his son; and, as we might expect, we find that M. Cato was a particular friend of Sulla, soon to be the special *protégé* of the Metelli against Marius.[78] Pompeius was also an intimate friend of P. Sulpicius Rufus, the prosecutor of Norbanus and friend of M. Drusus and C. Cotta.[79] Thus the

D

second marriage of Drusus' sister kept her well within the *factio*, which it helped to cement. Again and again careful study of the *factio* confirms its multiple interrelations—it is not a matter of basing sweeping generalizations on a stemma—and brings us back in the end to the trials of 95.

Let us return to the puzzling and all-important question of the date of Livia's divorce and re-marriage. Servilia (the mother of Brutus the tyrannicide) was born before 100[80] and can give us no help. But her brother Caepio, to whom Cato Uticensis was so much attached, may be more useful. There is a good case for holding that he was quaestor under Pompey in 67, the year of his death.[81] If so, we may put his birth in 98; for a man of his station would hold junior office *suo anno*. Thus Livia was probably still married to Caepio in 98. On the other hand, Cato Uticensis was probably born late in 95.[82] Thus Livia's divorce and re-marriage should be put (with a slight margin) in 97 or 96: there are only four or five years, and not a whole decade, between the personal estrangement of Caepio and Drusus and Caepio's emergence—with the prosecution of Scaurus in 92[83]—as the extreme enemy of the *boni*. That is no longer excessive: the road was a hard one for him to tread, and the spur of *dolor*—the injured pride of the Roman aristocrat, which turned so many old friends of the *boni* into bitter enemies (we need only mention Ti. Gracchus and Caesar)—will not necessarily at once have driven him to the very end. It is a pity that these years of Caepio's life are wrapped in obscurity. In 91 he appears to have been praetor.[84] That suggests an aedileship about the middle of the decade—the very years about which we should like to know more. If he did hold the aedileship—as, in the case of such an ambitious young man, is almost certain—96 is perhaps too early (an aedile of 96, of such high family, ought to have reached the praetorship before 91); 95 is excluded as the year of his trial; and 94 (or even 93) is possible. Unfortunately we cannot be sure. No aediles are actually named in our sources between 99 and 91, and of those conjectured none can be dated with any confidence. Caepio's position in 95 has often been misunderstood or ignored.[85] 95, the year of his trial, saw him at the crossroads: a year or two after his quarrel with Drusus and the attendant divorces, and perhaps the year of his candidature for the aedileship (unless he was contemplating it for the following

year), which was the key to high office. He had not yet openly
embraced the cause of his former enemies and deserted his friends;
but Drusus had their firm support and he himself their disapproval
—the immediate re-marriage of Livia with M. Cato (whose connection with the *factio* we have seen) contrasts with the absence—
in view of what Strabo tells us, hardly accidental—of any notice
of a new marriage by Servilia. The bitterness he felt was finally to
explode, in 92, in his attack on M. Scaurus, the head of the *factio*
and chief supporter of Drusus. This heinous act—Scaurus had
actually suffered physical injury in supporting Caepio's father[86]—
has for some reason never received the attention it demands. It
should now, however, be easier to see its importance in the history
of a troubled period and a troubled life. It also becomes clearer
why the attack of Caepio was made in 95; personally already
somewhat estranged from the *factio* and therefore isolated, he
seemed the weak point at which it might be attacked. Yet his fall
would have immediately involved his former friends, who were
too closely linked with him in the events of 103. So the consul
Crassus had to come to his aid. Perhaps this will help to explain
Cicero's puzzling reference to Crassus' speech;[87] for the consul did not
give of the best of his art, but merely delivered an extended *laudatio*.

L. Licinius Crassus[88] the orator, like his friend and *adfinis* Q.
Mucius Scaevola the Pontifex, seems less closely tied to the *factio*
than the men we have hitherto been considering. *Popularis* in his
youth, with his attack first on the turncoat Carbo and then (over
Narbo Martius) on the Senate as a whole, he had, like many others,
approached more closely to the *boni* once he had acquired *dignitas*
and raised his price. His speech in support of the elder Q. Caepio's
lex iudiciaria, from which we have a well-known fragment, marks
his conversion—and uneasy acceptance by the *factio*: Rutilius
distrusted his facile phrases.[89] In the nineties Crassus and Scaurus
were allies: it was Crassus and Scaevola—perhaps for the very
reason that they appeared to be more independent and untainted—
whom the *factio* entrusted with the task of dealing with the allies
who had been usurping Roman citizenship (as we shall see, not
without help from the friends of Marius);[90] and Scaurus may have
inspired their legislation.[91] It was Scaevola who, accompanied by
Rutilius (the man who appears again and again at the very heart
of the *factio*), went to Asia—probably on the motion of Scaurus—

in order to protect the suffering province from the *publicani* and from Marius.[92] Crassus, then, for both personal and good political reasons, had to support the son of his old associate Q. Caepio in 95; though he did so with little enthusiasm, perhaps already foreseeing the future: four years later he was to be one of the chief supporters of Drusus and enemies of the younger Caepio. As it happens, we know of another political case in which Crassus appeared about this time: he spoke against M. Claudius Marcellus, an old officer of Marius.[93] The trial is often[94] dated, without discussion or reason, in 91—a most improbable year. Though we cannot be sure, some time around 95 seems much more in keeping. It was, as we shall soon see, a time of reckoning with Marius and his friends. Like the lawyer Scaevola, however, the shrewd orator Crassus to a large extent preserved his freedom of action and insured himself against failure: the distrust of the uncompromising Rutilius for the versatile phrasemonger was not unjustified. Probably in 94 or 93, a daughter of Crassus and granddaughter of Scaevola the Augur was married off to the young son of Marius,[95] which made the latter an *adfinis* of both Crassus and Scaevola. Scaevola profited at once, gaining immunity from prosecution when Rutilius fell.[96] We may rest assured that, if Crassus had not died after his swan-song in 91,[97] he would—despite his association with the *factio*, to whose young members he acted as teacher and guide—have weathered the tempests of the following years as successfully as his friend Scaevola, who only died a martyr's death after a final miscalculation in 82.[98]

Thus we return to our starting-point. Though much, inevitably, remains dark—we should like to know the name of Caepio's prosecutor and the relative dates of the trials of Caepio and Norbanus (though here conjecture is possible)—much has become clearer. We now perhaps know more about the *factio nobilitatis* in the nineties—that circle, centred in the Metelli, which prosecuted Norbanus and was forced to defend Caepio. Patient inquiry can glimpse further connections; but some are not of major importance for this period, and in the case of others the details are shrouded in obscurity so far impenetrable. Other families and individuals were connected with the *factio*, at least for a while or in part. While we must not overstress mere *adfinitas*, unsupported by positive indications of collaboration, it is often the only evidence we have and at least invites conjecture. The family of the Claudii Pulchri, known throughout its history for *potentia* and *factio*, remains obscure. Ap. Claudius (*cos.* 143)—consular, censorian, *triumphalis* and *princeps senatus*, and thus one of the most powerful men of his day—was united with Metellus Macedonicus by hatred for Scipio Aemilianus.[99] These two great men also shared the good fortune of being inordinately prolific. Metellus had six or seven children—it is not certain which—and Cicero has preserved a roll-call of young *adfines*.[100] One of Appius' sons (the later *cos.* 79) married a Caecilia, granddaughter of Macedonicus.[101] It is a tenuous connection and we do not know whom the other son married. He, however, was the C. Claudius (*cos.* 92) whom Cicero[102] describes as 'propter summam nobilitatem et singularem potentiam magnus'; and though the words would come easily where one spoke of a Claudian, the connection with the Metelli and their circle must have been at least part of what was in Cicero's mind. It was this C. Claudius who, as consul, brought about Senatorial action (initiated by the *sententia* of L. Crassus) against Cn. Papirius Carbo[103]—and it is worth remembering that Carbo was later one of the leaders of the *Mariani*. By then C. Claudius was dead; but his brother Appius, husband of a Metella, was one of the few men against whom (in absence) strong measures were taken by the Cinnan government.[104] In 95 C. Claudius was praetor and was assigned the important *quaestio repetundarum*.[105] It would be illuminating to know what cases he tried. As we have seen, it is possible (though quite uncertain) that the case of Marcellus was one of them.[106] Another possibility—again the year is quite uncertain, but the middle of the decade is politically indicated—is the case of M'. Aquillius. This old colleague of Marius, who had been granted an ovation after concluding a servile war in Sicily, was accused by an obscure man and wretched orator called L. Fufius.[107] The date is nowhere stated. The Epitomator of Livy mentions the trial, which was dramatic enough to catch his fancy, at the beginning of book lxx. That book contains (as far as we can tell) the account of the years 99–92, and unfortunately the Epitomator, while normally keeping to chronological order within any one sphere, can never be trusted to reproduce chronology when changing from one theatre of action to another.[108] Thus, while we can be certain that the trial of

M'. Aquillius comes between the last and the next Roman happen-
ings mentioned (the return of Numidicus and the trial of Rutilius),
we cannot with any certainty relate it chronologically to the foreign events reported between it and the trial of Rutilius.[109] The
Epitomator likes to group by subject-matter (inefficiently enough),
and the main reason why the Aquillius trial has been attracted to
the beginning of book lxx is probably that the victories of Aquillius
conclude his book lxix.[110] We may be reasonably sure that neither
was the case in the text of Livy.

Aquillius was defended by M. Antonius, supported by C.
Marius, and acquitted. He had held the other consulship of 101,
when Marius, at the height of his glory, could have any colleague
he liked. Before that he had been Marius' chief legate in Gaul,[111]
and he was now preserved to become the man who—hardly without
Marius' approval—was to plunge Rome into war with Mithridates.[112] But his counsel, M. Antonius, deserves more comment.
Cicero, who greatly admired him, shows him to us in 91 as the
senior statesman and prominent member of the circle of the *boni*—
though at the cost of turning his defence of Norbanus into a piece
of flagrant dishonesty.[113] This presentation has misled modern
scholars, and his death after Marius' capture of Rome has seemed
to lend colour to it.[114] Yet we have seen that other notorious
executions on that grim occasion—those of two Caesares and of
Q. Catulus—were precisely those of old associates of Marius who
had turned against him and actively opposed him, and whom he
therefore considered guilty of betraying him. To these examples we
may now add another, not usually noticed. P. Crassus (*cos.* 97)—
who, like Catulus, anticipated execution by suicide—was not a
man very active in internal politics; his fame was acquired mainly
in war, and we know very little about him.[115] But he was married,
as Cicero happens to tell us, to a woman of the obscure, but
apparently wealthy, *gens Venuleia*—for, unlike another branch of
his family, he was not *Diues* either in name or in possessions.
Now, one of the very few Venulei known to us in the Republican
period (*RE* lists only three) is the man, almost certainly a senator,
whom Sulla proscribed.[116] That he was an *adfinis* of P. Crassus is
obvious; and we may thus add P. Crassus (who, with his sons,
helped to defend Rome against Cinna) to the list of ex-*Mariani*,
whose death was the reward of betrayal.

This survey of some of the victims of 87—we shall return to them later—puts M. Antonius in his proper place. We have already met him as the defender of Aquillius, in co-operation with Marius; and we next see him as the defender of C. Norbanus, one of the most notorious *populares* and firmly opposed by Scaurus; and we learn that Norbanus has been his quaestor in Cilicia.[117] It would be interesting to know—but the matter has never been satisfactorily investigated—to what extent such appointments, in this period, in fact depended (or could depend) on the choice of the commander.[117a] But we do not know. We learn, however, that this relationship founded *clientela* of a particularly sacred kind: Norbanus was to Antonius 'in liberum loco more maiorum' and was his *sodalis*.[118] Yet there is certainly more than *mos maiorum* and the accident of the lot: examples of quaestors who quarrelled with their superiors, some even to the extent of later prosecuting them, are numerous.[119] There is more to this friendship than Cicero knew—or will admit. We may note that in 92 (it seems) Antonius defended M. Marius Gratidianus in a civil case.[120] This man, nephew of C. Marius both by birth and by adoption, was closely connected with Antonius through his father M. Gratidius, who, after a career as a *popularis* in his native town of Arpinum, was killed while serving as a prefect under Antonius in Cilicia.[121] These Marian connections are confirmed by what we know of the circumstances in which Antonius attained the consulship for 99: Saturninus and Glaucia—who, of course, did not want to precipitate the breach with Marius, which ultimately proved inevitable —opposed the candidature of Memmius to the death,[122] but are nowhere mentioned as having done anything against that of Antonius. He, being outside the city with *imperium*, took no active part in the events that led to their destruction; but he certainly supported the action of Marius and the Senate at the time, and, as consul, opposed the surviving supporters of Saturninus.[123] That, however, was as a friend of Marius, not as a friend of the *factio* opposed to him; for, though it was well within his powers, and in spite of the moving pleas of so many noble Metelli and their *adfines*, he did nothing to further the cause of Numidicus' recall.[124]

In 97 M. Antonius and L. Valerius Flaccus were elected censors.[125] Flaccus was an old friend of Marius: he had been his

colleague in the consulship of 100, and Rutilius had contemptu-
ously called the Patrician 'more Marius' servant than his colleague'.[126] Under the Cinnan régime Flaccus, with others of his
family, was to be a prominent 'collaborator' (though moderate)
and was to become *princeps senatus*.[127] These, then, were the men
elected in 97. Marius himself had wanted the censorship, but
had not felt strong enough to stand.[128] A censorship of Marius and
Flaccus would have been opposed to the limit by the *factio*, and
Marius could not risk failure. So a bargain was struck: Marius
received the augurate[129] and his friend M. Antonius, more acceptable to his enemies, became Flaccus' colleague. We know very little
about the censorship, and no census figures survive; yet it is clear
that they must have registered masses of Italians as citizens, for
the *lex Licinia Mucia* followed under the next pair of consuls after
their *lustrum*.[130] Nor can such large-scale negligence on the part
of the censors have been accidental: having seen their personal and
political connections, we may safely compare the known generosity—stretching, on his famous admission, beyond the law—of
Marius.[131] It would be beyond our immediate scope to pursue
this subject further. But it is clear that the plans of Marius and his
friends aroused apprehension: the *lex Licinia Mucia* follows at once,
as does (whether it is to be put before or after that law) the trial of
Norbanus and perhaps, as we have seen, other trials affecting the
interests of Marius. But one of the most important of the latter is
one which we have not yet had occasion to mention: it is that
of T. Matrinius of Spoletium, arising out of the *lex Licinia Mucia*.

T. Matrinius[132] had been given the citizenship under an odd
provision of the colonial law of Saturninus as a member of one of
the colonies there envisaged; as the colonies were never actually
founded, it was submitted by the prosecution that Marius' grant
was null and void. What the legal position in fact was, we cannot
tell for certain; though both common sense and the only precedent
we know[133]—admittedly distant in time and not precisely corresponding—suggest that the prosecution had a very good case.
However, Marius had enough *auctoritas* to protect his client, and
the case failed. The prosecutor of Matrinius was a L. Antistius,
about whom Cicero tells us nothing except that he was a good
speaker. But is has been very plausibly suggested[134] that he was
none other than L. (Antistius) Reginus, who provided an *exem-*

plum of friendship by accompanying the elder Q. Caepio into exile at Smyrna.[135] Caepio's death should in any case be put before the date of the Norbanus trial,[136] and his friend will hardly have stayed on in Asia after.

The case was of importance far beyond its immediate scope: it was a test case of the first order, and hundreds, if not thousands, of new citizens must have been concerned in its outcome.[137] When Marius' *auctoritas* prevailed, they were safe—and more firmly attached to him than ever. But the trial of Matrinius, from the numbers and the issues involved, must surely be added to the great cases of the decade; and the link—through the person of the prosecutor, the best friend of the elder Caepio, whose policy of restricting the *ciuitas* is attested, though often ignored[138]—with the *factio* of the Metelli and their friends is welcome confirmation of the coherence of the pattern, and hardly unexpected even from more direct evidence: M. Scaurus sufficiently expressed the contempt of this circle for the new citizens.[139]

This brings us back at last to the trial of Norbanus. C. Norbanus was, it seems, not of Roman birth.[140] Münzer makes him a native of Norba. This may be true, but the evidence is not convincing. The story of Norba's desperate resistance to Sulla is based on a single occurrence of the name in Appian[141] (where, incidentally, it has been challenged and 'Nola' suggested); and in any case local *nomina* need not denote origin any more than local *cognomina* do: Norbanus need no more be a man from Norba than (say) the Terentii Massiliotae necessarily come from Massilia or the Aelii Ligures from Liguria. Münzer seems to think that Norbanus adopted his name on acquiring the citizenship; but it is unheard of for Italians to change their names when becoming citizens, except (and even this only at a much earlier period) for purposes of Latinization—and that is the one intention that would never have produced the *nomen* 'Norbanus'. On the other hand, it is inconceivable that he should have borne the name in his home town of Norba: in fact, however we look at it, the name itself is evidence against rather than in favour of (at any rate immediate) Norban origin. It is worth noting, however, that the name fits into a class of *nomina* perhaps of Etruscan origin, as does that of the Perpernae, the only non-Latin *nomen* to precede that of C. Norbanus in the consular *fasti*.[142] Etruria was to be the stronghold of the Marian

cause from Marius' landing there in 87 down to Sulla's terrible
vengeance after his victory. In any case, whether Norban or Etruscan, Norbanus was a new citizen (it seems) and had attached
himself to the cause of Marius. His trial, eight years after the
alleged offence,[143] was a move by the oligarchy, represented by the
prosecutor Sulpicius, in the attack on Marius and his friends,
which followed the censorship of L. Valerius Flaccus and M.
Antonius. It is no wonder that Antonius, Norbanus' chief friend
and protector, rushed to his defence; though, as we shall soon see,
we are fortunate in having this indication of continuing friendship
between Marius and Antonius at this time. Nor was Antonius the
only one interested: it has been plausibly argued that new citizens
flocked to Rome for the trial, and that it was on this occasion that
Scaurus (who testified against Norbanus) launched his insult against
them.[144]

It would be helpful if we could disengage and delineate the
factio of Marius in the nineties, as we can that of his opponents, and
as we can to some extent do for his following during the years of
Saturninus and again in 88–7. Unfortunately it seems impossible;
though perhaps there is still some evidence to be found in much-
read texts and discerned as relevant by more skilful research.
Meanwhile the picture cannot be as clear and meaningful as, for a
proper understanding of the period, it should. The *seditio* of
Saturninus and his associates had led to a disastrous split in the
Marian *factio*. This is not the place to examine the reasons—
solid and serious reasons, not usually given due weight in either
the ancient or the modern tradition—that led to the break between Marius and his associates and made him the saviour of the
Republic against them.[144a] But the results are important: the split
was deep, cutting through families and leaving bitter hatred.
The Patrician family of the Cornelii Dolabellae was related to
Saturninus. A L. Dolabella, perhaps not in Rome at the crucial
time, triumphs early in 98;[145] a Cn. Dolabella had remained with
Saturninus to the grim end.[146] On a lower social level the Labieni,
knights from Picenum, divide in a more tragic manner and brothers fight on opposite sides.[147] Their case, transmitted to us by mere
accident as pointing a barrister's invective, may be taken as
typical of many not thus recorded. For no one was later proud of
loyalty to Saturninus. Of the immediate associates, C. Appuleius

Decianus, a relative of the tribune, manages to survive. *Pietas*
causes him to attack the abominable P. Furius and a L. Valerius
Flaccus, related to Marius' friend and colleague.[148] For L. Valerius
Flaccus had, of course, supported Marius; so had M. Antonius,
who, as consul, strongly opposed the designs of Sex. Titius, another
surviving friend of Saturninus.[149]

The split, inevitably, transformed the Marian *factio*. We have
seen that at the height of his glory Marius had had the eager
co-operation of some members of the opposing circle—the Caesares, the Cottae, Q. Catulus, P. Crassus, and no doubt others.
But the breach with Saturninus did not mean a *rapprochement*
with the Metelli: as long as he could, Marius opposed the return
of Numidicus.[150] Yet the latter was recalled, and Marius, having
split his own following beyond healing and failed to prevent the
return of his chief *inimicus*, found his unlikely friends melting away.
Thus, as we have seen, he could not reach the censorship; and
he was forced into unseemly demagogy, like an unsuccessful
tribune.[151] We do not know precisely when each of his time-serving
noble friends deserted him. Catulus was probably one of the first;
having gained his consulship, and his military success, he found
Marius nothing but an obstacle in the way of proper appreciation
of his own achievements.[152] The poet Archias, who had begun by
singing the exploits of both of them, succeeding—with true Greek
tact—in delighting them both, was soon introduced by Catulus
into a circle that reads[153] like a list of the faction hostile to Marius.
P. Crassus was away from Rome[154] and will hardly have needlessly
committed himself before his return in 93. On the Caesares we
have no precise information. Hostility first appears openly in 89,
when C. Caesar Strabo, in an illegal (or at least questionable)
candidature for the consulship of 88, violently opposes Marius.[155]
But it may have begun earlier. Two Caesares were consuls in 91
and 90 respectively.[156] Nothing is known of the *cos.* 91 (Sex.
Julius C.f.—an uncle of the later Dictator, it seems) except that
he escaped assassination at the Latin festival; it seems inconceivable that in that eventful year a consul should not once be
mentioned in connection with internal politics, and we are forced
to conclude that he was abroad, while Philippus, his colleague,
looked after Rome.[157] Whether he ever returned to Rome, in order
to do his duty in the Social War, or whether he stayed in his

unknown province during those years and perhaps died there, we do not know: homonymity has produced inextricable confusion, and Sex. Caesar remains a figure of mystery.[158] L. Caesar, *cos.* 90, was a brother of C. Caesar Strabo, with whom Marius quarrelled in 89, and was to share his brother's fate in 87: with this branch of the family the breach, deepened (if not begun) by Strabo's irresponsible action, was open and unbridgeable, and events moved inevitably to their tragic conclusion.

Perhaps there is some more evidence in rather an unexpected place. When the Social War broke out, the two consuls were given their *prouinciae* and, as circumstances demanded, were assigned a body of *legati* representing all the military experience at the disposal of the Republic. The names of the *legati* under each consul make interesting reading.[159] Under P. Rutilius Lupus we find Cn. Pompeius Strabo, Q. Servilius Caepio, C. Perperna, C. Marius, and a Valerius Messalla; under L. Caesar Appian gives P. (Cornelius) Lentulus, 'a brother of Caesar', T. Didius, (P.) Licinius Crassus, (L.) Cornelius Sulla, and (M. Claudius) Marcellus. The consul P. Rutilius Lupus—not, as far as we know, closely related to that other Rutilius whom we have had occasion to notice so often and who was also a *nouus homo*—was a relative of Marius, to whom, no doubt, he owed his election; and we are told that he personally chose Marius as his legate.[160] There is no reason to doubt it and, as we shall soon see, every reason to believe it: the other *legati* were clearly also either selected by their respective commanders or at least so assigned as to meet the commanders' wishes. The lists are too neatly arranged not to attract attention; but from want of preliminary investigation they have not received adequate comment.[161] If our enquiry hitherto has borne any fruit, we should now be able to extract valuable information from the lists.

First, some names and identities. P. Lentulus, the 'brother of Caesar', has often—and rightly—been suspected: Q. Catulus was, of course, a brother of Caesar, and he was a legate in the War; it would be an odd coincidence if he were not mentioned, while P. Lentulus—bearing a name with the same ending—appeared as a brother of Caesar and a legate, though not otherwise attested in either of these classes. Coincidences may happen and our evidence is scanty; yet Catulus is the obvious candidate here. Either a scribe or even Appian himself will have been misled by *homoeoteleuton* in text or source into applying to Lentulus the phrase that rightly belongs to him. Thus in the original Lentulus' name will have been followed by that of Catulus, 'a brother of Caesar'.[162] Valerius Messalla and Marcellus cannot be determined with certainty. Marcellus comes very near it. He is the father of Aeserninus (we know of his heroic defence of Aesernia), and must surely be the old legate of Marius whom we have met in the *repetundae* court.[163] There is also an aedilician M. Marcellus available—a friend of L. Crassus, who was curule aedile in 91, when he must have been nearly forty.[164] But he has not the standing to be referred to here, among so many praetorians and consulars.[165] Messalla is much discussed, but exact determination is impossible and does not matter much for our present purpose. We need only notice that an obscure fragment of C. Caesar Strabo (brother of the *cos.* 90) establishes the Messallae as kinsmen of the Caesares, who appear to have quarrelled with them;[166] and Metellus Numidicus, at a date which is quite indeterminable, had prosecuted a Messalla *repetundarum*.[167] The Messallae, like so many others, in the end made their way successfully into Sulla's favour—in fact, more successfully than most. But it looks as though the charms of Valeria were exercised in the very real interests of a worried family; she had been divorced by her first husband, in spite of her beauty and high birth,[168] and we must conclude that there had been good reason, in the early days of the Sullan terror, for dissociating oneself from the family.

We can now look more closely at personal and political connections. The consul L. Caesar, as a brother of C. Caesar Strabo, would certainly be an enemy of Marius by 89; the list of his legates now documents this enmity for 90. Sulla and Catulus need no further comment. T. Didius was a *nouus homo* intimately connected with the Metelli: the *lex Caecilia Didia* links their names in one of the best-known oligarchic laws,[169] and as a tribune Didius had joined L. Cotta in defence of the elder Q. Caepio and determined opposition to Norbanus.[170] The anti-Marian tendency of Caesar's staff is thus *prima facie* sufficiently established to enable us to draw useful conclusions about the remaining *legati*. That P. Crassus, once Marius' friend, was rightly regarded as a bitter enemy in 87, we have noticed before.[171] Finding him in such company in 90, we

are justified in assuming that the estrangement was completed by
then. Lentulus and Marcellus are an interesting pair and must be
considered together: they are linked, in the next generation, by
the name of P. Cornelius Lentulus Marcellinus. Of this man we
know that he was the brother of Aeserninus, i.e. another son of the
Marcellus here mentioned, who—as we have seen—must be the
old legate of Marius.[172] The conclusion is almost inevitable that the
P. Lentulus who adopted him must be the Lentulus here found as
his father's colleague. This does not place our Lentulus unambiguously: the next generation brings a whole brood of Lentuli
who are *P.f.* and apparently not closely related.[173] But as this
Lentulus is the only one of his generation mentioned as having
attained any prominence, he must be identical with that other
prominent Lentulus whose execution Marius ordered after his
capture of Rome in 87.[174] We have seen the large number of his
fellow-victims who were ex-*Mariani*:[175] apart from the hostile
consuls Octavius and Merula, whose death comes in a special
category,[176] all the prominent victims of those grim weeks, as far as
we know anything at all about their associations, belong to this
class.[177] P. Lentulus, closely linked with Marius' old legate M.
Marcellus and (together with him) in the anti-Marian company of
L. Caesar's staff, may with confidence be added to that list of
renegades.

The legates of L. Caesar, like the consul himself, may be said
to be enemies of Marius, whether old irreconcilables or renegades.
Those of Lupus, the *propinquus* of Marius, may be expected to be
Marius' friends. We have already seen that Messalla—whoever he
was—probably belonged to that class. About Cn. Pompeius
Strabo's career before 90 we know nothing except a quaestorship
that reveals his character, but not his politics.[178] After his consulship in 89 he was put on trial, but somehow avoided punishment;
and an attempt by the *factio* to send Q. Pompeius Rufus (*cos.* 88),
whose connections we have already noticed,[179] to supersede him
in his command, failed owing to Strabo's unscrupulous resource-
fulness. He later fights—half-heartedly enough—against Cinna,
while plotting with him; and after his death his son is seen to have
the support of influential friends of Cinna, including Cn. Papirius
Carbo himself. When Sulla arrived, Pompey had to work hard to
live down his Cinnan connections.[180] Cn. Pompeius Strabo thus

certainly had connections among the *Mariani* and enemies among the *factio*: we may recall that he was *homo dis ac nobilitati periuisus*.[181] The case of C. Perperna is even clearer: this man of Etruscan descent will be a brother of M. Perperna (*cos.* 92), who was to be censor under the Cinnan government in 86 and whose homonymous son, after holding Sicily for the government in 82, survived to serve under Lepidus and Sertorius.[182] The Marian connection is obvious—and, as we have seen, not surprising in Etruria.

Q. Servilius Caepio, the last of the men on our list, deserves more detailed notice. As we have already seen,[183] he had travelled a long way since his quarrel with Drusus; *dolor* had driven him into violent opposition to the *boni*. In 92 he appears as the enemy of Scaurus, his father's friend, and in 91 he is the chief champion of the *Equites* and, with Philippus, the chief enemy of Drusus. This must, on both counts, have led to co-operation with Marius: the latter's friendship with the *ordo equester* had just been advertised in the trial of P. Rutilius Rufus, and Drusus—as should be clear from all the evidence we have surveyed—was the protagonist of the faction hostile to Marius. Caepio's place here, as the colleague of Marius on the staff of Marius' *propinquus*, decisively confirms—as far as he is concerned—the results of our previous analysis and lays the foundations for further inference, which must meanwhile be postponed.

Study of these lists of *legati* has helped us considerably: we may take it that one of the consuls (Caesar) with his staff represented the *boni*, the other (Lupus) the *Mariani*; and their staffs, probably personally selected, divide accordingly. Cn. Pompeius Strabo—an ambiguous character—may, as being in this company and hated by the nobility, be put among the friends of Marius. It follows that in 89 also one consul (L. Porcius Cato, on whose family we have commented)[184] represents the *factio* and one (Cn. Pompeius) their opponents, whom we may call *Mariani*. This, though it seems never to have been noticed in this form, is reasonable enough: for the duration of the War, just as the law-courts were suspended,[185] there was also to be *concordia* in elections. With victory certain—owing, chiefly, to the successes of Pompeius —*concordia* was ended and the oligarchy proceeded to claim the benefits: the *lex Plautia iudiciaria*[186] restored its preponderance in the law-courts to such an extent that the man who had won the

War could be put on capital trial a few weeks or even days after his triumph,[187] and the consulships of 88 duly went to Q. Pompeius and L. Sulla. That year was to prove unpredictably disastrous; but that is beyond our present scope.

The lists of *legati* also show us that most of Marius' noble friends had already deserted him by (presumably) 91. Of Q. Catulus, who will have been the first, we knew it before; but we now add the Caesares—at least the two later executed—P. Crassus, M. Marcellus, and probably a new name, P. Lentulus. M. Antonius, though not listed by Appian as a legate in 90,[188] must go with them. In 95 he had defended Norbanus. The next notice we have of him is his undignified behaviour when accused before the Varian *quaestio*.[189] It is not likely that this was after the reform that made the *quaestio* an instrument of the *boni*: the man who was their firm friend in 87 will hardly have been prosecuted by them on a capital charge in 88. We may take it that the prosecution belongs to 90, and that he was prosecuted along with Scaurus and others. Nor is this altogether surprising: M. Antonius was close to the family of the Caesares. His son (father of the Triumvir) was to marry a daughter of L. Caesar (the *cos.* 90); and though this was perhaps a few years later,[190] the betrothal, as was the custom, will date back to earlier years and thus to the orator's lifetime. M. Antonius had probably, at some time after 95 and before 91, followed the Caesares, as they had followed Catulus, into the camp of the *boni*. By 91 Marius had lost most of his aristocratic friends—though he had gained the alliance of Q. Caepio—and, as was soon to become evident, was cut off from the *boni* by an unbridgeable chasm.

It is time to end this survey. The nineties, under the placid surface of Livy's uninterested brevity and the mist of our inevitable ignorance, are by no means a happy and settled period: our suspicions about the decade that begins with the last convulsions of the *seditio Appuleia* and ends with the Social War and the *lex Varia* have been amply confirmed by careful analysis of the available evidence. In our tradition—such as it is—the year 95, with its great trials and the *lex Licinia Mucia*, is crucial, and investigation can most usefully start at that point. It reveals the existence and—to some extent—the composition of a *factio nobilitatis* (the term chosen to designate it does not matter much and has deliberately been varied), and of a faction of Marius and his friends.

Factions are not static—this, indeed, appears from every page of our survey—and personal profit and preference will change; the historian, especially where his evidence is so limited, must necessarily employ terms and delineate patterns of misleading precision. Yet the validity of the general picture is not thereby impugned, and the grand pattern that emerges is not merely that in the historian's own mind.

We have at times had to use the word 'tragic': it is metaphorical, but not inept. As the drama of these years is resurrected before our eyes by—inevitably—laborious patching of fragments, patience may begin to seem unrewarded; but then attention and interest are caught both by a series of minor characters—like the younger Q. Caepio, or Q. Catulus—who become more than names, and above all by the tragic figure of C. Marius. For he emerges from this study as different from the *callidissimus homo* of Passerini's great analysis[191] as from the blunt soldier of older historians. Much remains to be done before we can follow his personal tragedy; but the outlines have appeared. Eager for power, yet also—like many another *nouus homo*—for acceptance by the *nobilitas*, which he faced with the ambivalent attitude of fascinated admiration and proclaimed contempt, he exercised power with discretion, making it—through *beneficia*, which he found were eagerly sought for—a means for securing acceptance and respectability. In the process he decisively split his own following and undermined the foundations of his power. Yet when he saved the Republic from his former friends, he saved it for his enemies: as his power diminished, his *beneficia* were forgotten and those who owed their station and—like Q. Catulus—even their lives to him began to draw back. We have seen how his plans to base his power solidly on Italian support—plans which we see developing even before 100—were foiled by the *boni* in 95 and brought about a fierce counter-attack on his friends. The result of that eventful year was stalemate; and the marriage of Marius' son, bringing him *adfinitas* with both the consuls of 95, may de due to the firmness he had shown and the comparative success he had achieved. But it was not enough to arrest the general trend: P. Crassus and M. Antonius, at least, must have abandoned him after 95, and probably not long—if at all—before 91. We do not know the circumstances; the way in which, in 92, Marius seized his chance of striking at an old enemy

E

in the heart of the *factio*, while conspicuously sparing his new *adfinis* Scaevola, shows increasing bitterness and proclaims a warning. Success against P. Rutilius Rufus brought its own nemesis: his opponents, forced to take extreme counter-measures, threatened, in a bold stroke, to solve the Italian problem to their own advantage and to divide and disarm the *ordo equester*, which Marius had just successfully united behind himself against Rutilius. That Marius must have opposed M. Livius Drusus and his backers should surely be clear enough: though direct evidence is lacking, the indirect evidence—much of it surveyed in this study—is overwhelming. It was now—or, to be precise, a little earlier, when Drusus' plans became known—that Marius allied himself with the renegade Q. Caepio: their friendship is clearly attested in 90. And he used his Etruscan and Umbrian connections—for it is mainly in these regions that we have evidence for Marius' influence, and not in others, where it has unsuccessfully been sought—in order to dispel Livius' myth of Italian unity.[192]

Perhaps it was this that lost him some of his friends: the Italian problem had moved beyond the stage where it could be the plaything of party politics, and Marius must bear his share of the blame for the Social War. It is possible that M. Antonius, generous to the Italians in his censorship, now welcomed generosity from whichever side it came, and finally broke with his old friend. To Marius it would nevertheless seem betrayal.

Meanwhile Marius had tried, in the East, to stir up a great war that should again make it necessary for him to save the Republic and perhaps restore the happy conditions of 102–1.[193] As this is comparatively well attested, we may suspect that he faced the prospect of the Social War also with (at least) equanimity, and his intrigues against Drusus became more explicable. He succeeded in both his immediate aims: Drusus' plans were defeated and the Social War broke out; and in the East Mithridates was goaded into attack. But neither of these political victories bore the desired fruit. Embittered and frustrated and an ailing man, he retired from his command in the Social War.[194] In 88, however, after failing to get the Eastern command he hoped for, he seemed at last to have his opportunity of achieving what he wanted: P. Sulpicius Rufus, a friend of M. Drusus, tried to revive the latter's programme; but times had changed, and his elders thought they knew better. He could not carry his own friends with him and was opposed by the consuls and the *factio* which had secured their election. *Dolor* at this now drove Sulpicius, as it had once driven Q. Caepio, to join Marius—and all the more quickly and thoroughly, as Caepio had shown the way. With all this and its consequences we cannot deal here; though it also needs detailed investigation, for which this study may perhaps serve as a preliminary. We must conclude with a glimpse of a disillusioned old man, who had given away power only to find that friends vanished with it; who came to live, in the end, for the sole object of seizing power in order to use it better; and who, when he succeeded in this after his enemies had employed murder and high treason to stop him, lived to exact bitter vengeance and died an object of horror to his own friends.

APPENDIX

THE SUPPOSED CAMPANIAN FOLLOWING OF MARIUS

I. Prosopography

Gabba (*Athenaeum* N.S. 29 (1951)), in the course of an article that was nothing less than epoch-making in its approach to the problems of this period, advanced the thesis that Marius had a large following among Campanians, especially of the upper classes. On this particular point his reasoning seems to me mistaken; and so great is the importance of his article (and his work on the period in general) that it seems urgently necessary for disagreement to be voiced and reasoned, in order to prevent the thesis from becoming generally accepted without examination.

He collects the names of men whom he calls Campanian adherents of Marius (pp. 256 f.). As the list is crucial to his whole thesis, investigation must concentrate on it. For convenience of reference I have numbered the names.

(1) and (2) *Cn.* and *Q. Granius*

They *may*, of course, belong to the well-known Campanian family active in the East; but neither of these *praenomina* is actually found there! 'Cn. Granius' almost certainly owes his name to an error of scribe or historian: see *RE*, s.v. 'Papirius', no. 38, coll. 1024 f. As for Q. Granius, compare Q. Granius the *praeco* (*RE*, s.v. 'Granius', no. 8):

this man, active in Rome well before the end of the second century, is in Cicero (*Br.* 172) the choicest example of *sapor uernaculus* which the Italian could never hope to attain. Q. Granius was the equivalent of a Cockney.

(3) *Q. Rubrius Varro*

Gabba writes: 'che questi *Rubrii* [i.e. Varro and the colleague of C. Gracchus] siano campani sembra a noi poter ricavare dalla presenza di altri *Rubrii* in Capua in quell'età'—a most unconvincing argument, as the name is both common and widespread (cf. *RE*, s.v.).

(4) *M. Laetorius*

Gabba derives his Campanian origin (tentatively) from the *magister pagi* Cn. Laetorius (*ILS* 6302)—a very unsatisfactory argument, as the Laetorii happen to belong to the oldest Plebeian families of Rome, and several members of that family in fact have the *praenomen* Marcus (see *RE*, s.v.).

(5) and (6) *P. and L. Magius*

These may be accepted as of *ultimately* Campanian family. They are most probably the sons of Minatus Magius of Aeclanum (*RE*, s.v. 'Magius', nos. 6, 8, 10); they are therefore Campanian only by remote descent and tell us nothing about Campania of their generation.

(7) *Gutta* (App. *b.c.* i 90)

He is mentioned as a Capuan together with Pontius Telesinus the Samnite and M. Lamponius the Lucanian. This seems to show that he fought for the Confederate armies in the Social War and came to join the Marian camp with the survivors of *Italia*. How far he is typical in this, we cannot tell. In any case, there is no reason to assume friendship with Marius.

(8) and (9) *L. and C. Insteius*

[These men (belonging to the tribe Falerna) almost certainly are Campanians. On the Falerna, see now L. R. Taylor, *Voting Districts* (1960) 272. The name 'Insteius' is common in Campania (see *CIL* x, Index). C. Tarquitius Priscus, also in the Falerna, should probably also (despite Cichorius, *Röm. Stud.* 167 f.) be regarded as a Campanian.]

(10) *Helvius Mancia*

This son of a freedman from Formiae has in any case nothing to do with the Campanian upper classes (and little with native Campanians).

His vituperation of Pompey in the law-courts, probably in 55, tells us nothing at all about his part (if any) in the first Civil War. On all counts he is quite irrelevant to this question.

(11) and (12) *C. Flavius Fimbria* (father and son)

Gabba refers to a Flavius Fimbria at Cales and one at Anagnia in Imperial times. He is hesitant about accepting this as evidence; but in this case he is less than just to his thesis: the *cognomen* is very rare and the connection may well stand.

(13) and (14) *Cossutii* and *Pedii*

Their Marian allegiance is nowhere attested. They were connected with the Julii Caesares (cf. Syme, *JRS* 34 (1944) 93 f.); but, as we have seen, by 89 that does not prove friendship with Marius. As for the Cossutii, there is no Campanian connection either: the name and distribution are Etruscan (cf. Schulze, *Lat. Eig.* 158 f.) and examples are found in other regions (cf. Index to *CIL* ix 1). Gabba supports his claim for Campania with a reference to Dubois, *Pouzzoles antique*—where, however, we find (p. 47) 'nom rare en Campanie'!

The upshot is that of Gabba's numerous examples only the two Instei are even probable. The Magii may be accepted as of Campanian descent; many parallels will come to our minds to show that that hardly matters. The Fimbriae are perhaps reasonably supported—but, of course, they are not new citizens: the father was *cos.* 104, as an elderly man, after a difficult career (*RE*, s.v.). Among those who fled with Marius, Campanian connections are difficult to find; and Marius' experiences in Campania during his flight support this negative evidence. Among those who co-operated with Marius and his successors during the next few years, one (7) seems to have come into the faction by accident; two (5 and 6) are Campanian by descent only, with no known direct connection; one (10) is irrelevant; and of the two families (13 and 14) neither is known to be connected with Marius and one cannot be connected with Campania either. In the circumstances we are justified in saying that Gabba's thesis cannot be supported by prosopographical research.

II. SULLA'S COLONIES

Gabba (*op. cit.* 270 f.) lists Sulla's colonies and assignations, partly in support of his thesis. In fact, useful—but quite different—conclusions can be drawn from his list; and they support the interpretation suggested in this study (it will need proper development elsewhere). Of ten colonies listed as 'certe', four are in Etruria; i.e., as one of the ten is in Corsica (Aleria), nearly half of those on the Italian mainland. So is the only place listed as certain for assignations (Volaterrae)—a field in which the 'incerte' are *very* uncertain. Thus the outstanding contribution of Etruria to the Marian cause is again amply documented.

The case of Campania is again quite different. Gabba lists Nola, Pompei and 'Urbana' as certain, Abella and (for assignations) Suessula as uncertain. It seems impressive; but detailed inspection is called for. Nola, at the time of Sulla's return, was probably garrisoned by Samnites: it had never been reduced after the Social War, when the Samnites had taken it (see *RE*, s.v. 'Nola', col. 813). 'Urbana' seems to have been founded on part of the old territory of Capua (cf. Pl. *n.h.* xiv 62), where the Marians had founded a colony (Cic. *leg. agr.* ii 89 f.), which Sulla had somehow to deal with. Abella had been destroyed by the Samnite garrison of Nola during the Social War (Gran. Lic. 26 B (= 20 F)) and the colony must have been planted—whether, as is most likely, by Sulla, or, as is possible, by the Marian government a little earlier—on waste land and as a way of assisting the old inhabitants. For Suessula there is no worth-while evidence of any sort: 'uncertain' is an understatement. Thus there remains only Pompei; and here again we must not be misled by preconceptions about Marian sympathies, but go back to the Social War. For Sulla had besieged and taken the city (Vell. ii 16, 3; cf. *CIL* iv 5385) in one of his most glorious exploits in that war. Pompei, in fact, is closely linked with Nola in Sulla's campaign of 89, and it is anything but surprising to see the connection reappearing in the colonization of both of them. Thus, as is the case with the prosopographical evidence, closer scrutiny reveals no Marian sympathies whatever at the back of Sulla's—very limited—colonization in Campania.

We must conclude that the circumstantial evidence completely fails to establish a case for Marian connections in Campania; odd friends Marius will have had there, as elsewhere—but, as is clear from his adventures on his flight in 88, far more enemies. There is certainly no sign of such pervasive loyalty as we find in Etruria, both directly and circumstantially attested.

NOTES

[1] Last, *CAH* ix 173. Similarly, e.g., Ihne, *Hist. of Rome* (Engl. ed.) v 171.

[2] Which even Cicero could no longer understand (*ap*. Asc. 67 Clark). He only assumed the *toga uirilis* in 91 and his understanding of events before that year is limited.

[3] In a series of articles in *Athenaeum*, to which I am greatly indebted, even where I must express disagreement.

[4] *Br.* 162 (I shall cite Cicero's works without giving his name). This, at least, gives us a firm date.

[5] *ad Her.* i 21; ii 17.

[6] Sources for the events of 103 in Broughton, *MRR* i 563 f., with full discussion. To keep these notes within bounds, *MRR* and *RE* references will be given wherever this is practicable and saves space. Other modern views will not, in general, be discussed.

[7] Gran. Lic. 21 B (= 13 F).

[8] *Br.* 135.

[9] That the frumentary law—that stock device of demagogy—belongs to the first tribunate of Saturninus, and early in it, is recognized by all the best modern scholars. No good argument for 100 has ever been advanced. (Cf. *MRR* i 578, n. 3.)

[10] *MRR*, l.c. (n. 6, above).

[11] See below.

[12] See, e.g., Greenidge-Clay, *Sources*[1], 226.

[13] *de or.* ii 198.

[14] For a survey and discussion (favouring early 95) see Gabba, *Athenaeum* N.S. 31 (1953) 264, n. 4.

[15] Cf. Münzer, *RE*, s.v. 'Sulpicius', no. 92; *Hermes* 67 (1932) 231.

[16] Val. Max. viii 5, 2; *de or.* ii 203.

[17] *de or.* ii 197: he had, in fact, been struck by a stone.

[18] Sources in *MRR* i 212 f. Cf. Scullard, *Rom. Pol.* 36.

[19] See Münzer's stemma in *RE*, s.v. 'Servilius', coll. 1777–8.

[20] Sources *MRR* i 470 f. Only those consuls relevant are mentioned here. Of the other consuls of these years, Ap. Claudius Pulcher (*cos.* 143) was probably (despite Dio xxii 74—too vague to be evidence) connected with this group (see nn. 99 f., below, and text); Pompeius (*cos.* 141) was hostile, but later reconciled (see below and *RE*, s.v. 'Pompeius', no. 12).

[21] Val. Max. vii 5, 4; *vir. ill.* 61, 3.

[22] Three *repulsae* final: see Münzer, *Röm. Ad.* 196 f.

[23] Cf. Vell. ii 11, 3—corrected and expanded by Münzer, *RE*, s.v. 'Caecilius', col. 1202.

[24] Cicero (*Br.* 82) calls him 'ueterator'. He was the man who, as *tr. pl.*, had tried to use his sacrosanctity to evade his creditors (Val. Max. vi 5, 4).

[25] *Br.* 81. The trial was famous and is frequently mentioned.

[26] Val. Max. viii 5, 1; Cic. *Font.* 23.

[27] Oros. v 9, 4.

[28] *MRR* i 525; *RE*, s.v. 'Caecilius', no. 91.

[29] On these events, see *JRS* 46 (1956) 91 f.

[30] Plut. *Mar.* 4.

[31] He is not of the family of M. Cotta (see below). The Aurelii Cottae, apparently all descended from the *cos.* 252, are not a prolific family and a stemma embracing most of those known in the Republic can plausibly be constructed. The attempt is worth making, particularly as the *RE* entry, written before the days of Münzer, does not do so or even suggest relationships. I have added *RE* numbers after the names.

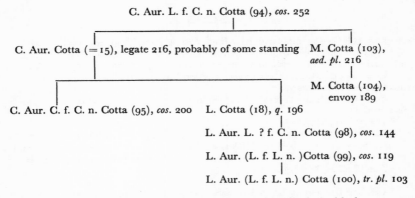

C. Aur. L. f. C. n. Cotta (94), *cos.* 252

C. Aur. Cotta (= 15), legate 216, probably of some standing   M. Cotta (103), *aed. pl.* 216

M. Cotta (104), envoy 189

C. Aur. C. f. C. n. Cotta (95), *cos.* 200   L. Cotta (18), *q.* 196

L. Aur. L. ? f. C. n. Cotta (98), *cos.* 144

L. Aur. (L. f. L. n.)Cotta (99), *cos.* 119

L. Aur. (L. f. L. n.) Cotta (100), *tr. pl.* 103

L. Cotta (97), mentioned as *tr. mil.* 181, is very probably identical with the *cos.* 144: his career was very likely to be retarded by his appalling reputation. The year 154 for his tribunate (*MRR*) is unsupported conjecture. It is worth noting that his son reached the consulship only 25 years later, which is a very short interval.

M. Aurelius Cotta, the father of three consuls (C. Cotta (96), *cos.* 75; M. Cotta (107), *cos.* 74; L. Cotta (102), *cos.* 65), is known only from the filiation of his sons. As their grandfather is nowhere mentioned, he cannot be attached to the family tree; say, a younger son of the *ueterator* (*cos.* 144). M. Cotta, *pro pr.* (?) in Sardinia in 49 (*MRR* ii 260), is almost certainly M. f. M. n., the son of the *cos.* 74. The *tr. pl.* 49 (Luc. *Phars.* iii 143) is not even given a *praenomen* and may be either a brother or a cousin of the last-named. Caesar's mother Aurelia cannot be securely attached either: that C. Cotta (96) is called his *propinquus* makes it unlikely rather than likely that she was a sister of the man (i.e. a daughter of M. Cotta): for such a close relationship Suetonius (*Jul.* 1, 2) would, more likely than not, have used the proper term 'auunculus'. I have not attempted to insert *monetales*, as no two experts agree to any extent about their times.

[32] *Br.* 137; *de or.* iii 42f.; *et al.*

[33] *de or.*, l.c.

[34] There had been no consular Catulus—and indeed no mention of a Catulus in a magistracy—since 220 (*MRR* i 235).

[35] *Planc.* 12. On the relationship see *RE*, x.v. 'Servilius', no. 98.

[36] Cf. n. 22 (above); *RE*, s.v. 'Lutatius', coll. 2074 f.

[37] *MRR* i 567.

[38] *RE*, l.c.; see especially *Tusc. disp.* v 56. He is said to have saved Catulus' life (App. *b.c.* i 74, referring to his ingratitude).

[39] Val. Max. vi 9, 13.

[40] *MRR* i 553; best discussed by Balsdon, *PBSR* 14 (1938), 98 f.

[41] Cf. his treatment of the *cos.* 105, the *nouus homo* Cn. Mallius Maximus (*RE*, s.v. 'Mallius', no. 13).

[42] The probable date of birth of the younger Marius (see *AJP* 75 (1954) 382, n.43).

[43] Plut. *Mar.* 6, 3; Suet. *Jul.* 6, 1.

[44] *MRR* i 577; ii 645; Gabba, *Athenaeum* N.S. 29 (1951) 15 f. (favouring 103).

[45] *de or.* ii 44; *off.* i 133.

[46] Cf. Syme, *CP* 50 (1955) 131.

[47] Suet. *Jul.* 1, 2.

⁴⁸ See n. 38 (above) and text.

⁴⁹ See *RE*, s.v. 'Lutạtius', col. 2077. Much of our tradition derives from Catulus' version.

⁵⁰ See n. 38 (above).—Mention must here be made (if only because it is expected) of the 'literary circle' of Q. Catulus, whose anti-oligarchic membership has often puzzled scholars (most recently Gabba, *Athenaeum* N.S. 31 (1953), 268 f.). The 'circle'— pleasant as it would be to use it here in support of our argument—is a myth that ought at last to disappear from our books, which tend to repeat it one from the other and all ultimately from Büttner. (See Bardon, *Litt. lat. inc.* i 123 f. for irrefutable argumentation direct from the evidence.) In particular, the identification of the noble Porcius Licinus (cf. the *cos.* 184), no doubt identical with a known *monetalis* (*MRR* ii 449), with a slave called Licinius because he was freed by Gracchus' widow (see *RE*, s.v. 'Licinius', no. 5), is a disgrace to scholarship. Its general acceptance (Bardon, *op. cit.*, is an honourable exception, though not familiar with the prosopographical arguments) cannot but cause surprise.

⁵¹ *Br.* 115; *de or.* i 220; Asc. 67 Clark. The filiation is given by the Capitoline Fasti for the years 75–4.

⁵² Cf. *MRR* i 528.

⁵³ *MRR* i 527.

⁵⁴ See Bloch, *Aem. Sc.* 23.

⁵⁵ Sall. *Jug.* 52 f.; cf. 86, 4; Plut. *Mar.* 10, 1. Before the quarrel Sallust assigns the chief role to Marius; that may be tendentious.

⁵⁶ Dio xxviii 97, 3.

⁵⁷ See n. 41 (above) and text.

⁵⁸ See n. 100 (below) and text.

⁵⁹ *RE*, s.v. 'Livius', no. 35.

⁶⁰ See discussion below.

⁶¹ Asc. 21 Clark; cf. *Athenaeum* N.S. 34 (1956) 117 f.

⁶² Pliny, *n.h.* vii 158; Val. Max. viii 13, 6.

⁶³ *de or.* i 227.

⁶⁴ See n. 61 (above).

⁶⁵ *de or.* ii 280.

⁶⁶ *RE*, s.v. 'Livius', no. 18, col. 863.

⁶⁷ *n.h.* xxxiii 1, 20.

⁶⁸ *Br.* 223.

⁶⁹ Dio xxviii 96, 3.

⁷⁰ iv 1, 13: the only reasonable meaning.

⁷¹ See Münzer's formidable collection of *testimonia*: *RE*, s.v. 'Livius', col. 863.

⁷² Cf. Syme, *Rom. Rev.* 33 f.

⁷³ Evidence and discussion *RE*, s.v. 'Livius', no. 35.

⁷⁴ Plut. *Cato Min.*, *init.* On the stemma of the Catones see Gellius xiii 20.

⁷⁵ That this marriage was the later one is clear from the evidence we have about the ages of the children (Münzer, *Röm. Ad.* 295 f.; cf. below).

⁷⁶ *MRR* ii 2–3. The date is there given as 99; as 100—and with certain ascription to L. Cato, without mention of the more likely M.—in *RE*, s.v. 'Porcius', no. 7. [On the date see App. *b.c.* i 32 f., with Gabba's notes (pp. 111 f.).]

⁷⁷ *RE*, s.v. 'Pompeius', no. 39; cf. *ibid.*, no. 12.

⁷⁸ Plut. *Cato Min.* 3, 2. Sulla's career cannot be treated in detail here.

⁷⁹ *am.* 2; *de or.* i 25.

⁸⁰ Brutus the tyrannicide was born *c.* 85 (*RE*, s.v. 'Iunius', no. 53).

⁸¹ Münzer, *RE*, s.v. 'Servilius', col. 1779. Oddly enough Münzer entirely fails to see the implications of this.

66 STUDIES IN GREEK AND ROMAN HISTORY

[82] *RE*, s.v. 'Porcius', no. 16, col. 168. Add Cic. *fam.* xvi 22, 1.

[83] See n. 61, above.

[84] *MRR* ii 24.

[85] Most recently, Gabba (*Athenaeum* N.S. 31 (1953) 271) calls him 'uno dei capi (allora) dell' oligarchia senatoria' and on the strength of this judgment puts his contest with T. Betutius Barrus of Asculum—which he makes a political case—in 95. Unfortunately nothing whatever is known about this case to give it any political significance: not even whether it was civil or criminal.

[86] *de or.* ii 197.

[87] *Br.* 162; see *ORF*², p. 245, defending the text.

[88] Sources for his career in *RE*, s.v. 'Licinius', no. 55.

[89] *ORF*², pp. 243 f. On Rutilius see n. 63 and text (above).

[90] See nn. 125 f. and text (below).

[91] Fraccaro, *RAL* Ser. v, 20 (1911) 178 f. [= *Opuscula* ii 132 f.]

[92] On this see *Athenaeum* N.S. 34 (1956) 104 f.

[93] *Font.* 24; Val. Max. viii 5, 3.

[94] Thus by Münzer (*RE*, s.v. 'Claudius', no. 226) and Hill (*Rom. Mid. Cl.* 129).

[95] Cf. *Athenaeum* N.S. 34 (1956), 112.

[96] In 92, when Rutilius was forced to go into exile, Scaevola remained unscathed (cf. last note).

[97] *de or.* iii 6.

[98] Livy, *per.* lxxxvi; App. *b.c.* i 88. That the four men whose execution on the younger Marius' orders is mentioned were indeed planning to desert the losing cause may safely be deduced both from the success of others (notably L. Philippus) in doing so just in time and from the fact that two of them—Scaevola himself and Carbo—were related to the consuls of the year and would be the last people exposed to arbitrary execution. But that belongs to the history—never yet properly written—of *Cinnae dominatio*. [See pp. 206–34 below.]

[99] On this man see *RE*, s.v. 'Claudius', no. 295. On his political position see especially *rep.* i. 31. That he had powerful backing is clear from the story of the triumph which he celebrated against the will of the majority of the Senate (*RE*, l.c.): there were limits to what even *Appietas* could have got away with unsupported.

[100] *red. in Sen.* 37; *red. ad Quir.* 6; *dom.* 123. Cicero (*fin.* v. 82), and after him Val. Max. (vii 1, 1), gives Macedonicus three daughters, all married. Pliny (*n.h.* vii 59) speaks only of six children, i.e. knows only two daughters. Münzer accepts Pliny, without discussion; but Pliny is no more infallible than Cicero, and there is the further possibility of an error in his text ('vii' having at some stage become 'vi'). If Cicero is right, it is not difficult to think of a husband for the third Metella: why not Q. Caepio, *cos.* 106, whose wife is not known? He, as we have seen, is closely linked with the *factio*, and his son, as well as those of P. Vatia, may be among the Servilii (Cic., ll.cc.) who pleaded for the return of Numidicus.

[101] *RE*, s.v. 'Caecilius', no. 135. One of the daughters, as is well known, was the wife of Ti. Gracchus; another was a Vestal Virgin—Appius had three, and it was one of his best investments, securing him his triumph (see *RE*, s.v. 'Claudius', nos. 384–6).

[102] *Br.* 166.

[103] *leg.* iii 42.

[104] *dom.* 83 f.

[105] *MRR* ii 11. For his career we have the interesting *elogium: Insc. It.*, xiii 3, 70b.

[106] See nn. 93 f. and text (above).

[107] References collected in *ORF*², pp. 227 f., 277 f.

[108] This is illustrated by many of the books where we have Livy. An obvious instance: *per.* xxxix, with its reference to Celtiberia and Macedonia at the very end.

[109] The victories of T. Didius in Spain, apparently of 97 (cf. Obs. 48); the testament of Ptolemy of Cyrene, of 96 (*ibid.* 49); and the successes of Sulla in the East, of 96 [see pp. 157 ff. below].

[110] For grouping by subject-matter, cf. (e.g.) book lxvii (the misfortunes of the elder Caepio all thrown together and followed by Marius' triumph, which was celebrated on January 1st, 104) and book lxix, *fin.* (Metellus' return from exile reported straight after Saturninus' death and before Aquillius' victories, which belong to 100, as we see from Obs. 45). That such grouping can extend from the end of one book to the beginning of another is made probable by (e.g.) xxxix *fin.* and xl *init.*, compared with Livy's text. The only indication of date that we have—a very slight one in *de or.* ii 195— suggests that a fair amount of time intervened between Aquillius' ovation and his trial: Antonius remembers and recalls his client's ovation (of 99), as he does his consulate (of 101), as something some way in the past.

[111] Plut. *Mar.* 14, 7.

[112] *MRR* ii 35–6. His colleague on that mission seems to have been T. Manlius Mancinus, who—as *tr. pl.* 107—had secured the Numidian command for Marius (Sall. *Jug.* 73, 7).

[113] *de or.* ii 198 f. ('uix satis honeste', as Antonius is made to admit).

[114] Thus Klebs (*RE*, s.v. 'Antonius', no. 28) writes that he 'während seines ganzen Lebens zur Partei der Optimaten gestanden hatte'—solely on the strength of his death. Cf. also the short entry in *OCD*.

[115] See *RE*, s.v. 'Licinius', no. 61.

[116] *Ibid.*, s.v. 'Venuleius', no. 1.

[117] *de or.* ii 202.

[117a] [See now L. A. Thompson, *PACA* 5 (1962) 17 f.]

[118] *Ibid.* 200.

[119] *div. in Caec.* 63 gives some instances, Caecilius himself, whatever his intentions in 70, had indeed quarrelled with Verres (*ibid.* 55 f.).

[120] *de or.* i 178; *off.* iii 67. [His connections with Arpinum are striking. See next note.]

[121] *leg.* iii 36; *Br.* 168. An *adfinis* of Gratidius, L. Tullius Cicero, was in Antonius' suite (*de or.* ii 2). Gratidius was 'Antoni perfamiliaris'. M. Cicero studied under him.

[122] Sources *MRR* i 576.

[123] *Rab. perd.* 26; and see below.

[124] *red. ad Quir.* 11; and see n. 100 (above).

[125] *MRR* ii 6.

[126] Plut. *Mar.* 28, 8.

[127] Cf. Livy, *per.* lxxxiii.

[128] Plut. *Mar.* 30, *fin.*

[129] *ad Brut.* i, 5 3.

[130] Gabba (*Athenaeum* N.S. 31 (1953) 262 f.) refuses to admit the connection as certain—but when, and in what manner, are we to assume that the flood of 'citizens', which suddenly necessitated the new *quaestio* at that very time, can have poured in, if not when the last lists were drawn up?

[131] Cf. the case of the Camertine cohorts (*Cic. Balb.* 48; Val. Max. v 2, 8; Plut. *Mar.* 28, 2) and that of the colonists under the *leges Appuleiae* (see below).

[132] *Balb.* 48.

[133] Livy xxxiv 42, 5; cf. Smith, *JRS* 44 (1954) 18 f.

[134] Niccolini, *Fasti* 213 f. (though his reconstruction is quite wrong).

[135] *MRR* i 563 f.

[136] Münzer, *RE*, s.v. 'Servilius', col. 1785.

[137] Whatever the reading in *Balb.* 48, where the text offers 'ternos' (never satisfactorily explained) and Ihne long ago suggested 'trecenos'. Had the case succeeded,

the Camertine cohorts would undoubtedly have been the next to be attacked: their enfranchisement was admittedly illegal (see n. 131, above).

[138] See *CR* N.S. 4 (1954) 101 f.

[139] *de or.* ii 257. That he applied the verses to *socii* become *ciues* is clear from the context (cf. Fraccaro, *RAL* Ser. v, 20 (1911) 180 f. [= *Opuscula* ii 133 f.]; Gabba, *Athenaeum* N.S. 31 (1953) 263 f.). The sting in the tail is precisely that Scaurus equates these respectable Italians with ex-slaves.

[140] On this man see Münzer, *RE*, s.v. 'Norbanus', no. 5; *Hermes* 67 (1932) 220 f.

[141] *b.c.* i 94, 6.

[142] Schulze, *Lat. Eig.* 88, 531 f.; Syme, *Rom. Rev.* 200.

[143] Münzer (*Hermes* 67 (1932) 229 f.) fails to explain the delay—and the point of the attack when it did come.

[144] See n. 139 (above).

[144a] [See my *For. Client.* (1958) 208 f.]

[145] *MRR* ii 5.

[146] Oros. v 17 ('Saturnini frater'—i.e. half-brother or perhaps cousin).

[147] *Rab. perd.* 20 f.

[148] *MRR* ii 4–5. On this see *JRS* 46 (1956) 91 f.

[149] *MRR* ii 2–3.

[150] See *MRR* ii 2.

[151] Plut. *Mar.* 32, 1; cf. *C. Gr.* 12, 1.

[152] See n. 49 and text (above). Jealousy began on the battlefield.

[153] *Arch.* 5–6 (cf. also 19).

[154] See n. 115 (above) and text.

[155] See especially Asc. 27 Clark; Diod. xxxvii 2, 12. Münzer (*RE*, s.v. 'Sulpicius', col. 848) puts the conflict a year later; but in view of the unanimous testimony of our sources that it was at the beginning of Sulpicius' tribunate this is unacceptable.

[156] Sources for what follows in *MRR* ii 20 f.

[157] That he was present at the *feriae Latinae* (Flor. ii 6, 8) is no argument against this (despite Münzer, *RE*, s.v. 'Iulius', no. 151): the festival was usually held early in the year, precisely in order to enable the consuls to get away (see *RE*, s.v. 'feriae Latinae', col. 2214).

[158] See *MRR* ii 27 and 31: certainty is impossible; but amid Appian's confusion it is very doubtful whether Sex. Caesar is ever heard of again. C. Caesar (*Diui Iulii pater*) may have been in Asia in or just before 91 (*MRR* ii 19, n. 2, and 22). In any case, he died peacefully as a praetorian in 85 (Pl. *n.h.* vii 181; Suet. *Jul.* 1). It is clear from this and from young Caesar's fortunes under Cinna that this branch of the family escaped serious quarrel with Marius. [See pp. 216 f. below.]

[159] App. *b.c.* i 40.

[160] Oros. v 18, 11; cf. Dio xxix 98, 2.

[161] Münzer (*RE*, s.v. 'Iulius', no. 142, col. 467) notices that Sulla and Catulus (see below) served under Caesar, and Marius under Lupus; he calls the former 'aristocratic' and the latter 'democratic'.

[162] *MRR* ii 31, n. 16. There is no justification for *substituting* Catulus for Lentulus: the names are too dissimilar to be confused, nor is Lentulus better known than Catulus. Nothing forces us to believe that the Senate (or Appian) assigned precisely five legates to each consul. Catulus as a legate: *Font.* 43.

[163] See nn. 93 f. and text (above).

[164] *de or.* i 57. He had accompanied L. Crassus to Asia, almost certainly before 108 (see *MRR* i 546), and was at that time very interested in philosophy.

[165] Cf. *Font.* 43.

[166] *ORF*[2], p. 274—nothing much can be got out of it.

[167] On the Messallae see Syme, *Historia* 4 (1955), 70–1, and *JRS* 45 (1955), 156 f.

[168] Plut. *Sulla* 35, 5.

[169] *MRR* ii 4.

[170] *de or.* ii 197.

[171] See nn. 115 and 116 and text (above).

[172] *Br.* 136. On Marcellus see n. 163 and text (above).

[173] *RE*, s.v. 'Cornelius', nos. 230, 238, 240—cf. Münzer's very tentative stemma (coll. 1359—60). He may well be right in his conjecture (no. 203) that the son of L. Caesar's legate is P. Lentulus Sura, the Catilinarian, who later married a daughter of this Caesar.

[174] App. *b.c.* i 72, *init.*

[175] Above, nn. 50 f., 115 f., and text.

[176] They were both guilty of high treason for their actions against the consul Cinna. Merula, indeed, was put on trial (no doubt for *maiestas*) and anticipated a just and inevitable verdict by suicide. Octavius would no doubt have suffered the same fate, had he not been killed by Censorinus (supposedly on Cinna's orders—see App. *b.c.* i 72) in the first fury of the capture of Rome.

[177] It will be convenient, at this point, to list the victims, marking (M) those whom we have found good reason for thinking former friends of Marius. The most complete list is given by Appian (*b.c.* i 72 f.):

> C. Caesar Strabo (M);
> L. Caesar (M—as brother of the preceding);
> (Sex. ?) Atilius Serranus;
> P. Lentulus (M?—closely associated with Marcellus);
> C. Numitorius;
> M. Baebius;
> P. Crassus (M) and his homonymous son;
> M. Antonius (M);
> * (M. Caecilius) Cornutus—escaped, but may be included;
> Q. Ancharius;
> Q. Catulus (M).

Other sources add S. Licinius or Lucilius—see *MRR* ii 47 and 52. Broughton (l.c.) says 'Licinius' must be rejected, 'since the praenomen Sextus does not appear in the Licinian family'; but see S. Licinius, *tr. pl.* 138 (Livy, *per. Oxyrh.* lv), whom we have no excuse for emending away. Thus the man's name cannot be known.

It is clear from this list—which includes both suicides and victims of assassination—that the only characters whom we cannot credit with Marian connections are those about whose associations we know nothing. Even in their cases, where any light appears, it seems to point in the same direction; but there is not enough to make it worth discussing.

* Broughton's index (*MRR* ii 538) wrongly gives this man's *praenomen* as C. The text of the work gives the correct form (see *Font.* 43).

[178] On the quaestorship, see *MRR* i 560.

[179] See n. 77 and text (above).

[180] On Cn. Pompeius Strabo see Gelzer's masterly study reproduced in his *V. röm. Staat* ii 56 f. It is interesting to find L. Iunius Damasippus (the infamous *pr.* 82) among Strabo's legates in 89 (see Cichorius, *Röm. Stud.* 141 f.). Whether L. Cinna (*Font.* 43; Livy, *per.* lxxvi) served under Strabo cannot be discovered (opposite opinions: *MRR* ii 36 and Cichorius, l.c.).

[181] Cic. *ap.* Asc. 79 Clark.

[182] On this family see *RE*, s.v.; especially numbers 2, 5, 6.

[183] See nn. 66 f. and text (above).

[184] See nn. 74 f. and text (above). His personal hostility to Marius is reflected in a nasty anecdote (Oros. v 18), invented to mask his military incompetence.

[185] *Br.* 309, supplemented by Asc. 73–4 Clark.

[186] Asc. 79 Clark.

[187] *Ibid.*; cf. *Insc. It.* xiii 1, 84–5.

[188] Nor in *MRR*. Yet it is clear from Cicero (*Br.* 304) that he did serve, as might *a priori* have been expected.

[189] *Tusc. disp.* ii 56. His defence of M. Marius Gratidianus in a civil case (*off.* iii 67; *de or.* i 138) may be dated about 92 (*de or.*, l.c.: 'nuper'). Though we cannot draw many conclusions from such a case, it does show that his estrangement from Marius cannot at that time have been complete.

[190] See *RE*, s.v. 'Iulius', no. 543. The Triumvir, to judge by the date of his quaestorship, should be born in 83. Cf. App. *b.c.* v 8 (perfectly reconcilable with that date) and Plut. *Ant.* 86, where, in view of this evidence, the lower age (giving the same date) must be correct.

[191] *Athenaeum* N.S. 12 (1934) 10 f., 109 f., 257 f., 348 f.

[192] App. *b.c.* i 36—a well-known crux, not improved by the wild speculations of moderns. Detailed treatment of this must be reserved for another occasion. Marius' connections with Etruria are clear from the events of 87 (his landing in Italy) to 81 (Sulla's punishment); there is also prosopographical evidence, a little of which has been mentioned above. As for Umbria, we have the Camertine cohorts and T. Matrinius of Spoletium, to mention the most obvious examples. On the supposed Campanian following of Marius, see Appendix to this article.

[193] See n. 112 and text (above).

[194] Plut. *Mar.* 33, *fin.*

Notes on Provincial Governors from the Social War down to Sulla's Victory

It is still too soon to write the story of the age of Marius and Sulla with the *akribeia* demanded by serious history. Some aspects have been covered with sufficient care,[1] but large gaps in our knowledge remain. Yet we need not despair of filling them. As Gabba has shown in the last few years,[2] a new approach will produce important new results from old sources. If the vague generality that too often passes for the history of this important period is to be banished from our books and lectures, it will have to be recognized in this instance, as it has in so many others, that dates and personalities form the backbone of history; for history is the account of human actions, and it develops in time. For this kind of basic enquiry we are now in a very fortunate position: the *Real-Encyclopädie* is almost complete, and Broughton's great work[3] has put much of the necessary information at the disposal of every undergraduate. Yet such works must not be left—against their authors' intentions—to halt enquiry and enshrine error in a *monumentum aere perennius*:[4] they must be made to serve as bases for further advance. Perhaps a few remarks on the provinces during the decade that extends from the outbreak of the Social War to Sulla's final victory will help to lay a foundation for the history that cannot yet be written. It may be expected that the ramifications of such an enquiry will extend deeply into Roman life and politics.

I. Africa

It is fitting, in an article published in this enterprising new journal,[5] to start with the province of most immediate interest to the continent in which it is to appear. As it happens, Africa in fact provides a very suitable starting-point. Not that we have adequate information: indeed, no names of governors are known for the nineties and for the time of the Social War. In 88 we find the province under P. Sextilius—a man who had hitherto kept out of political involvement and with whom Marius tried, and failed, to find refuge.[6] We do not know how long Sextilius stayed there, except that it was long enough for a twenty-volume work on agriculture (written in Greek) to be dedicated to him.[7] This suggests a tenure of some length, and some interest in local problems and local literary talent. If we may anticipate a later conclusion: it is quite likely that Sextilius was governor of Africa throughout the Social War. However, we have no firm evidence. Nor is he heard of again: for a more important man soon arrives upon the scene. Having declared against Marius, the governor will undoubtedly have admitted Q. Metellus Pius, when he fled to Africa after the Marian victory in Italy.[8] Henceforth Metellus, who probably had *imperium pro consule*, seems to have acted as the governor of Africa and he is generally recognized as such.[9] However, it is certain that he had no right to the appellation. His *imperium* (the revocation of which he might, with a show of legality, regard as invalid) had been bestowed on him for the Social War, not for the purpose of provincial administration.[10] Yet in spite of this, and in spite of his known hostility to the Government at Rome, the latter was unable to proceed against him for two years. This cannot be due to lack of troops: these years, as we are explicitly told, were years of peace, at least in Italy.[11] It is obviously due to a serious shortage of suitable commanders.[12] Not only had some of the nobles—though perhaps not as many as our anti-Cinnan tradition makes out—gone to join Sulla or at least to find temporary refuge in the provinces, but of those men of rank who stayed behind, many were most unwilling to commit themselves to irretrievable involvement with the present Government: they preferred to be men of peace, and those of them who survived in due course joined the victor in the Civil War.[13] Even when a man could at last be found to take on the task of acting against Q. Metellus, it was not a soldier of equal rank and distinction, but merely C. Fabius Hadrianus; and he, as far as we can see, found it easy enough to take over the province and expel the usurper.[14] After Fabius' violent death (probably late in 83)[15] there was apparently no regular governor until the Sullan régime settled down.[16]

II. C. SENTIUS IN MACEDONIA

This brief survey of the evidence for Africa has drawn our

attention to a fact that does not usually get the comment it deserves. The *regnum Cinnanum* was a time when we might expect a serious shortage of men able and willing to command armies and govern provinces on behalf of the Government. But the period that precedes—the time of the Social War—must, for different reasons, have seen an even more serious shortage: men able to lead armies were wanted nearer home;[17] yet the Social War was bound to, and in fact did, arouse the eager hopes of Rome's enemies everywhere, so that the provinces more than ever needed competent commanders. Thus the problem is a continuous one, lasting throughout the period we are here surveying, with, at the most, some momentary (and illusory) relief in 88. We are inevitably reminded of the time of the Hannibalic War—the only period during centuries preceding, which was at all similar; it seems obvious that the same principle would again have to be adopted in similar circumstances: prolonged commands and the minimum of change may be expected to characterize our decade, as they certainly do that of our only precedent. It is clear that this probability should be seriously considered by those[18] who attempt to compile the *fasti* of the period; yet, as far as can be seen, the standard works appear to be unaware of it. A general principle, of course, is not enough, however plausible it may be: we must attempt to test and check it. Evidence is not abundant; but that is all the more reason why what there is should not be ignored. And the case of the province of Africa is enough to show us that, once the right question is asked, the right answer may become obvious enough.

Let us next consider the case of C. Sentius. He, after being urban praetor in 94,[19] must have gone to his province in 93, i.e. *ex praetura*.[20] The urban praetor, like others who had important duties in Rome, could not be spared in the City during his term of office, and by this time—in fact, at least sporadically, much earlier —the familiar scheme by which, in the late Republic, praetors (and, as we shall see, probably consuls) usually spent their year of office in Rome and then proceeded to a provincial command with prorogued *imperium*, seems to be fully developed; though, of course, we have not enough evidence to say how many of the six praetors were in fact needed in the City before Sulla's reorganization of the law courts.[21] A welcome and obvious parallel is

F

provided by the case of Sentius' colleague L. Gellius Poplicola: he, after being *praetor peregrinus* in 94, went to an Eastern province with *imperium pro consule* in the following year.[22] Sentius' rank is not well attested. The Livian *Periocha* and Orosius, as well as Cicero, call him *praetor*.[23] As is well known, this is simply a general term for 'governor' or even 'commander':[24] that Sentius was not, in the technical sense, *praetor* is evident. Broughton thinks that the word must refer, at least *prima facie*, to praetorian *imperium* (i.e., a post *pro praetore*). But this is a mere guess. The *Periocha*, for instance, while frequently using 'pro cos.' (it does not seem to know the phrase 'pro pr.'), nevertheless can use 'praetor' for a holder of *imperium pro cos.*;[25] similarly, as Mommsen's collection of *loci* makes clear, Cicero, when not speaking technically, can use 'praetor' quite freely of the holder of *imperium pro cos.* Thus all we know is that C. Sentius went to Macedonia with *imperium* in 93. After this he is attested there on various occasions, defending his province against barbarian invaders. Finally, in what must at least be late 88 and is probably early 87, we find his legate Q. Braetius (?) Sura opposing Mithridates' invasion of Greece.[26] We shall see before long that he did not stay much longer: indeed, he was most unfortunate in having to stay as long as this. But his six years' tenure should certainly have more attention than it has usually attracted. As we have seen, he had to defend the province against the barbarians. In the course of this, in 92 (it is, for once, accurately dated), he suffered a defeat.[27] We may well believe that, had it not been for this, he might have been relieved in time to return to Rome before the outbreak of the Social War: we shall see later that his colleague L. Gellius did so. Most probably, therefore, it was Sentius himself who wished to stay on and avenge the defeat he had suffered. However, this happened to extend his stay up to the beginning of the Social War and—this is what we particularly want to notice—robbed him of his chance of relief until the War was over. It is only thus that we can explain the unprecedented length of his administration.

III. C. SENTIUS' SUCCESSOR

By 88 there was no longer any reason why Sentius should not hope for relief: the Social War (or at least the worst of it) had ended with the triumph of Cn. Pompeius Strabo; the Mithridatic War was an Asiatic matter and there was no reason to expect that it would impinge upon Europe. We may assume almost as a matter of course that one of the praetors of 88 would be given Macedonia as his province, at least *ex praetura*. Who was the man appointed?

It is, of course, possible that, when Mithridates invaded Greece, the arrangement (whatever it was) was cancelled and Sulla himself instructed to take over the province—possible, but not probable and certainly not necessary. For it was, of course, hoped that Sulla would soon carry the war to Asia: and in any case, while Sulla had to attend to the war against Mithridates, someone would have to fight the northern barbarians. There was room for a governor of Macedonia (perhaps with praetorian *imperium*, to avoid conflict) in addition to Sulla's special appointment. Now, as it happens, we have at this very period a man of praetorian standing who must at one time have held a position of authority in the province of Macedonia, about which we have no details. Could P. Gabinius, the man whose praetorian *tabulae* were never (we are told) taken very seriously[28] and who was later successfully prosecuted *repetundarum* at the request of the Achaeans[29]—could he be C. Sentius' successor? It is certainly easiest (as Münzer saw long ago)[30] to regard this man of praetorian standing as an ex-governor of Macedonia-Achaea. Nevertheless, P. Gabinius has not achieved inclusion in recent lists,[31] no doubt because the compilers would not face the problem of finding a place for him. Yet this problem—which Münzer, though he was aware of it, ignored—should be capable of at least a probable solution, since our Macedonian *fasti* for the late Republic are unusually full and reasonably clear.[32]

Prima facie one would expect a praetor to go to his province either in or (by now more probably) after his praetorship. We must begin, therefore, by fixing the date of his praetorship. He was a member of a college of praetors, the date of which is indicated in the first of the Ciceronian passages we have cited:[33] he and his colleagues (Cicero names Q. Metellus Pius and Ap. Claudius Pulcher) were charged with registering those who claimed citizenship under the *lex Plautia Papiria*. This is not the place to discuss that much-distorted law: clarified by Sherwin-White in an admirable discussion (though he unfortunately hesitated to push his arguments to their logical conclusion),[34] it is still constantly being misinterpreted by a singularly obstinate and ill-founded modern tradition.[35] But its date, at least, seems to be fixed by unimpeachable authority: Asconius[36] dates the tribunate of Plautius in 89. Modern scholars have been unanimous in regarding this as dating the *lex Plautia Papiria* in 89; and they have, apparently, been equally unanimous in taking the further step of dating the college of praetors[37] entrusted with receiving the *professiones* under this law in the same year, since, according to Cicero, the *professio* had to be made within sixty days.[38] Yet these conclusions, though each of them has statistical probability, are not by any means inevitable. For they depend on two concealed premisses, which should be brought out into the open; it will then be seen that, at least by the time the second conclusion (the date of the college of praetors) is reached, a very considerable element of uncertainty has been introduced into what the textbooks seem to regard as altogether beyond discussion.

The trouble is that, as is well known, the tribunician year did not coincide with the consular year, but began on December 10th. Since Asconius says that Plautius passed his *lex iudiciaria* in 89, this would normally mean, with high probability, that he was (as we usually say for convenience' sake) tribune for 89—i.e., from December 10th, 90, to December 9th, 89. It is possible, however, that he was tribune from December 10th, 89, to December 9th, 88, and passed his *lex iudiciaria* at the beginning of his year of office. Normally, of course, statistical probability must prevail, in the absence of contradictory evidence. In this case, however, an element of real doubt is introduced by a fact that deserves to be stressed: the *lex iudiciaria* was in fact passed late in the year 89. For the first case tried under its provisions[39] was that of Cn. Pompeius Strabo, who was consul in 89 and could not, therefore, be put on trial before 88. It is still possible that the law concerned was passed before December 9th, 89, but that there was no actual case under it (for reasons that might be conjectured) until the following year. But this concatenation of hypotheses begins to look very different from the careless assurance with which the date of Plautius' tribunate is usually put forward. The fact is that the evidence does not enable us to decide: if we ignore the weight of modern authority behind the usual dating and merely look at the ancient evidence, we must simply give up the task of dating Plautius' tribunate.[40]

We have examined the first concealed premiss. The second is quite independent of what date we prefer for Plautius' tribunate. If the *lex Plautia Papiria* was passed up to October 29th, 89, then only the praetors of 89 would be concerned in the *professiones*; if between October 30th and December 29th of that year (i.e., between October 30th and December 9th, if we prefer the earlier date for Plautius; between December 10th and 29th, if we prefer the later), then two colleges of praetors would be concerned; if after January 1st, 88, then only the praetors of 88. It will now be seen that the dating of the praetors named by Cicero as receiving the *professiones* is not by any means the simple matter that standard works appear to believe it. They will belong to 89 only if *either* the law was passed before October 30th of that year (which is itself possible only if Plautius was tribune at the time) *or* the law was passed between October 30th and December 29th (which makes no assumption about Plautius' date), but Archias got his *professio* in before the end of the year. But they will belong to 88 if *either* the law was passed in that year (which is possible only if Plautius was tribune at the time) *or* the law was passed between October 30th and December 29th, 89 (which makes no assumption about Plautius' date), but Archias did not get his *professio* in until the beginning of 88. It is as well that all this should at last be made explicit: conjecture is legitimate and inevitable, particularly when our evidence is so poor—but it should not masquerade as indisputable fact.

It should now be clear that we cannot hope to assign a certain date to the praetorian college Cicero mentions. But we must at least look at our evidence with renewed care, in order to see whether, in its present state, it appears to point to one date rather than the other. We cannot determine when the *lex Plautia Papiria* was passed; almost certainly, however, not until, with the Social War at least well under control, the Senate had time to think of legal niceties and rectify anomalies overlooked before.[41] The Social War, at least on the Northern front, officially ended with the triumph of Cn. Pompeius Strabo, which was celebrated on December 25th, 89,[42] and was the only triumph ever celebrated in connection with the War. The capture of Asculum, for which he was awarded the triumph, took place quite late in the year: on November 17th Pompeius was still distributing the rewards that his troops had earned.[43] It is thus most unlikely, at any rate, that the *lex Plautia Papiria* was passed early in 89; it would only be towards the end of the year that the Senate would have leisure for such things. If this is so, however, we can at once see (if we look at the possibilities enumerated in the last paragraph) that the scales now seem weighted in favour of 88—not by any means decisively, but enough to justify a preference for that date—as the date of the praetorian college we are considering. In 88, moreover, Q. Metellus Pius is called στρατηγός and 'praetor' by our sources. This again is not decisive: we have seen that this appellation should not always be regarded as technical; but it must again be borne in mind as another pointer in the same direction, especially in the absence of any contradictory evidence.[44] Broughton's statement that 'as Praetor he registered new citizens at Rome in 89, so the title *praetor* must refer to imperium as a promagistrate',[45] illustrates how the chronology of these events has too often been built up by circular argument. Unfortunately we have no knowledge of the activities of P. Gabinius and Ap. Claudius in 88; though we can be sure that Gabinius did not go to Macedonia in that year, since Sentius was still in charge there.[46] Whatever the date of his praetorship, he was still wanted in Italy in 88.

We have now seen that, on the whole, the evidence seems to favour 88 as the year of Gabinius' (and his two colleagues') praetorship, although we have not found any very decisive arguments. There is, however, another puzzle that has not aroused the curiosity it deserves: why, when claiming that the *tabulae* of Metellus were the only ones really counted as official for his year,[47] does Cicero support this by showing that those of two other praetors were untrustworthy? There were, after all, six praetors:[48] what about the other three? If the college was that of 89, I can find no plausible explanation: we must say—rather lamely—that Cicero knew nothing to the discredit of the other three and was hoping that his audience would not notice that he had named only two colleagues of Metellus instead of five. Cicero does undoubtedly use some naïve oratorical tricks; but this piece of inanity is probably more than we should lightly accept.[49] 88, on the other hand, was a troubled year. It was the year of Sulpicius' agitation and Sulla's march on Rome. Two praetors are known to have been on the wrong side in these troubles: a Brutus (known to be M. Junius Brutus) and a Servilius (who cannot be identified) were sent to stop Sulla's advance, and they did not mince words about it, with the result that they were roughly handled by his troops.[50] Brutus was one of the twelve prominent men who escaped from the City at Sulla's approach and (as we see in the case of Sulpicius) were stripped by him of all their offices and declared *hostes*. Brutus found a refuge in Spain, where his family had a good deal of influence.[51] Of Servilius no more is heard. But in view of the way in which he had compromised himself, there can be very little doubt that he was also one of the twelve who escaped: we only have nine names.[52] The *tabulae* of two of the praetors of 88 thus ceased to have any official standing. It now becomes quite possible (though it is nowhere mentioned) that a third praetor was similarly involved, whether or not he is among the nine men whose names—with no indication of their rank—we have. The events of 88, however, would be well known to both Cicero and his jury a generation later. If there were only three praetors, of the college of that year, whose *tabulae* had a legal claim to official standing (the *acta* of the others having been rescinded when they were declared *hostes*, as we know those of the tribune Sulpicius were), Cicero and his audience would take it for granted that only three praetors out of that college need even be mentioned in this connection. Cicero's peculiar 'blunder' now appears to be possibly not a blunder at all, and the difficulty caused (as so many in ancient authors are) simply by the fact that both the author and his audience took for granted matters about which we ourselves are only very imperfectly informed.

All this, I must repeat, cannot claim to be conclusive. But in view of the fact that there appears to be no solid argument for 89, while many pieces fall into place more satisfactorily on the assumption of 88, we are surely entitled—until someone makes out a real case for the earlier date—to put the college of praetors that contained Gabinius, Claudius and Metellus provisionally in 88; there is, at least, no doubt that they were on the right side in the civil troubles of that year: Metellus and Claudius were later among Sulla's most prominent supporters and were chosen by him for consulships,[53] while Gabinius was a relative (probably an uncle) of the military tribune A. Gabinius, who distinguished himself at Chaeronea and appears to be identical with the later *cos*. 58.[54]

P. Gabinius, then, was praetor probably in 88. There is no reason why he should not have crossed to Greece with Sulla in the following year, to take over his province, *ex praetura*, from C. Sentius, who is not heard of after this. In practice, of course, he would not take over until Sulla proceeded farther east and government in Rome disintegrated; but there is no more obvious course than to suppose that a man whom we know to have (*a*) held a praetorship at the right time, (*b*) been active in Greece at about the right time, (*c*) belonged to a family friendly to Sulla, so that Sulla would raise no objection to him, was with Sulla all this time, ready to assert a claim to the governorship of Macedonia as soon as political circumstances permitted. How long he stayed there we cannot tell. Dolabella took over *ex consulatu* in 80.[55] There is probably no need to interpolate another governor between the two.

There was indeed, during Sulla's stay in Greece, another governor of Macedonia. The Government seems to have tried to retain some influence in the province. In 85 we find L. Scipio (later *cos*. 83) fighting some Illyrian and Thracian tribes.[56] That he was titular governor of Macedonia—probably sent to supersede Gabinius—is obvious from the details our source gives us about his actions: of the tribes he dealt with, the Scordisci had been the constant scourge of Macedonia, while the Maedi and (probably) the Dardani could not be reached at all by a Roman commander except through Macedonia.[57] Another correlation of events now clamours for comment. L. Scipio, as Appian tells us,[58] solved the Scordiscan problem (this is an exaggeration), but made treaties with the Maedi and the Dardani—naturally there were allegations of bribery. However, in this very year 85,[59] while waiting for a reply to a message that Archelaus had taken to Mithridates, Sulla invaded Thrace from the portion of Macedonia under his control. He fought and won battles against several Thracian (and Illyrio-Thracian) tribes:[60] Appian gives three names—the Dardani and two minor ones; Plutarch mentions only the Maedi; Eutropius gives both tribes and two others (one of them certainly and the other quite possibly wrong); the *de viris illustribus* the

Maedi and the Dardani (defeated, it adds, 'in itinere'); Granius
Licinianus, in a more detailed account, says that Sulla had invaded the territory of the Maedi and received the submission of
the Dardani and the Denseletae, and that somewhat later his
legate Hortensius defeated the Maedi and the Dardani (which, incidentally, shows what Sulla's success had been worth).[61] We cannot
here discuss the problem of the sources of these different accounts;
but it is clear at once that the Maedi and the Dardani were in fact
the tribes chiefly attacked—according to Granius (well informed,
as usual) twice in one season. It cannot be accident that they are
the very tribes that were said (by whom, we wonder) to have
'bribed' Scipio, the Roman Government's representative, into
making peace with them. We cannot disentangle the precise
connection, since we have no clue as to the precise chronology
of these various Thracian campaigns. But it is perhaps worth while
recalling and stressing the undoubted fact (which we do know)
that at this very time the enemy of the Roman people, Mithridates,
was being saved from the Roman commander C. Flavius Fimbria,
who was on the point of destroying him, by L. Cornelius Sulla, who
wanted his help against the Roman Government.[62] Sulla, after his
victory in the Civil War that followed, would need to distract
attention from this undeniable fact. The governorship of L. Scipio
fits perfectly into the historical context.

Scipio, as is known, refused to take the chance Sulla offered of
joining the right side in time, as others of his birth and station
were doing.[63] As a result, he had to spend the rest of his life in
exile. P. Gabinius, however, was still in an honoured position in
Rome in 76: in that year he was chosen, perhaps in his capacity
of *quindecimuir*, as a member of an embassy sent to collect Sibylline
oracles from Erythrae.[64] He seems, in fact, to have been the senior
member of this sacred mission, which also included an unknown
Otacilius and a L. Valerius, who is probably none other than
Cicero's later client. It is clear that P. Gabinius was indeed at the
summit of *dignitas*, and he might well hope for a consulship in due
course. Yet six years later he had been convicted *repetundarum* and
was an example of *leuitas* as well as *calamitas*.[65] Can we explain the
long-delayed prosecution and the sudden reversal of fortune?

They are, in fact, anything but surprising. In 76 the Sullani
were firmly in power and opposition to them and attacks on them

were dangerous and foredoomed to failure. Young C. Caesar had tried it, picking as his victim the *consularis et triumphalis* Cn. Dolabella (perhaps, as we have seen, Gabinius' successor). This was apparently in 77.[66] He failed and in the following year tried again, limiting his ambition to a less distinguished malefactor, the ex-prefect C. Antonius.[67] Yet he failed again, through his enemies' machinations, although even the Sullani had not the face to deny Antonius' guilt. And such was the weight of *inuidia* that he had brought upon himself by these prosecutions that Caesar preferred to go to study under Molon at Rhodes.[68] The following years, however, saw the gradual weakening of the Sullan settlement, accelerated after 74, when Pompey's quarrel with the *boni* came out into the open.[69] It is in this political context that we must place the prosecution of P. Gabinius, not long before 70,[70] by that *uir fortissimus et innocentissimus* L. Piso—almost certainly L. Piso Caesoninus, just back from service in the East (where the Achaeans had come to know him) and just of the right age to acquire renown by a political prosecution.[71] This man, through quite unforeseeable vicissitudes of fate, was in due course to be consul in 58 as colleague (it seems) of the nephew of the man whose conviction he had secured, and he was to hear very different language applied to himself by the orator who had used the complimentary phrase in 70.

IV. THE FIRST TRIUMPH OF P. SERVILIUS VATIA

We have now seen, in the cases of Africa and Macedonia, that there is evidence to support the expectation one would form by a consideration of the character of this period and of the analogy of the Hannibalic War: the expectation that there was a serious shortage of men to take over provincial commands and that tenures of such posts, during the period here considered, are likely to have been much longer than is allowed by the orthodox conjectures in the standard works. Once this general principle is recognized, further support can be found in odd facts not of decisive significance in themselves, and we can at least begin the task of rewriting the *fasti*—and the history—of this period.

P. Servilius Vatia (the later Isauricus) triumphed *pro praetore*, from an unknown province, in October 88.[72] His return from a province at this particular time seems, in the circumstances, to call for investigation; and so does the fact that he triumphed: it is the only triumph (except for Cn. Pompeius Strabo's in 89, which is in a different category) between 93 and 81, i.e., during the whole of this decade of Social and Civil War. Fortunately we have enough of the triumphal *Fasti* to make this clear and to show how unusual we must think both the long period without triumphs and, within it, this solitary exception.[73] Yet nowhere in our extant literary sources—neither in Appian's various monographs, nor in Plutarch, nor in the Livian tradition, which reports so many minor wars in the provinces—do we hear of any victory (or even defeat) by Servilius that might have justified this special honour. The historian has all the more right to be curious. There is (as is generally agreed) one thing, about this time, that we do know about P. Servilius: he ought to have been consul in 87. Sulla backed his candidature together (it seems) with that of Cn. Octavius;[74] and this is not surprising, since Servilius was the son of a Metella, and Sulla, having married another Metella (the widow of Scaurus), was now at the heart of the factio that centred in that powerful family.[75] This makes it easier to understand why P. Servilius was not only allowed to return from his province (when men like C. Sentius and, as we shall see, even greater men were not), but was given a triumph unique in this period—for achievements that have left no trace in the whole of our tradition. He was wanted for the consulship of the following year, and the triumph, shortly before the consular elections, was intended to impress the People and secure his election. Unfortunately Sulla had alienated too many people, and the trick that would, in normal circumstances, almost certainly have succeeded, failed owing to his *inuidia*. As it turned out, the *triumphator* had to wait another eight years for his consulship, getting it finally when Sulla's will would no longer be resisted;[76] and only an anecdote in Plutarch and a suspicious entry in the *Fasti* have survived to tell us of this amusing episode.

It would be interesting at least to know what province Servilius had governed, and for how long. Neither of these questions can be answered with certainty; yet in both cases we have at least some pointers towards an answer. The former can be approached by elimination. As Broughton has seen, we may eliminate all those provinces whose governors in the years immediately preceding are known, as well as those whose governors usually have *imperium pro consule*.[77] Not many remain: Sardinia, Africa, perhaps Cilicia.[78] Sardinia (as Broughton points out) is the most likely, as a triumph-hunter could always find some mountain-tribes to worry. However, Africa no doubt offered similar possibilities, and if Sextilius was not there during the Social War, Servilius well may have been. As we have seen, we need not look for a province that offered genuine danger and opportunities for glory.[79] The other question —that of the duration of Servilius' command—is even more difficult. The standard works here tend to disguise the truth and present baseless conjecture as fact: his praetorship is put in 90, and this is at best hesitantly queried,[80] at worst bluntly asserted.[81] Yet it is simply a blind guess. And, as we have seen, it is not a very convincing one. Wherever he was, it is most unlikely that he would have gone out in 90 or even 89. C. Sentius, as we have seen, had been in his province since 93, C. Flaccus (a consular), as we shall see, since 92, and they were not relieved. Perhaps, if we want conjecture to be reasonable, we should look at his age and career. He seems to have had an elder brother, Gaius, who was praetor in 102.[82] Twelve years between the praetorship of two brothers is not unheard of, but sufficiently unusual to dissuade us from postulating it unnecessarily. Moreover, P. Servilius was born about 134,[83] and a grandson of Metellus Macedonicus should have had his praetorship before he was forty-four. That he could not stand for the consulship until 88 was no doubt due to the special crisis we have noticed: during the Social War he had to stay at his post. All that his connections could secure him was a return in 88, as soon as the danger was over, and—to compensate for his loss of time—a triumph in order to make his election a certainty. As we have seen, he was unlucky again; but we may confidently put his praetorship in 93 or, at the latest, 92, and his provincial command between 92 (or perhaps 91) and 88.

V. C. NORBANUS, GOVERNOR OF SICILY

C. Norbanus, friend and protégé of C. Marius and M. Antonius,[84] was in charge of Sicily about the end of the Social War. There is no doubt that this was during or after his praetorship;

but a study of the career of this *nouus homo* is, of course, quite use-less for suggesting a chronology. Thus his praetorship and his Sicilian administration cannot be precisely dated. There are, however, some indications that should not be altogether neglected. Broughton[85] gives him a—queried—praetorship in 88 and pro-magistracy in 87. That he was in Sicily about that time is true enough. Diodorus[86] describes his success in operations against a desperate venture by defeated Italian forces on the mainland: in particular, he saved Rhegium from an attack made after Sulla's departure from Italy. Now we know that Sulla left Italy early in 87, ignoring an attack made upon him in Rome, in his absence, by a tribune M. Verginius (or Vergilius).[87] But again we should extend the command upwards, we do not know how far. Cicero, in the *Verrines*, speaks rather slightingly of Norbanus, not men-tioning the fine achievements of which we read in Diodorus: Norbanus, he says, was not a military man, but had a perfectly peaceful time in Sicily while the whole of Italy was ablaze with the Social War.[88] This is tendentious and distorted; but it seems to be based on one fact—that C. Norbanus was in charge of Sicily during the Social War—which both Cicero and his audience must have known. Norbanus' achievements might be blotted out by a decade of hostile propaganda after Sulla's victory; but there was no reason why the date of his governorship should be. If someone else had governed Sicily during the Social War, being relieved by Norbanus (as our books posit) as late as 88, Cicero would never have dared (or needed) to mention Norbanus as the governor who was there at the height of the War. For, as the tri-umph of Cn. Pompeius Strabo indicates, that War was regarded as practically over by the end of 89. Though the Samnites and Lucanians remained in arms—and in fact did give some trouble to Norbanus—87 or even 88 could hardly be described as a time when the whole of Italy was ablaze with the War, before an audience which would clearly remember the War. We may safely say that Norbanus governed Sicily in 89 and therefore (since there is no reason to think that a change was made in the middle of the War) in 90. Beyond that we cannot go, on what evidence we have.

Nor do we know how much longer he stayed in Sicily. He must, of course, have been back some time in 84, in order to stand for the

consulship of the following year.[89] At the other end, we may regard it as certain that he did not return in the course of 87: a
distinguished praetorian, still *cum imperio* on his way back from
his province, could not fail to appear prominently on the Marian
side during that year of civil war. By 86, after Marius' death, the
regnum Cinnanum had secured peace, which lasted for about three
years.[90] Norbanus may have returned at any time during this
period, as soon as someone could be found to take over from him.
The next governor of Sicily of whom we hear is M. Perperna in
82.[91] We have no reason for thinking him praetor in that year[92]
and no indication of how long he had been there. He may have
been Norbanus' successor, or there may have been another governor between these two. We can only point out that, in view of
what we have seen, there would almost certainly not be *more*
than one.

VI. THE EASTERN PROVINCES

On the Eastern Provinces we have a good deal of information,
but not enough to establish their *fasti* with anything like certainty.
A large number of men known from various inscriptions can be
tentatively assigned to the first decade of the century.[93] Few of
them can be precisely dated. The only certain date—though
much ingenuity has been wasted in querying it—is that of Q.
Mucius Scaevola the Pontifex, who reorganized the province of
Asia in a brief but important tenure in 94, and whose legate
P. Rutilius Rufus continued to govern it in his name into 93.[94]
L. Valerius Flaccus (*cos. suff.* 86) must have held the province
at some time before the Mithridatic War: that much is clear from
the money collected for him at Tralles.[95] He should not, however,
on this account be rashly identified with the man whom his own
ex-quaestor M. Aurelius Scaurus was not allowed to prosecute:[96]
that case is put by Cicero into a series belonging to the last years
of the second century, and no indication is given of the province
concerned.[97] The province cannot be conjectured; the date,
however, fits in so well with the known career of L. Valerius
Flaccus, consul in 100 and friend of C. Marius, that there can be
no doubt that the incident concerns that man's praetorian (or
post-praetorian) province. This may be of some relevance to that
much-disputed subject, the dating of the coins on which the name

of M. Aurelius Scaurus appears. But it should be clear from a glance at the widely divergent opinions expressed on that subject that the coins must not on any account be used to tear L. Flaccus' command out of the context in which Cicero so clearly puts it.[98] Perhaps that L. Flaccus owed his acquittal to his friendship with Marius, then embarked upon his unprecedented series of consulships.

To return to his namesake, the *cos. suff.* 86: the last office of which we have certain knowledge before his consulship is the aedileship (apparently in 99), which brought him a prosecution by C. Appuleius Decianus.[99] It is possible—though not by any means certain—that he was praetor in 96 and Q. Scaevola's predecessor in the province. We also have a very probable successor to the Pontiff in L. Gellius Poplicola, who, when in Athens *pro consule ex praetura*, offered the philosophical schools his mediation in their disputes. This learned man, as we happen to know, was *praetor peregrinus* in 94, as a colleague of C. Sentius, and will have reached his province some time in 93[100]—just in time (as we have seen) to take over from the legate P. Rutilius Rufus. It would be natural enough for a praetor of 94 to succeed the consul of 95. It is, indeed, conceivable that L. Gellius was on his way to Cilicia and not to Asia.[101] But Magie has shown—as far as the present evidence goes, convincingly—that 'Cilicia', at this time, appears to have been merely the name for an *ad hoc* command, entrusted to men like M. Antonius or L. Sulla for the execution of some special commission: there is no reason to think that apart from these two there was any governor of Cilicia, until Q. Oppius was sent to watch Mithridates.[102] L. Gellius, unlike his colleague C. Sentius in Macedonia, was lucky enough to get back to Rome before the outbreak of the Social War. He probably remained for no more than a year, like Q. Scaevola himself,[103] and left the province in 92: Asia, unlike Macedonia, was a peaceful province, especially now that it had been reorganized by Q. Scaevola,[104] and it did not need long-continued commands under normal circumstances. His successor—still able to return before the Social War—was probably C. Julius Caesar (*Pater Diui Iulii*): his praetorship, as Broughton has shown, cannot come early enough to make him a predecessor of Scaevola, and should probably be put in 93, which would put his proconsulate in 92–1.[105] The next governor we find

is C. Cassius, who opposes Mithridates in 89 and 88. We do not
know when he was appointed; but it is perfectly possible that he
was another unfortunate stranded in a province by the outbreak
of the Social War.[106] He may be Caesar's successor who arrived
in 91. But we cannot be certain. After his tenure comes the black-
out of the Mithridatic War.[107]

VII. C. Flaccus: Spain and Gaul

On Further Spain we have no information at all for our period.
P. Crassus who triumphed in 93[108] seems to have been succeeded
by a P. Scipio Nasica, about whom we know very little except
that he was the father of Metellus Scipio.[109] After him we have no
more evidence down to the Sertorian War. In view of the evidence
we shall consider later, it is quite probable that, during the shortage of commanders, the two Spains were under the nominal
supervision of a single governor: Sertorius, at any rate, does not
seem to have found a resident governor (of either faction) in
Ulterior. And C. Annius, sent against him by Sulla, similarly
seems to have been in charge of the whole Peninsula.[110]

We must next consider the case of C. Valerius Flaccus, who, in 81
(or possibly 80), triumphed over Celtiberians and Gauls.[111]
He had been consul in 93, and soon after (it seems) we find him
successfully fighting in Spain.[112] That he went there after and not
during his consulship is virtually certain. This, indeed, seems by
then to have been the normal practice; and no consul is attested
as fighting in Spain between Scipio Aemilianus and Caesar. As it
happens, we know that the year of Flaccus' consulship was a
peaceful one, certainly not calling for a consul's presence in a
province.[113] Normally he would probably have returned in 90.
But, as in the case of C. Sentius (who went to his province a year
earlier, but was unlucky), the Social War seems to have tied him
to his post. It is theoretically possible that he did return later,
remaining *ad urbem* to safeguard his right to triumph, and was then
sent out again to govern Gaul (as we shall see he did). But this,
in itself a most improbable reconstruction, is made even more
unacceptable by the fact that we do not hear of him during the
Civil War, in which his brother (the *cos. suff.* 86) was so prominent;[114] nor do we know of any other governor for Citerior—

indeed, as we have seen, for Spain—until Sertorius takes over without opposition,[115] we do not know from whom. Sertorius' quick success, and the absence, in our sources, of any hint of the presence of a governor in Spain at the time (not to mention a reference to a named man), indicate a serious weakness in the administration of the provinces of Spain. There can be no doubt that it must be connected with the shortage of suitable men, which we have already noticed; but it may be possible to define this particular weakness more accurately and thus further to illustrate that general point.

C. Flaccus appears as *imperator* in Gaul in 83: this date is explicitly given by Cicero.[116] But it is most likely (and indeed generally agreed) that he was already holding this command two years earlier, when his nephew L. Flaccus (Cicero's client) took refuge with him and served under him after the murder of his father by Fimbria.[117] Thus it looks as if C. Flaccus was in charge of Gaul at least from 85 until the end of 82, the earliest date for his return to Rome.[118] But Cicero's language, in referring to C. Flaccus, is decidedly odd. He does not say that Flaccus was in Gaul as governor (we might expect 'praetor' or the verb 'praeesse'), but simply 'qui tum erat in prouincia'. Yet Flaccus was not just visiting there: he was there with his army, and the faithful and honourable Massiliots got to know his nephew very well during his service there.[119] Clearly Flaccus' status was rather odd and deserves further investigation. It is, in fact, extremely likely that he was looking after the province (at least the Transalpina), to which Cicero explicitly refers) while still in charge of Spain or, at least, of Citerior. Transalpine Gaul was a peculiar *prouincia*: not annexed or organized after its conquest in the second century, it provided, during the German invasions, a striking example of the dangers of Senatorial unwillingness to extend Rome's administrative responsibilities.[120] Even in the first century, when we hear of the province, its administration is usually combined with that of some other province—normally Cisalpina: right down to the age of Caesar it is not by any means unusual to find a united *prouincia Gallia*.[121] But in times of emergency commanders in Citerior were much concerned with the province that formed their land link with Italy.[122] Pompey is the best example: his achievements there are perhaps not always sufficiently appreciated in the

G

modern tradition.[123] Thus, although it was far from an ideal solution, it would be quite natural, during a time of emergency, when no other suitable man could be spared or found, to entrust the supervision of this province to the governor of Citerior. C. Flaccus, consular and *imperator*, governing Spain and (as we shall see) a man whom the Government thought it could trust, would quite naturally be asked to keep an eye on the Transalpina, and this would explain Cicero's odd phrase about his presence there. It will also explain what we have noticed above: the weakness of the central administration in Spain when Sertorius arrived there. Flaccus, amid his multiple responsibilities, was perhaps unable to oppose him effectively either on his passage through the Transalpina or in Spain—or perhaps, as we shall have to suggest, he was unwilling to. That Flaccus held *imperium* in two provinces (at least in succession) from 92 to 81 seems undeniable. That, in the emergency of the *regnum Cinnanum*, he received a cumulation of provinces that recalls some of the later 'special *imperia*' is, at least, the most economical interpretation of our evidence and is not contradicted by anything we know.[124]

At this stage we must consider the administration of the Transalpina before Flaccus. As we have seen, he was almost certainly there by 85 and quite possibly a good deal earlier. The last Roman commander mentioned there before him is the man who, in 90, won a victory over the Salluvii.[125] Broughton lists him as C. Caelius and makes him a praetor or promagistrate.[126] The rank cannot be accurately determined, as our source does not give it. The name appears in various forms.[127] Rossbach, for reasons he does not vouchsafe us, printed 'Cae⟨ci⟩lius'.[128] The manuscripts divide between 'Caelius' (Nπ) and 'Coelius' (P[arisinus]). The manuscripts of the *Periocha* are, unfortunately, all sadly corrupt. In general, Nπ, which form one group, seem about equal in value to P: Rossbach, though he prefers the former, has to admit that 'tamen non minor eorum locorum numerus est, ubi lectiones [of P] iis, quas N habet, praestent'.[129] Münzer and (following him) Broughton opted for 'Caelius', rightly dismissing the contemptible 'Caecilius'; and this, therefore, has become the form in which the name generally appears.[130] But perhaps we can do better than entrust the choice to Heaven. On the principle of the *difficilior lectio* 'Coelius' seems far preferable. It is well known that

'Caelius' is the form in which both these names usually appear in the literary tradition. In particular, the only consular Coelius, C. Caldus (*cos.* 94), appears as 'Caelius' in codices and texts of Cicero and once even in MRR,[131] and other members of his family seem to be equally unlucky.[132] Thus it is well worth while, in this case, to consider the quality of the manuscript that gives the rarer form. As it happens, P is a manuscript very little plagued with 'emendation'—Rossbach particularly comments on this fact and on its value.[133] There is therefore every reason, before we even start prosopographical investigation, to accept 'Coelius' as palaeographically preferable. As for possible identities, no one has ever found a Caelius with whom the victor over the Salluvii could be identified. Yet there is, on the other hand, an obvious C. Coelius—none other than the *cos.* 94, a man of some military fame.[134] We are entitled to assume that the reference here is to him. It is not impossible that he went to Gaul *ex consulatu*, in the usual way, and stayed there until after the Social War: there is, as far as we can see, no reason why he should not have returned in time to avoid being caught there; but we have not enough evidence to judge of these matters. The case of C. Sentius in Macedonia is a warning example: praetor in the year of Coelius' consulship, he went to Macedonia in the following year and, as we saw, had to stay until 87. Similarly (it seems) C. Flaccus in Spain (though he only went in 92) does not appear to have been able to return for over a decade. Neither of these cases would have been believed if they did not happen to be attested; and they should, at any rate, teach us not to reject such possibilities too lightly. There is no mention of Coelius during the events of 91, although he was a competent orator,[135] nor any mention of him in connection with the Social War, although he was an experienced soldier.[136] He may well have been caught in his province by the outbreak of the Social War and forced to stay on: we simply cannot tell. But even if that is not so, we need not be surprised to find him fighting the Salluvii in 90. Spain was among the most important provinces during the Social War.[137] Fortunately, as we have seen, an experienced consular was in charge there (at least in Citerior) and acquitting himself well. But it might well be thought necessary to entrust to another experienced consular and military man the difficult task of guarding the vital land link with the

Peninsula.[138] The presence, and the military activity, of C. Flaccus in the same province a little later perhaps helps to make this even more probable. We may, therefore, safely adopt the course recommended by palaeographical considerations and proceed to identify the victor over the Salluvii with the *cos.* 94, although we cannot tell whether he was specially sent to the province to safeguard communications with Spain during the Social War or whether he had been there ever since 93.

That he stayed to the end of the Social War we may regard as certain. But one wonders whether he was not still there in 87. In that year we find a P. Caelius (thus spelled) in charge of the garrison of Placentia, trying unsuccessfully to defend it against Cinna's forces.[139] He was a man of senatorial rank who, fortunately for the historian, had a dog.[140] But that is not the end of the story. Münzer, with his incomparable flair for such things, noticed that this story is also told by Aelian about a man called Κάλβος, said to have died during a civil war.[141] He rightly concluded that the man must have been a P. Coelius Caldus. It is a pity that this characteristically brilliant reconstruction seems to have been forgotten; it is well worth restating.[142] Placentia,[143] a vital road junction, was the key fortress in Lombardy, and its commander—being, as we have seen, a senator—should be assigned a higher rank than that of prefect. He will, in fact, be a legate. We are told by Valerius Maximus that he was assigned his post by Octavius. This item of information appears to receive some indirect support from Appian,[144] and in the absence of contrary indications it must be accepted. But, whatever the status of the Cisalpina between 89 and 81,[145] there was clearly a close historical connection between the two Gauls. Quite recently L. Crassus may have had both of them *ex consulatu* (i.e. in 94);[146] a little later, M. Lepidus was to have both the Gallic provinces; and there are other examples in the age of Cicero, where our evidence is better.[147] It is an attractive conjecture that Crassus' successor in the consulship, C. Coelius Caldus, also succeeded him in his province of Gallia. However that may be, it is certainly likely enough that in 90, when we find him fighting the Salluvii, his authority extended to the Cisalpina: someone would have to ensure the obedience of that district, and we do not know of any other senior magistrate or promagistrate in charge there. When, moreover, in 87 a relative of C. Coelius appears as a legate in charge of Placentia, one cannot help wondering whether he was not (at least originally) a legate of the governor of Gaul.[148] This does not contradict his being assigned his post by the consul Octavius: the consul's authority was superior to that of any provincial governor, and he could intervene in any province as he saw fit—so, at least, one might argue, if it suited one's case.[149] And since P. Coelius proved his friendship for Octavius and his cause by his death, there is not likely to have been any disagreement between them on this question.

Nor is it surprising to find the Coelii Caldi on the side of the *boni* against the Mario-Cinnans. We do not know very much about the career of C. Coelius Caldus, except that he was a *nouus homo* who made his way to the top after a hard struggle, helped by some military and oratorical ability.[150] As a tribune he had been *popularis*, passing a *lex tabellaria*. But that does not mean much: even distinguished nobles (not to mention new men) were allowed by custom to sow some wild oats in politics; having thus raised their price, they could count on grateful acceptance by the *boni* when they chose to 'settle down'. We need only mention, as examples of this about the time we are concerned with, the orator L. Crassus, who had bitterly attacked the Senate over the foundation of Narbo,[151] and L. Philippus, who, when tribune, had threatened to stir up social revolution.[152] It seems that C. Coelius also, when of maturer years, came to terms with the *boni*. The *commentariolum petitionis* gives us invaluable information on his struggle for the highest office: Coelius had two noble and very distinguished competitors, and he managed to defeat one of them.[153] Their merits may be exaggerated, to point a moral; yet it is clear that Coelius—like another *nouus homo* with a *popularis* past, a generation later—must have had powerful noble support to defeat them. But who were his competitors? One, of course, was successful—his colleague L. Domitius Ahenobarbus. Very little is known about this man, but more about his family. Two Cn. Ahenobarbi deserve mention: the *cos.* 96, his elder brother, whose quarrel with L. Crassus came to a head in their joint censorship in 92[154]—and Crassus, of course, with the caution indicated by his shrewdness, was in the circle of the *boni* and one of the chief supporters of M. Drusus[155]—and, more important still, Cn. Ahenobarbus, who must be the son of one of the two consulars, and who married a daughter of Cinna and fought for the Marians in Africa until he was killed by Pompey.[156] Thus it may be regarded as certain that by the middle of the nineties the Ahenobarbi were enemies of the *factio*. This accounts for one of Coelius' competitors. Who was the other? The quest might seem fruitless, yet, oddly enough, we can arrive at a highly probable answer. A noble who expected the consulship as his birthright would, if defeated, normally stand again in the following year. Now we happen to know the candidates for the consulship of 93—the successful ones were C. Flaccus and M. Herennius,[157] and the unsuccessful one was L. Marcius Philippus (later *cos*. 91). His defeat by the *nouus homo* Herennius was the surprise of the year.[158] This was clearly Philippus' first candidature: had he stood in the previous year as well, his defeat by two *noui homines* (Coelius and Herennius) in succession—unlikely enough in itself—could not have failed to arouse additional comment. Herennius, on the other hand, cannot be the noble and distinguished candidate mentioned as Coelius' competitor. This leaves C. Valerius Flaccus; and here, beyond reasonable doubt, is our answer. His distinguished birth is beyond question, and his achievements (we must remember that in due course he was to win a triumph) would certainly justify the language used. Defeated at his first attempt, he topped the poll at the second. In common decency he had a right to expect it.[159] Now C. Flaccus, as is well known, and as we have had occasion to indicate in passing, came of one of the foremost pro-Marian families.[160] There can be no doubt that he and Ahenobarbus were what we may call the Marian team in the elections for 94. The year 95— a crucial one—had, on the whole, turned out successful for Marius and his friends; yet they had suffered reverses and had to make concessions, and this one may now be added to the list.[161] The *factio*, having (as it happened) no one better to put up—for these things were inevitably to some extent a matter of chance—united in support of C. Coelius Caldus and pushed him into office. As we have already noticed, a more distinguished *nouus homo* was in due course to profit by a similar chance to gain the consulship of 63—and there, fortunately, we have enough evidence to be able to observe how it was done.

It is time to gather up the fragments and try to piece them together. And, as so often happens in this difficult but rewarding period, they will be seen to fall into place to form a pattern hitherto unsurmised, yet shown by its very clarity and coherence to be true. C. Flaccus (we may say) went to Citerior *ex consulatu* and, caught by the Social War, had to stay there, as, for instance, C. Sentius (being even more unfortunate) stayed in Macedonia and as (we have good reason to believe) other governors stayed in their provinces. His predecessor, C. Coelius Caldus, may have suffered the same fate in Gaul—if so, he there succeeded his predecessor in the consulship, L. Crassus. In any case, whether retained or specially sent there for the purpose, C. Coelius is found guarding that key province in 90 and no doubt continued to do so in 89; as might be expected—and as we can see where there is any evidence at all—governors tended to be left at their posts for the duration. In 87 we find a relative of his[162] at Placentia, probably as a legate, supporting Cn. Octavius and opposing the Mario-Cinnans to the death. This, as we have been able to deduce, fits in very well with the fact that C. Coelius gained his consulship with the help of the anti-Marian faction. But Cn. Octavius—like P. Coelius—was defeated and killed. If—as the presence of his relative as a legate in the Cisalpina suggests—C. Coelius was still in charge of Gaul (which was so often a single *prouincia*), the victors cannot have looked with pleasure upon the continuing presence of their enemy in an important province, cutting their communications with Spain. But a firm friend, C. Flaccus, was near at hand, governing the adjoining province of Citerior. He, as it happened, was also (it seems) an *inimicus* of C. Coelius, who had defeated him in the elections for 94. What happened next, we cannot tell. C. Coelius certainly disappears from history: we hope he died a natural death. In any case, the Government did the obvious thing and asked C. Flaccus to intervene in the neighbouring province: as we have seen, this is not the only example of a governor of Citerior doing so. By 85, the *imperator* C. Flaccus is firmly installed in Transalpina (though even a polite orator cannot really call him the lawful governor of it), while, almost certainly, retaining Citerior. In fact, in view of the Government's proved shortage of reliable commanders and administrators, and in view of the weakness of the administration in Spain at the time when Sertorius reaches it, it is not impossible that no suitable commander could be sent to Ulterior either and that Flaccus had to do his best there as well.[163] Flaccus, however, no doubt became rather less friendly towards the Government after his brother's unavenged death early in 85; he would hear all about it from his brother's son, to whom he offered a refuge. By 83, doubts of his loyalty must have been serious: Q. Sertorius, a more trustworthy supporter, was designated to take over Spain. In his case the sources are unanimous in saying that it was the whole of Spain, as indeed his actions there also make clear. Yet moderns have been eager to limit him to Citerior.[164] In view of the facts we have surveyed, there is no reason to doubt the sources, which are further confirmed by the fact that Annius' command also seems to have extended over the whole Peninsula.[165] These attested facts make it all the more likely, in turn, that the absence of any mention of a separate governor of Ulterior during our period is not accidental and that Flaccus was expected to look after it, which he could not do efficiently. It is perhaps significant that Sertorius, who had to travel by land, reached his province without serious opposition:[166] the *imperator* in Gaul, who could at least have tried to stop him, perhaps had not quite made up his mind which side to take. But before long he must have taken the right decision, and Sulla's weakness for Patricians did the rest: his triumph in 81 (or 80) bears eloquent testimony. Yet it is worth noting that the *imperator* and *triumphator* was not given another command: they were reserved for more reliable followers of the winning cause.

APPENDIX

It will be convenient to summarize the information gained and suggestions made above. I have made no attempt to indicate degrees of probability, which can be gathered from the full discussion in the text and notes. Parentheses indicate the lowest upper and highest lower dates known or deducible; e.g. (91)–(87)=from 91 (or earlier) to 87 (or later).

Province	Name	Dates	Remarks
Sicily	C. Norbanus	(90)–(87)	
	M. Perperna	? – 82	Upper date unknown
Sardinia	?P. Servilius Vatia	(91)– 88	Sardinia most probable province for him
	Q. Antonius Balbus	? – 82?	Upper date unknown

Spain	C. Valerius Flaccus	92 – 81	Probably in charge of the whole of Spain[167]
	Q. Sertorius	82 – 81	His first tenure; sent to succeed Flaccus?
Macedonia	C. Sentius	93 – 87	
	P. Gabinius	87 – ?	Lower date unknown
	L. Cornelius Scipio	(85)– 84	*Cos.* 83
Africa	P. Sextilius	? –(87)	Probably from 90 at least, if Servilius is rightly placed in Sardinia
	Q. Caecilius Metellus	87 – 84	Not governor, but *cum imperio*
	C. Fabius Hadrianus	(84)– 83	Possibly died early 82
Asia[168]	L. Valerius Flaccus	95 – 94	The most probable dates
	Q. Mucius Scaevola	94 – 93	Including his legate's term
	L. Gellius Poplicola	93 – 92?	
	C. Julius Caesar	92?–91?	Dates conjectural
	C. Cassius	(89)– 88	Possibly from 91
Cilicia	Q. Oppius	(89)– 88	Found quite early in 88; must have arrived by 89, if not earlier
Gaul	L. Licinius Crassus	94	The whole of Gaul
			Dates not certain
	C. Coelius Caldus	(90)–(87?)	Possibly from 93, as Crassus' successor
	C. Valerius Flaccus	(85)– 81	In charge of Transalpina; Cisalpina apparently administered directly by the Government

NOTES

[1] Though here, as elsewhere, there has recently at times been a tendency to regard source criticism as an end in itself and neglect the historian's main and proper task.

[2] In an important series of Articles in *Athenaeum*, the first N.S. 27 (1949) 173 f., the most important (so far) N.S. 32 (1954) 41 f. and 293 f. Though it is fortunate that these important studies are all in one periodical—and in one readily available to all scholars—it is to be hoped that they will in due course be collected into a book.

[3] *The Magistrates of the Roman Republic* (cited *MRR*).

[4] See Syme's judicious remarks in his review of *MRR* (*CP* 50 (1955) 127 f.).

[5] [*The Proceedings of the African Classical Associations*, to the first number of which this article was contributed by invitation.]

[6] *MRR* ii 41. Plutarch says that Sextilius had neither friendship nor enmity for Marius.

[7] Varro, *r.r.* i 1, 10.

[8] App. *b.c.* i 80 (reading Λιβυστίδι for the indefensible Λιγυστίδι).

[9] *MRR* ii 58 and 61 (but cf. 54); Jashemski, *Origins and History of the Proconsular and the Propraetorian Imperium to 27 B.C.* (1950) 59 and 132 (henceforth cited by the author's name only). [I have modified my views on this; see 'Waiting for Sulla', pp. 221, 225, below. Acceptance of the *communis opinio* is a constant snare for the student of this period.]

[10] Thus clearly Appian, l.c.

[11] Cic. *Br.* 308.

12 [It appears to be chiefly due to the conciliatory policy of Cinna's government; see 'Waiting for Sulla', pp. 206 ff., below.]

13 Cf. Cic. l.c.; Livy, *per.* lxxiii; App. *b.c.* i 77 f.

14 *MRR* ii 60 f.

15 *MRR* ii 69. For the date, see Oros. v 20, 3 (under 83); Livy, *per.* lxxxvi (after the younger Marius' election to the consulship).

16 On Cn. Domitius Ahenobarbus see *MRR*, l.c.

17 Cic. *Font.* 43; cf. App. *b.c.* i 40 (not complete—see *Historia* 6 (1957) 338, n. 162; 341, n. 188). See also below, on the *Fasti Triumphales* for these years.

18 E.g. Jashemski, Appendices III–X (and cf. XVI), and Broughton, *MRR*.

19 *MRR* ii 12.

20 *MRR* ii 14 (n. 3), 15, 16 (n. 5); his predecessor, most probably, was L. Julius Caesar (*cos.* 90): see *MRR* ii 13, 14 (n. 3); *RE*, s.v. 'Iulius', col. 466.

21 [I should now think that most of them were: see *Historia* 11 (1962) 207.]

22 *MRR* ii 12, 15, 16 (n. 4). Cf., somewhat earlier, the case of C. Marius (*pr.* 115); though Plutarch (*Mar.* 5 f.) does not tell us his *prouincia* in that year, it was clearly one that kept him in the city. On Gellius, see further, section VI, below.

23 References *MRR* ii 15.

24 See Mommsen, *Staatsr.* ii³ 240, n. 5, with ample documentation from good authors. Insufficient attention to this (as well as insufficient scrutiny of the evidence on L. Caesar) has led Münzer badly astray (*RE*, s.v. 'Sentius', col. 1510). Unfortunately this elementary point of Latin (including Ciceronian) usage is also often ignored in *MRR*, and this has resulted in some glaring improbabilities.

25 E.g. *per.* xxxiii, compared with Livy's text, xxxiii 25, 8 (C. Sempronius Tuditanus); cf. Broughton's discussion (not quite accurate) of M. Crassus' position in 72 (*MRR* ii 121, n. 2). Clearly no conjecture on the nature of a promagistrate's *imperium* is normally worth making, unless we have other pointers; nor can we decide (unless we have other evidence) between praetorship and promagistracy.

26 *RE*, l.c.

27 Livy, *per.* lxx.

28 Cic. *Arch.* 9.

29 Cic. *div. in Caec.* 64.

30 *RE*, s.v. 'Gabinius', no. 13.

31 Jashemski, 130 (and index); *MRR* ii 33, 38 (n. 2): his praetorship, but no mention of a province.

32 See Jashemski, l.c.—sound in outline.

33 *Arch.* 9.

34 *The Roman Citizenship*, 132 f. (on the meaning of *adscriptio*). There is no reason to believe that Cicero is *not* quoting the main provision of the law. As Sherwin-White says, it was probably meant to rectify anomalies in previous legislation (necessarily passed in some haste); and though there may well have been others, we have no warrant for saying so, and no knowledge of actual cases.

35 Broughton (*MRR* ii 34), like many other recent writers on the subject, does not seem to know Sherwin-White's discussion. [Little has changed in this respect: see *Historia* 11 (1962) 227 f.]

36 Asc. 79 Clark.

37 Sherwin-White (*op. cit.* 133) misinterprets the phrase 'apud praetorem' as meaning 'before the praetor' (i.e. the *praetor urbanus*) 'at Rome'. In fact it means 'before a praetor' (anywhere): that is quite clear from Cicero's discussion; for Archias could have made his *professio* before P. Gabinius or Ap. Claudius, as indeed others seem to have done.

38 Cic. l.c. (n. 30).

[39] Cic. *ap*. Asc. l.c.

[40] [Mr G. V. Sumner has suggested to me that the laws on *promulgatio* normally made it impossible for a tribune to pass legislation before January 1st. It is to be hoped that further investigation will confirm this and settle the dates of numerous tribunes.]

[41] See n. 34 and text (above).

[42] *Inscr. It*. xiii 1, 84 f.

[43] *ILS* 8888 (the most obvious interpretation).

[44] App. *b.c*. i 53; *vir. ill*. 63, 1.

[45] *MRR* ii 45 (n. 6). Metellus' military activities in 88 would not, of course, have prevented him from receiving his friend's *professio* before he set out: Archias was eager to profess before his patron (cf. n. 37, above).

[46] See n. 26 and text (above).

[47] *Arch*. 9: 'quae *solae* [tabulae] ex illa professione collegioque praetorum obtinent publicarum tabularum auctoritatem' (my italics, for emphasis).

[48] Vell. ii 16, 3.

[49] It is very similar to the sort of thing that, in the case of the elder Curio, Cicero stigmatizes as a serious fault of *memoria* (*Br*. 217).

[50] Plut. *Sulla* 9, 2.

[51] See my *Foreign Clientelae* (1958) 266, 315.

[52] App. *b.c*. i 60; cf. Livy, *per*. lxxvii.

[53] *MRR* ii 79, 82.

[54] On A. Gabinius, see my discussion in *Philologus* 103 (1959) 87 f.

[55] See *RE*, s.v. 'Cornelius', no. 134.

[56] App. *Ill*. 5. For the date see *MRR* ii 59 (n. 2): the emendation of τριακοστὸν to τριακοσιοστὸν makes easy and obvious sense.

[57] Cf. *RE*, s.vv. 'Scordisci', 'Maidoi', 'Dardani'.

[58] App. l.c.

[59] Not 86 (thus *RE*, s.v. 'Maidoi'). The date is quite certain: see *MRR* ii 58.

[60] Livy, *per*. lxxxiii.

[61] App. *Mithr*. 55; Plut. *Sulla* 23, 5; Eutr. v 7, 1 (the Dalmatae are obviously impossible (read 'Denseletae'?) and the Scordisci suspect); *vir. ill*. 75, 7; Gr. Lic. 34–5 B = 28 F (the Scordisci are introduced into the text by the Bonn editors).

[62] See *Foreign Clientelae*, 241, 272.

[63] See *RE*, s.v. 'Cornelius', no. 338 (not entirely satisfactory).

[64] *RE*, s.v. 'Gabinius', no. 13; *MRR* ii 95.

[65] Cic. *div. in Caec*. 64.

[66] Suet. *Jul*. 4. Tac. *dial*. 34 (*ad fin*.) is wrong; cf. Asc. 26 and 74.

[67] Asc. 84; Plut. *Caes*. 4, 1.

[68] Suet. l.c.

[69] This cannot be discussed in detail here. Cf. the *leges Aureliae* of 75 (*MRR* ii 96)—an unsuccessful attempt at compromise—and the tribunates of Cn. Sicinius (*ibid*. 93), L. Quinctius (*ibid*. 103), C. Licinius Macer (*ibid*. 110), and finally M. Lollius Palicanus (*ibid*. 122). For Pompey's letter of 74, see Sall. *hist*. ii 98 M; cf. *Foreign Clientelae*, 279 f. C. Caesar's election to a pontificate is another instance of the policy of conciliation that, in the hope of defending the main principles of the Sullan settlement, the *Sullani* were compelled to adopt. (Cf. Taylor, *CP* 36 (1941) 117 f.—rightly stressing its importance, but failing to recognize the change it betokens.) On hearing of it, Caesar, who had previously preferred to go to study under Molon (see last note), at once hurried home (Vell. ii 43, *init*.). The trials of A. Terentius Varro should also be mentioned in the series of attempts to bring various *Sullani* to book. (See *MRR* ii 97, 102, 108 (n. 4). Cf. also Magie, *RRAM* ii 1125, n. 42—where, however, the arguments for making the man a proconsul are not at all cogent.)

[70] Cicero says 'nuper' (*div. in Caec.* 64).

[71] At the time of the Social War Piso was 'grandis iam puer' (Cic. *Pis.* 87). If he got his consulship *suo anno*, he was born in 101 and would become eligible for the quaestorship in 71—which makes excellent sense. Cicero's compliment implies military service; and, taking it together with the fact that the Achaeans asked him to be their *patronus*, we may without hesitation place that service in the East. It is an attractive conjecture (which, at present, cannot be proved) that he was with his father-in-law P. Rutilius Nudus (on whom see *MRR* ii 105, and *RE*, s.v. 'Rutilius', no. 30).

[72] *Inscr. It.* xiii 1, 84 f., 563.

[73] *Ibid.* The fact that his command had been *pro praetore* suggests (*prima facie*, at this period) that it was not a very important one.

[74] Plut. *Sulla* 10, 3 (Mommsen's emendation is obvious and uncontested). See *MRR* ii 43; *RE*, s.v. 'Servilius', col. 1812.

[75] For an analysis of that *factio* in the nineties, see *Historia* 6 (1957) 318 ff. [=pp. 34 ff., above].

[76] *MRR* ii 82.

[77] *MRR* ii 30 (n. 5), against Münzer, *RE*, l.c. As Broughton makes clear, this excludes Spain.

[78] Africa and Cilicia have governors in 88 (on Africa, see section I, above, on Cilica, section VI, below), but they are not attested earlier. Oppius, however, was in Cilicia too early in the year to be regarded as a newly-arrived governor; moreover, Cilicia almost certainly had a governor with the higher *imperium* (attested for Oppius, as for M. Antonius earlier): Broughton's assertion to the contrary (*MRR* ii 19, n. 6) is entirely unsupported.

[79] For the military possibilities of Africa, cf. Plut. *Sert.* 9. However, as we have seen, it is quite likely that Sextilius was there for some time. In Sardinia we do not hear of a governor until Q. Antonius Balbus is defeated and killed there by L. Philippus (Livy, *per.* lxxxvi). This event cannot be precisely dated, since the Epitomator includes it in a job lot of provincial and Italian events. The one mentioned just before is the death of C. Fabius, which belongs to 83 (see n. 15, above); the one just after is the *foedus* of Sulla with the Italians. If, as is quite likely, this return to Italy marks the beginning of the new consular year (the next Roman events undoubtedly belong to 82), the Sardinian episode will belong to 83 (at least in its beginnings). But 82 cannot be definitely excluded. Broughton (*MRR* ii 67) puts Balbus' praetorship (during which he is known to have coined in Rome) in 82; but this is exceedingly unlikely. At the latest, it will be 83, and it may well be 84 or even earlier, since we do not know how long Balbus was in Sardinia.

[80] *MRR* ii 26, 35, 43 (and in Index); but not queried 72, 82, 215, *et al.*

[81] Münzer, *RE*, l.c.: '90 war er Praetor'.

[82] *RE*, l.c. (and coll. 1762 f.).

[83] *RE*, l.c. (combining Cic. *Phil.* ii 12 with Ael. fr. 110; cf. Dio xlv 16).

[84] On this man and his connections see *Historia* 6 (1957) 318 f. [= pp. 34 f., above]; cf. Münzer, *Hermes* 67 (1932) 220 f. and *RE*, s.v. 'Norbanus', coll. 927 f.

[85] *MRR* ii 41, 45 (n. 3), 48.

[86] xxxvii 2, 13 f. (with the name decapitated).

[87] Plut. *Sulla* 10, *fin.*; cf. Cic. *Br.* 179. The name of the tribune is 'Verginius' in Plutarch, 'Vergilius' in the best (but not the whole) of the Ciceronian tradition. The *Florentinus* has 'Virgilius', demonstrating the influence of the poet's name. Perhaps, therefore, 'Verginius' is better, as the corruption can be explained so very easily. There is a *monetalis* VER about this period (*MRR* ii 455, 459); unfortunately that is no help!

[88] 2 *Verr.* v 8: 'cum bello sociorum tota Italia arderet.' *Ibid.* iii 117 adds nothing to the point.

[89] *MRR* ii 62.

[90] Cic. *Br.* 308.

[91] *MRR* ii 67, 73 (n. 4). On his name, see Syme, *CP* 50 (1955) 135.

[92] That Diodorus calls him ὁ τῆς Σικελίας στρατηγός (i.e. 'governor') means very little.

[93] See *RRAM* ii 1579. Magie, while right in his rejection of 'Cilicia' (at this time) as a territorial province, is wrong in rejecting the traditional designation of Sulla (in his promagistracy after his praetorship) and of Oppius as proconsuls of 'Cilicia': if not a province, it could still be—and undoubtedly was—a *prouincia*.

[94] See my discussion of his administration in *Athenaeum* N.S. 34 (1956) 104 f. I now think that there is good reason for believing that Scaevola went to the province *ex consulatu* (i.e. in 94, not in 95): not only was it by now becoming quite exceptional for a consul to go to a province during his year of office (and we know that Scaevola transacted important business in his); but the fact that Rutilius was prosecuted in 92 suggests that he returned, at the earliest, late in 93.

[95] See Münzer, *RE*, s.v. 'Valerius', no. 178.

[96] Cic. *div. in Caec.* 63. The identification—made without reservation by Münzer (l.c.)—is rightly rejected in *MRR*, where there is, however, no recognition of Cicero's context and its implications (see n. 98, below).

[97] Münzer (l.c.) erroneously states that Asia is referred to.

[98] Cicero, fortunately for the careful reader, inserts this case between two others securely datable to the last years of the century, so that no doubt is really possible. On the coins, see *MRR* ii 432, 457 (dates ranging from 118 to 92!). Broughton identifies the would-be prosecutor with the *cos. suff.* 108 and is thus forced both to ignore the context in Cicero and to invent an otherwise unattested L. Flaccus, whom he makes praetor or proconsul in 117. But such *ad hoc* hypotheses fail to save the vicious theory. Broughton's treatment of the *monetalis* is hesitant and not entirely convincing. (See *MRR*, ll.cc. and Index (p. 536).)

[99] On this see *JRS* 46 (1956) 95 f.

[100] *MRR* ii 16 (n. 4). He has been unfortunate enough to miss inclusion in Magie's lists, probably because his province is not actually specified. But there is, of course, no serious doubt that he must at any rate be put within Magie's field of study.

[101] *MRR*, l.c. Broughton's statement that the governor of Cilicia had *imperium pro praetore* has no support whatever in the sources.

[102] *MRR* ii 42: the date is quite uncertain, except that he appears quite early in 88 and must therefore almost inevitably have been there in 89. (Cf. C. Cassius in Asia, below, for whom this is attested.) In view of what we have seen, 90 may therefore be regarded as certain and 91 as probable enough.

[103] Including the administration *per legatum*.

[104] See *art. cit.* (n. 94, above).

[105] On the career of this man, see the important article by Broughton in *AJA* 52 (1948) 323 f. He makes it clear that the most convincing reconstruction of the well-known *elogia* compels us to put the main part of Caesar's career in the first decade of the first century. But Broughton overlooks the fact that Caesar's agrarian commission (which precedes his quaestorship) may be dated in 103 with at least as much probability as in 100: Gabba (*Athenaeum* N.S. 29 (1951) 15 f.) even considers 100 impossible. If the commission is put in 103, the quaestorship may come in 102, and there is then no possible objection to a praetorship in 93. Broughton's collection of known *cursus* for this period (*art. cit.* 329, n. 35) should, incidentally, be used with extreme caution.

[106] *MRR* ii 42, 45 (n. 7); *RRAM* ii 1579 and 1100, n. 22, suggesting that he may have been C. Cassius Longinus (*cos.* 96)—which is possible if the Senate was expecting

serious trouble, but not otherwise. He is not anywhere called a consular, which would have greatly heightened the pathos and indignity of his defeat.

[107] The three men mentioned as στρατηγοί in *Inschr. v. Priene* 121 (see *RRAM* ii 1579 —unaccountably putting them all before 94) may or may not have been governors: it is perhaps most probable (since a quaestor of L. Murena concludes the list) that they were legates under Sulla. Cf. Münzer, *RE*, s.v. 'Plautius', coll. 15–6; Syme, *Historia* 4 (1955) 58.

[108] *MRR* ii 15.

[109] *Ibid.* 14; cf. *RE*, s.v. 'Cornelius', no. 351.

[110] See further below.

[111] *MRR* ii 77 f. See *Inscr. It.* xiii 1, 563, and cf. *Hermes* 83 (1955) 118.

[112] App. *Hisp.* 100; *MRR* ii 14 and 19 (n. 7) (useful discussion).

[113] Obs. 52: 'totus annus domi forisque tranquillus fuit' (this is not considered by Broughton).

[114] *RE*, s.v. 'Valerius', no. 178.

[115] He got his *prouincia* not before 83 (*MRR* ii 63).

[116] See *MRR* ii 58–9, 60 (n. 3).

[117] *MRR*, ll.cc. Cf. Cic. *Fl.* 63. The elder L. Flaccus seems to have been killed early in 85 (see *RE*, l.c., col. 30: certainly within a very few weeks either way, and most probably not in his consulship).

[118] Rightly thus in *MRR*. Jashemski (126 and 141) is quite unintelligible, Münzer (*RE*, l.c.) ambiguous on C. Flaccus' task and status.

[119] Cic. ll.cc.

[120] On this, see my discussion in *Foreign Clientelae*, 264, n. 3.

[121] *Ibid.*: and cf. below.

[122] On this aspect of Transalpina, see Syme, *Buckler Studies*, 302.

[123] E.g. *MRR* ii 90, 104—cf. Cic. *leg. Man.* 30; *Font.* 14.

[124] Broughton, while rightly recognizing the connection of the triumph 'ex Celtiberia et Gallia' with the Spanish proconsulate (*MRR* ii 19 (n. 7)), omits to list C. Flaccus as a promagistrate between 91 and 86 (inclusive). That is flagrantly inconsistent: the triumph inescapably implies continued *imperium*. [It is corrected in the *Supplement*.]

[125] Livy, *per.* lxxiii.

[126] *MRR* ii 25, 27.

[127] See discussion in Jashemski 141.

[128] Livy, l.c. (*T. Livi Periochae*, p. 83, with apparatus).

[129] *Ibid.* p. xiii, with numerous examples. This, of course, largely vitiates his expressed preference.

[130] See Jashemski, l.c. (also adopting it). Stella Maranca is the only important exception (*Fasti Praetorii*, 320), printing 'Coelius'. But he has no discussion and the choice is probably accidental. Münzer has no proper discussion, Broughton none at all.

[131] 2 *Verr.* v 181; *Mur.* 17; *comm. pet.* 11 (all in the OCT series). It is only the epigraphic and numismatic evidence that has revealed his true name. The same error is accidentally found in *MRR* ii 3 (n. 2).

[132] See, e.g., Vell. ii 120, 6.

[133] Rossbach, l.c. (n. 129, above).

[134] See *RE*, s.v. 'Coelius', no. 12.

[135] Competent, but not inspired: Cic. *Br.* 165; *de or.* i 117. It is a pity that Malcovati has omitted him in *ORF*[2].

[136] See *RE*, l.c.

[137] The importance of Spain in the Social War, obvious enough *a priori*, happens to be attested in the Asculum decree (*ILS* 8888).

[138] On this function of Transalpina, see Syme, l.c. (n. 122 above). That the province, at this time, was not as settled and peaceful as it had become a generation later is clearly shown by the revolt of the Salluvii and, even well after our period, by the campaigns of Cn. Pompeius Magnus. (See n. 123, above).

[139] Val. Max. iv 7, 5; *MRR* ii 51.

[140] Pliny, *n.h.* viii 144. See Syme, *CP* 50 (1955) 134.

[141] Ael. *hist. an.* vii 10. Similarly Plut. *mor.* 969c, where, however, the name has dropped out altogether.

[142] *RE*, s.v. 'Coelius', coll. 196–7. The chief reason for the neglect is probably that earlier, when he wrote the entry 'P. Caelius' (s.v. 'Caelius', col. 1255), Münzer had not yet discovered the importance of the dog; and after he had discovered it (s.v. 'Coelius', l.c.), he did not refer back to the earlier entry and mark it as superseded. But there can be no doubt that this was his intention. Broughton seems to have failed to notice the later entry.

[143] See *RE*, s.v. 'Placentia', col. 1903.

[144] App. *b.c.* i 66: Octavius and Merula send to Cisalpina for reinforcements—showing that, whether *de facto* or *de jure*, their authority extended to Cisalpina.

[145] Miss Ewins has recently revived the case for organization as a province in 89 (*PBSR* 23 (1955) 73 f.)—not quite successfully, as there is no real evidence for it. App. *b.c.* i 66 (see last note) and 86 certainly implies a connection with Italy; and though one can argue (as Miss Ewins does) that it is merely a *de facto* one, there is in fact nothing whatever to set against these indications. It seems almost certain, as far as we can tell, that between the *bellum Octauianum* and the *bellum Sullanum* Cisalpina was connected with Italy, just as it is *in* each of those civil wars. That Verres was assigned to Carbo as his quaestor does not (as Miss Ewins claims) show that Cisalpina was a province: at most, it was Carbo's *prouincia* (and perhaps not even that—he may have had Italia); but the consul, being *militiae*, would in any case have a quaestor.

[146] Cisalpina (Cic. *Pis.* 62; *inv.* ii 111); but Valerius Maximus tells us that his province was simply 'Gallia' (iii 7, 6), and Crassus' interest in the Transalpine province is well known: it dates back to the foundation of Narbo Martius and is confirmed by the prominence of Licinii in the nomenclature of the province (see my discussion in *Foreign Clientelae*, 264 f.). On the date, Valerius Maximus ('ex consulatu'—i.e. 94) is almost certainly right against Cicero (*inv.* ii 111: 'consul'—i.e. 95): Crassus, like his colleague Scaevola, was busy in Rome during his consulship (in fact more so, since he also defended Q. Caepio—see *Historia* 6 (1957) ll.cc. [pp. 43 f., above]), and moreover Obsequens tells us (50) that 95 saw peace at home and abroad. Cicero himself would have been the last person to regard the *de inventione* as altogether trustworthy (cf. *de or.* i 5)! My allusion to this matter in *Athenaeum* N.S. 34 (1956) 106 f. had better be forgotten.

[147] Cf. *Foreign Clientelae*, l.c.; add C. Piso (*cos.* 67): see Larsen, *CP* 26 (1931) 427 f.

[148] Cf. the perfect parallel of the Murenae (Cic. *Mur. passim*; Sall. *b.C.* 42).

[149] Cic. *Phil.* iv 9 (cf. *Att.* viii 15, 3).

[150] See above.

[151] Cic. *Br.* 160; *Cluent.* 140.

[152] Cic. *off.* ii 73.

[153] *comm. pet.* 11.

[154] *MRR* ii 17. Cf. *Foreign Clientelae*, l.c.

[155] See *Historia* 6 (1957) 328 f. [=p. 44, above].

[156] *MRR* ii 69, 74. For his wife, see Oros. v 24, 26.

[157] *MRR* ii 14.

[158] Cic. *Br.* 166.

[159] It may seem rash to confine enquiry to the candidates of 94 (for 93): defeated

candidates did sometimes wait a year before trying again. But that almost certainly did not happen in this case. Of the *coss.* 92, the only one whom the language of the *commentariolum* would fit was C. Claudius Pulcher; and he had been praetor in 95 (Cic. 2 *Verr.* ii 122) and certainly not a candidate for the consulship in that year. M. Perperna, though his father had probably held the consulship (*MRR* i 501), was not of the highest nobility and, in fact, was said by his enemies (whatever the truth of the scandalous story!) to be an alien (Val. Max. iii 4, 5). It is so unlikely as to be almost incredible that the distinguished man defeated by C. Coelius in 95 stood again in 93, only to be defeated again by a man like Perperna—and all this without our hearing of it. The argument for Flaccus is overwhelming.

[160] See *Historia* 6 (1957) 333 [=pp. 47 f., above].

[161] See my discussion (*art. cit*).

[162] The son of this P. Coelius (a very old man in 87) must be the *pr.* 74, whom Cicero happens to mention (see *MRR* ii 102).

[163] For the state of Ulterior after Cinna's death, see Plut. *Crass.* 6—certainly suggesting the absence of ordered government.

[164] E.g. *MRR* ii 63. Jashemski (126) does so with a reference to *CAH* ix 320, where it is stated without evidence or argument. I have not found either in support of this limitation; but cf., against it, App. *b.c.* i 86; Plut. *Sert.* 6; and, of course, Sertorius' actions.

[165] Recognized (hesitantly) *MRR* ii 77. But cf. Jashemski, l.c. ('Ulterior'—without discussion or plausibility). Annius also is active in both parts of the Peninsula, and no other senior magistrate is recorded as being there at the same time.

[166] He was opposed only by some barbarian tribesmen in the Pyrenees (Plut. *Sert.* 6, 2 f.)—which proves that he passed through the Transalpine province without opposition.

[167] [Cf. the arrangements during the war with Perseus (Livy xliii 15, 3; xliv 17, 9 f.).]

[168] A man described as Γναῖον 'Οκτάϊ[ον] Γναίου στρατηγὸν 'Ρωμαίων (*I. de D.* 1782; cf. *BCH* 31 (1907) 446 f.) is identified by the editors with the *cos.* 87 and described as praetor *c.* 90. (Thus also, with location in 'an eastern province', *MRR* ii 26.) In fact the Greek leaves it very doubtful whether he was praetor or promagistrate at the time (cf. n. 107, above); and the identification is anything but certain, since the man honoured may well be the *cos.* 128, about whose career we know nothing. The form of the name in the Greek on the whole favours the earlier date; and there were obviously many Roman commanders in the area about 130.

Mam. Scaurus Cites Precedent

In A.D. 22 C. Junius Silanus was accused of extortion in Asia and—to discourage possible advocates, Tacitus tells us—of *maiestas*.[1] By far the most important of the accusers was Mam. Aemilius Scaurus, who had probably been consul in the previous year.[2] It was a most unpopular thing ('infamis opera') for a senior statesman to do: even in Cicero's day, long before the emergence of the *delator* as the *bête noire* of the aristocracy, the prosecution of senators had, on the whole, brought discredit upon the prosecutor, unless he was a younger man furthering his own career.[3] Naturally enough, Scaurus had to find good precedents. He cited three: 'L. Cottam a Scipione Africano, Seruium Galbam a Catone censorio, P. Rutilium a M. Scauro accusatos.' Tacitus bitterly remarks that those great men were not involved in *that* kind of case (referring, no doubt, to the added *maiestas* charge); but how good were the precedents in all other respects?

The first two were well-known *repetundae* cases. That of Galba —one of Cato's most celebrated cases—belongs to 149 B.C. and offers no difficulty. (See *ORF*[2], pp. 79 f.) Cotta is slightly more puzzling. Cicero calls him *ueterator*, and his life was a disgraceful example of prodigality and insolvency. He was prosecuted *repetundarum* by Scipio Aemilianus in 138 B.C. and acquitted (it seems) through jealousy of his prosecutor's power.[4] Unfortunately we are not told the scene of his depredations. The prosecution comes too late to be referred to events that had taken place in his praetorship and must refer to those of his consulship in 144 (and subsequent proconsulship, if any). In that year Scipio had already shown his hostility to Cotta by preventing his going to Spain; but it is clear from his *bon mot* on that occasion that Cotta, unlike his colleague Galba, had at that time not yet had a *repetundae* case in his reprehensible past.[5] In 142 (−141) B.C. Scipio was censor, and we know that he took his task very seriously. In 140 he had to defend himself against a charge brought by a disgruntled tribune, Ti. Claudius Asellus; and straight after this—as far as we can tell—he was sent to the East as the head of a Senatorial commission with an extensive itinerary. It is not surprising, therefore, that it was only in 138 that his case against Cotta came to trial.[6] If, however, the charge did refer to his consulship, it is difficult to find a province to which he may have been sent. We have seen that it was not Spain; and Spain, as far as we know, was at this time the only part of the Empire that needed a consular governor for major warfare. Consuls, at this time, were not normally sent to perfectly peaceful provinces. And if Cotta had had a war to fight, whether in Macedonia (where there was intermittent fighting under attested praetorian governors) or even just beyond the borders of Italy against Gauls or Illyrians, we should expect a mention of it in the *Periocha* of Livy and the Livian tradition, which meticulously records even minor skirmishes. In fact, we have no reason to think that Cotta did any fighting at all in his consulship. He may have found odd jobs to do in Gaul, just beyond the borders of Italy. But we may well suppose—in the absence of any record of an alternative possibility—that, when both the consuls of 144 B.C. contended for Spain, that was because there was no other province (in the later sense) for them; and that, when neither of them actually got Spain, neither of them got any province at all. In that case the usual practice was to assign the consuls 'Italia' as their *prouincia*. It will be recalled that an attempt was made to do something of the sort to Caesar in 59 B.C.[7] I have not been able to find another instance of a prosecution *repetundarum* for offences committed against *socii* in Italy; but there is, of course, no reason why a charge should not lie on those grounds; and in view of Scipio's known interest in the Italian *socii* (and especially their upper classes), whom he was to defend so effectively in 129 B.C.,[8] it is not at all surprising that he should have brought such a case against an *inimicus*. Though Gaul cannot be excluded, *Italia* is historically an attractive suggestion.

It is, however, the last of Scaurus' precedents that is the most difficult and the most interesting; and it has been unaccountably neglected. M. Scaurus, later *Princeps Senatus*, prosecuted P. Rutilius Rufus for *ambitus* in 116 B.C., after defeating him in the consular elections for the following year and securing acquittal on a similar charge brought by Rutilius against himself. All that we know about the case, apart from these 'background' facts, is a single joke by one of Rutilius' counsel (Cic. *Br.* 113; *de or.* ii 280). In view of Rutilius' later career it may be regarded as certain that he was acquitted.

Is this the case to which Mam. Scaurus is referring? Commentators seem to have universally assumed that it is. Yet how is this case relevant as a precedent for Scaurus? The other two cases have certain features in common, all of them very much to the point that he was making in order to justify his prosecution of Silanus: (*a*) they are both *repetundarum*; (*b*) consequently they are both attempts to defend *socii populi Romani* against oppression; (*c*) they are both made by senior statesmen at the height of their authority and power; (*d*) finally, they are both *causes célèbres*, reported as such—even in our scrappy tradition on the worst-documented period of the later Republic—by a multiplicity of sources. Let us now compare M. Scaurus' prosecution of Rutilius under these heads: (*a*) it was *ambitus* and therefore not a proper precedent; (*b*) it was undertaken as an act of private vengeance for a similar action by Rutilius; (*c*) the prosecutor, at the time consul designate, was as yet far from being a senior statesman, particularly as he was practically a *nouus homo*;[9] he was not nearly as high in rank as his noble and consular descendant in A.D. 22; (*d*) finally, though Cicero mentions the case in his rhetorical works, it was clearly of no importance either in legal or in political history—being only a private quarrel between two bad-tempered men (cf. Cic. *Br.* 113)— and no other source bothers to refer to it. Surely this is an odd precedent for Mam. Scaurus to cite in the same breath with the other two.

It should now be obvious that there is something wrong with this example. Once we recognize that Mam. Scaurus can hardly have intended to refer to the *ambitus* case of 116 B.C., we may proceed to look for what he did have in mind. This—as will be clear from our analysis—must be a notorious *repetundae* case: nothing else would have fitted into the series and served his own purpose. Now, though M. Scaurus at times gave evidence in such cases, we do not actually know of any *repetundae* case in which he prosecuted: thus the approach through the person of the prosecutor is unrewarding. Let us, however, consider the accused: the name of P. Rutilius Rufus calls to mind one of the best-known of all

repetundae cases.[10] After serving as Q. Mucius Scaevola's legate in
Asia, Rutilius was prosecuted and condemned through the
machinations of Marius and the *Equites*. His conviction and exile
helped to shape the programme of M. Livius Drusus for his
tribunate (Asc., p. 21 Clark) and thus led to—though, of course,
it was not properly the cause of—the Social War.[11] If we make the
assumption that M. Scaurus was the prosecutor of Rutilius in
this famous case, everything at once falls into place most admirably: Scaurus, by that time, had been *princeps senatus* for a generation and was one of the most powerful men in Rome (cf. Cic.
Font. 24)—far higher in dignity and power than any private citizen
could hope to be under the Empire; and the case was a *repetundae*
case of outstanding importance and fame. Admittedly, Rutilius
was claimed to be the victim of a miscarriage of justice, and en-
comiastic tradition—based ultimately on his own writings and
those of Cicero, the pupil of his friend Scaevola—finally prevailed.
But a descendant of the prosecutor, in ordinary *pietas*, quite apart
from the interest of the moment, would have to claim that his
ancestor had championed a just cause against a guilty man;
and the audience would take that implication for granted. The
conclusion seems inevitable: it must have been this case—*the* case
of P. Rutilius Rufus, in the memory of men—that Mam. Scaurus
was citing as his precedent, implying that his great-grandfather
was the successful prosecutor.

We seem to have arrived at a fact of cardinal importance for
the interpretation of Roman politics at the beginning of the
first century B.C.—of such importance, indeed, that, since it
is not anywhere directly attested, the witness must be carefully
examined.

He does not stand up well under examination. Not only does it
seem unlikely that the old *princeps senatus*, crippled with gout,
would voluntarily have taken upon himself the strain of a major
political prosecution[12]—and this without arousing any comment
whatever in the numerous sources on the trial;[13] but, as it happens,
we know the name of Rutilius' prosecutor: he was a man called
Apicius—no doubt a member of the equestrian clique whom
Rutilius and Scaevola had annoyed—whose reputation has
suffered accordingly.[14] This evidence, both positive and negative,
is further confirmed by analysis of the political situation in the

nineties (for which, see my article cited above): by then the old quarrel between Scaurus and Rutilius had long been forgotten amid the continuous shifting of political alliances; they were both in the same closely knit faction, centred in the Metelli and opposed to Marius, who had tried to strike at them through the trial of Rutilius (Dio, fr. 97.3); in fact, Scaurus, so far from being one of Rutilius' enemies, was marked out to be the next victim after his fall.[15] The weight of all this varied evidence is decisive: M. Scaurus cannot have prosecuted Rutilius in 92 B.C.

Yet, as we have seen, only the assumption that he did will make sense of Mam. Scaurus' list of precedents. Is Tacitus wrong? It would not be the only time: as a source for Republican history he is not above inaccuracy and is, at the best, as good as his source in each case.[16] Here, however, his source was probably reliable enough: for an important debate in the Senate he would either look up the *acta Senatus*[17] or at least rely on 'scriptores senatoresque eorundem temporum'. We may take it that Mam. Scaurus did recite his list of precedents and must be held responsible for it. Can we attribute such an error to the great-grandson of M. Scaurus himself?

There is no reason why we should not. About the character of Mam. Scaurus many harsh things were said, not only in his own day and century,[18] but in fact centuries later.[19] *Suggestio falsi*, never alien to Roman oratory even in its most virtuous exponents, would not surprise us in his case. In an action that was bound to make him unpopular, a *domesticum exemplum* of this kind was worth having: if he found a reference to his ancestor's prosecution of Rutilius in the family archives (as we have seen, the case was probably no longer a matter of general knowledge), he was not above moulding it to his purpose by means of a little *contaminatio*. Yet, on the whole, a more lenient view suggests itself as more probable: from what we know of the man, simple ignorance is the best explanation. For though he was by nature one of the most gifted speakers of his time, we learn from the elder Seneca that laziness was his besetting sin: he would often prepare his cases when actually in court. As a result he missed true greatness: 'eo illum longa, immo perpetua, desidia perduxerat ut nihil curare uellet, nihil posset.' Nor was this confined to his forensic speeches: his *libelli* (whatever they were) 'caloris minus habent, neglegentiae non minus'.[20] It is only to be expected that such a man, when citing precedent, should fail to verify his references and should confuse his facts. Nor is it surprising that, being the man he was, he should be ignorant of the details of his own great-grandfather's career. We remember another well-known great-grandson—degenerate perhaps, but hardly in the same class as Mam. Scaurus—who was guilty of much more flagrant public ἀνιστορησία: none other than Q. Caecilius Metellus Pius Scipio Nasica (see Cic. *Att.* vi 1, 17).

Thus we have lost our unexpected 'fact' from the history of the late Republic. Yet our enquiry has not been in vain. It has not only made sense of a passage of Tacitus, but thrown some light on the character of Mam. Aemilius Scaurus; and it has quite unexpectedly illustrated one of the elder Seneca's judgments, which only too often we have to take on trust.

NOTES

[1] Tac. *ann.* iii 66. I should like to thank my friend Mr R. Sealey for pointing out to me that the passage needs explaining and for discussing my explanation with me.

[2] *PIR*², A 404; Degrassi, *Fasti Cons.* 8.

[3] Cic. *off.* ii 49; cf. *div. in Caec.* 1 and 66 f.; Quint. xi 1, 57.

[4] Sources in *ORF*², pp. 129 f. Livy, *per. Oxyrh.* lv gives the date; oddly enough, Cicero did not know it—any more than the Loeb editor of Tacitus (*ad loc.*). That the case was *repetundarum* is clear from *div. in Caec.* 69. App. *b.c.* i 22 may refer to this Cotta or (thus Cichorius, *Röm. Stud.* 78) to his son, later *cos.* 119. On the elder Cotta and his circle see also *Historia* 6 (1957) 319 f. [=pp. 36 f., above].

[5] Val. Max. vi 4, 2: 'neutrum, inquit, mihi mitti placet, quia alter nihil habet, alteri nihil est satis.' The latter must be Galba, who had been accused *repetundarum* (see above) and was known to be guilty; the former is Cotta, who, as tribune of the plebs, had tried to use his sacrosanctity to avoid paying his debts (Val. Max. vi 5, 4).

[6] On Scipio's duties in the years 142–139 B.C., see *MRR* i 474 f. [Cf. now A. E. Astin, *CP* 54 (1959) 221 f.]

[7] Suet. *Jul.* 19, 2. This, incidentally, is often misunderstood. It is clearly a traditional formula and means the suppression of brigandage in Italy such as occurred even in the second century B.C. For a proconsul doing odd jobs in Gaul, see the inscription of Sex. Atilius Saranus, the consul of 136 (*ILS* 5945). But we do not know what his *prouincia* had been—*Italia* is as likely as Gaul.

[8] App. *b.c.* i 19. For what Roman magistrates could do in Italy, cf. C. Gracchus *ap.* Gell. x 3, 2 f.

[9] On Scaurus' family and his struggle to establish himself, see Bloch, *M. Aemilius Scaurus* (1909) 3 f.

[10] *MRR* ii 8–9 lists over thirty references to the case.

[11] On all this see *Athenaeum*, N.S. 34 (1956) 104 f., especially 117 f.

[12] On his state of health see Asc., p. 22 Clark. His *delatio* of Q. Caepio in 92 was a tactical manoeuvre, not meant to result in a real trial.

13 See n. 10 (above). The argument from silence here surely seems justified. Cf., e.g., Cic. *Br.* 110 f.: a parallel treatment of Scaurus and Rutilius, describing their clash in 116, then going on to discuss Rutilius' showing at his trial in 92 without a word of Scaurus.

14 Posidonius *ap.* Athen. iv, 66 (168 D): this cannot really mean anything but that Apicius was Rutilius' prosecutor. That the *princeps senatus* acted as *subscriptor* to a Roman knight is inconceivable.

15 Asc., l.c.; cf. *Athenaeum*, N.S. 34 (1956) 117 f.

16 For random examples of inaccuracy and misleading formulation, see *ann.* iii 26 f. (a 'history' of legislation in Rome); xi 22 (a history of the quaestorship); xii 60 (the judiciary laws); and, on a minor biographical matter, xiii 6 (Pompey's age).

17 Cf. *ann.* ii 88. Tacitus' methods are treated in all the standard editions. [See now Syme, *Tacitus* (1958), Index, s.v. '*acta Senatus*'.]

18 Apart from Tacitus (l.c., and vi 29: 'uita probrosus'), see especially Sen. *ben.* iv 31.

19 Tert. *de pallio* 5, *fin.*, must refer to him.

20 See Seneca's long discussion of him in *contr.* x, *praef.* 2–3.

Rome and Antiochus the Great:
A Study in Cold War

I. Friendship to Cold War

THE story of Roman relations with Antiochus III prior to the outbreak of the Syrian War has often been told;[1] yet it has a peculiar fascination for the present-day reader, and, regarded as a study in diplomacy and propaganda, it may reveal some facets of great interest in the understanding of the history of the unification of the Mediterranean world. If, as the old saying has it, history must be rewritten for each generation, there is surely no period of history which our generation should be more competent to rewrite.

While Rome, in the West, had been dealing with Hannibal, Antiochus had overcome the rebels in his kingdom and, despite a temporary setback at Raphia, had established his authority over a larger area than any Seleucid king since the founder of the dynasty.[2] By 201 B.C. the Aegean world, the traditional theatre of Greek politics, was flanked by two great powers, in East and West respectively. Only a generation earlier the picture had been quite different: there had been two great powers (Rome and Carthage) in the western half of the Mediterranean and three (Antigonids, Seleucids and Ptolemies) in the eastern half; in each half, though there was little good will, there was the peace established by balance; and—as had indeed been the case, on the whole, for centuries—neither half had very much impinged upon the other. Now Rome was supreme in the West and, by Philip V's attack upon her in the course of the Hannibalic War, had been forced to turn her attention eastward; while in the East Antiochus had acquired overwhelming strength and, having settled his kingdom as far as the Indus valley, must necessarily now turn towards the West. The balance in the Aegean was further upset by the death of Ptolemy Philopator, who was succeeded by a child; the Ptolemies, for the moment, had ceased to count, and Antiochus marched into Syria. Philip V, of course, would not miss his chance: unable or unwilling to see the shift in balance, which had reduced his kingdom to the second rank of powers, he had also acquired an exaggerated opinion of his own strength in his First Roman War; and he now thought he could still prevent Rome and Antiochus from becoming overwhelmingly strong. Thus he also embarked on a policy of expansion. Whether or not it was co-ordinated with that of Antiochus,[3] it was bound to appear so to the smaller states; Pergamum and Rhodes, with the traditional balance of power in the Aegean area crumbling before their eyes, decided to call in Rome—a distant and therefore apparently less dangerous great power—in order to redress it.

We are not here directly concerned with the perplexities of the causes and origins of the Second Macedonian War.[4] It is sufficient for us to note, against those who ascribe to the report of a pact between the two kings a decisive influence in persuading the Senate to go to war, that throughout the troubled period that precedes the war, and indeed throughout its actual course, there is no sign of Roman hostility to Antiochus. We know something about their diplomatic relations: Holleaux[5] has drawn up a list of the embassies that passed between them. The first is dated 200[6] and is said to have been sent to make peace between Antiochus and Ptolemy. For this statement two references to Livy and three to Polybius are cited by Holleaux as evidence. But the Livian passages tell of a mission sent to Alexandria for various specified purposes—no mention is made of the war between the two kings;[7] while Polybius mentions the presence of the Roman embassy in Athens and Rhodes, but says nothing about its ultimate purpose or even destination.[8] In fact, the story rests on evidence not cited by Holleaux in his table; and it is annalistic tradition of the worst sort. Appian, in one of the most confused chapters of his *Macedonica*,[9] mentions an order to Antiochus 'not to attack Egypt'. But the report is vitiated, not only by its failure to get the ultimatum to Philip right, but also by its stress on the Aetolian embassy that failed to get Roman help—a tale that certainly does not belong in 201 and is probably invented by an annalist.[10] Apart from Appian, only Justin[11] mentions the Roman 'order' to Antiochus, which he connects with Lepidus' appointment as *tutor regis*. Now, whatever the truth of this difficult matter,[12] the appointment of M. Lepidus to the guardianship of the king and the administration of the kingdom at this time, when he himself was probably only about

twenty, is out of the question.[13] So, of course, is the 'order' to
Antiochus: not only had the Senate neither right nor, what is
more important, power to give orders to the ruler of the East; but
we shall see that, although Antiochus made no move to evacuate
the Egyptian possessions he had conquered, a little later he and
Rome are on the best of terms. This alone is enough to condemn
the 'order' to Antiochus: it is another annalistic fabrication,
meant to show Roman *constantia* and *magnitudo animi*. As far as the
purpose of the mission to Alexandria is concerned, there is probably nothing to be added to Livy's formulation: this is annalistic
tradition at its best; and it is clear, consistent, and—having no
special point to make—credible.[14] It is, however, quite possible
that the mission had a friendly interview with Antiochus: we shall
see that he was soon to be considered *amicus populi Romani*. But,
with or without such a visit, we need hardly be surprised that the
order to Antiochus was later invented for this mission, probably by
contaminatio with that of 196 (see below) and with the more famous
one of C. Popillius to Antiochus IV.[15]

The next diplomatic contact is the embassy which (we are
informed) politely asked the king to withdraw his troops from
Attalus' territory. This is dated by Livy to 198 B.C.[16] Holleaux,
having had no qualms about the order to Antiochus in 200, rather
perversely refuses to accept this embassy or even to include it in
his table, in which he does list (in brackets) other embassies
admittedly spurious. His reason is that he will not believe in
Antiochus' invasion of Attalus' territory in the first place.[17] He
argues, briefly, that in Livy's report Attalus' envoys ask the Romans
to permit him to go home with his forces, while in fact we know
that he spent the winter at home; and this fact alone would make
an invasion by Antiochus at this time unlikely. The latter argument is quite invalid: not only is it possible that Antiochus
wanted to meet Attalus himself in the field and shut him up in his
capital, but it is also possible that he did wait until Attalus had
left and then proceeded to attack—in which case we may confidently assume that Attalus did not wait for the Senate's permission before returning.[18] Knowing neither Antiochus' aims nor
Attalus' movements, we should be guilty of plain absurdity if we
argued from both of these to the falsity of a statement in our
source. Nor is Holleaux's principal argument much better. As we

have seen, it is quite possible that Attalus was on his way to joining the consul when he heard of the invasion; he would then, naturally enough, send an embassy asking the Senate's formal permission to return, and, safely anticipating a favourable answer, return as fast as he could. But in any case speeches in Livy must not be pressed in this way: we know how he likes to heighten oratorical effect, and the actual wording of this speech may well be his own, whatever his source.[19] The *fact* of Attalus' appeal for help must not be rejected, even if the wording in Livy can be impeached; and if we seem to labour this elementary point of source criticism, it is because its neglect has been responsible for much *a priori* history. If we have to choose, it is the Senate's answer rather than the envoys' request that we should elect to trust; for it is in plausible official style and may well go back to good material. This answer, however, does not refer to the king's absence from home, but merely permits him to have his *auxilia* back; and it is not by any means unlikely that, when Attalus went home for the winter, he in fact left part of his forces with the Roman commander. In favour of the whole report there is the noticeable absence of the Roman blustering that often characterizes annalistic fabrications: the Senate refuses to use or threaten force or to try to issue orders to Antiochus, whom it describes as a 'friend of the Roman people'.[20] In fact, it is hard to see why anyone should ever have doubted the truth of this report—which is further confirmed by a later reference, probably ultimately based on archival material, to Attalus' gratitude for Roman assistance[21]—and the incident should be firmly reinstated in our accounts of the period. Antiochus, having settled accounts with the Ptolemies in Syria, and planning his advance through Asia Minor, would naturally make a demonstration against Pergamum. But for the moment it was probably not very seriously meant; he seems to have withdrawn as soon as he received the polite Roman request to do so.[22]

He had, in fact, nothing to gain by provoking Rome at this point and everything to gain from her favour; and he must have gladly seized this chance of obliging the Senate. At any rate, in the course of 198[23] he sent an embassy to Rome. The occasion is not mentioned in the sources and did not arouse Holleaux's curiosity; but we may now be reasonably certain that it was sent in order to announce to the Senate the king's ready compliance with its request. At this time Antiochus was preparing the expedition he launched in 197; and as he must have been aware that it would take him into the Roman sphere of influence, it was essential for him to try to conciliate the Senate in advance and, of course, to arrive at an estimate of its attitude towards him. He certainly had reason to be satisfied with the immediate result: in Livy (P.) he refers to the Senate's 'honorifica in se decreta responsaque', and we need not ascribe to the Fathers the Machiavellian reasons for them which Livy delights in giving. As we have seen, the embassy had a signal act of complaisance to announce, and the Senate can have had no inkling of what Antiochus was preparing. But Antiochus drew the wrong conclusion: finding the Romans friendly, he at once, on the return of his envoys, set out on his great expedition westward.[24]

It is well known how the Rhodians courageously asked him to withdraw; the fact should be beyond dispute, although the heroics may be discounted.[25] We have seen how fear of collaboration between Philip and Antiochus had haunted the smaller states a few years earlier, terrified as they were at seeing the traditional balance of power destroyed by the sudden decline of the Ptolemies. The Rhodians had called in Rome to redress the balance; it is not surprising that now, seeing Antiochus moving westward with large forces, they jumped to the conclusion that their worst fears were realized and that he was hurrying to save his ally Philip from defeat. As Livy (P.) tells us, at this very time they happened to receive the news of the battle of Cynoscephalae and they at once desisted from seriously trying to impede Antiochus. With Philip decisively defeated, the fear of active collaboration between the two kings was gone; Rome could be left to balance Antiochus' power.

Naturally enough, Antiochus' rapid advance, news of which would not be minimized by their friends, aroused the Romans' apprehension. It may well have appeared to them that he had deliberately misled them by means of his embassy, and they could not but wonder what his real intentions were. This contrast (as it might seem) between words and deeds, which Livy stresses in connection with Antiochus' next embassy, undoubtedly intensified the effect that the advance as such was bound to have. The first result was seen at once: Antiochus' advance was one of the main reasons for Flamininus' decision to give Philip a quick and relatively lenient peace. As Polybius says,[26] it was important to liquidate the war in Greece as soon as possible; and we may add that Flamininus was already forming the scheme for a balance of power in an unoccupied Greece that was to be his chosen political weapon against Antiochus during the next few years: the defeated enemy would make a necessary ally against excessive Aetolian power.

Antiochus, all this time, seems to have refrained from renewing diplomatic contact with the Romans. He might have hastened to congratulate them on the victory of Cynoscephalae and reassure them about his intentions; but in fact he waited while the cities of Asia Minor surrendered to him. It is clear that he was hoping to confront the Senate with the accomplished fact of the conquest of southern Asia Minor and the crossing into Europe. This alone can explain why, when things did not go according to plan and Smyrna and Lampsacus held out against both persuasion and force, he nevertheless, in the spring of 196 (when an embassy to the Romans, as we shall see, could no longer be delayed), decided to leave them unconquered in his rear and hurry to seize a bridge-head on the European side of the Hellespont: it would be much more difficult for the Romans to make him evacuate what he already held than to forbid him to go farther. At the very time when the king was leading his forces into Europe,[27] Hegesianax and Lysias were at last sent to Corinth to congratulate Flamininus on the victory of which Antiochus, like the Rhodians, must have heard during the previous campaigning season; they were also to assure him of the king's pacific intentions.[28] Livy stresses the contrast between words and deeds,[29] as it must have struck the Romans; and they were indeed thoroughly frightened. Flamininus must have reported his suspicions of Antiochus to the Senate, when he recommended the signing of the treaty with Philip; nor had those more directly affected by the king's advance failed to appeal to the only possible champion. We know from a remarkable inscription[30] how Lampsacus asked for Roman protection and how its envoys—and we need not doubt that they were not the only ones—arrived at Corinth about the same time as those of Antiochus, having been sent on to Flamininus by the Senate. It becomes clear now why Antiochus, though not quite ready with his accomplished fact, had been unable to delay the sending of his embassy any longer.

The effect of all this can be seen in the decree that the ten commissioners brought to Corinth in 196: the Greeks of Asia, as well as those of Europe, were proclaimed free; and a letter was at once dispatched to Prusias, asking him to free Cius.[31] Moreover, the Senate now decided to support Ptolemy in his war against Antiochus and to try to settle the war by 'arbitration' in the former's interest.[32] It was in this atmosphere of suspicion that Hegesianax and Lysias arrived at Corinth, and the new policy was at once proclaimed to them. Antiochus was asked to withdraw from all the Greek cities (those autonomous and those previously under Philip or Ptolemy) that he had occupied or was attacking, and to refrain from crossing into Europe; for (the Senate proclaimed) he was not to bring back war and 'enslavement' to kings into the Greek world just freed from them by Rome.[33] Thus Rome had reacted to Antiochus' policy by launching a war of propaganda and at once seizing the initiative in it. Having successfully played the champion of Greek freedom against Philip, she saw no reason why such a role was not to be equally successful and equally advantageous against another king. At the same time, it is obvious that the Romans had no intention of provoking a war: there was no blustering or threat of force, such as had been used against Philip before the outbreak of the war against him; and in fact Flamininus and the ten commissioners promised to send a counter-embassy to Antiochus in order to negotiate.[34]

At this stage neither side wanted war. Antiochus, having, as he thought, assured himself of Roman favour by prompt compliance with a Roman request that he might well have ignored, kept reiterating his peaceful intentions towards the Romans and no doubt felt sure that he would be able to convince them of the truth of his protestations. Though, as his actions show, he foresaw a certain amount of Roman opposition to his crossing of the Hellespont, the Senate would no doubt, once thus convinced, abandon its attempts to reverse the irreversible and *amicitia* would be restored. That the king had no intention of attacking Rome will be clear enough from subsequent events. As for the Senate, though worried by the king's rapid advance and even more by his apparent duplicity, it was to make its desire for peace equally clear by the evacuation of Greece. Yet the atmosphere had been poisoned; and cold war, once begun, was to precipitate the two powers, inevitably, into what both wanted to avoid.

The Roman envoys duly went to see the king, whom they met at Lysimachia, which he was then rebuilding. They were joined there by the Senate's envoy L. Cornelius Lentulus, who had been sent out to 'arbitrate' between Antiochus and Ptolemy.[35] On their way they had hastily proceeded to 'free' various cities once subject to Philip. It is interesting that these were Bargylia in Asia Minor and Thasos (and other cities) in Thrace—i.e., precisely those places in which Antiochus might be expected to be interested before long.[36] Having freed them, the Romans would have a moral right, or even duty, to defend their freedom if it were threatened: Antiochus should not, at least, advance farther than he already had. At the same time Hegesianax and Lysias, Antiochus' envoys to Corinth, also arrived at Lysimachia. It is worth while attending to this little point. The Romans had transacted a great deal of business, both at Corinth and on their way, since these men had left Corinth; yet they arrived at Lysimachia about the same time. Unfortunately we are not told how they had spent the interval; but it is scarcely hazardous to conclude that, after receiving Flamininus' hostile terms, they had spent some time, on their return journey, making contacts in Greece on behalf of the king. These contacts were to be useful before long.

At Corinth the Senate's envoys and Flamininus had openly embarked on cold war. At Lysimachia, now, the personal atmosphere still remained friendly, and diplomatic courtesies were observed;[37] but the negotiations were conducted in that peculiar manner (perhaps partly with a view to settlement, but largely with a view to propaganda effect outside the conference room) that seems so familiar to us. The Romans had three demands to make, with varying degrees of justice; and Polybius carefully distinguishes the manner in which each was made. They asked the king to evacuate the cities belonging to their ally Ptolemy, which he had occupied; they solemnly protested that he should evacuate those belonging to Philip, whom they had defeated; and they exhorted him to keep his hands off those that were free. This last, of course, they had no right to demand, but propounded by virtue of their *susceptum patrocinium libertatis Graecorum*; in fact it conflicted with their first demand, which implied the return of some Greek cities to Ptolemy. But it fitted in with the role which Rome had assumed and about which we shall have more to say. Finally, the envoys asked the king to explain what worried them most—his presence in Europe. But Antiochus, heir to generations of Hellenistic diplomacy and forewarned of the new Roman game, was ready for them. First, he denied their right to intervene in Asia at all, just as he would not dream of interfering in Italy. The implications of this were clear: he regarded Asia as being under his hegemony, just as Italy was under that of the Romans; and it would follow that all the intervening region should be neutral ground between them—a very different picture from that painted by the Romans, with Europe their exclusive sphere of interest and Asia Minor the meeting ground of the two powers.[38] As for the cities that had belonged to Philip and Ptolemy and his crossing into Europe, he claimed historical rights: he was only reoccupying territory that had belonged to Seleucus Nicator (long before the Romans had ever thought of these regions!) and had been lost owing to the troubled times through which the dynasty had passed; and now Lysimachia was being rebuilt as a residence for his son Seleucus—i.e., he had no intention whatever of abandoning it. So far all was orthodox diplomacy, meeting claim with counterclaim: Antiochus had affirmed that he was not prepared to withdraw, but that, on the other hand, the Romans, if they acquiesced, need not fear his advancing beyond reasonable limits (though these limits, as befitted the situation, had been very elastically defined for the present). Now the king proceeded to his final blows. As for Ptolemy, whom they were protecting, he had good news for them: his differences with Ptolemy had been amicably settled and the young king had agreed to become his son-in-law;[39] and as for the autonomous cities of Asia Minor, he was quite willing to leave them 'free'—provided the freedom were clearly recognized to be his own gift and not that of the Romans. At this stage the envoys had few weapons left; it appeared that their protégés did not need a champion. There was only one hope of reversing the impression. To brand Antiochus' offer of freedom to the Greek cities as false, they introduced ambassadors from Smyrna and Lampsacus to declaim against him and make it clear to the attentive Greek world whom Greek cities really regarded as their champion and whom as their enemy. But Antiochus was again prepared. He cut short the very first harangue, offering to submit all his differences with these cities to the arbitration of—Rhodes! A fairer offer could not be imagined. This Greek city, quite recently hostile to him (as we have seen), was traditionally the enemy of the kings' excessive pretensions.

This was the end of the conference of Lysimachia. The scene of high comedy that actually led to its break-up[40] was a convenient accident. In fact there was nothing further left to say. The round had gone to Antiochus. He had made it clear that Rome need not fear his attacking her, but that he himself was not afraid, if Rome wanted war, and that threats would not move him. Moreover, if Rome did want war, she would be branded as the aggressor: he was not, as Philip had been, ready to present her with a good catchword. We shall have to analyse the background of the cold war in more detail. But we can see at once that, if Rome had wanted to fight at this point, she would have had to fight for the freedom of cities that Antiochus was quite willing to declare free, for the settlement of disputes that he was willing to refer to arbitration, and for the return to Ptolemy of cities that Ptolemy apparently did not want back. On these terms Rome could not hope for much sympathy in the Greek world. She would be branded as the barbarian aggressor, and the freedom of Greece would have been proclaimed in vain. Antiochus at once dispatched another embassy to Flamininus, asking for a treaty of alliance. Of course, nothing came of it, and nothing can have been expected to. Flamininus non-committally referred the envoys to the Senate, and they did not even bother to go.[41] It was merely another gesture, proclaiming the king's desire for peace both to the Romans and to the neutral states; and the effect was achieved. The next move was up to the Romans.

The Senate, though afraid of Antiochus' power, seems to have been convinced that for the moment he meant no harm.[42] The difficulty for them was that they would soon have to make up their minds what to do with their army in Greece; should they ignore Greek opinion, or should they fully implement the declaration of freedom and withdraw their forces? For the moment the decision could be put off. Nabis presented a good opportunity for another year's campaigning, while the situation might become clearer.

I

On this there could hardly be any difference of opinion. Thus Flamininus (carefully leaving the actual declaration of war to a Greek congress, to avoid the appearance of armed intervention in Greek affairs) proceeded to deal with Nabis, in which task he could rely on the sympathy of the greater part of the Greek governments.[43] But with that campaign over, and the tyrant—humbled, but not destroyed—left in power as a counterweight to the Achaeans in the South, as Philip had been to the Aetolians in the North, the great decision had at last to be faced. Early in 194 the question came up for discussion in the Senate.[44] The great Scipio, himself consul, wanted to have Macedonia and an army: Lysimachia had shown the failure of cold-war techniques, and more orthodox measures of security were indicated. But the majority of the House opposed him. Flamininus' friends carried the decision to evacuate Greece.

II. COLD WAR TO WAR

It is now time to analyse this difference of opinion in the Senate (parallel to that between Flamininus and the majority of the senatorial commission)[45] and to discuss its causes and its nature in greater detail. We have no reason to think, as has sometimes been stated, that it is a mark of serious disagreement as to the danger threatening from Antiochus. That danger, as Polybius tells us, was indeed obvious; and we have seen that Flamininus himself was one of the first to recognize it and be influenced by it. The only difference was on how to deal with the situation. One party—that sharing Scipio's view—preferred to negotiate from positions of strength, i.e. to subordinate diplomacy to strategy; the other—that of Flamininus—propounded a policy of diplomacy and propaganda, with the backing of force (necessarily present in the background) deliberately played down. If peace could be saved—and there was no serious reason to believe in an imminent attack by the king—this policy was more likely to save it; while if it could not, its propounders thought it more advantageous even for war than that of their opponents. The keystone of Flamininus' policy was the evacuation of Greece, and it was this that for years he laboured to impose upon the suspicious opposition.[46] Modern accounts, neglecting the political background of the war with

Philip (at least after its actual outbreak), too often fail to appreci-
ate the fundamental change in Roman policy from the ultimatum
presented by Lepidus to Philip at Abydus, i.e., the demand that he
should give up his recent gains and cease attacking Greeks,[47]
through Flamininus' dramatic and (to Philip) totally unexpected
announcement at the Aous Conference that he must begin by
freeing the Thessalians,[48] to the Isthmian declaration and the
evacuation of Greece.[49] Roman policy between 201 and 194
tends to be presented as consistently and unchangingly demanding
the 'freedom of Greece', and it is only the genuineness of that freedom that is debated. In fact, as we know, the very commission
charged by the Senate with 'securing the freedom of the Greeks'[50]
wanted to do so by leaving garrisons in the 'fetters of Greece';
and Flamininus had difficulty in persuading it to evacuate even
the strategically quite valueless city of Corinth.[51] Flamininus,
unlike the commissioners and those who shared their opinions,
realized that with her entry into the Hellenistic concert of powers,
Rome, if she was to succeed, had to adapt herself to its traditional
methods and techniques and combine them with those developed
by herself, which had brought about her successes in the West.
One of the outstanding features of Hellenistic history was the
importance of Greek public opinion: the most powerful monarchs
deferred to it and wooed its favour with demonstrative courtesy.[52]
In particular, they had been 'freeing' Greek cities from one
another since Polyperchon freed them from Cassander's garrisons
—or Alexander from those of the Persians. It was to this tradition
that Flamininus wanted to adapt Roman policy.

That this adaptation was not as difficult as has sometimes been
thought—that Rome, in fact, had in her own diplomatic arsenal
forged the weapon of 'freedom' that Flamininus now used with
such *éclat*—has been pointed out elsewhere.[53] The 'freedom of
Greece' was a profoundly Roman idea, often used before in other
areas, and now dressed up in Hellenistic trappings. But it is the
latter[54] that are important for our present purpose. Flamininus
took Greek public opinion as seriously as any Hellenistic ruler did,
and in this important respect he may indeed be called philhellenic;
it is the grain of truth in Tenney Frank's view,[55] which reaction
against that view has since tended to obscure. Where the protago-
nists of East and West were so evenly matched that no one could

predict the outcome of a war, Flamininus realized the importance of attaching what we should nowadays call the uncommitted nations to the Roman cause. If war came—and we know that Flamininus was bearing the possibility in mind as early as 197–6—one or two isolated garrisons surrounded by a hostile population might be a liability rather than an asset; but the support of the Greek world would be a solid advantage, worth buying at some apparent cost. That all this was hard-headed political calculation, and not sentimentalism or misguided idealism, is obvious enough from the context of Flamininus' policy. It is well known—and we have already had occasion to notice it—how he saved Rome's defeated enemies (Philip and Nabis) from her allies (the two Leagues) in order to preserve a balance of power in the peninsula that he intended to leave ungarrisoned. This balance of power was the hard prerequisite for his apparently generous policy. On this point he would stoop to any chicanery[56] and would not allow any compromise or concession, even for the sake of Rome's good name or his own.[57] It is this fundamental inconsistency—this lack of the courage, ultimately, of his own convictions—that relegates Flamininus, in the last analysis, from the class of statesmen to that of mere politicians and that was responsible, first before the war with Antiochus and then again after, for the final failure of Roman policy in Greek lands. But once the balance of power was established, he knew that Roman troops were not needed. In view of Aetolian propaganda, working on the distrust of their 'liberators' that the Greeks had acquired in over a century of 'liberations', the evacuation of Greece had become a political necessity.[58] This time freedom was, conspicuously, to have no strings attached.[59]

Moreover, in this form the 'freedom of the Greeks' offered further diplomatic possibilities against Antiochus; and this brings us back to Lysimachia and the story of the cold war. We have seen how the 'freedom of the Greeks' was extended to those in Asia. At small cost to herself, Rome could now pose as the champion of Greeks everywhere and call upon Antiochus to adopt her conception of Greek freedom—very much to his disadvantage. Marginal to Rome's interests, the Greek cities of the eastern world were of the very essence of his own; and if he now withdrew from Asia Minor, he might next be called upon to give up his Greek cities everywhere. On the other hand, he could not allow himself to be forced into the position of one branded as bringing war and enslavement to the Greek world.[60] Such was the dilemma the king faced at Lysimachia. We now understand the Romans' confidence, after the proclamation of their policy, in sending ambassadors to meet the king. However, as we saw, he was equal to the occasion. The implications of his arguments now became even clearer and provide the connection with what was to follow. It was not for nothing that he compared his position in Asia with that of Rome in Italy: Italy also had Greek cities—as both the king and the Greek world in general well knew, even though the Romans conveniently forgot it—and this fact had its obvious political uses.[61] Yet even in Asia he was willing to concede freedom and arbitration—provided it were made clear that this *beneficium* (contrasted, by implication, with Roman behaviour in Italy) was his own and that he, and not the Romans, was entitled to the gratitude for it. With Roman influence removed from Asia, the freedom of the cities concerned would, whatever their legal status, become nugatory.[62] Another Roman point was skilfully twisted to the king's advantage: if he had crossed to Thrace (a step to which, as we have seen, he claimed to have every right), it was in order to protect the Greeks there against the barbarians.[63] It was he who was the real philhellene.

In the face of complete diplomatic defeat Flamininus nevertheless persisted in his policy. The balance of power in Greece was assured with the defeat of Nabis and the Roman *patrocinium* established,[64] and a reversal of Roman policy at this point would be fatal to any hope of future assistance from the Greeks and further use of the slogan of freedom. In view of this fact, immediate strategic considerations (not necessarily sound in any case) were of minor importance. Even the arrival of Hannibal at the court of Antiochus in 195,[65] though it had scared the Roman electorate into giving Scipio Africanus a second consulship,[66] made no essential difference to the situation. With the first hysteria over, it was seen that the king had no intention of letting the exile push him into immediate war, and Flamininus' clearer head prevailed. Roman troops withdrew from Greece.[67] This step not only proclaimed the Roman conception of Greek freedom; both to Antiochus and to the Greek world it showed that Rome had no intention of starting a world war. To Antiochus it seemed to indicate that a permanent settlement was possible on the basis of his position at Lysimachia. He had followed up his diplomatic triumph there by inordinate diplomatic activity aimed at attaching neighbouring kings, tribes, and cities to himself;[68] and having, on the whole, succeeded in this and thereby further improved his bargaining position, he now sent Menippus and Hegesianax to Rome, at the time when envoys from the whole of the Greek world were flocking there to hear—and, if possible, influence—the Senate's decision on Flamininus' *acta*. He wished to have a treaty between Rome and himself included in the settlement. Again, as in 198, the king had misinterpreted Roman actions. This time he had taken an act of cold war for one of acquiescence and surrender.

There followed the Conference of Rome,[69] held, behind closed doors, between Flamininus and the ten commissioners (whom the Senate had constituted a committee with full powers for the purpose) on the one hand and the king's envoys on the other, while the embassies from the Greek world anxiously waited for what the great powers might decide. We are fortunate in being comparatively well informed of its course. As so many prominent Romans were on the committee concerned, Polybius, when lapse of time had done away with the need for secrecy, seems to have found it possible to get detailed information. The king's position was simple: regarding the Roman evacuation of Greece as a retreat, he hoped for recognition of his gains at no cost to himself; and he considered himself fully Rome's equal in status and power. With his claims apparently *de facto* conceded, he probably thought that Rome would strike some face-saving bargain acceptable to himself. In any case he was clearly quite unprepared for what happened. For Flamininus, no longer forced to negotiate in public and to think of his wider audience, dropped all pretences and made the Roman position clear: if the king evacuated Europe, he could have Asia to himself and Rome would not worry about the freedom of the Greeks there; but if he insisted on staying in Thrace, Rome would continue to be interested in their freedom. The envoys, having no instructions to meet this new situation, hedged and complained that the king's honour was at stake in Thrace; but Flamininus retorted that Rome's honour was committed to defending the freedom of the Greeks: either they should both abate their honour somewhat, or, if the king refused, the Roman point of honour would appear much more honourable than his! The envoys had no power to accept the offer, although they asked that negotiations should continue. Flamininus, with his usual flair for theatrical action, made the most of the situation. On the following day he invited all the embassies, which had been anxiously waiting for the outcome of the talks, to attend the Senate meeting at which he was to report. Assured of his audience (which would broadcast his words as far as anyone could hope to), he proclaimed to the House that the Roman people intended to liberate the Greeks from Antiochus with the same good faith that they had shown in liberating them from Philip.[70] Antiochus' envoys were trapped. Having no powers to start a war (in fact, it seems, instructions not to do so), they were now seriously afraid that it might be declared at once.[71] For fear of precipitating a declaration of war, they could not, therefore, speak up to expose Flamininus' trick. They had to hear their king branded as the enemy of Greek freedom and could only plead that negotiations should not be broken off. Flamininus had brilliantly avenged the defeat of Lysimachia.

Though diplomatic courtesies were still preserved,[72] it was clear that peace now hung by a thread. Both the king and the Romans had repeatedly shown that they did not want war; yet mutual suspicion and the monster of their own cold-war techniques were slowly driving them into it. And the effect of these causes was cumulative, so that it became more and more difficult to escape from the vicious spiral. We have seen how, when Rome first turned hostile, the king's envoys seem to have retorted by making contacts in Greece. Now, on their return from Rome, we have actual evidence that they did so. They called in at Delphi[73] and thus established contact with the Aetolian League, now the leading anti-Roman power in Greece. Fearing a Roman declaration of war, they could hardly leave Greece entirely attached to the Roman side; this time it was quite essential to make contact with potential allies there. Yet this step, forced upon the king's envoys by Flamininus' diplomatic success at Rome, was to do more than any other to precipitate the war the king wanted to avoid. To the mutual fears and suspicions of the great powers, and their struggles for advantages in diplomacy and politics, there was now to be added the pressure of a minor power deliberately aiming at involving them in war for the sake of its own advantage. At its meeting held a little later, in the spring of 193, the Aetolian League decided, encouraged by the interest the king had shown, to send envoys to him, to Philip, and to Nabis, in order to form a grand coalition against Rome. Although this ambitious plan failed, Nabis at least was persuaded to attack the Roman settlement of Greece. The cold war had been ignited at one point.[74]

Meanwhile a Roman embassy had reached Asia Minor by the summer of 193.[75] Its chances of success, never high, were further reduced by two accidents: first, the envoys called on Eumenes, who—like the Aetolian League on the other side—hoped to gain by war and did his best to promote it; next, the king's son died. We do not know the arguments used by Eumenes; but there was an obvious one that the crafty ruler will hardly have neglected: Antiochus had recently offered him a marriage alliance, which, carefully weighing up the chances, he had been wise enough to refuse;[76] there was no doubt that, if he considered himself deserted by Rome, the offer would still stand open. In any case, Livy (P.) stresses his influence on the Roman mission. The death of the younger Antiochus was perhaps even more disastrous. It broke up the first talks and made it impossible for the king himself to attend further negotiations or even take a personal interest in them. His minister Minnio, who took over, could not make concessions, even if he wanted to (which he probably did not); and the resumed talks came to nothing. But it is doubtful whether even the king's presence could have made a difference. Resentful after the trick played upon his envoys in Rome, he was now being further incited to war not only by Hannibal and the war party that naturally existed at his own court, but by the Aetolian envoy Dicaearchus, who must have reached him about this time.[77] Although there is no sign of his giving the latter any further encouragement, all these circumstances must inevitably have hardened his attitude.[78] Thus the vicious spiral took another turn. Even so, the Roman envoys sensibly reported to the Senate that they had seen no preparations for war; the Senate took action only against Nabis and allowed the consuls of 192 to go to their *prouinciae* in northern Italy. Not even the arrival of Attalus, Eumenes' brother, could move them from their cautious attitude; they merely adopted a few purely defensive measures.[79] As for the king, Livy tells us that after the departure of the Romans he at once held a council and, on its advice, decided upon war. But this is patently absurd. It is well known how, when he did decide to invade Greece (we shall soon see how and why), the Great King, ruler of the East, could muster only 10,000 infantry, 500 cavalry, and 6 elephants.[80] There are few cases in history of two great powers entering upon war with each other so unprepared and so demonstrably against their own (at least immediate) intentions.

Yet events were pursuing their course. The politicians on both sides could not control the spirits they had summoned. In Greece, so recently settled by the Romans, class conflict combined with inter-state rivalry into an explosive mixture, which the Aetolians easily succeeded in igniting. The Romans had firmly established the oligarchic parties in power; as a result, the lower classes and their leaders now looked to Rome's enemies. In Peloponnese this alignment was reinforced by the conflict between Nabis and the Achaean League. The leaders of the latter, traditionally opposed to Spartan revolutionaries ever since the days of Agis IV, had been thoroughly frightened by Nabis' much more dangerous revolutionary programme;[81] and the renewal of war between these two antagonists was bound to sharpen all the hatreds and conflicts throughout Greece. The Senate, however, did not depart from Flamininus' policy. Except for a force sent (at their own request) to assist the Achaeans against Nabis, no armed forces were dispatched to Greece: the freedom of the Greeks was to be scrupulously and conspicuously observed. All that the Senate did was to send a mission headed by Flamininus himself, to reassert Roman authority: it seemed that no one except the Achaean League could now be trusted.[82] The mission was, on the whole, successful. Its very appearance was enough to overawe the anti-Roman parties by demonstrating Roman interest and reminding them of Roman power, and thus giving their opponents a chance of tightening their own grip on the various cities. At Chalcis there were difficulties, but they were overcome. Only at Demetrias was there serious trouble. There the Romans were caught in the toils of their own complex diplomatic web. Since the end of the war with Philip, they had been trying to make an ally of him against Antiochus: a combination of the two kings would still be formidable,

and yet it had been necessary (as we have seen) to leave
Philip on his throne on generous terms. There was good hope of
success for Rome, since Philip had much more cause to fear
Antiochus' ultimate success than to hope for it.[83] Thus the policy
of concessions to Philip, begun to re-establish his power against the
Aetolians, had recently been continued in view of the danger from
Antiochus. These concessions, however, had frightened the citizens
of Demetrias, who believed, whether rightly or wrongly, that
Philip had been promised their city as the price of assistance.
Flamininus, asked to deny this in their assembly, would not do so.
We do not know whether the rumour was in fact true. But
even if it was not, the whole laborious attempt to entice Philip
might fail, if a limit to the concessions he might expect were proclaimed in public at such a time. This was the nemesis of Flamininus' unwillingness to rely wholeheartedly on the 'freedom of the
Greeks': his diplomacy had overreached itself, and his dilemma at
Demetrias was inescapable. The freedom of the Greeks, the balance of power, the hope of gaining Philip's alliance—all these
strands could not be woven into a single web. For the moment
Flamininus' presence, and a few ready phrases about Demetrias'
debt of gratitude to Rome, saved the situation. But in fact tension
remained. At Demetrias Flamininus had failed; and this failure,
comparatively unimportant though it might seem at the time,
was to lead in a direct line to the outbreak of war.

If Rome was rapidly losing control of the cold war on which she
had engaged, Antiochus' fate was very similar; but for him the
consequences were to be disastrous. When the Roman envoys
left him, late in 193, he had not been thinking of war. The Aetolians,
however, continued to work for its outbreak. Having persuaded
Nabis to break the peace, they sent Thoas (*strategus* for 194–3
and leader of the anti-Roman party) to Asia to report this success.
He found the king, after the departure of the Roman mission,
almost despairing of peace and more inclined to listen to him than
he had been to listen to his brother Dicaearchus a few months
earlier. On that occasion he had, as far as we know, done nothing
at all. This time he thought it inexpedient to show no interest.
Thus he sent Menippus with Thoas, in order to assure the League
of the king's interest in them and, incidentally, of his power and
resources.[84] There is no mention, even in Livy's prejudiced

account, of Menippus' actually pressing for war; and he is not included in Polybius' list of those who seduced the Aetolian people or in the lists of those whose extradition the Romans were later to demand from Antiochus.[85] Menippus merely promised the Aetolians that Antiochus would restore their freedom (and that of the rest of Greece), which, he claimed, had *de facto* been destroyed by the Romans. This was no more a declaration of war, or an exhortation to it, than the precisely corresponding declaration by the Romans that they would free the Greeks of Asia Minor from the king. Indeed, the parallelism is so close that it cannot be accidental; the king was taking the cold war a stage further and turning the tables on the Romans. Yet the effect, on a people like the Aetolians, was bound to be quite different from that which the Romans had achieved in Asia. The moderating influence of Menippus appears in the actual decree passed by the Assembly: avoiding a declaration of war, it merely called upon Antiochus to free Greece and to arbitrate between the Aetolian League and Rome. This was precisely what the king wanted; it strengthened his diplomatic position without committing him to anything definite. But the Aetolian leaders did not intend to leave it at that. Their *strategus* Damocritus at once showed that they could no longer be held back. He refused to inform Flamininus of the contents of the decree, adding that he would soon tell him in arms on the banks of the Tiber.[86] Flamininus could only conclude from this that war had been decided upon; and even when the text became known, the Romans were bound to believe that there was at least a secret decision to that effect and—a necessary corollary—that Menippus, on the king's behalf, had secretly agreed to it. Damocritus' action, in view of the known aims and methods of the Aetolian League at this time, can only be held to be deliberate. Having promised Menippus not to declare war, and having kept the letter of his promise by an agreed and non-committal decree, he had done his best to break the spirit of it by his attendant action. War had been brought appreciably nearer by this suggestion to the Romans that their enemies had decided upon it.

With the Assembly dismissed and the foreign envoys out of the way, the *apocleti* could proceed to makes its coming certain. They decided to attack the Roman settlement of Greece at what the recent Roman mission had revealed to be its weakest points: they would

try to seize Chalcis and Demetrias. Moreover, as Nabis had failed
to hold his own even against the Achaeans, they would eliminate
him and garrison Sparta themselves.[87] At Chalcis and Sparta they
failed; but at Demetrias the unstable rule of the pro-Roman
faction, patched up by Flamininus, was easily overthrown. Not
that the citizens wanted war with Rome; Demetrias had nothing
to gain by that. They only wanted complete independence and,
above all, security against being sacrificed to Roman policy. But
the Roman envoy Villius, incensed at their 'ingratitude' to the
liberators of Greece and, no doubt, believing war imminent, re-
sorted to threats and thus made the estrangement complete.[88]
This played into the hands of the Aetolians. With Demetrias in
their power, they had at once dispatched Thoas to the king to
report the success and persuade him to cross to Greece.[89] He
found the king anything but prepared for this—so far had he been
from considering an invasion of Greece as the necessary consequence of his message to the League that he had hardly any
forces ready; and of the small force he had, part was destined for
quite a different action: it was to help Hannibal stir up trouble in
Carthage.[90]

Hannibal, ever since his arrival at Antiochus' court, had been
intriguing with anti-Roman elements at home. One of his envoys,
clumsy enough to be caught, had created a public scandal and
almost an international incident;[91] and there is no reason whatever to think that he was the only one Hannibal sent. Antiochus,
as befitted the technique of cold war, had done nothing to stop
these intrigues, which might create a welcome diversion in the
West at no cost to himself; on the other hand, he had never committed himself to public support of Hannibal (which might have
made all the difference to the latter's success). At his own court,
too, he had kept the exile at arm's length, as he distrusted his
motives and did not share his bellicosity any more than his
strategic imagination.[92] It was only now, in 192, with the situation
rapidly worsening, and hope of a permanent settlement with Rome
practically at an end, that he decided to give Hannibal some
support. Even so, it was very limited—far from what Hannibal,
almost ever since his arrival, had been asking for.[93] We hear only
of open ships, and they cannot have been many. It had taken the
king some time to get them together; and even for his own crossing,

a little later, he had no more than sixty available.[94] It is significant that the forty cataphracts also available are not mentioned as being offered to Hannibal, although Hannibal had specially asked for cataphracts. And though we have no indication at all of the number of men Hannibal was to have, it cannot have been large; it must have been well below the small total that the king himself later raked together for his own crossing into Greece.[95] Thus, by the time of the Aetolian occupation of Demetrias, the king not only had not collected an adequate force for invading Greece—he had moved no farther than permitting Hannibal his venture, on a much smaller scale than the Carthaginian wanted, in the West. This, however, was intended to avoid war for the king himself rather than to bring it about. If it succeeded, it would keep the Romans far too busy to allow them to interfere with him; while if it failed, the status quo in the West would merely be restored, and there was no reason to think that Antiochus' very limited participation in the venture would tempt the Romans into that attack on him which they had shown every sign of wanting to avoid. Hannibal's mission to the West was merely another act of cold war; no other explanation will satisfactorily account for Antiochus' actions that have puzzled generations of scholars.[96]

The news brought by Thoas changed everything. Demetrias was one of the strongest places in Greece; the northernmost of the 'three fetters' that had long assured Antigonid domination of that country, it was the city from which Antigonus Gonatas had set out to win his kingdom. With the anti-Roman party in power, and neutrality made impossible by Villius' threats, the inhabitants were ready enough to welcome any champion who could protect them against Philip's renewed domination and the Romans' wrath; and, once there, Antiochus would not easily be driven out. What was most important, this opportunity might not be open for long. It appeared from Villius' threats that the Romans had every intention of punishing the city for its 'ingratitude'. Time, if Antiochus delayed, could only work against him. It was thus that this most cautious of monarchs was persuaded to alter his course of action and cross to Greece. Holleaux, who more than any other scholar appreciated Antiochus' temperament and understood his aims, calls his action in accepting Thoas' invitation 'téméraire pour la première fois'.[97] Yet it is doubtful whether, had he rejected it, he would have gained anything but censure for excessive caution.[98] Both sides were the victims of their own policies, and war could by now hardly be avoided.

With Antiochus' occupation of Demetrias, where he was welcomed by the citizens in the autumn of 192,[99] we may conveniently end this survey. Though it was later claimed that war did not officially break out until a Roman detachment was defeated by Menippus at Delium,[100] the *de jure* beginning of the war is as obscure as it is unimportant. *De facto* it undoubtedly began with the occupation of Demetrias. This was recognized by the Achaean League when, in declaring war on Antiochus and the Aetolians, they gave as their official reason that they considered themselves to have the same friends and enemies as Rome.[101] The war itself has often been examined[102] and the comedy of it duly appreciated. Fought by both sides for the liberation of Greece, it found the Greeks, on the whole, singularly unenthusiastic about both their liberators. Though class antagonism and inter-state rivalries naturally produced tension at its beginning, it soon became evident that Antiochus was not the true friend of the downtrodden; and the Greeks, whatever their convictions, soon agreed in gladly joining whichever side, at the moment, appeared the stronger.[103] With the Roman victory at Thermopylae this question was settled; and, except for the Aetolian League (too deeply committed to hope for mercy), the attitude of the Greeks was settled correspondingly.[104] It is obvious that, had the fortunes of war been different, Antiochus would have been received with the same cowed resignation that greeted the Romans. With victory in Asia won, the Roman claim to be fighting for the freedom of *all* the Greeks was quietly buried. Eumenes and Rhodes, on the whole, shared the spoils of Asia Minor, and the former even received Lysimachia and other possessions in Europe.[105] The *fides* of Rome, long pledged to free the Greeks from Antiochus, had turned out to be as elastic as that of any great power. It was only in European Greece that the 'freedom of the Greeks' continued to retain a limited political value as a slogan.

Much more can, and should, be said about the origins and history of *libertas* as a diplomatic concept of the Romans; but this is not the place for it.[106] This study has been concerned with a particular diplomatic and political conflict, one between the two great powers of East and West, which led, without aggressive intent on either side, to one of the decisive wars of history. In the course of our analysis we have come across situations and techniques only too familiar to us; and, to avoid facile moralizing, we may claim to have seen that, just as ancient history is not irrelevant to present-day problems, so present-day problems have their lessons for the ancient historian.

NOTES

[1] See M. Holleaux, *Études d'épigraphie et d'histoire grecques* (1938–), v 156 (bibliography by L. Robert). This volume will be cited by the author's name only. [I regret to say that, at the time of writing this article, I did not yet know H.-E. Stier's interesting discussion in chapters 5 and 6 of *Roms Aufstieg zur Weltmacht* (1957).]

[2] On the general background see the accounts in the standard works (on Antiochus, especially M. Cary, *History of the Greek World*² (1951) 69 f., 113 f.).

[3] Magie's arguments, more often ignored than answered, have made the existence of such a pact very doubtful (*JRS* 29 (1939) 32 f.).

[4] See pp. 22f., above.

[5] l.c. (n. 1) and f.

[6] On the chronology see *MRR* i 322 (n. 4).

[7] Livy xxxi 2, 3 f.; 18, 1.

[8] Pol. xvi 25, 27, 34.

[9] *Mac.* 4.

[10] I have discussed this matter in *Latomus* 17 (1958) 208 f.

[11] xxx 3, 3 f.; xxxi 1.

[12] See W. Otto, *6. Ptol.* (1934) 27 f. (not altogether convincing); cf. C. Cichorius, *Röm. Stud.* (1922) 22 f.

[13] On his age, cf. Philip's quip at Abydus (Pol. xvi 34, 6 = Livy xxxi 18, 3); note that he was πραγμάτων ἄπειρος, which would hardly qualify him for *tutela*.

[14] 'Senatsbeschlüsse gehören zum wertvollsten Bestand der Annalistik' (M. Gelzer, *V. röm. Staat* (1944) i 84).

[15] See *MRR* i 430.

[16] Livy (A.) xxxii 8, 15–16; 27, 1.

[17] *Études* iii 331 f.

[18] Thus, apparently, E. V. Hansen, *Attalids* (1947) 61—vitiated by acceptance of 198 as the date of the battle of the Panion, which Holleaux has put out of court (see n. 22).

[19] H. Nissen, *Krit. Unt.* (1863) 25 f.

[20] That such *amicitia* does not imply a treaty has been made clear by A. Heuss, *Völkerrechtl. Grundl.* (1933), *passim*.

[21] xxxii 27, 1. Holleaux tries to discredit this embassy by claiming that, if genuine, it ought to have arrived earlier in the year! The absurdity of this argument is underlined by the fact that Livy gives no precise indication of the date; for all we know, the embassy may have come as soon as the consuls had left Rome.

[22] As the battle of the Panion can no longer be dated 198 (see Holleaux, *Études* iii 321 f.), we must indeed ascribe Antiochus' withdrawal to the Roman intervention. As we shall see, this return to our sources at last makes the history of these years a little more intelligible.

[23] Livy xxxiii 20, 8 f.; cf. *ibid*. 34, 2 f. It may have consisted of Hegesianax and Lysias; but Livy's language (at xxxiii 34, 2) does not, as is usually thought, necessarily imply this.

[24] Livy xxxiii 19, 6 f.; for the envoys' return see 20, 9.

[25] *Ibid*. 20. See Passerini, *Athenaeum* N.S. 10 (1932) 117 f. (I should like to acknowledge my general indebtedness to that careful study.)

[26] Pol. xviii 39, 3 f.

[27] The chronology is certain: Pol. xviii 47, 2 shows that he had not yet crossed when they set out; *ibid*. 49, 3 that he had already done so when they returned.

[28] Pol. xviii 47; Livy xxxiii 34, 2 f.; App. *Syr*. 2.

[29] xxxiii 34, 2. It must have been as obvious to the Senate as it was to him.

[30] *SIG*³ 591.

[31] Pol. xviii 44, 2. See further below.

[32] See below (n. 35 and text).

[33] οὐδένα γὰρ ἔτι τῶν Ἑλλήνων οὔτε πολεμεῖσθαι νῦν ὑπ' οὐδενὸς οὔτε δουλεύειν οὐδενί (Pol. xviii 47, 2).

[34] Rightly stressed by Passerini, *op. cit*. 121–2.

[35] *MRR* i 337 gives full sources and discussion.

[36] Pol. xviii 48, 2; 50, 1. (I have not, in general, given references to other sources based on a surviving Polybian account.)

[37] Pol. xviii 50, 4. Polybius gives a careful account of the conference.

[38] This policy of recognized spheres of influence is often said to have been borrowed by Rome from Hellenistic practice; but it is, in fact, thoroughly Roman. We need only mention the first two treaties with Carthage (Pol. iii 22 f.), the treaty with Tarentum, and the later example of the Ebro treaty with Hasdrubal. The Peace of Phoenice (205 B.C.), though not explicitly fixing spheres of influence, created a similar *de facto* situation [see pp. 21 f., above]. We shall see this view, in a marked 'geopolitical' form, coming out into the open at the Conference of Rome.

[39] This detail is mentioned by Appian (*Syr*. 3, *fin*.) and Diodorus (xxviii 14, *fin*.); our text of Polybius, here based on the *Excerpta antiqua*, mentions only ἀναγκαιότης. It is difficult to say where the derivative sources got their information. An 'intermediate source' as its origin seems too facile an assumption; yet it is odd that they should both have independently supplied the detail from their own knowledge (cf. Livy xxxv 13, 4). Is the tradition of the *Excerpta*, usually reliable enough, here at fault?

[40] Livy (P.) xxxiii 41: both sides hear a false rumour that Ptolemy has been killed, and each, thinking the other ignorant of it, tries to disengage itself from the talks in order to reach Egypt before the other.

[41] Livy xxxiii 41, 5; xxxiv 25, 2. Cf. Holleaux 164 f.

[42] Cf. Livy xxxiii 45.

[43] Nabis was a dangerous revolutionary (see below). The Aetolians saw through the Roman game (Livy xxxiv 23, 10); but Flamininus had cleverly made the tyrant's occupation of Argos the *casus belli*, and the Achaeans and their friends swallowed the attractive bait. They were to discover too late that the liberation of Sparta would have been a more profitable war aim.

[44] Livy xxxiv 43, 3 f.

[45] Pol. xviii 45, 7 f.; Livy xxxiii 31, 4 f.

[46] Some of their suspicions have penetrated (probably through the Scipionic family tradition) into Polybius' account of Flamininus' motives and thus colour the whole subsequent tradition. In modern times they were brilliantly revived by Holleaux. There is probably a good foundation for them; Flamininus' motives and character were complex enough. But the purely political and diplomatic aspect of his policy, which gives it its chief interest, has tended to be obscured and neglected.

[47] Pol. xvi 34, 3 f.; similarly in the ultimatum handed to Nicanor in Athens.

[48] Livy xxxii 10, 7.

[49] See my *Foreign Clientelae* (1958) 66 f.

[50] Pol. xviii 42, 5.

[51] *Ibid.* 45, *fin.*

[52] This can be followed especially in works like A. Heuss, *Stadt u. Herrscher* (1937).

[53] *Op. cit.* (n. 49).

[54] Clearly apparent, e.g., from the form of the Isthmian proclamation (Pol. xviii 46, 5).

[55] Especially in his famous chapters in *Roman Imperialism* (1914).

[56] See Klaffenbach's remarks in his edition of the treaty of 211 (*SBAW* (1954) No. 1, 12 f.).

[57] Cf. Livy (P.) xxxiv 48, 5 f.

[58] Pol. xviii 45, 9.

[59] For the success of Flamininus' theatrical gesture see Polybius' description of the scene at the Isthmian Games of 196 (xviii 46).

[60] See n. 33. On the difficulty of limiting the idea of 'freedom' to a fixed area and the dangers of letting it spread too far, see Eumenes' illuminating remarks (Pol. xxi 19, 9).

[61] Livy (P.) xxxv 16, 3 f.; cf. xxxi 29, 10 f.

[62] Some scholars have been unnecessarily legalistic in their interpretation of this, as of Antiochus' other offers at Lysimachia. Claims advanced at international conferences need not be viewed in terms of systems of strict law, especially when their merits cannot be adjudged by any tribunal.

[63] Pol. xviii 51, 7; cf. Livy xxxiii 38, 10 f.; xxxiv 58, 5; App. *Syr.* 1.

[64] Cf. Livy xxxiv 50.

[65] For the date see Holleaux 180 f.

[66] Rightly seen by H. H. Scullard, *Roman Politics* (1951) 196.

[67] Defensive measures were taken in Italy (Livy xxxiv 45; cf. Frank, *Rom. Imp.* 170).

[68] App. *Syr.* 5–6.

[69] Livy xxxiv 57 f.; Diod. xxviii 15; cf. App. *Syr.* 6.

[70] Livy (59, 5) here adds 'nisi decedat Europa'; and as Diodorus has a similar phrase (15, 4), it is usually said to go back to Polybius and therefore accepted. But source criticism must here be supplemented by common sense: it is quite inconceivable that Flamininus, having so carefully set the stage, proclaimed to the assembled Greeks that *unless* Antiochus evacuated Europe Rome would show the same *fides* to the Greeks in Asia (to whose liberation her *fides* was already pledged—see Pol. xviii 44, 2 and *passim*) as she had shown to those in Europe; he cannot have thus declared in public that it depended on Antiochus' evacuation of Europe whether Rome would keep her word in Asia. It may be that Polybius himself, or even his informant, failed to understand Flamininus' manœuvre and mistakenly brought the account of the public proclamation into line with that of the secret negotiations, where they in fact diverged. But there is reason to believe that the mistake may not go back to Polybius after all. Appian says that the Senate's reply to the king's envoys was that he must leave Europe *and* free the Greeks in Asia. Though his account is very much abbreviated, it is recognizably from Polybius; and this particular section, as it makes perfect sense, may well represent the true Polybian tradition. The facts, fortunately, are clear enough, as the false account—besides being silly—is self-refuting: if the 'unless' clause had indeed been part of the official statement, the envoys had no reason to fear an immediate declaration of war and plead (as Livy so graphically represents them as doing) for continued negotiations.

[71] Livy xxxiv 59, 6.

K

[72] An amusing sidelight on this, and on the king's and the Senate's competitive philhellenism, is provided by *SIG*³ 601 : Menippus, one of the envoys, had been charged with procuring a Roman *asylia* decree for Teos, and the Senate was eager to oblige the little city. The stylized phrases of courtesy to Menippus show that the two powers were officially still far from considering war.

[73] *SIG*³ 585, lines 43 f. (193 B.C.).

[74] Livy xxxv 12.

[75] *Ibid.* 13, 6–17, 2.

[76] App. *Syr.* 5; cf. Pol. xxi 20, 8.

[77] Livy xxxv 12, 15; cf. n. 84 below.

[78] App. *Syr.* 12, *init.* reports an offer by Antiochus, apparently at the beginning of these talks, to leave Rhodes, Byzantium, Cyzicus, and all the Greeks of Asia except the Ionians and the Aeolians free, if the Romans would give him a treaty. This is usually rejected without inquiry; but it may well be true, at least in outline. It would mean that the king offered to guarantee the freedom of the bigger cities (i.e. to commit himself not to attack them) and to withdraw from the Greek cities of the south coast of Asia Minor, if he were allowed to keep the rest. As there is no mention of Europe, the offer would be unacceptable to the Romans. If true—and there is no good reason why it should not be—this shows that at the beginning of the talks the king was ready to make concessions.

[79] Livy xxxv 17, 2; 22, 1–3; 23, 11–10.

[80] *Ibid.* 19, *fin.*: 'ex consilio ita discessum est ut bellum gereretur'; but cf. *ibid.* 43, 6 (late 192 B.C.): 'uix ad Graeciam nudam occupandam satis copiarum.'

[81] Livy xxxv 34, 3; cf. xxxiv 51, 4–6. On the Spartan revolution see the standard works (most conveniently M. Cary, *op. cit.* 153 f., 192 f.).

[82] Livy xxxv 31.

[83] Not only had Antiochus failed to assist him against Rome, but his often repeated claim to the whole of the kingdom won by Seleucus Nicator from Lysimachus must have made a Macedonian king very uncomfortable: Macedon had been just as much part of Lysimachus' dominions at the time of his defeat as Thrace, and it is quite likely (though not certain) that Seleucus proclaimed himself King of Macedon before his death. Antiochus' co-operation with the Aetolians could be trusted to be the last straw.

[84] The chronology of the Aetolian embassies is of crucial importance, yet difficult to ascertain from Livy's sketchy account. Nor can we be certain whether the Aetolian meeting that sent out the three envoys (Livy xxxv 12) was, as is quite likely, the *Panaetolica* of 193 or a special assembly. (On Aetolian assemblies, see Larsen in *TAPA* 83 (1952) 1 f.) In any case, considering the number of events that were still to take place in Greece in the course of the year, it must have been held in the spring of 193. Thus we may put the arrival of Dicaearchus at the court not later than August. For the Roman envoys we have the landmark of the younger Antiochus' death, which took place not earlier than summer 193 (see Holleaux 388, n. 3, with Robert's note). Thus Dicaearchus' arrival may precede the Conference of Apamea (the talks with Antiochus) and must precede that of Ephesus (the talks with Minnio). Thoas' mission is not mentioned by Livy until his return with Menippus, just before the *Panaetolica* of 192 (xxxv 32). It is very likely, therefore, that he went out very soon after his brother's return, in order to retrieve the latter's comparative failure by means of his news of developments in Peloponnese.

[85] Pol. xxi 31, 13; 17, 7; 43, 11.

[86] Livy xxxv 33, *fin.*

[87] *Ibid.* 34, 2 f. That Antiochus was about to come to Greece in any case (*ibid.* 1) seems to be Livy's own inference.

88 *Ibid.* 39, 6 f.

89 *Ibid.* 42, 4; App. *Syr.* 12 (confusing the Aetolian embassies).

90 Livy xxxv 42.

91 Aristo of Tyre in 193 (Livy xxxiv 60 f.).

92 The tale that the Roman mission of 193 succeeded in making the king suspect Hannibal of pro-Roman sentiments until the account of Hannibal's famous oath reconciled them (Pol. iii 11 and the Polybian tradition) is belied by the facts. Antiochus never at any stage (with the single exception here considered), either before or after, had much use for Hannibal's advice; the fact, which—after what we have seen of Antiochus' aims, methods, and character—need not surprise us, is indeed pointed out by the sources at crucial moments, usually with a twist against the king (e.g. Livy xxxvi 8, 1; App. *Syr.* 9, *fin.*, 14, *fin.*).

93 Livy xxxiv 60, 5: 100 cataphracts and 11,000 men.

94 Livy xxxv 43, 3.

95 See n. 80 and text, above.

96 The explanation, simple as it seems to us, might well have appeared absurd (had it ever occurred to them) to scholars of a past generation, accustomed to operating with neatly distinguished concepts of 'peace' and 'war', 'aggression' and 'defence'.

97 Holleaux 179.

98 Such as he gets from Holleaux, 397–8, in another connection.

99 Holleaux 179 (cf. 396).

100 The Roman version of this impious massacre (Livy xxxv 51, with heightened pathos) tends to be repeated by moderns without investigation. In fact, as Livy himself tells us, the Roman troops at Delium were about to embark for Euboea, in order to garrison Chalcis against Antiochus; and as we can see from Livy's account, they had gone to Delium in order to avoid Menippus' superior forces at Aulis and take deliberate advantage of the *asylia* of the place. They had about as much immunity as military transports marked with the red cross. For a Greek view of such behaviour see Thuc. iv 97 (also concerning Delium).

101 Livy xxxv 50, 2. This motivation (which, via Polybius, will go back to the prescript of the actual decree) shows that the Achaean League already considered Rome at war with Antiochus and the Aetolians. It thus throws grave doubt on the Romans' later use of the massacre of Delium as a convenient official ἀρχή for the war.

102 Never better than by Holleaux 397 f. (the original of his contribution to *CAH* viii).

103 The Epirots, at one stage, openly said so (Pol. xx 3); the Boeotians, who had good reason to be anti-Roman, received Antiochus only when his military superiority seemed demonstrated (*ibid.* 7, 3 f., compared with Livy xxxv 50, 5). This was reasonable behaviour—and shows the absence of any unreasonable emotion.

104 Livy xxxvi 20, 1 *et al.*

105 Pol. xxi 43 f.

106 Some of it has been said in the book cited in n. 49 above.

Caesar's *Cursus*
and the Intervals between Offices

THE puzzle of C. Julius Caesar's date of birth and *cursus honorum* has never been satisfactorily solved. The facts can be stated quite simply. All but two of the sources referring to his age imply 100 B.C. as the date of his birth, and the date of his quaestorship agrees with this; yet he held the senior magistracies two years earlier than, according to what we know of the normal *cursus*, that date would allow.[1] Are nearly all the sources wrong (as Mommsen thought)? Or did Caesar at some time get a special dispensation, which no one has bothered to mention (as the majority opinion would now hold)? Or is there another explanation of a more general kind, fitting Caesar into a class of exceptions (as Afzelius proposed)?[2]

Of these three types of proposed solutions the first two are plainly unsatisfactory. The first owes any consideration it has received solely to the *auctoritas* of its propounder. This has been amply demonstrated by Deutsch, and it simply will not do to reject the consensus of reliable ancient tradition for the sake of what is, after all, only a thinly supported hypothesis of modern scholars: we must make our theories fit the evidence and not vice versa. The second kind of solution, however, is not, in point of method, one to be lightly adopted. Cicero's proposal for L. Egnatuleius[3] shows, in a context full of patent illegality, that precedents for such dispensations could be found; but that was after Caesar's *regnum* and need hardly surprise us. It is not good evidence for the position more than twenty years earlier. We know, indeed, that the tribune C. Cornelius tried to abolish, and succeeded in restricting, the Senate's power of granting dispensations from laws;[4] but we need not believe[5] that this power was used mainly, or even at all commonly, in the case of the *leges annales*, or that the Popular tribune was specially concerned with the strict observation of these particular laws. Other explanations of the crucial passages can readily be suggested,[6] and only the scrutiny of known instances would be able to impose such an interpretation.

Yet the cases that have actually been adduced are not at all parallel to that of C. Caesar.[7] That of Pompey, of course, is known to be altogether exceptional.[8] That of L. Lucullus[9] seems to belong to a special class of exceptions and thus, if anything, supports the third rather than the second type of explanation for Caesar as well: Lucullus, like other *Sullani*, had lost time owing to his political allegiance in the eighties, and it was only just that special legislation should be passed—we note that it was not a dispensation by the Senate—to enable these men to regain the time lost.[10] M. Aemilius Scaurus remains the only· genuine parallel cited by those[11] who have recently discussed the matter: he, indeed, will occupy us before long. But it should be clear that the view that such dispensations from the *leges annales* were common in the early sixties—so common that nobody bothered to remark that young Caesar, as yet far from distinguished, obtained one—would need a good deal more support than it has so far had in order to become acceptable.[12]

This rapid survey has shown that the third type of explanation, first proposed by Afzelius in his brilliant article, is on the whole most satisfactory. We know that recognized classes of exceptions did exist: the case of L. Lucullus is enough to prove it, and in any case the phenomenon need occasion much less surprise than a hypothetical proliferation of individual exemptions. It remains to find a suitable class into which Caesar's case would fit. There Afzelius is much less satisfactory. He assumed a difference between a 'civil' and a 'military' *cursus*, taking Cicero's case as the type of the former and Caesar's as that of the latter. But the distinction between 'civil' and 'military', in the Republic, is hard to draw: Afzelius did not succeed in finding a satisfactory sense in which Caesar's career can be described as 'military', while Cicero's cannot; nor did he give parallels from other known careers that support such a distinction. At the time when his article appeared that was perhaps difficult to do. But now Broughton's monumental work has enabled us to approach the matter systematically.[13] This is the main reason why there is much to be said for another survey of the old problem.

Taking Cicero's career as the norm,[14] we may note departures from it among known careers from 81 to 49. (The events of Caesar's *regnum* and the precedents it established should, as we have seen, not be used in this connection.) Though our lists are far from complete, we may expect this procedure to shed some light on the question. Apart from Caesar himself (*q.* 69, *aed.* 65, *pr.* 62, *cos.* 59), the following men in Broughton's lists show a shorter interval than Cicero's somewhere in their careers (M. Tullius Cicero, for comparison: *q.* 75, *aed.* 69, *pr.* 66, *cos.* 63) :[15]

L. Aemilius Paullus,	*q.* 59?,	*aed.* 55?,	*pr.* 53,	*cos.* 50;
M. Aemilius Scaurus,	*q.* 66?,	*aed.* 58,	*pr.* 56;	
P. Autronius Paetus,	*q.* 75,			*cos. des.* 65;
Q. Caecilius Metellus Scipio,		*aed.* 57?,	*pr.* 55,	*cos.* 52;
M. Caelius Rufus,		*aed.* 50,	*pr.* 48;	
C. Claudius Marcellus,	*q.* 87?,		*pr.* 80;	
P. Clodius Pulcher,	*q.* 61,	*aed.* 56,	*cand. pr.* 52 (and see below);	
P. Cornelius Lentulus Sura,	*q.* 81,		*pr.* 74,	*cos.* 71;
L. Domitius Ahenobarbus,	*q.* 66?,	*aed.* 61,	*pr.* 58,	*cos.* 54;
Q. Gallius,		*aed.* 67,	*pr.* 65;	
Q. Hortensius Hortalus,	*q.* 80?,	*aed.* 75,	*pr.* 72,	*cos.* 69;
L. Licinius Lucullus,	*q.* 87?,	*aed.* 79,	*pr.* 78,	*cos.* 74;
P. Nigidius Figulus,		*aed.* 60?,	*pr.* 58 (see below);	
Cn. Plancius,	*q.* 58,	*aed.* 54;		
P. Servilius Isauricus,	*q.* by 60,		*pr.* 54,	*cos.* 48;
Q. Tullius Cicero,	*q.* 68?,	*aed.* 65,	*pr.* 62;	
L. Valerius Flaccus,	*q.* 71 or 70,		*pr.* 63;	
L. Valerius Triarius,	*q.* 81,		*pr.* 78?;	
P. Vatinius,	*q.* 63,		*pr.* 55,	*cos.* 47.

Before this list can be usefully analysed, it must first be critically discussed, with special reference to the doubtful dates, where they are relevant.

L. Aemilius Paullus. His quaestorship could as easily be 60: when Cicero refers to him as quaestor in Macedonia in 59 (*Vat.* 25), he may be speaking loosely (for 'pro quaestore'). It was common (though not necessary) for a quaestor to accompany a new governor, and C. Octavius went to Macedonia in 60.[16] His aedileship should be accepted (see *MRR* ii 216).

Q. Caecilius Metellus Scipio. His aedileship in 57 must be accepted, since the date of the funeral games for his father cannot be satisfactorily explained in any other way (see *MRR* ii 201).

C. Claudius Marcellus. The date of his quaestorship depends on his identification with the AARCELLUS honoured in Samo-thrace,[17] and on the further assumption that 'his career in the period of Sulla roughly paralleled that of [L.] Lucullus'.[18] As Lucullus was *q.* 88 and *pr.* 78 (see above), such a parallel should, starting from Marcellus' praetorship in 80,[19] produce 90 or 89 for his quaestorship. In any case, it will be seen that such specula-tion is hardly worth while.

L. Domitius Ahenobarbus. The date 66 for his quaestorship depends on an emendation in Asconius (p. 45 Clark). The text there says that he opposed the tribune Manilius 'in praetura', which was emended to 'in quaestura' by Manutius. This, though received into the text by Clark, is quite arbitrary, as that quaestor-ship is nowhere attested. It is much simpler, as Münzer saw, to assume a reference (probably somewhat garbled in transmission) to Cicero's own praetorship, which did fall in 66.[20]

Q. Hortensius Hortalus. Cicero, in 70, described his quaestorship as 'nuper'.[21] The word is vague, and, as we know that he was aedile in 75, he cannot in any case have been quaestor later than 77, and probably held the office even earlier [see now *Historia* 12 (1963) 133]. We must follow Broughton in refraining from speci-ous precision, and we cannot use his quaestorship for our purpose.

L. Licinius Lucullus. See above.

P. Nigidius Figulus. Towards the end of 60 he spoke in a *contio*, threatening action against jurors who favoured C. Antonius.[22] This is the sole support for the conjecture that he was aedile in 60 or (thus Broughton) tribune in 59.[23] As he was praetor in 58, a tribunate in the previous year would have been highly irregular (though perhaps not impossible). But there is no warrant for assuming any office: he may well have been *productus* in a *contio* by one of the tribunes for 60 (one of those, unknown to us, who vetoed the attempt to transfer P. Clodius to the Plebs).[24]

P. Servilius Isauricus. All we know is that in 60 he seems to have spoken among the quaestorians.[25] This gives 61 (not 60) as a *terminus post quem non*, but tells us nothing about the actual date.

Q. Tullius Cicero. Münzer conjectured a quaestorship about 68, as Quintus was away from Rome about that time.[26] In view of the extreme irregularity that this would import into his *cursus* without any positive evidence, the conjecture should be abandoned.

We do not even know how long Quintus had been away at the time when Cicero wrote his letter, nor how far away he was.

L. *Valerius Triarius*. It could be held that he was another of the returned *Sullani* and that this accounts for the short interval between quaestorship and praetorship. But in fact the identification of the quaestor and the praetor is probably wrong—at least, there is no evidence for it. The quaestor is a L. Triarius (Cic. 2 *Verr*. i 37). The praetor—not attested as such, but as propraetor in Sardinia in the following year[27]—has not had his *praenomen* recorded in our sources. He is, however, almost certainly identical with C. Valerius Triarius, the legate of L. Lucullus, who was (to judge by his responsibilities) a man of praetorian standing.[28]

Thus seven names may be eliminated, and we are left with twelve. Of these we may ignore L. Lucullus, as we happen to be informed of his special status (or rather, it seems, that of his class). When we look at the remaining eleven, the first point that attracts attention is the fact that in five cases (L. Paullus, M. Scaurus, Q. Metellus Scipio, M. Caelius Rufus, Q. Gallius) there is only one year between the aedileship and the praetorship, and in three cases (L. Paullus, Cn. Plancius, P. Clodius Pulcher) a shorter interval than expected *before* the aedileship. This naturally raises the question of how the aedileship (which we know was not compulsory) fitted into the *cursus* after Sulla.[29] The only direct information we have on the Sullan *lex annalis* does not mention the office.[30] There is, however, a well-known passage in Cicero's *Letters*, in which a *biennium* between aedileship and praetorship is referred to. This passage, a new interpretation of which has recently been proposed,[31] must now be considered. Cicero is trying to dissuade C. Furnius from standing for the praetorship of 42. After appealing to the precedent of others who stayed at their posts and sacrificed speed of advancement, he continues: 'quod eo facilius nobis est, quod non est annus hic tibi destinatus, ut, si aedilis fuisses, post biennium tuus annus esset. nunc nihil praetermittere uidebere usitati et quasi legitimi temporis ad petendum'. He goes on to say that L. Plancius' consulship in 42 would be a great advantage to Furnius, if he postponed his candidature to that year. This is usually taken to imply that Furnius had failed to get the aedileship for 44[32] or 43[33] and that Cicero is telling him that, if he *had* obtained it, he would now have had to wait until 42 (or 41) in any case before being entitled to stand for the praetorship (of 41 or 40). Unfortunately, those who advance this interpretation have never yet provided a translation of the passage and it is difficult to see how such a sense can be got out of the Latin. Perhaps simple translation will make the meaning of the text clear: 'This is all the easier for us, since this year is not marked out for you, as (if you had been aedile) *your* year would be marked out for you two years later (or: " . . . it would be *your* year two years later," with no significant difference of meaning). As things are, you will not appear to be letting any customary and indeed almost obligatory time for your candidature pass by.' Cicero is saying that, if Furnius had been aedile in 45 (with no implication as to whether he had actually stood for the office then), he would now be *expected* to stand for the praetorship of 42; as, however, he never was aedile, there is no such moral obligation. That this is rather dishonest special pleading is obvious. But we must accept the implication that, when a man obtained the aedileship, that was tantamount to an announcement that he would stand for the praetorship not more than two years later (i.e., to hold it three years later). That is reasonable enough: a man who went to the expense of becoming aedile would hardly be likely to let his munificence be forgotten, before standing for higher office. But, as Afzelius saw,[34] Cicero explicitly states that the actual interval was customary and not legal. And we may add that Cicero in fact refers to it, if anything, as a maximum, not as a minimum: if Furnius had been aedile, there would have been something disgraceful (as in the circumstances there was not) in his postponing his candidature for the praetorship until 42.[35] The passage, as Afzelius saw, makes it clear that there was no statutory *biennium* between aedileship and praetorship: custom merely expected a man not to wait *more* than two years. This, of course, perfectly agrees with the fact that in Appian[36] the aedileship is completely ignored in the account of Sulla's *lex annalis*. And it is fully confirmed by the evidence of known cases: as we have seen, in five cases the *biennium* is known not to have been observed as a minimum and there are three more cases—though, as we shall see, here there may be a different explanation—of a shorter interval *before* the aedileship. Now, for the whole of the period we are considering, Broughton lists only forty-five aediles, eighteen of them not securely dated and twelve not known in any other magistracy after, so that we cannot test the presumed 'rule' in their cases. The number of 'exceptions' (certainly five, possibly eight, out of fifteen) is, therefore, too significant to be ignored; and a casual reference shows us[37] that there will have been men who stood after an interval of one year and failed, as indeed we might expect if such candidatures were permitted. Thus the sources do not justify the modern hypothesis of a compulsory *biennium* between aedileship and praetorship: between praetorship and consulship the *biennium* is attested without exception.

This investigation has left us, at last, with our hard core of special cases, who are worth listing again at this point (for their *cursus* see the previous list): L. Aemilius Paullus, P. Autronius Paetus, P. Cornelius Lentulus Sura, C. Julius Caesar, L. Valerius Flaccus, P. Vatinius.

To them we may provisionally add P. Clodius Pulcher, who, as Cicero informs us at great length, was eligible for the praetorship of 53.[38] We shall discuss his case in due course.

It is *possible*, of course, that all these men were given special dispensations after the quaestorship, of which we do not happen to be informed. It is possible, too, that other men were given similar dispensations even before they held the quaestorship, so that even knowledge of their *cursus* will not help us to discover the abnormality. But, as we have seen,[39] there is no evidence for the view sometimes advanced that such dispensations were in fact quite common, and there is at least some (the *lex* passed for men like L. Lucullus) to suggest that they were not: such an *ad hoc* explanation is not to be welcomed except as a last resort. There is certainly something odd in positing unattested dispensations indiscriminately for men as different as C. Caesar, L. Paullus, L. Flaccus, and P. Vatinius. Let us explore alternatives.

The first that suggests itself is one that, in one form or another, has been urged by many scholars:[40] if the *lex annalis* of Sulla laid down minimum ages and not minimum intervals, a man who did not get one office (say the quaestorship) *suo anno* might obtain higher office after a shorter interval than was customary. This explanation would be very attractive in the case of low-born characters like P. Vatinius: he may well not have dared to stand for the quaestorship *suo anno* (he was barely elected when he did stand), while on the other hand we know that by the time he was ready for the praetorship he had gained the support of the dynasts, who pushed him into it.[41] Do the texts permit this interpretation; and, if they do, does it satisfactorily explain *all* our cases?

The sources for the original *lex annalis* certainly refer to minimum ages only; indeed, it has been held (notably by Afzelius) that the qualification was never laid down in any other form.[42] This extreme view probably goes too far: the *biennium* between praetorship and consulship is fully and invariably attested as a minimum throughout the late Republic—too much so for it to be due merely to custom, even of the prescriptive Roman kind. We must constantly remember, in any investigation of this difficult subject, that we depend on a balance of inadequate literary sources and imperfectly known careers: certainty is unattainable, but we must be guided by the facts such as we know them. As Astin has shown, these facts seem to point to the sudden introduction of a compulsory *biennium* after the praetorship early in the second century; and all the evidence, from a mass of careers in the post-Sullan age, suggests that this requirement was retained. It is open to anyone to say that it was merely '*quasi* legitimum': but that is an argument about words rather than facts. We have seen in the case of the aedileship that we can expect the *absence* of such a legal requirement, even in a less abundantly attested office, to appear unmistakably from the evidence.

The case of the quaestorship, however, is different. Statistical evidence for the second century is inconclusive,[43] and we know of at least one man (his name unfortunately corrupted to 'Q. Caelius') in the pre-Sullan period, who did not hold that office at all.[44] In the post-Sullan age we do, as we have seen, find exceptions to what may be regarded as the normal interval after the quaestorship. There is thus every reason to consider seriously the view that Sulla's law, which made the quaestorship compulsory, laid down a minimum age for it, but no minimum interval after it.

Against the facts we have noticed there stands one passage in Cicero that seems to imply a fixed interval rather than a fixed age: in proposing honours for Octavian in 43, he proposes 'eius rationem, quemcumque magistratum petet, ita haberi, ut haberi per leges liceret, si anno superiore quaestor fuisset.'[45] This implies that the holding of a quaestorship in 44 would enable a man to stand for other magistracies at fixed intervals from that year, whatever his age. It has been plausibly suggested[46] that Cicero meant to combine two privileges: Octavian was to be deemed (a) to have held the quaestorship (which was a prerequisite for the higher magistracies); (b) to have been of an age to do so in 44 (i.e. born in 75—a benefit of twelve years). This is not what our text actually says; but Astin has pointed out[47] that Cicero may well have tried to deceive Octavian by deliberate ambiguity: we remember his remark that the young man was 'laudandus, ornandus, tollendus.'[48]

This suggestion deserves serious consideration: Cicero was a master at handling the Roman constitution, and the *Philippics* show his mastery at its highest. Moreover, when proposing (straight after our passage) a similar, but less ambitious, benefit for L. Egnatuleius, he expresses it quite clearly as permission to stand for and hold every magistracy 'triennio ante legitimum tempus'. He could, therefore, be clear enough when he tried. Yet we must also consider the alternative that there may be something wrong with our text. Ursinus long ago suggested 'praetor' for 'quaestor' (i.e. permission to stand for the consulship of 41). As we have seen, the legal *biennium* between praetorship and consulship should be accepted, so that this emendation would remove our particular difficulty. There are other points in its favour: (a) Octavian is also to be allowed to speak in the Senate 'inter praetorios' (which Nipperdey therefore emended to 'inter quaestorios'—but see the next point); (b) in his long justification of his proposals, Cicero recalls ancient heroes who were consuls as *adulescentes* and argues that it is desirable for young men of exceptional qualities to be allowed to reach the consulship very early; but he does not mention the praetorship. Neither of these points is decisive, but together they are enough to make us wonder about the text. Perhaps, however, it would seem too revolutionary a proposal to attribute to Cicero, even in such an exceptional case.[49] There is a simple emendation that would at least remove all ambiguity. If Cicero had said 'si anno superiore *anno suo* quaestor fuisset', this would clearly express the two privileges that he apparently meant to confer on Octavian; and the dropping out of 'anno suo' after 'anno superiore' need not occasion surprise.

We must confess that we cannot be sure what Cicero meant in

this difficult passage, or even what he said. Whatever it is, it must not prevent us from following the factual evidence: a minimum age for the quaestorship after Sulla (who first made it compulsory) best covers the facts of the actual careers we know: it is the best explanation of how two *noui homines* (Autronius and Vatinius), both of whom acquired powerful connections in the course of their careers, can show a shorter interval than what (from Cicero's case) we may regard as the norm between quaestorship and senior magistracy. Indeed, in the case of P. Autronius there is decisive confirmation, which does not hitherto seem to have been noticed in this connection. In the *Brutus*, Cicero mentions him in such a way as to leave no doubt about his age:[50] he is explicitly said to be the *aequalis* of Q. Pompeius Bithynicus, who was 'biennio fortasse maior' than Cicero himself; and this in a context where Cicero is using the word 'aequalis' precisely. There can thus no longer be any serious doubt that Autronius got his quaestorship (in which he was Cicero's colleague) two years later than he was entitled to, and that this did not prevent him from standing for the consulship *suo anno*.

The view that there was a minimum age for the quaestorship and no fixed interval after it, during our period, thus seems well established.[51] Will it explain *all* our cases? Clearly it will not. In C. Caesar's case we can be sure of that: quite apart from the improbability of his failure to reach the quaestorship until two years after his proper year—a difficulty that Mommsen, Carco-pino, and their followers have never really faced—we can in fact, as we have seen, deduce the year of his birth from the best sources with all but certainty; and it leaves no room for this explanation. We may add that, satisfactory as it is in the case of men like Autro-nius and Vatinius (and in that of Autronius demonstrably correct), it will not really do for the *nobiles* whom we now have to consider. No doubt in an odd case even a *nobilis* would fail to reach a junior magistracy *suo anno*; but that five of them, in our scrappy record, should have done so, and that the list should include a L. Aemilius Paullus and a C. Julius Caesar, or even Cicero's client L. Valerius Flaccus, who in his youth had a very distin-guished military career[52]—that hypothesis rather strains credulity. These five cases (L. Paullus, P. Clodius, P. Lentulus Sura, C. Caesar, and L. Flaccus) need further consideration.

Let us first consider the actual intervals. C. Caesar was quaestor in his 31st year, praetor in his 38th and consul in his 41st.[53] This interval (seven years between quaestorship and praetorship, ten between quaestorship and consulship) is reproduced in the case of P. Lentulus Sura. In the case of L. Paullus it is six/nine or seven/ten years,[54] in that of L. Flaccus seven or eight to the praetorship:[55] as the interval of seven/ten years is certain in two and possible in all four cases, they tend to support one another and it becomes probable in all of them. In the case of P. Clodius the interval is certainly a minimum of eight years: he was quaestor in 61 and entitled to be praetor in 53. He is also odd man out in another way: he is the only one of these men who (at the time when he became eligible for the praetorship) was not a Patrician. But the case of Clodius is probably a red herring that we owe to Cicero. In fact, as is known, he only stood for the praetorship of 52; we have only his enemy's word for it that he was eligible for that of 53 and refused to stand—because he would not have had enough time to use the office for stirring up trouble![56] The whole passage, composed after Clodius' death, is highly suspicious: it looks like a lawyer's trick. For 53, as Cicero stresses, was an odd year: no praetors for it were elected until half-way through the year itself. As a motive for Clodius' refusal to stand, this is not very plausible; praetorian standing (i.e., a gain of a year in his *cursus*) would seem to be an advantage that far outweighed the loss of a few months of actual office. But the fact of Clodius' supposed eligibility is probably closely bound up with it. It seems very likely that what the *leges annales* actually laid down was the age and/or standing required for the *professio*, rather than that for holding the office.[57] P. Clodius was entitled to submit his *professio* in 53. That would normally have meant standing for 52; but owing to the unusual conditions, it *could*, in 53, have meant standing for 53 itself. This (if it was legal) would have given him a very short run of office and probably no gain at all in his *cursus*. He therefore preferred not to do it: or so Cicero was to say (or rather, write) with no fear of contradiction. It is best to omit the case of P. Clodius from our calculations.[58]

There remain the names of four men, two certainly and two probably showing an interval of seven/ten years, where Cicero himself has nine/twelve, and all four of them Patricians. This result is surely significant, in view of the small number of Patrician families surviving in the late Republic. It becomes even more so, if we look at some statistics of careers. During the period we are surveying, Broughton lists only fourteen Patrician quaestors.[59] Three of them cannot be traced to any higher magistracy, so that no conclusions on their *cursus* are possible;[60] one more, though known to have been quaestor, cannot be dated with any accuracy;[61] of the remaining ten, four show the irregularity we have noticed. It is surely in this context that the problem of C. Caesar's career should be treated: it suggests the answer that Afzelius sought along the right lines, but failed to find owing to the difficulty of collecting the relevant material. We can at last catch a glimpse of a class of exceptions to the *leges annales*, to which Caesar's case seems to have belonged. Perhaps, if scholars—before Afzelius and even after—had not been dazzled by Caesar's name into asking the wrong question, it would have been found sooner. In any case, it should no longer be ignored.

It is known that, when Augustus reorganized the *cursus honorum*, Patricians were given a great advantage: they could move straight from the quaestorship to the praetorship.[62] We do not know whether any gain in time went with this privilege.[63] In any case, custom and practice before long overrode whatever the law on these matters was; and there Patricians—though not they alone— had notable advantages, particularly in the speed of promotion to the consulship.[64] Some of this may have been traditional. Nor would it be unreasonable. Aedileships were hard to get for Patricians in the late Republic, and praetorships even harder for those who omitted the aedileship—as L. Sulla found; it would only be fair to give them the chance of an early candidature. Naturally, it would only be the most successful men who reaped the full benefit of this advantage: we could hardly expect to be able to trace it in more than four cases out of ten.

Whether this privilege was introduced by Sulla (who greatly favoured Patricians), or whether it existed in the second century, we cannot hope to discover with any degree of certainty. While curule aediles were still only elected in alternate years,[65] it would seem to have been even more necessary than later. But our evidence for the pre-Sullan period is too scrappy for serious use.[66] That after Sulla, at any rate, Patricians had an advantage of two years over Plebeians in the minimum ages required for the senior magistracies may, in the present state of our evidence, be confidently accepted. It explains not only the puzzle of C. Caesar's career (which, for some reason, did not puzzle his contemporaries enough to elicit comment), but also some similar facts, long familiar, but apparently never connected or discussed.

APPENDIX

Q. †Caelius† in *Planc.* 52. A man whose name appears in this form is said by Cicero to have become consul after failing to obtain the quaestorship. Emendations have usually been proposed without due regard for the context or historical probability, and Astin (*op. cit.* 29 f.) is rightly cautious. Some negative points, at any rate, can confidently be made: (i) C. Coelius Caldus (*cos.* 94), who still appears in most editions, is impossible. Not only is the corruption in the *praenomen* difficult to explain (that in the *nomen* is common in our texts), but— and this is decisive—the man concerned is here called 'clarissimus adulescens'. C. Coelius Caldus, however, is the very type of the *nouus homo* who made good (*de or.* i 117; 2 *Verr.* v 181; *Mur.* 17). (ii) Q. Caecilius is impossible. Cicero never refers to a Metellus in this way: with few exceptions, *nobiles* were normally referred to by *praenomen* and *cognomen*, not by *praenomen* and *nomen* (cf. Syme, *Historia* 7 (1958) 217 f.). Moreover, such a reference would be ludicrously ambiguous: four Q. Metelli were consuls between 123 and 80 alone. (iii) Q. Aelius (Paetus, *cos.* 167) is most unlikely: as Astin points out, all the other men named in this passage (there are five of them) reached the consulship in or after 105 B.C. In the context that is natural enough: Cicero would hardly assume in his audience a detailed knowledge ('scimus') of the career of a far from outstanding consul of 113 years previously. It is doubtful whether he could even refer to the man simply as 'Q. Aelius' without baffling the audience; and he always studiously avoids displays of erudition. We may well doubt whether Cicero himself would be so familiar with the *cursus* of a man like Paetus: compare and contrast his floundering over the career of a much more recent and much more distinguished consul, C. Sempronius Tuditanus, *cos.* 129 (*Att.* xiii 30 and 32).

This will at least clear the ground. Positive suggestions cannot be made as confidently. Mr Astin has suggested to me that the *praenomen* Q. may be due solely to the word 'quaestor', which precedes it. If that is so, the passage becomes practically *insanabilis*. Otherwise an obvious suggestion would seem to be Q. Catulus, despite the ambiguity (*coss.* 102 and 78): the *younger* Catulus must still have been well known to Cicero's audience.

NOTES

[1] Sources collected in M. E. Deutsch's article 'The Year of Caesar's Birth', *TAPA* 45 (1914) 17 f. (with bibliography). Tacitus' date (*dial.* 34: 98/7) is certainly wrong; Eutropius (vi 24) implies 102: but see Deutsch's comments (l.c.). Deutsch argues very convincingly for 100 as the date implied by the other sources. J. Carcopino (*Mél. Bidez* (1934) 35 f.) argues ingeniously, but less convincingly, for 101: see Renders, *AC* 8 (1939) 117 f., for some comments. In particular, Carcopino's handling of the Suetonius and Plutarch passages (47 f.) is very poor; he is unable (63 f.) to explain, or explain away, Cicero's repeated claim to have been made consul *suo anno* in 63; and he does not satisfactorily account for the implication that Caesar failed to get the quaestorship until two years after his year. (Cf. n. 52, below.) On an ingenious, but mistaken, attempt to arrive at Caesar's age by dating his marriage to Cinna's daughter (Suet. *Jul.* 1) in 84 (thus, especially, De Sanctis, *RFIC* 12 (1934) 550 f.), see H. M. Last, *CR* 58 (1944) 15 f. [Carcopino (*Profils de Conquérants* (1961) 241 f.) has defended his view at great length and attacked me for basing mine on a survey of the extant evidence instead of following authority. The decision can be left to the reader.]

[2] See Deutsch, *art. cit.*; L. R. Taylor, *CP* 36 (1941) 125 f.; Afzelius, *C & M* 8 (1947) 263 f.; A. E. Astin, *The Lex Annalis before Sulla* (1958) 33 (= *Latomus* 17 (1958) 51), withholding judgment.

[3] *Phil.* v 52 f.

[4] If indeed that was the aim of his laws (for the sources, see Taylor, *art. cit.* 128, n. 65).

[5] As Taylor does (l.c.). Dio xxxvi 39 does not appear to refer to dispensations from laws (*annales* or others).

[6] Cf. Taylor, *art. cit.* 129, n. 69; W. McDonald, *CQ* 23 (1929) 200 f. (the best account of C. Cornelius' tribunate).

[7] Instances collected and discussed by Taylor, *art. cit.* 127 f.; Astin, *op. cit.* 16 f. (= *Latomus* 16 (1957) 599 f.).

[8] As Cicero tells us (*leg. Man.* 62). The case of Aemilianus (actually cited by Taylor in this connection) cannot be seriously considered as a parallel.

[9] Cic. *ac. pr.* 1: 'licebat ... legis praemio.' As *priuilegia* were illegal, this shows, *prima facie* at least, that a class was affected.

[10] L. Lucullus was quaestor in 88 (*MRR* ii 52, n. 5 [he was almost certainly the 'one quaestor' who followed Sulla in his march on Rome]), so that a praetorship in 78 was no more than his due. References to the 'acceleration of his career' obscure this fact. None of the prominent *Sullani* except Pompey (and we know the careers of a number of them) can be shown to have had his career specially accelerated.

[11] Taylor and Astin, ll.cc. (n. 7, above).

[12] Taylor quotes two other possible parallels: M. Crassus and M. Cato. Neither of them is sound. M. Crassus needed no exemption in 71: Broughton rightly refuses to date his praetorship in 72 (see his discussion, *MRR* ii 121, n. 2); it may even be earlier than 73, since Appian's account of his appointment to the Slave War (*b.c.* i 118, *init.*) strongly suggests a special grant of *imperium* to a *priuatus*. As for M. Cato in 56, the dispensation he was offered had nothing to do with the *leges annales* (see *RE*, s.v. 'Porcius', col. 183). We may add an argument from silence that is at least worth considering: if Caesar had been granted a dispensation, it is odd that Cicero does not lament the fact in (say) 60 or 59 B.C.

L

[13] Astin (*op. cit.*), in a careful survey, has recently arrived at important results for the period before Sulla.

[14] Since he seems to have held the magistracies *suo anno* (sources collected and discussed by Astin, *op. cit.* 31 f.).

[15] Partial list in Astin, *op. cit.* 39. M. Junius Silanus is listed by him as *q.* 84, *pr.* 76. The latter is probably wrong (Broughton gives 77: *MRR* ii 88 and 94), the former almost certainly: although Broughton lists him under 84 (*ibid.* 60), his Index more cautiously says 'by 84' (*ibid.* 577); as all that we know is that Silanus, at an undetermined date, served under Murena in the East, he was probably elected in 88 for 87 (cf. Broughton's discussion of Murena himself: *ibid.* 62, n. 4).—I have ignored the tribunate of the Plebs, which was certainly not fitted into the regular *cursus* so as to impose a *biennium* after it. There are about a dozen examples that establish this point and it is universally accepted.

[16] The date is fixed by his predecessor's dilatory return (Cic. *Att.* ii 2, 3).

[17] *CIL* i² 2, 662b (quite undatable).

[18] *MRR* ii 52, n. 4.

[19] *Ibid.* 79 (cf. 84).

[20] The whole matter is carefully discussed by Münzer, *RE*, s.v. 'Domitius', coll. 1334 f. Broughton, while referring to the evidence, unfortunately lists the fictitious quaestorship without query.

[21] 2 *Verr.* iii 182.

[22] Cic. *Att.* ii 2, 3.

[23] Broughton (*MRR* ii 193, n. 5) gives as the noteworthy fact, not Nigidius' appearance in a *contio*, but his threat to *compellare* defaulting jurors. But anybody could do that (see *TLL*, s.v. 'compellare', iii 2028 B 2).

[24] *MRR* ii 184.

[25] Cic. *Att.* i 19, 9; *MRR* ii 184.

[26] See *MRR* ii 139.

[27] Sources *MRR* ii 91. Though this depends on an emendation in Exsuperantius (which would not normally be worth much), the Asconius passage seems to lend it support.

[28] Rightly *RE*, s.v. 'Valerius', coll. 232 f. Broughton is curiously inconsistent: the praetor is called 'L.' and identified with the quaestor on pp. 91 and 631 (Index), but is called 'C.' and identified with the legate on pp. 120 and 134; the quaestor L. is identified with the legate C. on p. 77. (Some of these identifications are queried, but without comment.) [This has been corrected in the *Supplement*.]

[29] In most cases we cannot determine whether the curule or the Plebeian office was held; by this period, we need not assume any difference. The two Patricians were certainly curule aediles, Cicero probably Plebeian aedile (cf. L. R. Taylor, *AJP* 60 (1939) 194 f.). On the *biennium* after the aedileship in the pre-Sullan period, see Astin, *op. cit.* 9 f.

[30] App. *b.c.* i 100: καὶ στρατηγεῖν ἀπεῖπε πρὶν ταμιεῦσαι, καὶ ὑπατεύειν πρὶν στρατηγῆσαι. See Gabba's edition, pp. 342 f., for other sources and discussion (with bibliography).

[31] Cic. *fam.* x 25. See Astin, *op. cit.* 14 f. (with bibliography).

[32] Astin, l.c.: 'Cicero's line of thought can be as follows: "This year (i.e. 43) is the first in which you are legally entitled to stand for the praetorship, but it is easier for you to postpone your candidature, in that if you had been aedile (in 44) your year would have been two years later (i.e. Furnius could not have stood till the elections in 42 for 41) ... ".' Other commentators have not even given this much of an indication of how they take the passage.

[33] Afzelius, *art. cit.*

34 *Art. cit.* However, we are not entitled to draw conclusions from this to other stages of the *cursus*, especially the interval between praetorship and consulship.

35 For Cicero's use of 'quasi legitimus', cf. 2 *Verr.* v 57; *fat.* 2.

36 See n. 30 (above).

37 C. Favonius, probably *aed.* 52, wanted the praetorship of 50 (*MRR* ii 240, n. 2).

38 *Mil.* 24.

39 See above, pp. 81 f.

40 Notably by Afzelius (*art. cit.*).

41 Cic. *Vat.* 11; *MRR* ii 216.

42 Afzelius, *art. cit.* On this, see Astin, *op. cit.* (with discussion of earlier views).

43 Astin, *op. cit.* 29.

44 *Ibid.* (with discussion). The passage needs renewed consideration (see Appendix).

45 *Phil.* v. 46.

46 Astin, *op. cit.* 41 (citing Karlowa).

47 l.c.

48 Cic. *fam.* xi 20, 1.

49 Yet he might not have altogether disliked the prospect of a consulship of M. Tullius Cicero II, C. Iulius Caesar! (Cf. Syme, *Rom. Rev.* 182 f.)

50 240 f.

51 This is also Astin's conclusion. It will, of course, in some cases explain the shorter interval between quaestorship and aedileship. It may now be asked whether *all* the irregularities in the case of the aedileship could not be satisfactorily explained by a similar hypothesis about that office. But that will not work well in every case. It would involve the further hypothesis that men like the younger M. Scaurus and Q. Metellus Scipio failed to get the aedileship *suo anno*, but succeeded in the case of the praetorship (not to mention the ambitious M. Caelius Rufus, in whose case there are further problems). It is certainly much easier to hold that Sulla's *lex annalis* had nothing to say about the aedileship, though it would naturally fall under the general rule forbidding *continuatio* of magistracies.

52 On his early career, see *RE*, s.v. 'Valerius', no. 179. P. Lentulus Sura (*q.* 81) could be one of the *Sullani* whose career had been delayed; but that will not explain the other cases, and the identity of interval (see below) is striking.

53 That he was quaestor in 69 may be regarded as certain after L. R. Taylor's demonstration (see *MRR* ii 136, n. 7).

54 See p. 142, n. 16 and text (above).

55 See *MRR* ii 123, 129 (but cf., more accurately, 629); cf. *ibid.* 121, n. 1. There is not enough evidence to decide.

56 Cic. *Mil.* 24.

57 Or perhaps both: it might make no difference in our case. See Renders, *AC* 8 (1939) 117 f.

58 [There is also another reason: Patricians who became Plebeians were always in an odd position. Thus Q. Metellus Scipio was at one time *tr. pl.*, at another *interrex* (*MRR* ii 189, 229).]

59 Excluding P. Clodius and those (quite undatable) in Appendix II.

60 P. Cornelius Lentulus Marcellinus, *q.* 75 or 74 (if this mysterious person should be either deleted or identified with P. Spinther, our statistics are not affected in any relevant point); P. Sulpicius (Rufus ?), *q.* 69, whose identification with the censor of 42 is anything but certain (see *MRR* ii 136, n. 8; cf. Syme, *CP* 50 (1955) 132 and 135); and Faustus Cornelius Sulla, *q.* 54, who did not advance to the senior magistracies.

61 M. Valerius Messalla (Niger), whose quaestorship is known only from his *elogium* (*Inscr. It.* xiii 3, 77).

62 Mommsen, *Staatsr.* i³ 554 f.

[63] Dio lii 20 (an imaginary speech by Maecenas, which is our only literary source for the details of Augustus' *ordinatio*) does not mention the special privilege of Patricians at all. It appears from known careers.

[64] See Syme, *Tacitus* ii, Appendix 19.

[65] Cf. Mommsen, *op. cit.* ii 482.

[66] Astin, *op. cit.* 34 f. Mr Astin has kindly pointed out to me that, such as it is, it suggests that the privilege did not exist before Sulla. See, especially, the career of Scipio Aemilianus—I would add, perhaps, that of L. Sulla himself; but that is another story.

Sulla's Cilician Command

THE task of drawing up a scheme of chronology for Asia Minor at the beginning of the first century B.C.—*periculosae plenum opus aleae*—was attempted and, in outline, magnificently carried out by Th. Reinach seventy years ago.[1] Basing himself on the coin finds, with practically no literary tradition (except Justin) to establish a framework, he succeeded far beyond the achievement of any of his predecessors in building up an unexpectedly solid and self-supporting structure. In this he was able to make use of the long-established 'fact' that Sulla's praetorship could be dated 93 and his Cilician command 92.[2] This traditional date has become, explicitly or by implication, one of the hinges of Asian and Roman chronology for this period, and it appears without doubt or query in all our standard works.[3] Who first arrived at it, and by what process of reasoning, is a problem that would by now be difficult to solve and hardly worth the effort.[4] But since the source passages cited in most of the modern works in support of the date are (as we shall see) either irrelevant or, where relevant, not easy to interpret as pointing to the date they are intended to support, one cannot help suspecting that the date has simply gone on being transmitted, without verification, from one scholar to another. Thus the whole matter is of considerable interest in illustrating the distortion to which unquestioning acceptance of modern authority can lead, and often has led, even in the comparatively well-documented field of the late Republic. Yet it is not by any means a minor point: the nineties are a crucial period, unduly neglected by historians (ancient and modern) more interested in spectacular events than in the interaction of personalities and purposes that forms the stuff of history.[5] And as the evidence for this period is both abundant and fragmentary, care must be taken to fit each piece into its proper place in order to construct a picture that is coherent and true.

I. THE PRAETORSHIP

Though the facts of Sulla's praetorship and Cilician command are mentioned by several sources, the date is given in precise form by only one—Velleius Paterculus. It is ironical that this solitary attempt at precision is so obviously wrong that it has never been believed by anyone and may safely be ignored.[6] For Velleius, referring to Sulla in his list of Roman commanders in the Social War (the outbreak of which he dates in 90 B.C.),[7] puts his praetorship 'anno ante', i.e., in 91. This date, intrinsically impossible (for it would leave far too little time for his Cilician command and his return to Rome before the Social War), is refuted by the Livian *Periocha*. This work, like the rest of the ancient tradition, gives no actual date; but, as usual, it permits us at least to deduce certain limits. Sulla's activities in the East are mentioned before the Rutilius trial and after the victories of T. Didius in Celtiberia and the testament of Ptolemy Apion.[8] As it happens, we know that Livy's account of T. Didius belongs to 97 and his account of Apion to 96.[9] The Rutilius trial almost certainly belongs to 92 and cannot be later.[10] As the Epitomator normally relates foreign affairs *after* the domestic events for the year (sometimes, indeed, collecting the foreign events of several years together, often at the end of a book), the year 92 is in fact excluded for Sulla's Cilician command; which makes it all the more remarkable that the *Periocha* is invariably cited in support of it by those who accept this standard date. Though unable to furnish a precise date, it does at least, by exclusion, narrow the field of enquiry: the date must be between 96 and 93 (both included).

Fortunately Plutarch is more helpful. At the beginning of chapter 5 of his *Sulla* he tells of Sulla's failure in his first attempt to gain the praetorship and his success when he stood again in the following year. The account appears to be based on Sulla's own: we are told that he himself blames the populace for his failure, saying that they had expected him to be aedile first and give magnificent games. This citation immediately follows the account of his unsuccessful candidature. We are therefore entitled (not to say compelled) to believe that this account, including Sulla's motive for standing, is itself from the same source. This, however, must mean that it is factually accurate: indeed, it is obviously an unimpeachable source for the facts of the case. Now, this is what

Plutarch says: ὁ δὲ Σύλλας, οἰόμενος αὐτῷ τὴν ἀπὸ τῶν πολεμικῶν δόξαν ἐπὶ τὰς πολιτικὰς πράξεις διαρκεῖν, καὶ δοὺς ἑαυτὸν ἀπὸ τῆς στρατείας [against the Germans] εὐθὺς ἐπὶ τὴν τοῦ δήμου πρᾶξιν, ἐπὶ στρατηγίαν πολιτικὴν ἀπεγράψατο καὶ διεψεύσθη. In other words, Sulla himself seems to have put his candidature straight after (εὐθύς) the German wars and given his confidence in his military glory as his reason for omitting the aedileship. This, however, cannot be made to square with the *communis opinio*; for if he was praetor in 93, his first candidature must come in 95; and this is so far from being 'straight after the war' and the reputation he had won in it that he can hardly in his most optimistic moments have hoped that his military glory, after five years of idleness and obscurity, would suffice to ensure his election. Yet this passage also is commonly cited as supporting the accepted dating.[11]

A study of Sulla's *cursus* leads to a similar conclusion. He was born, almost certainly, in 138[12] and was quaestor, perhaps *suo anno*, in 107.[13] There followed practically continuous military service until 101. Sulla's first lawful opportunity of standing for the praetorship would probably be in 99 (for 98).[14] We have no reason to think that an ambitious man, after a distinguished military career, would miss that opportunity, only to revive his ambition four years later. 99, however, would fit in very well with Plutarch's (i.e., probably Sulla's) account of the candidature: the glory won in the German wars that ended in 101[15] must have been very much alive when he started his canvass (which would certainly be in 100). There is another relevant point. Sulla's proper year for the curule aedileship would appear to have been 101.[16] Thus he had an excellent alibi: in that year he had been away on active service, and the earliest year in which he could in fact have stood for the aedileship was 100 (for 99).[17] If he had gained the office and held it in 99, the operation of the law against *continuatio* of magistracies would have compelled him to miss his year for the praetorship (98); indeed, as it now seems likely that there was a law enforcing a clear *biennium*, he could not have been praetor until 96.[18] It would be manifestly unjust to expect a man to lose two years, merely because he had been away on active service, and had distinguished himself in the field, when he might have been standing for the aedileship. Thus Sulla had a good case to put to the People, and Plutarch's words begin to make proper sense: impatient to pursue his career—and indeed, he had been continuously active since first entering upon it in 107—he expected his military distinction to secure him his praetorship *suo anno*, since he had missed the aedileship in the interests of his country.

On the accepted dating of his praetorship none of this makes proper sense. If he was in no hurry to be praetor, there was nothing to prevent him from holding the aedileship after his return from the war: as we have seen, he could still have been praetor earlier— after holding an aedileship in (say) 99—than (on this dating) he was. It was only the hurry to reach high office—a legitimate ambition—that would give him a fair excuse for cheating the People of their games. We are asked to believe, then, that Plutarch's εὐθύς means that he did nothing for five years, letting his name fade from public memory, letting his year pass and abandoning all ambition; that, having been idle for five years—for the first time since embarking upon his public career—he suddenly decided, in 95, to resume his political progress; and that, missing out the expense of an aedileship, he aimed straight at the higher office, expecting the distinction won in the field six years previously to carry him into office despite that omission. If that was so, his failure is certainly easy to understand; what is incredible is that any skilled Roman politician should have behaved so irrationally and expected to succeed.

If there were good evidence for all this, we should—as is so often the case—have to accept it and despair of understanding. But as we have seen, there is in fact no evidence at all for such a view, while what evidence we have points positively, and almost irrefutably, to his adopting a course that makes perfect sense: not only does Livy seem to exclude the date commonly accepted, but we appear, via Plutarch, to have Sulla's own word for it that he stood for the praetorship *suo anno* in 99, was defeated (since the Roman People expected their pound of flesh), and, after finding the compromise solution of promising lavish *praetorian* games, finally secured election without further loss of time in 98 for 97.

II. SULLA IN CILICIA

Having restored Sulla's praetorship to 97, where he himself probably put it, we must next see how this squares with what we know of his provincial command after his praetorship and of the history of Asia Minor during this period.

The sources for the command are collected and discussed in the standard modern works.[19] The first points to be settled are the technical questions of the name and nature of the command. Two sources clearly describe Sulla as in charge of Cilicia, and they are such that we need not doubt the accuracy of the information.[20] As Magie has pointed out,[21] this does not necessarily mean that there was at this time a province (in the territorial sense) of Cilicia, such as we find a generation later. 'Cilicia' had been the command given to M. Antonius against the pirates who were based there; we know that P. Servilius Vatia was later sent there to fight the pirates,[22] and it is legitimate to conjecture that before him Cn. Cornelius Dolabella had been sent there for the same purpose.[23] Though it is customary to date the establishment of the territorial province of Cilicia to Sulla (or Murena),[24] there was not really much to govern before the conquests on land that earned P. Vatia his name; however, whether or not there was a small coastal strip (before Sulla as after) to serve as a base, there were certainly allies from whom assistance could be demanded: Sulla used mainly 'allied' troops in his Cappadocian campaign, and Dolabella (and his subordinates) made a fortune out of the allied cities.[25] There is no sign of any fundamental change around 80 B.C., such as is commonly assumed: at the most Sulla and the Senate, after the experiences of the Mithridatic War, had hardened in their determination to deal with the pirate problem, which had proved a serious military danger in an unstable area. At any rate, it seems that immediately after Sulla's dictatorship, as certainly before it, Cilicia meant pirates: it was not so much a province as a *prouincia*. There can be no serious doubt that Sulla's task in 96 was to be that particular war.[26] As far as we know (and admittedly our information is not complete), it was the first time since the indecisive campaigns of M. Antonius that anyone had been given that particular assignment. His title for the task—i.e., the nature of his *imperium*—cannot be recovered with complete certainty; but the same known precedent, and perhaps the analogy of the later appointments we have noted, makes it very likely that he was sent *pro consule*.[27]

Sent to Cilicia, almost certainly to deal with the pirates,

Sulla (as is known) ended up by performing quite a different task. He restored Ariobarzanes to Cappadocia, apparently at the special request of the Senate.[28] This has caused more surprise that it need have.[29] We know of a governor of Cilicia, forty-five years later, who was asked by the Senate to keep an eye on Cappadocia and its royal family: if events had developed a little differently, M. Tullius Cicero would have had some serious fighting to do there.[30] Sulla's province of Cilicia must have been assigned to him, in the usual fashion,[31] in the year of his praetorship. As we have seen, it was not a regular territorial province and it suggests that, in 97, the Senate was thinking of the pirate problem and not yet of Cappadocia. At some time between the assignment and (most probably) Sulla's arrival in the East in 96, the restoration of Ariobarzanes must have been decided upon as a more urgent task. As holders of *imperium* were not numerous, it was an easy step to entrust this task to the commander who had drawn the *prouincia* nearest to the area concerned. Unfortunately we cannot be certain of the precise date of the decision. The fact that Sulla had to rely mainly on allied troops[32] suggests that he was not able to levy troops in Italy before his departure, i.e., that the new development only took place after he had left; for the magnitude of the task, as we shall see, was such that Roman forces would have been called for. It is a slender clue: the Senate, as so often, may have been unaware of the seriousness of the situation. But it is reinforced by the fact that the name of Sulla's command was not changed: as we have seen, it would have been perfectly easy to make his *prouincia* 'Cappadocia', and in the face of an emergency this could have been done after the assignment as well as before. Again, this is far from decisive. But where pointers are so few, the convergence of these two deserves attention. It entitles us to prefer early 96, after Sulla's departure for his province, as the date when the Senate decided to entrust him with the Cappodocian commission. We shall return to this question later.

III. THE STATE OF CAPPADOCIA

Meanwhile we must approach the problem from another direction and investigate the history of the monarchies concerned. Here matters are far from simple. Our only narrative source is

Justin—inadequate as usual—and we have stray references in other authors; but above all, the evidence of coins has had to be fitted together to produce a proper picture. As we saw at the beginning of this study, the task was performed with masterly skill by Th. Reinach two generations ago, and no modifications of any consequence appear to have been made in his conclusions.[33] He was, however, assuming the date 93 for Sulla's praetorship (and 92 for his Cilician command), which even in his day was too firmly established for him to question or attempt to prove it. This naturally influenced the way in which he fitted the uncertain evidence together: it led him to the conclusion that Ariobarzanes was restored in 92. As we have noticed, this runs counter to the date for Sulla's command implied by the *Periocha* of Livy, and it will certainly not square with Plutarch's evidence on his praetorship. But so firmly was the *communis opinio* fixed in Reinach's mind that—like many others—he actually cites both these passages as evidence for the date 92. Since this was a matter that did not need proving, he was—to some extent unconsciously—above all concerned with making the evidence on Asia fit in with it. With the presupposition removed, the whole history of the kingdoms of Asia Minor during this period must be re-examined, at least in outline. It will be seen that the precision at which Reinach arrived is to a large extent illusory: we cannot pinpoint events to within a year by what internal evidence we have, and a reasonably tight scheme of chronology can only be worked out (if at all) by reference to dated Roman events. This is, of course, implicit in Reinach's attempt; but it must be made explicit if we are to avoid deceiving ourselves.

The basic account in Justin runs, in outline, as follows:[34] Mithridates and Nicomedes (III) both covet Cappadocia, where Mithridates has for some time been trying to establish his influence; each of them puts up a pretender and sends to Rome to obtain the Senate's recognition for him; the Senate, however, declares Cappadocia (and Paphlagonia, which does not concern us here) free; the Cappadocians refuse this freedom and ask for a king, and Ariobarzanes is appointed by the Senate to rule them; Mithridates now stirs up Tigranes, recently become King of Armenia, to attack Ariobarzanes, and the latter flees to Rome; at the same time Mithridates himself attacks Bithynia, where Nicomedes (III) has recently died, and his successor, Nicomedes (IV), also flees to Rome; the Senate sends Aquillius and Maltinus [*sic*, it appears] to restore the two kings, and Mithridates prepares for war. This account ignores the activity of Sulla: in fact, at first sight it seems to leave no room for it. It is chiefly for this reason (for the Eastern command of Sulla is, as we have seen, very well attested) that it has been regarded as seriously defective.

Appian, in his *Mithridatic Wars*, unfortunately adds little of importance.[35] It is chiefly Plutarch who enables us to supplement Justin.[36] He tells us that Sulla was commissioned to restore Ariobarzanes, but was also intended to curb Mithridates' ambitions; Sulla killed many Cappadocians and Armenians who came to help them, drove out Gordius (whom Justin mentions several times, *i.a.* as negotiating with Tigranes on behalf of Mithridates), and appointed Ariobarzanes king; then comes Sulla's famous interview with a Parthian envoy. The only other addition to our information is made by Strabo, who tells of the offer of freedom refused by the Cappadocians and adds the important fact that the Senate thereupon permitted them to choose one of their own number as king, and that they then chose Ariobarzanes.[37]

The usual way of reconciling Justin and Plutarch is simple and, up to a point, undoubtedly correct: Ariobarzanes was expelled twice before the Mithridatic War and restored twice: Justin has omitted the first restoration (by Sulla) and consequently the second expulsion (soon after Sulla's departure), so that the second restoration (by the mission headed by M' Aquillius) follows straight upon the first expulsion. In part this must be correct, since Sulla's mission undoubtedly precedes that of Aquillius (which we know led immediately to the First Mithridatic War) by some years, and yet both are clearly reported as being concerned with the return of Ariobarzanes. But the postulate that the first restoration and the second expulsion are simply omitted in Justin, so that the remaining pieces dovetail neatly into each other, is a little artificial: such purely mechanical explanations are not to be adopted except as a last resort, since in fact neither source (neither Justin nor Appian) mentions *two* restorations of Ariobarzanes to his throne. In this case careful reading of the sources suggests a much more satisfactory explanation.

When Plutarch describes Sulla's successful intervention,

though he speaks of the commission to 'restore' Ariobarzanes to Cappadocia (καταγαγεῖν), he then merely says that Sulla appointed him king (ἀπέδειξεν).[38] There is no doubt that the word ἀπέδειξεν should refer to the *first* placing of Ariobarzanes on his throne, and καταγαγεῖν in no way contradicts this or prevents us from taking the word in its normal sense: Plutarch, who knew (and tells us) that Ariobarzanes was being restored to his country,[39] would certainly have known (and almost certainly have told us) if he had also been restored to his throne. The distinction is important for a proper understanding of these events: it means, in fact, that Ariobarzanes had not taken possession of his kingdom at all until Sulla installed him. Sulla's task was not (as modern accounts say) the restoration of a king to his throne, but the installation of a king designated by the Senate and kept out of his appointed kingdom. As we saw, it is clear from Strabo that Ariobarzanes was a Cappadocian noble,[40] and there is no reason whatever for postulating a restoration to his throne, where the sources do not necessarily imply more than a restoration to his country.

Having clarified this important point, we can begin to rewrite the history of these events in a way that keeps much closer to the sources and makes much better sense of our information. Mithridates had long ago installed a young son of his as pretender, giving him the title of Ariarathes (IX) Eusebes: his accession, at the age of eight, can be dated around 100—with the necessary caution.[41] He 'ruled' Cappadocia with Gordius as his guardian and regent for about five years.[42] There can be no doubt that he was actually in occupation when the Senate's edict reached the country. What followed, though to be found in the sources, has been entirely misconstrued in most modern accounts, owing to their misunderstanding of the nature of Sulla's action. We know that Ariarathes (or rather Gordius) was unpopular, and his enemies had already tried to end his rule by appealing to the last surviving member of the old royal family. That move had been defeated by Mithridates, and the man concerned had died soon after.[43] When, as a result of the developments we have noticed, 'freedom' was imposed by the Senate, neither party was willing to accept it: the Pontic faction was naturally unwilling to give up what it had so long possessed; their enemies knew that a 'free' Cappadocia was at the mercy of Mithridates' troops. Since a Pontic faction, of course, did exist, he would have no difficulty in finding a suitable moment for intervention. Thus an embassy was hurriedly dispatched to Rome, asking for permission to elect a king: in this the two parties may even have agreed.[44] Permission was granted, and while we know that the Pontic faction wanted the rule of Gordius to continue, their enemies, sure of Roman support, chose Ariobarzanes. It does not seem to have been a good choice: *segnis admodum,* as we know him from Justin and from his own deeds, he was hardly the man who would defend his country against Mithridates. But one can see reasons for the choice: on the one hand he was probably already known as pro-Roman and therefore a suitable candidate for attracting the Senate's help (as in fact he did); on the other hand, he was a Cappadocian noble, the peer of the men who elected him, and, like most aristocracies anywhere, they were no doubt unwilling to risk imposing a tyrant on themselves, the more so after the ruthless administration they had recently experienced. Thus the choice was made and another embassy dispatched to Rome to ask for the recognition of Ariobarzanes. All this time, as we have seen, Gordius will have remained in occupation, at least of as much of the country as he could hold. The modern account here lands itself in its crowning absurdity: it has to assume (though the assumption is not always made explicit) that Gordius (and the boy king, whom, for practical purposes, we can ignore) evacuated the country after the Senate's order, only to invade it again almost at once, in time to be expelled (as Plutarch tells us he was) by Sulla. There is no reason to assume such dithering. Gordius had an excellent pretext for simply staying on, and he is not likely to have missed it: we happen to know that (as might in any case have been expected) the election of Ariobarzanes was anything but unanimous and that the Pontic party voted for the continuance of Gordius' administration. Gordius, it seems, was to claim that the election of his enemy was invalid, and that *he* had been chosen by the Cappadocians. Nor was this idle propaganda: we remember the 'large number of Cappadocians' whom Sulla had to kill.[45] In the circumstances, Ariobarzanes can have had no chance of making good his claim. If he was not in exile before (as a prominent anti-Pontic noble easily might be), he would certainly have been well advised to

leave the country now: it is clear that he had no intention of
fighting for himself, and his best place was in Rome, trying to
persuade the Senate to intervene on his behalf by stressing the
danger from Mithridates (which we know was the chief reason
for Sulla's commission). It was in this situation that the proconsul of Cilicia was entrusted with the task of restoring Ariobarzanes to his country and installing him on his throne (καταγαγεῖν and ἀποδεῖξαι). It was only Sulla (as Plutarch makes clear) who
succeeded in overcoming Gordius and the 'large number of
Cappadocians' supporting him after his long tenure of power.
Justin, in fact, has not conveniently omitted an expulsion and a
restoration of Ariobarzanes, which, luckily, we happen to pick up
from Plutarch: he has simply given us a concise, but (for his
purposes) correct, account of what actually happened. Naturally,
he is not interested in Ariobarzanes until his appearance as king,
and the installation of Ariobarzanes on his throne (which was
Sulla's act) is simply not separated, as in his brief summary it need
not be, from Ariobarzanes' appointment. Not being either a biographer or a panegyrist of Sulla (or even concerned with Roman
actions for their own sake), he has no reason to stress his intervention: what mattered was that Ariobarzanes became king. The
corollary of this is that the alliance of Mithridates and Tigranes
of Armenia, which led to Ariobarzanes' flight to Rome and his
restoration by M' Aquillius—a sequence that we need no longer
doubt—must come *after* Sulla's action. In fact, in his account of
the latter Plutarch nowhere mentions the great Tigranes,[46] and
one wonders whether, if that great monarch had indeed been in
occupation of Cappadocia, Sulla's motley force would have won
the easy victory it did win—and without any special mention of
the feat in Sulla's *Memoirs*, which Plutarch used.[47] For Tigranes,
despite his collapse in the sixties, was in his day a greater ruler than
Mithridates Eupator; and Sulla, while engaged on his Mithridatic
War in the eighties, must have heard of Tigranes' outstanding
achievements, which appear to be contemporary. In fact, it is
quite likely that, at the time when Sulla may be presumed to have
been writing his account, Tigranes was at the height of his power
and glory.[48] We can be certain that Sulla, far from playing down
his achievements, would rather exaggerate them: the 'numerous
Armenians', whom he claims to have defeated when they 'came

to the aid of' the Cappadocians, need not have been a large force: in any case, the wording makes it clear that they were not an occupation force, and the facts show that their defeat had no further consequences. They were not the army of Tigranes that expelled Ariobarzanes. In fact, we may be able to conjecture how they got there. Tigranes, for long a hostage in Parthia, had bought permission to succeed to the vacant throne of Armenia in 96 or 95; and he at once turned on his western neighbour, the kingdom of Sophene, and overran it.[49] That kingdom had a long common frontier with Cappadocia, and, as might be expected, it was not a settled frontier; thus the fortress of Tomisa (probably east of the Euphrates—but Strabo is not very clear) seems to have changed hands between the two kingdoms. It will have been along this disputed frontier that Tigranes' outposts, arriving from the East, engaged in a skirmish with Sulla's men arriving from the West.[50] Finally the upper Euphrates (to which we know Sulla advanced) seems to have been agreed upon as a frontier. Sulla thus had no pretext for claiming that he had defeated the future King of Kings; however, he was to make what he could of his fighting with Armenian forces.

Thus, as a result of Sulla's intervention, Ariobarzanes was duly crowned King of Cappadocia. Mithridates accepted the situation (no doubt mindful of Marius' famous advice, given not long before) and, for the moment, did nothing to restore his son.[51] But before long—we cannot tell precisely when—he began those negotiations with Tigranes that led to their marriage alliance and, when Rome was engaged in the Social War, to the combined attack on Cappadocia and Bithynia. This attack, which seems to have taken place in 90,[52] is, of course, the one related by Justin and our other relevant sources.

IV. THE COURSE OF EVENTS

We can now hope to draw up a time-table for the events we have been discussing—remembering that at many points precision is impossible[53]—and must then consider its implications for the connection of events. One warning, however, must be given at the outset: we must avoid exeessive reliance on regnal years derived from coins. It is Reinach's great merit to have used these dates to best effect; but it is his chief fault that he relied on them too much. As he himself must in the end confess, we often do not even know from what calendar date the regnal year of a monarch is computed, and therefore how the official figure is related to chronological years.[54] Nor is it permissible to equate gaps in a series with a ruler's exile (as Reinach generally does),[55] or its end—in our collections—with his death: no argument from silence could be more vicious, since the evidence often consists of small collections and is necessarily furnished by chance finds. Thus, while regnal years on coins are undoubtedly useful, e.g. in calculating the approximate length of a reign (especially a long one),[56] the use of this evidence must be firmly circumscribed, and the margin of error must, where this is important, be made explicit.[57]

With this word of warning we may embark on the task. We start with the firmest date we have—that of Sulla's praetorship, about which (as has been shown above) there can be little real doubt. Praetor in 97, he would go to his province in 96. Here our difficulties start: we do not know precisely when he would leave Rome or arrive in Cilicia. There is a tendency, in modern works, to underestimate the time it would take a promagistrate to get to a distant province. Yet we have numerous certain examples from the Ciceronian age (when the practice of leaving after one's year of office was almost invariable)[58] to remind us of the facts.[59] It will be instructive to look at Cicero's own case. He left the city on May 1st, 51, and Italy about June 10th; and he arrived in his province on July 31st. We may think that he was not in a particular hurry to get there (though this is not true, since he had to stay for a year and wanted to get back to Rome as early as possible).[60] But there can be no doubt of his eagerness to get back to Rome after; yet he left his province on July 30th, 50, and only reached Brundisium on November 24th.[61] Illness and contrary winds could cause long delays[62] and men were helpless against them. Of course, not everyone was in a hurry: commanders going to, or returning from, the Greek East liked to travel *antiquitatis cognoscendae*, and we find their names attested in Athens, Delos, Rhodes, and every other centre of Greek culture.[63] Thus, though we cannot be certain when Sulla arrived, it would be rash indeed to suggest a date before April 96,[64] particularly in view of the equinoctial gales. Again, we cannot tell whether he stayed precisely

M

a year—though we have no reason to assume the contrary, since his task turned out much less formidable than it might have appeared. He will thus have left the province in the late spring or summer of 95 and arrived back in the summer or autumn of that year.

This is as near as we can get to it. Yet even this turns out to be of some importance, as indeed must every approach to a proper chronology of this important period. After his return, Sulla was prosecuted by a C. Censorinus, who later dropped the prosecution.[65] Censorinus must be the later Marian adherent, who was to kill Cn. Octavius and attempt the life of Q. Scaevola.[66] Those who date Sulla's return in 91 are hard put to it (where they consider the matter) to explain the prosecutor's change of mind in that year of increasingly bitter conflict.[67] In fact, as we can now see, the prosecution was probably launched in the last months of 95. That year, as we happen to know, was eventful and crucial. Marius' enemies had made a series of attacks upon his *auctoritas*, and his friends had taken counter-measures. The end was stalemate: though the *lex Licinia Mucia* was passed, T. Matrinius was acquitted and the legality of Marius' grants of citizenship was vindicated; and the acquittal of C. Norbanus balanced that of Q. Caepio.[68] Into this year of thrusts and counter-thrusts the prosecution of L. Sulla fits well enough. In 95—the fact, for once, is unambiguously attested—C. Claudius Pulcher was *praetor repetundarum*. Firmly rooted in the *factio*, he will have done his best to protect Sulla as long as he was in office.[69] Yet this is probably not why Censorinus gave up. Just as the prosecution fits into the year of conflict, so its abandonment (as we have seen, it cannot be earlier than very late in 95 and may well belong to 94) fits into the uneasy *concordia* that was its outcome.[70] But Sulla did not escape scot-free: he had to abandon all thought of the consulship, until the Social War wiped out the memory and the Metelli needed a strong candidate.[71] By 89 he was indispensable to the *factio*.

Let us now turn our attention to the events that preceded Sulla's intervention in Cappadocia. The Senate's instruction to him probably, as we saw, belongs to early 96. If we want to work back from that date, we must allow a few months for the embassy that asked permission to elect a king and the one that announced the result of the election and asked for ratification.

Precision, therefore, is quite impossible; but we shall not be far out, if we assign the Senate's decision to free Cappadocia and Paphlagonia to early 97. Our attention is now caught by a chronological coincidence too striking to be accidental. C. Marius, after the discredit he had incurred in 100, was unable to prevent the recall of Q. Metellus Numidicus late in 99.[72] To avoid having to witness the acclamation of his enemy's arrival (in 98), he decided—particularly as he knew he now had no chance of reaching the censorship—to visit Cappadocia and Galatia.[73] The choice of Cappadocia can hardly be accidental: it had for years been a trouble-spot. It was there that, no doubt some time in 98, he met Mithridates, who at the time controlled Cappadocia and was just sending an embassy to Rome to obtain official recognition for his nominee; and it was there that he gave the King the famous warning to obey Rome or to be stronger than Rome. We are not informed when Marius returned to Rome.[74] But there is no reason to think that he stayed away more than a year, long after Metellus' return had ceased to be topical. The augurate conferred on him in absence—a signal honour[75]—restored his *dignitas*, and it probably belongs to 98; it is clearly a compensation extorted by his friends for the censorship to which he would normally have been entitled.[76] Marius now had every reason to return as soon as possible. In 97 his associates L. Flaccus and M. Antonius were censors and embarked on a policy—which can be shown to be that of Marius—of generosity to the Italians in the matter of the franchise.[77] Moreover, the consuls of 97 were Cn. Cornelius Lentulus and P. Licinius Crassus. Nothing of any importance is known about Lentulus, to whom Münzer devotes only seven lines;[78] but P. Crassus, as analysis shows, was connected with the faction of Marius.[79] With a friendly consul in office, Marius can safely be presumed back in Rome quite early in 97. With the same friendly consul to consult the House, Marius' report on the state of affairs in the East must have carried a good deal of weight; and we know his suspicions of Mithridates. Thus the enormity of the Senate's decision on Cappadocia (which Marius had just visited) and Paphlagonia can at last find a proper explanation and its proper place in the series of events. Marius reported the danger from the kings (we remember his interview with Mithridates) and threw his *auctoritas* behind the moves to curb their ambitions; and the recognition and effective protection of Ariobarzanes is the further consequence of this.

In what it regarded as a potentially dangerous situation, the Senate had taken a grave decision early in 97: the two kings— Mithridates and Nicomedes—were to be directly challenged. Next it had to be made clear that the Senate meant business and would see that its word was obeyed. Thus a mission was sent out to Asia, headed (most probably) by the *Princeps Senatus* himself: I have had occasion to point out before[80] that it is this political context that best suits the mysterious *legatio Asiatica* that was to bring M. Scaurus so much *inuidia*. The mission will have left Rome some time early in 97, soon after the Senate's decision.[81] But on its return—which must be later in the same year or early in 96— it brought grave and unexpected news: not only were the kings dangerous, but the province of Asia was seething with justified discontent and resentment under a corrupt administration, and it would be an easy prey for an enemy's intrigues. This fact C. Marius, with his Equestrian connections, had failed to report: to judge by his behaviour in the case of P. Rutilius Rufus, we can be sure that he did not altogether welcome the report. But the Senate acted on the *auctoritas* of its *Princeps*: it could hardly take the grave risk of ignoring the state of affairs with which he acquainted it. Thus the province of Asia was assigned to one of the consuls of 95, when, in accordance with the *lex Sempronia*, the allocation of provinces came up for discussion in 96.[82] As it happened, that year would have a consul—certain of election— ideally suited for the task of reform. Nor was that hope disappointed: to the chagrin of those who profited by corruption, Q. Mucius Scaevola, with the help of his equally learned and upright friend P. Rutilius Rufus, performed the task so well that his arrangements became a model for later governors in that province and others.[83]

APPENDIX

It may help, if the chronological scheme here suggested is drawn up in tabular form.

> $c.$ 100: Ariarathes Eusebes (i.e. *de facto* Gordius) rules Cappadocia.
>
> 99: *Late*: Marius leaves Rome for the East.

98: Marius meets Mithridates; he is given the augurate and decides to return to Rome. Mithridates and Nicomedes send embassies to Rome.

97: Consulship of P. Crassus; censorship of L. Flaccus and M. Antonius; praetorship of L. Sulla (he is assigned Cilicia for 96).

Early: Marius returns (perhaps late 98) and reports; the Senate decides to free· Cappadocia and Paphlagonia; departure of M. Scaurus' mission; Cappadocian request for permission to elect a king.

Late (or early 96): M. Scaurus returns and reports. Cappadocian vote divided between Ariarathes and Ariobarzanes.

96: *Early*: Sulla goes out as proconsul of Cilicia. The Senate recognizes Ariobarzanes and orders Sulla to instal him in Cappadocia.

About June (?): Asia assigned to one of the *coss.* 95.

Later: Sulla's intervention in Cappadocia. Tigranes occupies Sophene. (We cannot establish the chronological order of the last two items.)

95: Year of party strife in Rome. Q. Scaevola consul.

Late: Sulla returns to Rome and is prosecuted.

(Probably) 94: *Early*: *Concordia* restored; Sulla's prosecution dropped. Q. Scaevola's administration of Asia, followed, for three months, by that of his legate Rufus. (This overlaps into 93, but we cannot tell how far.)

NOTES

1 *Trois royaumes de l'Asie Mineure* (1888) (cited *T.R.*). The conclusions there reached are reproduced, in a slightly amended form, in his *Mithridate Eupator* (1890) (cited *M.E.*).

2 *M.E.* 106 (with n. 2).

3 E.g. Drumann-Groebe ii 366; *RE*, s.v. 'Cornelius', col. 1527; *MRR* ii, 14, 16 (n. 3), 18, 19 (n. 6); *CAH* ix 237; Magie, *Roman Rule in Asia Minor* (cited *RRAM*) i 206 f. (with notes in vol. ii); Mommsen, *R.G.* ii 275.

4 It is certainly found as early as 1830 (Clinton, *Fasti Hellenici* iii 140).

5 See *Historia* 6 (1957) 318 f. [=pp. 34 f., above].

6 ii 15, 3. Rightly ignored at least ever since Clinton (l.c.).

7 15, 1 (*init.*).

8 Livy, *per.* lxx.

9 This is clear from Obsequens 48, *fin.*, 49, *fin.*

10 This date is generally accepted (see *MRR* ii, 8; 9, n. 6). It cannot be later, as in the *Periocha* the defeat of C. Sentius by the Thracians intervenes between it and the tribunate of M. Drusus. The latter, however, must undoubtedly be the first event recorded for 91.

[11] The incongruity is well illustrated by the Loeb edition, where (*Plutarch's Lives* iv 333) we find the following note on this passage: 'He returned to Rome in 101 B.C., and was elected praetor in [=for?] 93 B.C.' Users of that edition must find this rather baffling.

[12] The sources, as usual, tend to be a little careless in computing his age. Velleius (ii 17, 2) says he was in his 49th year when elected consul (late 89), Plutarch that he was 50 years old (*Sulla* 6, 10). Similarly Valerius Maximus (ix 3, 8) puts his death (early 78) at the beginning of his 60th year, while Appian (*b.c.* i 105) says that he was then 60 years old. Allowing for the usual confusion between year of life and years completed, and noticing that Valerius Maximus seems the only one of these authors who found a precise statement, we may put Sulla's birth late in 138.

[13] *MRR* i 551: *suo anno* on the assumption that the rules for the quaestorship were already the same as in the age of Cicero. See now, however, Astin, *The Lex Annalis before Sulla* (1958) 44 f., arguing that the minimum age was probably much lower before Sulla's reforms.

[14] See Astin, *op. cit.* 31 f. This assumes the normal rules of the *cursus*, as there is not enough evidence to justify a contrary hypothesis. For Sulla's career, see the summary in *MRR* ii 557.

[15] The battle of the Raudine Plains took place on July 30th, 101 (Plut. *Mar.* 26, 4). We do not know the date of the joint triumph of C. Marius and Q. Catulus.

[16] See Astin, *op. cit.* 31 f. We do not know whether the alternation between Patrician and Plebeian curule aediles, known earlier in the second century, was still observed at this time. (On this alternation, see Mommsen, *Staatsr.* ii³ 482: it had certainly disappeared by 91 and probably—cf. *MRR* i 489 f.—as early as 135.) But even if it was, the year 101 would have been a 'Patrician' year, and so would 99, the first year for which he would have had time to stand. See also Cichorius, *Unt. zu Lucil.* 235 f.

[17] See last note. Marius, after his victory, had time to gain the consulship of 100; but that was quite different, as he needed no prolonged canvass.

[18] For the *biennium*, see Astin, *op. cit., passim.* [But there was no such rule after Sulla: see pp. 144 f., above.]

[19] *MRR* ii 18–19; *RRAM* i 206; 284; ii 1099 (n. 17); 1163 f. (n. 14).

[20] App. *Mithr.* and *vir. ill.* On this and what follows, see *RRAM* ii 1163 f.

[21] *RRAM*, l.c.

[22] *Ibid.*

[23] See *RRAM* i 286: he certainly had some forces meant against an enemy, and we do not hear of any other enemy at the time.

[24] Thus, e.g., Magie, l.c. (n. 20, above).

[25] See Magie, ll.cc. On Sulla, see Plut. *Sulla* 5, 3.

[26] Magie (l.c., n. 20, above) rightly points out that 'it is difficult to see why an official sent to carry out a mission in Cappadocia should have held the same title as a commander [i.e. M. Antonius] despatched against the Cilician pirates'. Since Cilicia does not appear to have been one of the regular provinces, it would certainly have been just as easy for the Senate to make Sulla's command "Cappadocia" as 'Cilicia'. But Magie goes on to reject the name of the command, although it is well attested. He does not seem to notice the alternative conclusion, which (since it does not conflict with our evidence) is obviously preferable: that the Senate originally meant Sulla's command to be of the same nature, and for the same purpose, as that of M. Antonius had been.

[27] It is hard to see on what grounds this can be doubted. Broughton, who lists Sulla as *pro praetore* (similarly Jashemski, *Procons. and Propraet. Imperium* (1950) 68), appears to cite in support of this the fact that he is called *praetor* in *vir. ill.* and *praetorius* by Cicero and Eutropius. The references to Cicero and Eutropius seem to have got in by mistake and should be deleted: they refer to Sulla's rank at the time of the Social

War, which is neither in doubt nor relevant here. The term *praetor* cannot be taken as defining the nature of the *imperium*: it is the common (and perhaps correct) general term for a holder of *imperium* who is not actually a magistrate of senior standing (thus even in Cicero, Livy, and other good sources—see Mommsen, *Staatsr.* ii³ 74, n. 2; 240, n. 5). There is thus nothing to set against the analogy from M. Antonius and later commanders in Cilicia.

[28] For the sources, see above. Plutarch (*Sulla* 5, 3) mentions a special commission to that effect, which can only have been given by the Senate.

[29] Thus, e.g., Magie, l.c. (n. 26, above).

[30] On Cicero and Cappadocia, see *Att.* v 18, 1 and 4; 20, 6; *fam.* ii 17, 7; xv 2, 1 f.; 4, 4 f. Cf. Plut. *Luc.* 6, 1.

[31] There is little precise evidence (see Marquardt, *Staatsverw.* i² 522). Cf. n. 59 (below).

[32] Plut. *Sulla* 5, 3.

[33] Magie on the whole follows Reinach. The latest study of this area that I have seen (Vitucci, *Il Regno di Bitinia* (1953)) offers nothing new on these events; the recent popular work on Mithridates Eupator by A. Duggan departs from the accepted account only by accident and in error.

[34] xxxviii 2–3.

[35] *Mithr.* 10. See further below.

[36] *Sulla* 5, 3 f.

[37] Strabo xii 2, 11 (p. 540). He makes this point quite clear by contrasting the appointment of Ariobarzanes with that (by Antony) of Archelaus, who was a foreigner.

[38] Plut. l.c.

[39] κατάγαγεῖν does not imply more than the restoration of an exile to his country; naturally, it *could* be used of the restoration of a king to his throne; but Plutarch here proceeds to make it clear that he does not mean it.

[40] See n. 37 (above). Reinach, in discussing the family of Ariobarzanes, ignores the explicit Strabo passage.

[41] Justin xxxviii 1, *fin.*–2. Cf. Reinach, *T.R.* 51 f.; *M.E.* 98 f. See further below.

[42] Reinach, ll.cc. (from regnal years on coins).

[43] Justin, l.c. Justin is not usually excessively hostile to Mithridates: the dissatisfaction in Cappadocia may be accepted.

[44] See above. The most dramatic account is in Strabo (l.c.).

[45] Plut. *Sulla* 5, 3. Mithridates' claim that the Cappadocians (i.e., of course, the pro-Pontic party) asked for Gordius as ruler: Justin xxxviii 5, 9. (Justin says 'king'; but that will merely be a minor slip. Trogus probably had some word like ἄρχειν, and Gordius, of course, was the effective regent.) Such a vote was inevitable in the circumstances. Fortunately it is attested and we need not rely on conjecture.

[46] See Plut. l.c.

[47] Calabi (*MAL* (1950) 268 f.) denies that Plutarch is here using the *Memoirs*. But both her arguments in support of her contention are weak: (i) that Plutarch's account of the Cappadocian mission is vague— she stresses the failure to report Sulla's official title; this is due entirely to Plutarch's usual lack of interest in constitutional detail: he does know and report the name of Gordius and even that of the Parthian envoy (probably also correct, since that of Gordius is) and must therefore have had a precise source; (ii) that Sulla himself had no reason to 'write up' his interview with the Parthian envoy, while later writers would be likely to do so; but Sulla, while in the East, must have heard of the fame of Mithridates the Great (even if, for unintelligible reasons, the Senate had not)—there is no reason to doubt that he would think his proud treatment of the great King's envoy one of the highlights of the Cappadocian expedition. On the positive side, Plutarch's source, besides being (as we saw) well

informed, is one that exaggerates Sulla's exploits (e.g. in the insistence on the large enemy losses); and the detailed account of the Chaldaean's prophecy at the end of the interview points unmistakably to Sulla himself as the source: his interest in such things need hardly be discussed.

⁴⁸ See *RE*, s.v. 'Tigranes', coll. 970 f.

⁴⁹ Strabo xi 14, 15 (p. 532); see *RE*, l.c. The date of Tigranes' accession depends entirely on Plut. *Luc.* 21, 6: at the time of his interview with Ap. Claudius Pulcher he is said to have been on the throne for twenty-five years. The figure, in the context, is obviously not warranted precise; nor can we decide for certain whether he saw Ap. Claudius in 71 or in 70. Appius was sent by L. Lucullus before the capture of Amisus (*ibid.* 19) and returned to him before the siege of Sinope (*ibid.* 23). For a time-table of operations, see *RRAM* i 334 f.; ii 1213 f. The year 95, commonly given without query for Tigranes' accession (thus, e.g., by Reinach), is therefore a mere approximation.

⁵⁰ See *RE*, s.v. 'Tomisa', col. 1701. Note that Lucullus later gave the place to Ariobarzanes. It is possible that Sulla tried to cross the Euphrates and was repulsed by the Armenians: he admits (*ap.* Plut. l.c.) 'lingering' (διατρίβειν) upon its banks. But we cannot be sure of this, any more than of the exact chronology. The statement in the text is merely intended as an approximation, sufficient for our purposes.

⁵¹ App. *Mithr.* 10; cf. 57 (Sulla's address to Mithridates). It should be pointed out that Sulla, in his speech, knows only one expulsion of Ariobarzanes, namely that which led to his restoration by M' Aquillius. Before that he has nothing to say except that he restored Ariobarzanes to his country (ἐς Καππαδοκίαν κατήγαγον, explicitly). He adds that *that* was the occasion when Mithridates ought to have protested, or for ever held his peace. Thus Sulla (in his speech) sees himself as the *first* to deprive Mithridates of Cappadocia, so that the King's acquiescence on that occasion is a precedent. This completely rules out the usual modern account, according to which Mithridates at first permitted the installation of Ariobarzanes as King of Cappadocia, only to change his mind and expel him later: acquiescence in his installation is precisely the precedent Sulla wants; yet he has no act of acquiescence to record before his own appearance in Cappadocia. This is well worth pointing out; though, since it occurs in a speech, I have not insisted on it in my principal argument. On Marius' advice to Mithridates, see further below.

⁵² Justin and Appian, ll.cc. Armenian participation in *this* attack is admitted (see, e.g., *RE*, s.v. 'Mithridates', col. 2168; *CAH* ix 238; Reinach, *M.E.* 115 f.). Thus the *communis opinio* must assume, not only the omission in Justin, so conveniently filled up from Plutarch (see above), but also an unattested 'renewal' of the treaty between Mithridates and Tigranes and of their agreement to invade Cappadocia (Reinach, l.c., exemplifies this). The only *attested* agreement of this sort is that (concluded after much negotiation) which led to Ariobarzanes' flight to Rome and ultimately to the mission of Aquillius. This, of course, is long after Sulla's action in Cappadocia.

⁵³ This is nicely illustrated by the way in which Reinach changes his mind about the date of Ariobarzanes' accession, according to the way in which he wants it to fit into the background he has prepared for it (97 B.C. in *T.R.* 184; 95 B.C. in *M.E.* 101), although he claims in each case to have established it from independent and self-contained evidence (incidentally, the same in each case, but differently interpreted).

⁵⁴ *M.E.*, l.c. (Cappadocia—but it applies generally).

⁵⁵ Notably in the case of Ariobarzanes (*T.R.* 60 f.) and in that of Ariarathes Eusebes (*ibid.* 54 f.). But this at once leads to difficulties, which he does not even mention. Thus, if (*T.R.* 61) the lacuna from year 4 to year 12 in the series of Ariobarzanes corresponds to his long exile in the First Mithridatic War (yet can one seriously claim that the King was away from Cappodocia for nine whole years on end?), why is the Third Mithridatic War represented by a gap of only one year (23); and why is there a lacuna of four

years (17 to 20) in Reinach's series at a time (*c.* 80 to 76) when by all accounts Ariobarzanes was for once safely at home?

⁵⁶ Naturally, the margin of error decreases in importance with the length of the reign. Reinach uses these regnal years to make it quite clear that Justin's account of the reign of Ariarathes VII Philometor is over-compressed and thus appears foreshortened (*T.R.* 49 f.); and the fact that we have coins of Ariarathes IX's 13th year (and we happen to know that he died in 87—it is chiefly this independent information that enables us to use the numismatic evidence at all!) effectively traces the story of Mithridates' intervention in Cappadocia back to *c.* 100 (*ibid.* 54 f.; cf. *M.E.* 99).

⁵⁷ The limitations of the method are well illustrated by Reinach's attempt to use it in order to arrive at the dates of Ariobarzanes' reign. His argument is that we have coins up to Ariobarzanes I's 34th year and up to his son's 11th. The son died shortly before Cicero's arrival in Cilicia (see n. 30, above), i.e. in 51; his accession took place when his father abdicated in his favour in front of Pompey, i.e. by late 62 (Val. Max. v 7, *ext.* 2); and Ariobarzanes I himself had gained his throne when Tigranes was already King of Armenia, i.e. after 95 (the falsehood of this statement has, I hope, been demonstrated above). It all fits together well enough, and would be even more convincing if the answer had worked out the same each time. (Cf. n. 53, above.) But on investigation we find that we do not know how long before Cicero's arrival Ariobarzanes II had died, or whether the touching scene recorded by Valerius Maximus took place in 62, in 63, or even earlier; and finally that Justin's account is very summary, as usual, so that, when he says (after reporting Ariobarzanes' appointment to the throne) that Tigranes was 'eo tempore' King of Armenia, we do not know whether he means the time of the King's election by the Cappadocians, that of his recognition by the Senate, or that of his installation (by Sulla, as we have seen)—Justin does not distinguish. Thus it will be found that the coins in this case add nothing whatever to what we can painfully gather from our scattered literary evidence and do not even cut down the margin of error imposed by its inadequacy. This is an extreme instance of Reinach's self-deception.

⁵⁸ Not quite: see Balsdon, *JRS* 29 (1939) 57 f.

⁵⁹ Mrs Atkinson has now usefully drawn attention to this problem, at least as it affects the early Empire (*Historia* 7 (1958) 310 f.). Unfortunately she is quite mistaken in her passing reference to the date of the sortition of provinces in the late Republic: the year 61 (which she cites as typical—though calling it, by a slip, 58) was in fact made very unusual by the delay imposed by the Bona Dea affair and perhaps other matters (see Cic. *Att.* i 13, 5 and 14, 5).

⁶⁰ Cf. Atkinson, l.c.

⁶¹ Sources conveniently collected in *RE*, s.v. 'Tullius', coll. 976 f.

⁶² Thus Cicero suffered a long delay at Ephesus.

⁶³ A random contemporary example is L. Gellius Poplicola, who, while in Athens, offered to reconcile the philosophical schools. He was travelling *pro consule ex praetura* (Cic. *leg.* i 53), almost certainly to Asia.

⁶⁴ Cf., e.g., the case of Q. Cicero in 61—though we do not know how representative it is.

⁶⁵ Plut. *Sulla* 5, 6.

⁶⁶ C. Censorinus (see *RE*, s.v. 'Marcius', col. 1550).

⁶⁷ Thus Münzer (*RE*, l.c.) says: 'vermutlich unter dem Druck der allgemeinen politischen Lage'. But the outbreak of the Social War (if that is what he means) cannot be responsible, since all *iudicia* (except the Varian *quaestio?*) were then suspended (Cic. *Br.* 304; Asc. 73–4 Clark), and Sulla's case would simply not have been proceeded with under this general ordinance. Before the suspension, however, mutual antagonisms were at fever pitch, as the Varian *quaestio* itself shows.

[68] See *Historia* 6 (1957) 319 f. [=pp. 35 f., above].

[69] See *MRR* ii 11 and cf. *Historia, art. cit.* 330 [=p. 45, above].

[70] *Ibid.* 329; cf. my *Foreign Clientelae* 213 f.

[71] Cf. Vell. ii 17.

[72] On the chronology, see Gabba's commentary (pp. 110 f., 114 f.) in his edition of Appian *b.c.* i (1958).

[73] On this and what follows, see Plut. *Mar.* 31; cf. Cic. *ad. Br.* i 5, 3 (the augurate in absence).

[74] The trial of M' Aquillius, usually regarded as a *terminus ante quem*, cannot be dated (see *Historia*, l.c.).

[75] Cicero (l.c.) makes this clear.

[76] See *Historia, art. cit.* 333 [=p. 48, above].

[77] *Ibid.* Cf. *Foreign Clientelae* 211 f.

[78] *RE*, s.v. 'Cornelius', no. 178.

[79] See *Historia, art. cit.* 332 [= p. 46, above].

[80] *Athenaeum* N.S. 34 (1956) 120 f. The conclusions there reached are assumed as the basis of the present investigation.

[81] This corrects the chronology proposed l.c.: I was there unwise enough to take over the accepted chronology of events in Asia Minor without closer scrutiny.

[82] Thus the question left open, *Athenaeum, art. cit.* 115, n. 4, receives a satisfactory answer.

[83] See *art. cit.* 116. I should like to thank the Durham Colleges for continued financial support of my work, and Mr I. J. C. Foster, Librarian of the Durham University School of Oriental Studies, for his constant readiness to give me the benefit of his encyclopaedic knowledge of the ancient East.

Ancient Alexandria

WHEN Alexander the Great came to take possession of Egypt in 332 B.C., he was struck by the lack of a first-class port and commercial centre, despite the opportunities offered by the Egyptian village of Rhacotis and its environs, on the western edge of the Nile Delta. He at once decided to build a city on that site—one of the dozens of Alexandrias that were to arise along the conqueror's route as far as Chodjend and the Indus valley. It is doubtful whether he foresaw how much more important than its namesakes it was to be; and, by the time of his death in 323, little progress had been made with the building. Ptolemy, his successor in Egypt, at first resided in the historic capital Memphis. But before long he brought off a *coup* that was to have decisive consequences. When the cortège of the great King arrived in Syria on its way to Macedonia, he succeeded in diverting it to Egypt on the pretext that Alexander had wished to be buried in the oasis of the god Ammon. But the body never reached the oasis. In its sarcophagus of carved gold, it lay in Memphis, while Ptolemy had a great mausoleum, the *Sema*, built for it in the centre of Alexander's city. It was the transfer of Alexander to this resting-place that marked the beginning of the city's greatness. Alexandria now became Ptolemy's capital and was soon regarded as the centre of the Hellenistic world, which continued to dream of the King who had once united it under his rule.

In due course, Ptolemy himself was buried there, near the *Sema*; and the burial-places of his successors clustered around these two, until Cleopatra built a mausoleum for herself and Antony, fittingly placing it at some distance from the others. That city of the royal dead, with the *Sema* at its centre, retained the name of Demas (from a Greek word for 'body'), which has passed into Arabic as Kom ed-Demas. There, perhaps right down to the sixteenth century, the Moslem conquerors honoured the tomb of the 'King and Prophet Iskander', probably where the Mosque of the Prophet Daniel—connected by Arab legend with the foundation of Alexandria—now stands. The search for the tomb has occupied the thoughts and dreams of many men. About A.D. 1850, a Greek claimed to have seen the body underneath the Mosque; but excavation has proved fruitless. A more reliable witness—an Egyptian scholar—not long afterwards, claimed to have come across some ruins, perhaps belonging to the royal necropolis, in the vicinity. Possibly the area round the Mosque and the site of the fort of Kom ed-Dik has not yet revealed all its secrets. But whatever may one day be found, it is not likely to be the body of Alexander. The splendid golden sarcophagus was removed by a Ptolemy in financial difficulties, and one made of glass substituted. It is improbable that this fragile container can have protected the royal body through so many centuries of troubled history. In fact, even John Chrysostom no longer knew it about A.D. 400.

The city itself was laid out by the Rhodian architect Dinocrates, on a rectangular grid, with all its streets wide enough to take wheeled traffic, and two majestic central avenues, over 100 feet wide, probably intersecting at the *Sema*. The chief avenue—the Canopus Road—followed the line of the present Route d'Aboukir and its continuations. The city lay between the sea and Lake Mareotis (now Mariout). The Lake was connected with the Nile and with the Mediterranean, and the Nile with the Red Sea, by means of navigable canals; so that Alexandria stood at the head of the ancient equivalent of the Suez Canal. Excellent port and dock facilities were the foundation of its prosperity. A large harbour on the Lake, said to have been even busier than the sea harbours, sheltered ships coming from the Nile and the Red Sea. In the North, the island of Pharos (Ras el-Tin) provided a natural breakwater for a sea harbour. On its eastern tip the first two Ptolemies built the great lighthouse that became one of the seven wonders of the world and has immortalized the name of Pharos in many modern languages. It was made of white stone, in three storeys of different shape, and its total height was certainly over 400 feet. The ramp leading up to the first platform, over half-way up, was wide enough for two horsemen to pass each other.

The island was joined to the city by the Heptastadion, a causeway carrying a road and an aqueduct, pierced by two openings wide enough to permit the passing of sea-going ships between the two harbours thus created—the Great Harbour to the East and the Eunostos, or 'Safe Return', to the West. In the Middle Ages, the Heptastadion silted up and became the centre of the surviving township. Napoleon found about seven thousand people living there—all that was left of Alexandria; and it is still a populous 'old city' in modern Alexandria.

The centre of the city, in the district called Brukhion, roughly between the present railway station and the sea, was a Royal City not unlike that of Imperial Peking. Every Ptolemy tried to add something to its splendour, and it finally covered an area of over a square mile. It was this, even more than the colonnades and monuments of the wealthy city outside, that gained for Alexandria the epithets 'golden' and 'fair'—the latter, indeed, became almost its stock epithet. In addition to the palace buildings—the administrative centre of Egypt as well as the King's residence—it contained the gardens (including a zoo, for which rare animals were imported from every country of the then known world), the Museum and the Library.

The Museum was technically a temple of the Muses, governed by a priest whom Ptolemy appointed. But the Muses, of course, were the goddesses of the arts and sciences, and their temple was intended, even by Ptolemy I, to become a centre of literature and learning. Under the guidance and personal interest of the first two Ptolemies, it became an Academy of Letters and Science, whose members—at times as many as a hundred—received generous emoluments. An Alexandrian was later to write, with pardonable exaggeration, that it was in Alexandria that Greek culture had been preserved during the unsettled age of the early Successors.

The Library attached to the Museum soon became the greatest in the Greek world, as the early Ptolemies spent vast sums to enrich it with rare originals and complete its collection of Greek books. By the time it was burnt down, during Caesar's war against the Alexandrians, it numbered approximately a million volumes. About the middle of the third century B.C., the poet Callimachus classified the collection and compiled a catalogue—the first systematic catalogue in Western history, and an outstanding achievement even by Alexandrian standards. When complete, it filled one hundred and twenty volumes, and each entry gave historical and critical information about work and author. Much of our knowledge of lost Greek literature ultimately goes back to this scholarly librarian.

The Fellows of the Museum were the King's employees, and they were not allowed to forget it. The poets among them had to produce Court inanities that would make a modern Poet Laureate refuse his pension. The engineers had to entertain the Court with mechanical toys. An outstanding mathematician and astronomer, Conon of Samos, surpassed them all in flattery: when a lock of Queen Berenice's hair, which she had dedicated in a temple, disappeared, he discovered it as a constellation in the sky, and the poets then had to rush to immortalize the miracle in verse. There were more onerous official duties and more grievous limitations. When Ptolemy II decided to marry his sister—an Egyptian custom as abhorrent to Greek opinion as to ours—the poets had to win over public opinion by comparing the union to that of Zeus and Hera. A philosopher's courses (probably far from first-rate) were stopped as contrary to public policy. Scholars might suddenly lose the royal favour, particularly after a change of monarch: thus Demetrius of Phalerum, who had organized the Museum for Ptolemy I, died in disgrace under his successor. The struggles of literary and academic coteries were embittered by attempts to secure royal intervention.

Oratory, speculative and moral philosophy, and the serious study of history could not flourish in this atmosphere. But, up to a point, it proved to be ideal for other branches of study: philology, literary scholarship, mathematics and science. To the modern mind they make odd bedfellows. But the fact that in these, and in these alone, the Alexandrian achievement was unsurpassed during antiquity is explained by the important qualities they shared: lavish expenditure of money could build up research schools and traditions, and could attract the best men in those fields from many different countries; and, above all, such studies were politically innocuous.

The serious study of language and literature was born at Alexandria. The categories and terminology of grammar, as they are still taught in our schools, were first properly worked out there; and generations of work culminated in the Greek grammar of Dionysius Thrax, written in the second century B.C. and still used as a textbook in Victorian schools. As Gilbert Murray has observed, its record almost equals that of Euclid. Aristophanes of Byzantium—the names alone show how men from all over the Greek world flocked to the Museum—introduced the marking of accents and punctuation, though centuries passed before these great reforms firmly established themselves outside Alexandria. He also compiled a dictionary of word usage—the ancestor of the *New English Dictionary* and of Fowler! All this philological work was based on a thorough knowledge of Greek literature. Most of our Greek texts, especially of poets, ultimately derive from the work of Alexandrian scholars using the resources of their Library. Works were edited with detailed commentaries, and monographs appeared on everything that could possibly be made the subject of detailed inquiry. A modern Arts don would have felt quite at home.

Literature, however, was not only discussed, but produced. Alexandria at once became the centre of living Greek poetry, and writers flocked there to enjoy the congenial atmosphere and the kings' munificence. New literary movements arose, and the faction fights of literary coteries were carried on with as much vigour and, among a small sophisticated public, aroused as much excitement as in modern Paris. The most famous quarrel was that between Callimachus and Apollonius. Apollonius defended and practised the writing of epic as the highest literary form, though he adapted it to the interests—chiefly in love and in travel—of his contemporaries. Callimachus, the scholarly librarian—like many a modern don, he had started life as a schoolmaster before winning a Fellowship at the Museum—aimed at a different kind of poetry. Himself one of the greatest of the Alexandrian poets, he showed that he was well able to write works in the ancient manner. But he came to think 'a big book a big evil'; and he specialized in shorter works, finished with elaborate care and art and impeccable in every word. In this great quarrel, their fellow writers ranged themselves on either side. As was natural in Alexandria, it soon developed political implications, and Apollonius had to leave the country and settled at Rhodes.

Alexandrian literature, on the whole, henceforth followed the path of Callimachus. But it is unlikely that the victory of Apollonius would have made much difference in the long run. The vigorous literary life of Alexandria was confined to a small circle of intellectuals, most of them both scholars and poets, who wrote only for one another and for the few like them elsewhere. Before long, they made the writing of poetry a specialized, esoteric craft, far removed from the business of ordinary life and the concerns of ordinary readers: they did not have to worry about the sale of their books. During the first two or three generations, admirable work was produced. In addition to Callimachus, we need only mention the Sicilian Theocritus, whose *Idylls* range from artificial pastoral poems to scenes of Alexandrian life and panegyrics on Ptolemy II and his kingdom. But gradually poetry degenerated into an erudite game, not unlike some branches of modern art. In due course it was played out, and—as the political decline of the Hellenistic world became irrevocable—there was not enough interest left to change the rules and start again. The atmosphere of literary Alexandria at its best, however, is immortalized in Callimachus' epitaph on his friend, the poet Heraclitus—the poem that, in Cory's sensitive translation, is probably better known to the English reader than any other Alexandrian literary product.[1]

The Alexandrian achievement in mathematics and science has naturally attracted a great deal of attention in our scientific age. The Museum incorporated the tradition of Aristotle. Demetrius of Phalerum, who had known the Master, was one of the first pupils of his successor, the philosopher and naturalist Theophrastus. Strato 'the Physicist', another pupil of Theophrastus, whom he ultimately succeeded in Athens, spent several years in Alexandria, where he was appointed tutor to Ptolemy II. As we have seen, there were good reasons why Demetrius' chief interests, philosophy and oratory, could not take root: Demetrius' own fate was a clear warning. Thus the scientific element in the Aristotelian tradition prevailed. Euclid, during the reign of Ptolemy I, laid a solid mathematical foundation, establishing Alexandria as the centre of this branch of study, in which the Greeks had for centuries been interested. It was here that Apollonius of Perge invented conics; and the great Syracusan Archimedes went to study at the Museum and dedicated several of his works to friends he had made there. The chief application of mathematics was in the field of astronomy. Aristarchus of Samos, who first tried to measure the distance of the sun and the moon, and who discovered the rotation and revolution of the earth, was probably one of the Alexandrian circle, whose members he knew well. Hipparchus, the greatest of ancient mathematical astronomers, worked in second-century Alexandria, when the initial brilliance was already fading. It was he who discovered the precession of the equinoxes, and calculated the length of the solar year to within a few minutes, and of the lunar month to within a second. In geography, the greatest work was done by Eratosthenes, who for half of his long life was Chief Librarian. He first used observations of latitude and longitude to measure the earth, attempted a map of the world as he knew it, and—most important of all—described the products and the inhabitants of its various regions. Geography was only a very small part of the interests of the greatest polymath after Aristotle. In his own day and for long after, he was equally well known as a poet, philosopher, historian, literary critic and grammarian, mathematician and astronomer. Better than any other man, Eratosthenes epitomizes the intellectual life of early Alexandria. But scholarship had already advanced beyond the stage when such omniscience was possible, or even an ideal widely aimed at: the academic backbiters of Alexandria give him the nickname of 'Beta', apparently because none of the experts considered him first-rate in any single field. His like was not seen again until the Italian Renaissance.

Many names could be added, well worthy of comparison with the great figures of modern science. But enough has been said to show the genius of the Alexandrian achievement. Yet the modern reader cannot help asking why that achievement was not greater still. Why, in fact, did Alexandria not anticipate the modern development of science, with all its social and political consequences? In the case of the first flowering of Greek science—in early Ionia—the question is fairly easily answered by reference to political history: the Ionian cities lost their independence, and their upper class exhausted its strength in useless attempts to regain it. Fifth-century Athens, which inherited their achievement, for various reasons could not provide an atmosphere that encouraged scientific research and progress. Where Alexandria is concerned, in some important respects the answer is very much the same, although the process of political decline was less spectacular and cataclysmic. By 200 B.C., Ptolemaic Egypt, and before long the whole Hellenistic East, was coming under the

N

tutelage of Rome; and Rome—the new centre of, and heir to, Hellenistic politics and civilization—was a society singularly ill-suited to scientific inquiry.

The decline of Alexandria, in particular, was due largely to its own kings and citizens. The latter exhausted themselves by taking sides in the fratricidal wars of the former and often choosing the wrong side. The city mob, as in other unsettled states, acquired the habit of turbulence and king-making. The kings, when they gained the upper hand, retaliated. Citizens were massacred and—more important in the long run—the privileges of the body politic were whittled down. The Royal City, of course, had always been outside the civic jurisdiction. But, in the city itself, as in other Hellenistic cities, the Greek element must originally have been supreme, and the non-Greeks—Egyptians and Asiatics, of whom there were large numbers in the cosmopolitan capital—merely resident aliens with certain corporate privileges. By the end of the Ptolemaic era, the evidence reveals a very different state of affairs. The Greeks still had the highest status and might alone call themselves Alexandrian citizens; but they had lost their Council (which they in vain petitioned the early Roman emperors to restore) and thereby, to a large extent, the power of co-ordinated political action. Egyptian infiltration into the citizen body became difficult to restrain; and the Jews—the largest of the foreign communities—were strongly organized and formed a city within the city.

This background of royal poverty and instability, and of civic turbulence and decline, did not favour the continuation of outstanding research work. Though an isolated genius like Hipparchus, after 150 B.C., could still produce great work, on the whole the glories of the third century were no more equalled in science than in literature. The scientific tradition showed more life than the literary, and it continued until well into the Roman period, after 30 B.C. But various factors combined to prevent real progress. Three hundred years after Hipparchus, the geographer Ptolemy admiringly based his treatise on that distant predecessor. Little—and less that was of any value—had been done in the interval. As is well known, less still was added during many centuries after Ptolemy.

The question arises, in an even more obvious form, with regard to the applied sciences. Heron, whose dates are unknown, but who may have lived after the beginning of our era, besides doing some important work in mathematics, developed mechanics with remarkable success. He anticipated many modern inventions, particularly those based on the compression of air and of steam. But his vacuum pumps and steam-engines—for they fully deserve the modern names—were used in elaborate toys, and in temple 'miracles' to impress the ignorant. The modern student is utterly baffled by the failure of Heron and his contemporaries to grasp their potential importance. Why did a government that was continually seeking devices for keeping the profits from its controlled economy on the highest level fail to perceive the vast increase that might result from some simple form of mechanization? Why did private citizens and their associations fail to seize the opportunity? The stock answer—if we may ignore writers who like to postulate the existence of mysterious 'historical forces' —is that slave and serf labour was working so satisfactorily that those who used it had no incentive to look for anything better. Yet this is no more true of Alexandria than of England in the age of the Industrial Revolution. If an industrial revolution *had* occurred in Alexandria in the first century A.D., historians would quickly have identified all the conditions that made it 'inevitable'. While the Egyptian countryside soon began to show the marks of the cold-blooded Roman exploitation, with the peasants driven beyond endurance, Alexandria, together with a few of the smaller towns, was a prosperous centre of commerce and industry. Brought by merchants sailing before the monsoons or crossing the desert along the caravan routes, then carried up the network of Egyptian canals, the cargoes of the East continued to pour into the city, for manufacture and often for re-export. Indians were a common sight on the quaysides of Alexandria in the first century A.D. Alexandrian glass—both mass-produced and luxury ware— spread all over the Empire and well beyond it. Imported metals were worked into manufactured goods that spread as far as Gaul and India. East Africans, whose descendants, centuries later, were to be dressed in Lancashire cottons, wore garments specially produced for their tastes in the workshops of Egyptian towns and of the great city itself.

Yet, although for some time prosperous, Alexandria was never free from competition. In most of her markets other regions competed, usually with increasing success. An industrial revolution, led either by the Government on the land, or by private industrialists in the city, might well, in retrospect, seem inevitable. Yet, of all who applauded Heron's machines, no one envisaged a practical application for them. To this, as to other major historical puzzles, a complete answer is hardly possible. But some of the important factors that were responsible for this omission, as for the decline of science, are worth stressing. Literature ended by becoming an erudite game; and science, though probably somewhat later, followed the same course. Played according to traditional esoteric rules within a small circle, it had no contact with the world at large; and by the time of Heron both sides had lost the capacity to imagine any contact between the two. Scientists themselves tended to be more interested in the game than in the truth—though, at their best, they recognized that the truth was part of the game: in Ptolemy's geography ingenuity often seems to count for more than truth, and his very admiration for Hipparchus is for the masterly player rather than for his discoveries. Political factors worked in the same direction. Alexandria, however prosperous, was merely a provincial city in the Roman Empire. Among responsible citizens, the long decline had produced a longing for stability, combined with an admiration for the glories of the past. The Romans had brought stability and prosperity. The glories of the past were still admired; but responsible citizens accepted their new position and were grateful for it; and the mentality thus produced made revolutionary departures in any sphere psychologically impossible. Behind its prosperous façade, Alexandria was a middle-aged provincial city.

It was the Alexandrian populace, cut off from scientific or economic development, that understood that the prosperity was hollow. The Ptolemies themselves had had to curb the spirit of their city. Yet, when Caesar reached Alexandria, and again when Cleopatra, for the last time, made the city a great capital, the ordinary citizens united behind their rulers against the foreign invader. But, on both occasions, they had again joined the losing side. Just as important—the Jews of Alexandria, on both occasions, joined the winning side; and Caesar and Augustus showed their gratitude by confirming and extending the privileges of the Jews.

As a result, anti-Semitism became a feature of Alexandrian life and politics. While great philosophers like Philo, within the highly Hellenized Jewish community, were trying to establish a synthesis of Greek and Jewish thought, and were, it seems, socially accepted by the Greek upper class, mob orators kept rousing the populace against the Jews as symbols of the foreign domination. At the same time, the attitude of the Roman masters was anxiously watched. The death of Tiberius (A.D. 37) brought young Gaius ('Caligula') to the throne, a prince with a family tradition of friendship for the Alexandrian Greeks; at the same time, the Governor, Avillius Flaccus, endangered by Court intrigues, sought their good-will by withdrawing his protection from the Jews. The result was the first pogrom in Western history—and, if we may believe Philo's account, one not often surpassed in ferocity. It ended with the removal of Flaccus; and soon after Gaius himself was dead, assassinated by his own Guard. Claudius, who succeeded him (A.D. 41), wrote a stern letter to the Alexandrians, Greek and Jewish. Friendly up to a point, but giving a firm warning to troublemakers, it is one of the most valuable documents we have, both on Alexandrian history at this time and on the Emperor. Henceforth, though tension remained, superficially there was calm, until the Jewish revolt in the second century, in which the Alexandrian Jews became involved, led, after much bloodshed and damage in the city, to a final solution on Hitlerian lines.

Alexandrian anti-Semitism was merely an aspect of the political frustration felt by the populace, and was closely bound up with its resentment of Roman domination. This is shown by those remarkable documents, the *Acts of the Pagan Martyrs*, which, in varying degrees, combine anti-Jewish and anti-Roman feeling, the latter being distinctly and without exception the more important and often explicitly the basis of the former. This *genre* of popular Alexandrian literature—far beneath the notice of serious writers—has come down to us in papyrus fragments, extending over more than two centuries. They show that the appeal of these stories—which, with all their naïveté, have a life that was singularly lacking in 'serious' literature—was not dulled, any more than that of modern thrillers or romances, by endless repetition of stereotyped characters and situations. They tell the story of the heroism of Alexandrian Greeks accused before the Emperor's Court Tribunal;

and since we know something—not usually to their credit—about several of these heroes, it is clear that they are a kind of historical romance. The long popularity of such pot-boilers shows, as nothing else can, the frustrated resentment of the ordinary Greek citizens of Alexandria under their provincial prosperity.

That prosperity did not last long. The city shared in the fortunes of the Roman East and knew many vicissitudes. There as elsewhere, Hadrian indulged his passion for building; and during his reign Alexandrian prosperity probably reached its summit. With the mad Caracalla, who ordered a massacre there half a century later, it came to an end. Aurelian dismantled the city's fortifications (A.D. 279); Diocletian captured it after a siege (297) and put up the triumphal column now known, by a quirk of tradition, as 'Pompey's Pillar'. Yet the city long remained 'fair Alexandria', one of the wonders of the world. The hero of a late Greek novel, on entering Alexandria, is overcome by its beauty, which he describes in some detail, with particular stress on the *Sema* and the colonnades. Byzantine Alexandria, the seat of one of the most powerful bishops, regained much of its political importance and continued its tradition of resentment against the Imperial power. Athanasius, in the fourth century, is only the greatest of many of these ecclesiastical politicians—in turn persecutor and persecuted, absolute ruler of Egypt and fugitive in the desert, honoured by emperors who needed his support and attacked by emperors who feared his power and ruthlessness. But renewed political importance did not revive the spirit that had inspired the first century of the city's life. In a disintegrating world, neither the Empire nor the Church encouraged advance or adventure; and under the Christian Empire great men did not devote themselves to science and letters. The Christian city spent its new energy in sectarian civil war and alternating persecutions, while literacy and the standard of living decreased, and the glories of Alexandrian architecture became quarries for building materials.

The end came in 642, with the Arab conquest. The Arabs, at this time, were interested neither in the sea nor in Greek tradition. For the first time, Alexandria found itself under the rule of an entirely different civilization and turned inward upon Egypt. It ceased to be a cosmopolitan city and, as the great new capital of Cairo eclipsed it, soon sank to provincial level. The discovery of

America and of the Cape of Good Hope finally destroyed what commercial importance it had managed to regain over the centuries, leaving a miserable fishing village. It was only the rise of modern Egypt, in the nineteenth and particularly in the twentieth century, that brought new life to Alexandria. The fishing village has grown into a modern city. But the Suez Canal now inevitably prevents it from fully regaining its ancient importance, even within the Mediterranean. And no foreseeable development seems likely to make the Mediterranean again the centre of the Western world.

NOTE

[1] The poem is found in many standard collections (e.g. *The Oxford Book of Greek Verse in Translation*, p. 584, no. 513).

Alexander the Great and the Loneliness of Power[1]

FEW episodes in history have fascinated as many readers and listeners as the bright star of Alexander the Great shooting across the firmament, to mark the end of an era and the beginning of another. From schoolboys wide-eyed at the great adventure to old men moralizing on philosopher kings, we all interpret the great drama in terms of our experience and our dreams. It has gained a secure standing among the Myths of Ancient Greece, ranking (one may say) with the story of Odysseus or of Oedipus. Needless to say, the history of Alexander III of Macedon has to some extent been lost underneath the myth-making, and some aspects of it can perhaps no longer be salvaged. But the tragedy of the historical Alexander is at least as fascinating as the best of both the ancient and the modern legends; and it is this that, across the fragments of the history, I want to sketch on this occasion.[2]

Macedonia, during twenty years or so in the fourth century B.C., had been raised by Philip II from a semi-barbarian feudal state on the borders of civilized Greece to the leading rank among the powers of the Greek world. But, as so often in the history of nations rising to sudden greatness, this had done little to civilize the primitive passions and ways of thought of the people and even of the ruling class. Philip had tried to Hellenize his court, where Greeks and Macedonian nobles mingled freely; but their mutual suspicions were not eliminated, particularly as the Macedonians, on the whole, provided the soldiers and administrators, while the Greeks, on the whole, provided the cultural prestige. As far as the Macedonian barons themselves were concerned, Philip had tried to curb the traditional feudal anarchy by methods not unlike those of the French crown in the seventeenth century. The nobles had to some extent been brought under the direct control of the court; but their connection with the feudal levy of their districts was not broken, and the feudal rivalries were merely transmuted into court intrigues.

One of these intrigues finally led to a serious estrangement between Philip and his wife Olympias and crown prince Alexander. Olympias, Alexander and their adherents had to leave the country; and though Alexander himself was apparently allowed to return, his chances of retaining his position were not rated very highly either by himself or by others competent to judge. Then, in 336 B.C., Philip was assassinated in very mysterious circumstances. We cannot quite penetrate the mystery; but in any case, Alexander was the one who profited.[3] Antipater (one of the most prominent nobles) had everything all prepared and at once produced the young man to the army, which swore allegiance to him. The opposing faction (led by one Attalus), which only a little earlier had carried all before it, was taken entirely by surprise. Charged with having instigated the assassination (which was absurd, in the circumstances), it was wiped out even to infants in arms, and Alexander's rule was made secure.[4]

The King was secure, but far from all-powerful. We must not think of this boy of less than twenty in terms of the great leader he turned out to be. For the moment he was a youth raised to power by a clique of powerful nobles, who no doubt expected to rule through him. So, in addition to his numerous foreign problems (barbarian invasions, Greek insurrections, and the war against Persia that Philip had already begun and from which his successor could not withdraw even if he had wanted to), Alexander, on a long view, was faced with an even more formidable internal problem: how to assert his independence and to become King in fact as well as in name.

The most powerful of all noble families was that of Parmenio. He had been Philip's most trusted general and had followed his master in turning to the faction headed by Attalus, who had, in fact, become his son-in-law. Philip's assassination took him entirely by surprise. He was away in Asia at the time, commanding the advance guard that had secured a bridgehead there, and Attalus was with him. As a result, they seem to have been a little out of touch with the intrigues at court—and this, perhaps, cost Philip his life. However, once they were confronted with the accomplished fact of Alexander's succession, they had to submit or rebel. Rebellion was dangerous, with the home army firmly won over to Alexander; and with wars to fight on all frontiers,

Parmenio was probably too much of a staunch Macedonian to consider treason. Moreover, unlike Attalus (whose case was now hopeless), he was not irretrievably committed: Alexander would welcome his allegiance and be prepared to pay for it. Parmenio swiftly decided to throw his full weight behind Alexander. He personally saw to the elimination of his son-in-law Attalus and in return secured his own terms. When Alexander crossed to Asia in 334, after settling all wars and revolts in Europe, Antipater (his chief sponsor) was left behind with half the Macedonian forces to look after Europe; but Parmenio and his family and supporters were firmly entrenched in the army that went with the King. Parmenio's eldest son Philotas commanded the famous Macedonian cavalry (the 'Companions'); his second son commanded the most important infantry force (the 'hypaspists'); his brother Asander was in charge of the light cavalry; and many known adherents of the family (we need only mention Coenus, a son-in-law of Parmenio, and his brother Cleander, probably Parmenio's trusted aide) held other high posts. Parmenio himself was in charge of the whole infantry force and acted as the King's second-in-command and chief of staff. In view of his experience and Alexander's age, it was no doubt expected that he would take practical charge of the war against Persia.[5]

The loyalty of these men, in the war against Persia, was not in question. For one thing, it was their own war, begun, with their enthusiastic agreement, under Philip, and waged by Parmenio long before Alexander's accession. Alexander was merely following in his father's footsteps. Moreover, nearly all possible pretenders had now been killed off, and there was no one who could rally support in a bid for the throne. But Alexander found himself in a position intolerable to a man of his temperament. Screened off from personal command of his forces, he was the puppet of a faction of powerful nobles, ruling at their mercy.

The next few years saw Alexander's great victories, in which the main forces of the Persian Empire were defeated and Darius left a fugitive (finally killed by his own nobles), while Alexander emerged as the unchallenged ruler of the Empire west of the Euphrates and eastward well into Iran.[6] Throughout this period of his greatest glory he was ably supported by his commanders. But as he became better known and showed those qualities of courage and leadership that won him the enthusiastic allegiance of his men, he carefully used all opportunities of undermining the position of his excessively powerful subordinates. After the first victory, soon after the crossing to Asia, Parmenio's brother Asander was moved from his field command to become governor of the first province of the Empire to be taken over by the Macedonians (that of Lydia). It was, of course, a great honour; but in fact it turned out a loss rather than a gain to Parmenio. The field command was lost to him, while his brother was soon merely one governor among many and, in spite of distinguished service in his province, was before long inconspicuously removed from it and given a minor assignment. Moreover, those in Alexander's confidence now apparently began to spread rumours distinctly unfavourable to Parmenio. (These can be traced back to the Greek Callisthenes, a nephew of Aristotle and an enthusiastic admirer of Philip and Alexander, who had joined the expedition in order to sing its praises to the Greek world.) It was said that on various critical occasions Parmenio had given Alexander advice that the King had ignored—luckily for himself, as it had turned out; and that in battle Parmenio was no longer up to his old strength and had had to be rescued from defeat by Alexander. All this was far from true; but it was given a shadow of plausibility by the fact that in battle Parmenio normally had the difficult assignment of holding the enemy's main forces on one wing, while Alexander made the decisive breakthrough on the other. In this way, gradually, Alexander won the loyalty of the army away from him. At the same time, his adherents were kept under close watch: we know that Philotas' mistress was suborned to spy on her lover and report to one of Alexander's trusted officers.[7]

As the victorious advance continued into Iran, tension between Alexander and many of the great nobles increased. They had no intention of going on fighting and marching for ever. After gaining glory and plunder, they wanted to settle down to rule the conquered and enjoy the fruits of victory. Alexander, on the contrary, now claimed to be the lawful successor of the Persian kings (he even charged Darius with having been a usurper!) and would certainly not be satisfied with anything less than the conquest of the whole of the Empire up to the Indus. Moreover, he knew that he would have to conciliate his new subjects and win their support;

and this applied particularly to the Persian aristocracy, who were the traditional administrators of the Empire. Above all (perhaps), he liked being Great King, with all the pomp and ceremonial that went with the title. In his relations with Asiatics (many of whom were now promoted to positions of honour and responsibility) he behaved entirely as they expected their Great King to behave. Naturally, this policy could not be fully carried out until Parmenio's power had been dealt its final blow: his family were among the most vocal objectors to it.

It is hard to separate personal antagonism from political opposition in all this. But the result, in any case, was to increase tension and make conflict inevitable. In Media Alexander took an important step: he left Parmenio behind in charge of the lengthening supply-lines. The general had no reasonable grounds for objecting to this; but it meant, in effect, that the King had got rid of his overpowering presence. Soon after, Parmenio's younger son, who had commanded the hypaspists, died. Philotas, his elder brother, had to stay behind to see to his funeral. This was clearly Alexander's chance, and he seized it at once. A few days after Philotas rejoined the camp, a 'conspiracy against the King' was discovered. The alleged instigator (a very obscure person) was killed while resisting arrest, but Philotas was somehow implicated. In a tense and anxious situation Alexander staged his *coup d'état*. We have a vivid description of it in our sources. Some of the King's trusted boyhood friends, in the meantime promoted to minor (though not yet major) commands, were detailed to surround Philotas' quarters with their own detachments. Struck out of the blue, Philotas could not resist and was arrested. The King at once put him on trial for high treason before the army. The army, of course, was stunned by the incident. Since the massacre at the beginning of the reign, there had been no outward sign of conflict among their commanders. But although no proof of Philotas' implication in the conspiracy could be produced, the King made it a question of confidence between himself and Philotas and demanded the death penalty. He thought that he could now use the army for the final overthrow of Parmenio's power. As usual, he had judged rightly. It is noticeable how in politics as in fighting Alexander's character appears consistent and unmistakable: never rushing things, always carefully planning further ahead than the enemy could see, but never missing the chance of striking the decisive blow when it presented itself, and then leaving the enemy no hope of resistance or recovery. Some of Parmenio's old adherents had been won over to abandon the declining cause. Coenus, for instance, was one of the most eager prosecutors. This must have helped to persuade the army. Philotas was condemned and at once executed.

A more delicate task remained. Parmenio could not be tried before his own men for crimes which there was no evidence that he had committed. The King could not risk failure. It was only after his death that stories of his planning treason appeared, and it was even said that Philotas had confessed this. But at the time there was only one thing to do. Fortunately Coenus (as we have seen) had been won over, and with him his brother Cleander, who was Parmenio's second-in-command in Media. This facilitated matters. A secret messenger was sent to assassinate the old general, with Cleander's co-operation. Though this provoked ominous unrest among the army, there was nothing the men could now do. Alexander had finally gained his independence. In Europe, Antipater remained, too powerful to be touched from a distance. But that could wait: at least he was too far away to interfere with the King.

There followed a series of spectacular trials of Parmenio's adherents. Not all were convicted: Alexander could not afford a wholesale slaughter of the Macedonian nobility and, as in military pursuit, he knew where to call a halt. But the final result was a clean sweep. All those who had not left the faction in time, or could be trusted to submit quietly now, were eliminated, and the King's trusted friends—especially those prominent in the *coup d'état* against Philotas—were promoted. The chief of these men, Hephaestion, whom Alexander called his *alter ego*, now became commander of half the Companion cavalry. The other half, in a characteristic gesture, went to a dour old Macedonian, Clitus.[8]

Naturally, much bitterness remained. Not long after, this erupted in an ugly incident at Samarcand. At a drinking party (such as were common at the half-barbarian court of Macedon) Clitus took offence at a casual remark of Alexander's. Tempers flared up, stimulated by alcohol, and finally Alexander killed Clitus with his own hand. The deed itself was merely manslaughter, significant (apart from the light it casts on the Macedonian court) only as a symptom of continuing tension. But what followed was of outstanding importance. It shows, more than almost any other incident, Alexander's ability to seize a chance offered and turn it to decisive advantage, even where (as in this instance) he had not planned to prepare it.[9]

Alexander now shut himself up in his tent and proclaimed overwhelming remorse for what he had done, and a determination to expiate it by fasting to death. The army was utterly thunderstruck by this. But gradually the realization began to sink in of what it would mean to them, if the King died; they would face an almost hopeless retreat from Samarcand, with no one to command them and the barbarians taking full advantage of their weakness. So, on the third day, they sent envoys to plead with Alexander to change his mind. When they passed a resolution posthumously convicting Clitus of treason, and thereby legitimizing Alexander's action, he let himself be persuaded. He now knew that he could rely on the army against anyone—and so did whoever might be concerned. As the historian Curtius remarks, the death of Clitus was the end of freedom. Alexander now regularly wore an adaptation of Persian royal dress, and before long he married an Iranian princess. This would have been unthinkable a few months earlier.

However, he now went too far. Pressing home his advantage, he tried to unify his court ceremonial on a Persian basis. Hitherto he had had to keep up two entirely separate establishments: a traditional one, in which he was the first among peers, for Greeks and Macedonians, and an elaborate Persian one, in which he was the Great King, for Asiatics. He now tried to take the major step towards abolishing the former by making prostration (the ordinary mode of saluting the Great King) compulsory for Europeans. His friend Hephaestion undertook to arrange the first precedents informally at a dinner-party. He probably did not expect any serious opposition. But things went unexpectedly wrong. The Greek Callisthenes, now thoroughly disillusioned with Alexander, who from being the leader of the Greeks had become an Oriental despot, refused to perform the ceremony; and when the Persian nobles one after another duly performed it, falling on their faces in all their stately robes, a Macedonian officer burst out laughing. In a rage, Alexander had to call it off.[10]

It was his first serious setback. As usual, he had been quick to learn by his mistake and had cut his losses. But the defeat had been beyond disguise. Callisthenes' part was significant: it was clear that Alexander had lost the sympathy of thinking Greeks—even of those who had once hailed him enthusiastically as a divinely appointed leader. Callisthenes, of course, could not live much longer. He was soon executed on a trumped-up charge of having instigated some page-boys to assassinate the King.[11] But this, though it satisfied Alexander's resentment and demonstrated his power, merely made the hatred of most Greek intellectuals for him permanent and incurable. He was now committed to looking chiefly to Asia.

The memory of purges and murders could best be wiped out by military success. In a brilliant campaign in India, the army was reunited behind its invincible leader. He seems also now to have reorganized it in such a way that the four trusted men who had taken part in the arrest of Philotas became the marshals of the Empire. Hephaestion, the chief of them, combined the positions of second-in-command and Grand Vizier.[12] At the same time, the training of natives in the Macedonian fashion was begun.[13] This, at the time, aroused little attention. But Alexander was again thinking far ahead.

Then there came another disappointment, and a warning. After weeks of marching through the monsoon, with no end in sight, as Alexander, with the defective geographical knowledge of his age, pursued an elusive Ganges (or perhaps even the end of the in-habited earth)—after weeks of unimaginable and apparently pointless hardships, the men, one day, simply refused to go on. Alexander had discovered the limit of what he could expect of them. But there was worse still. The spokesman for the mutinous soldiers was none other than Coenus—the man who, once Parmenio's son-in-law, had helped to wipe out the power and the family of his benefactor and who, in due course, had become one of the four marshals. Coenus was clearly not a man to be trusted if things began to go wrong. The King, who had used the army to break the power of the nobles, was suddenly faced with the spectre of co-operation between the army and a scheming noble against himself. For the moment, nothing could be done. Alexander tried to threaten and browbeat; but the men, this time, would not yield: they knew that he could not do without them and that they had good support. Finally Alexander had to retreat down the Indus valley to the sea.[14] During the next few months, he gave the men harder fighting and marching than ever before, though from a military point of view it was now unnecessary.[15] And it is clear from our accounts that they no longer followed him as eagerly as before. To regain their loyalty, the King himself was always in the front line; and once, when storming a city, he was so severely wounded that no one thought he could survive. This at last brought the men back to their old worship of their leader. But Alexander never wholly recovered from the shock he had received. He had no sooner achieved his objective of gaining untrammelled power than he found that he was more than ever dependent on others, and that absolute power meant eternal vigilance.

As for Coenus, he died in action soon after. Alexander gave him a splendid funeral, but is said to have inveighed against his memory.[16] We cannot be certain as to the circumstances surrounding the death of this sinister man. But those who remember the fate of Rommel are entitled to be cynical—especially in view of what happened before long.

After Alexander regained full control of his men, he decided to test them in a march through the desert of southern Iran. He was well informed of the nature of that region; but the test turned out more severe than he had expected, and after incredible sufferings, worse than any endured in actual fighting, the remnants of the grand army straggled to safety in the cultivated land southwest of the plateau. Naturally, the King was quick to suspect treason as the cause of the disaster; and to his increasing distrust there was now added the need to find a scapegoat. The result was a bloody purge that went on for months. Among the first to suffer—and this is what makes us suspicious of the manner of Coenus' death—was Coenus' brother Cleander, who had arranged Parmenio's assassination and thus earned promotion. He and three of his associates among the army commanders were now summoned to bring reinforcements to the King. On their arrival they were arrested and soon executed on charges of maladministration. Altogether more than a third (perhaps two-thirds) of all the provincial commanders shared their fate, and one or two others seem to have barely averted it. The armies under the command of the provincial governors were dissolved (at the price of causing mass unemployment that led to grave social problems), and unknown men who owed everything to Alexander were appointed to the vacant posts.[17]

Then Alexander began to put into execution a great scheme that he had long been bearing in mind. He now realized that he could not count on the absolute submission of the present generation of nobles or men. In the spring of 324, at Susa, Alexander and eighty of his principal courtiers and commanders (chief of them Hephaestion) married Iranian princesses. What these nobles thought of it became clear after his death, when most of them repudiated their wives. But at the time they had to submit, and the marriages were celebrated with unprecedented pomp. Alexander wanted nothing less than a new ruling class of mixed blood, which would be free of all national allegiance or tradition. At the same time, 10,000 unions of Macedonian soldiers with native women were recognized as valid marriages (which meant legitimation of the children and rich wedding-presents from the King): clearly such associations were to be encouraged. That this was not from any humane motive was made clear at once. After putting the young natives trained in the Macedonian fashion through their paces, Alexander proceeded to dismiss (with rich rewards, of course) a large number of Macedonian soldiers; and he asked them to leave their native wives and children with him, in order not to cause trouble with their families in Macedon. His purpose, ultimately, was the creation of a royal army of mixed blood and no fixed domicile—children of the camp, who knew no loyalty but to him. At this point the Macedonian army rebelled. But Alexander was now ready for them: there was no major war in prospect, and he had them at his mercy. It might even be thought that he had deliberately provoked them at this point in order to see whether they would mutiny: if they did, he wanted them to do so when it suited him, so that he might avoid a repetition of his Indian experience. At any rate, he at once calmly told them that they were all dismissed and could make their way home by themselves: he would make do with Oriental troops. The men had no option but to ask his pardon—which he readily granted, since they were his best fighters. But he had won decisively, and after a grand banquet to celebrate the reconciliation he carried out his plans without change.

o

It is clear that the failures in India and in the desert had caused a severe psychological reaction in Alexander. He had discovered the insecurity of power, which all his successful scheming could not overcome. His success in the purges, and in the Susa marriages and his dealings with the mutineers, only increased the resulting instability. He took refuge from the insecurity of power in the greater exercise of power: like a god intervening in the affairs of mortals, he would order the fate of princes and of nations. He had always liked and encouraged the story that he was the son of the god Ammon (a Libyan god whom the Greeks identified with Zeus and whose oracle he had visited). The myth had been useful to inspire loyalty, particularly in Greeks, whose religion had a place for such things. But he now actually began to believe in his own divinity. About the middle of 324, he sent envoys to Greece demanding that he should be worshipped as a god. There are many anecdotes about the reluctance with which the Greeks complied. We have seen that educated Greek opinion was already largely estranged from him; and this act of blasphemy—for such it clearly was, even for the polytheistic Greeks, as many of our sources circumstantially assure us—would not endear him to them. Nor had he anything to gain by deification of this enforced sort: divine status would give him no significant political rights in a Greek city state,[18] and men's opinion of him would not change for the better. There is no escape from the conclusion that he wanted deification purely for its own sake, for psychological and not for political reasons. As for the Greeks, they had to obey. The famous decree passed by the Spartans and later quoted as an admired example of 'Laconic' speech expressed their feelings: 'Since Alexander wishes to be a god, let him be a god.'

One man, however, remained a danger to the King and god. Antipater, viceroy of Europe, the man who had made Alexander king, had no love for this new Persian King, who had murdered so many Macedonian nobles. And since the homeland, after ten years, knew him much better than it had ever got to know the King, he could count on a great deal of support. Alexander now sent one of his marshals home to supersede Antipater and ordered Antipater to report to him in person. At the same time he began to prepare the ground for what was inevitably to follow by listening with patience and obvious favour to the complaints of Greek embassies about Antipater's oppressive government. But Antipater was neither ingenuous nor easily frightened: he was, after all, the man who had manipulated Alexander's accession to the throne; and after the King's death he was to show himself, in his sure-handed and solid way, far abler than any of the more mercurially brilliant successors. Antipater simply refused to come, but sent his eldest son to negotiate on his behalf. In the meantime, he began to insure himself by entering into negotiations with the most powerful of the Greek states, which he knew to be hostile to the King.[19]

About this time Alexander suffered his most serious blow. In the autumn of 324, Hephaestion, the only man he fully trusted, drank himself to death. Alexander now approached more and more closely to insanity.[20] Hephaestion was made a demigod, and his memory was celebrated with incredible splendour and magnificence. But there was no one to take his place. It is significant that, although his duties had to be carried out, Alexander never again bestowed his titles on anyone. Henceforth the reign visibly declines. There is still some brilliant fighting. There are still some great schemes, befitting the King's new conception of his status. In fact, there are *too* many. We hear of plans for the conquest of the western Mediterranean, for the conquest of Arabia, for vast buildings and movement of populations. Historians have found it difficult to believe our evidence, though its source seems reliable enough. The fact appears to be that Alexander, amid the grandeur of divine dreams, had no real purpose left. He had won all the power he could. There was nothing left that was worth doing.

So the last few months dragged on until, about midsummer 323, at the age of 32, Alexander fell ill. Whatever the nature of his illness (and poison was, of course, suggested; but this can be neither proved nor disproved), he aggravated it by heavy drinking, until finally all hope was abandoned. He was urged to designate a successor; but he refused to the end. There is a story that, when he was asked for the last time whom he wanted to succeed him, he replied: 'The strongest'. Alexander was, essentially, not interested in a future without himself. And there was no one left about whose personal future he cared enough to help him succeed.

This is not, of course, the whole story of Alexander's reign. His military and political greatness is beyond question, and he retained his masterly touch in these fields to the end. But on the personal level, the story of Alexander the Great appears to us as an almost embarrassingly perfect illustration of the man who conquered the world, only to lose his soul. After fighting, scheming and murdering in pursuit of the secure tenure of absolute power, he found himself at last on a lonely pinnacle over an abyss, with no use for his power and security unattainable. His genius was such that he ended an epoch and began another—but one of unceasing war and misery, from which only exhaustion produced an approach to order after two generations and peace at last under the Roman Empire. He himself never found peace. One is tempted to see him, in medieval terms, as the man who sold his soul to the Devil for power: the Devil kept his part of the bargain, but ultimately claimed his own. But to the historian, prosaically suspicious of such allegory, we must put it differently: to him, when he has done all the work—work that must be done, and done carefully—of analysing the play of faction and the system of government, Alexander illustrates with startling clarity the ultimate loneliness of supreme power.

NOTES

[1] This is the text—slightly revised—of a lecture delivered at the Universities of Wellington and Canterbury in September 1961, and at the Universities of California (Berkeley) and Chicago in October 1961. The author wishes to thank the editor of *AUMLA* for his offer to print it.

[2] Inevitably, much that needs detailed discussion will have to be briefly touched on or taken for granted. For detailed treatment of several relevant problems, see *TAPA* 91 (1960) 324 ff. and *JHS* 81 (1961) 16 ff.

[3] [See now my discussion of this in *Phoenix* 17 (1963).]

[4] Plutarch, *Alexander* 9, 4 f.; Diodorus xvi 91 f., xvii 2 f.; ps.-Callisthenes i 26.

[5] See *TAPA*, art. cit. (n. 2 above) 327 f.

[6] This story is told in all the standard accounts, e.g. (Sir) W. W. Tarn, *Alexander the Great*, vol. i, 15 f.

[7] See *TAPA*, art. cit. (n. 2 above) 328 f.

[8] On the *coup d'état* against the house of Parmenio, see *TAPA*, art. cit. (n. 1 above) 330 f.

[9] On the death of Clitus, see Arrian, *anabasis* iv 8 f.; Plut. *Alex.* 50 f.; Curtius viii 1, 30 f.

[10] Different versions of this story in Plut. *Alex.* 54 f.; Arr. *anab.* iv 10 5 f.; Curt. viii 5 f. It is much discussed in both ancient and modern works.

[11] Arr. *anab.* iv 12, 6 f.; Plut. *Alex.* 55; Curt. viii 6 f.

[12] See Tarn, *op. cit.* (n. 6 above) 82 f.

[13] Diod. xvii 108, 1 f.; Arr. *anab.* vii 8, 2.

[14] Curt. ix 2, 10 f.; Arr. *anab.* v 25 f.

[15] On these campaigns, see Tarn, *op. cit.* 100 f.

[16] Arr. *anab.* vi 2, 1; Curt. ix 3, 20 f.

[17] For the great purge and the story of Alexander's last year, see *JHS*, art. cit. (n. 2 above). In view of the charges of maladministration and oppressive government that were used against most of these men, it is interesting to observe that one of the few who were never in any danger was Cleomenes, the governor of Egypt, known (from good evidence) for extortion and oppression.

[18] Modern apologists have surpassed themselves in ingenious attempts to deny this. But cf. (decisively) J. P. V. D. Balsdon, *Historia* 1 (1950) 363 f.

[19] On all this see *JHS*, art. cit.

[20] On this see especially J. R. Hamilton, *CQ* N.S. 3 (1953) 151 f.

Waiting for Sulla[1]

Estragon: *Who believes him?*
Vladimir: *Everybody. It's the only version they know.*
SAMUEL BECKETT

THERE are many periods of history—and unfortunately not always the least important—that survive, for us, entirely or mainly in one version. Ever since the development of modern critical historiography it has been recognized that it is the historian's duty to test that version, and highly skilled methods in the use of evidence have been worked out in order to enable him to do so. We all know some of the outstanding results in our field: the age of Augustus, once seen through the eyes of court literature; the ages of Tiberius and Claudius, once known only through the resentment of those who had suffered under tyranny—one could name many other periods that have gained a new reality in the last few generations and that now stand out in three dimensions.

Surprisingly, the age of Marius and Sulla does not appear to be among them. Until quite recently it could hardly be said that new methods had been brought to bear upon it: we seemed still to be in the pre-scientific age of historiography, when, if there were several ancient judgments, the historian was free to make up his mind according to his prejudices, and where this convenience of a ready-made alternative was not vouchsafed, the consensus had to be followed. In recent years this has begun to improve. The foundations for a proper history of the period are at last beginning to be laid, even though that history has not yet been—perhaps cannot yet be—written.[2] However, those crucial years in the eighties of the first century B.C., when for the first time the governing oligarchy of the Roman Republic had to face, not a mere demagogue, but a Patrician general at the head of a victorious army—those years, oddly enough, have so far failed to challenge scholars to probe behind the screen of the ancient literary tradition. Yet a study of that testing-time must inevitably have much to contribute to a proper evaluation of the late Republic, of the character and morale of its rulers and the causes of its downfall.

It is symptomatic of the widespread unawareness of recent progress in the study of this age—of the way in which these gains have failed, so far, to find their due place in the general scholarly tradition—that for the whole age of Marius and Sulla the arbitrary and haphazard treatment in the *Cambridge Ancient History* can still be cited—not only in the obscurity of schools and lecture-rooms, but in a penetrating article by an eminent scholar (*JRS* 50(1960) 144 f.)—as a 'masterly account', which is said to be central to later investigation. This being so, we must inevitably start the re-examination of the years with which we are here concerned by looking at that standard account.

The ninth volume of the *CAH* devotes five pages (264–9) to the 'Domination of Cinna'. This provided an opportunity for two page-headings. And these are the headings that, according to author and editor, summarize and capture the essence of those important years: 'The Mice at Play' and 'A Stab at Sulla's Back'. Surely these are strange words to use of the Senate and People of Rome facing a rebellious proconsul. Nor does the treatment belie the spirit of the summary. When the Government's decree outlawing the man who had failed to come to Rome to stand fair trial comes to be reported (the fact itself is barely and misleadingly mentioned), it is opined that 'by this senseless decree the greatest figure in the Roman world was forced into hostility with the government at home'; and the leaders of that government are called 'a contemptible troop, none of them effective and most of them corrupt'. (Not that there is any attempt to support this charge of corruption: the condemnation seems ultimately to rest entirely on the crime of failure.) It is not surprising that, in the introduction to that chapter, the events of those years are called 'a sordid story', whose study 'ill repays the trouble'.

So much for what is still regarded as the standard and central treatment. Some more recent works have arrived at a more balanced estimate. The best textbook (Scullard, *From the Gracchi to Nero*[2] (1963)) gives due credit to Cinna's government for measures of political and economic justice.[3] Yet even here we find no mention of some crucial events: e.g., right at the outset, the refusal of Sulla's officers to follow him in his first march on Rome, and his contumacy when he was summoned to stand his trial in Rome at a time when the city was not by any means dominated by his enemies—a vastly different situation from that in which Caesar later refused to face the sort of court that had convicted Milo. And just as even the origin of *Cinnae dominatio* is thus inadequately presented, there is no real recognition of the importance of that period. But a textbook, however excellent, could not transmit what had not been established in specialized investigation. And it is noteworthy that, even though we now have *The Magistrates of the Roman Republic* and Pauly is almost complete, there has been no such investigation. Münzer and Syme, for all the use that has in this instance been made of their methods, have laboured in vain. Must we still regard those years as a period whose study ill repays the trouble? Perhaps we should now take the trouble and see how we are repaid.

An obvious difficulty at once arises. It might be claimed that the comparative neglect of this period in modern works has been due to the inadequacy of the sources. Appian was concerned with war and bloodshed: we have many pages of graphic detail on murders, proscriptions and the *bellum Sullanum*, but little on what Cicero called the *triennium sine armis* (Cic. *Br.* 308). Plutarch wrote the lives of great men: we have a moralizing and fanciful portrayal of the last days of Marius, we have Sulla's war in the East and victorious return. But none of Plutarch's heroes, as it happens, was in Rome at this time and old enough to do much that was worth recording. Thus, apart from Cicero's scattered reminiscences, Livy becomes our main informant; but unfortunately, of course, he survives only in his various excerptors. Orosius and Eutropius have precisely one sentence on events in Italy between the death of Marius and Sulla's return; Florus has nothing at all; and various minor authors (especially the *Vir. ill.*) offer one or two odd points. The *Periocha* is best and must, in fact, be our main source. It has a long account of Marius' last days in book lxxx; Eastern wars in lxxxi and lxxxii; finally a great deal about warlike preparations by Cinna and Carbo and attempts at pacification by the Senate in books lxxxiii and lxxxiv. This shows a surprising interest in our period. For Livy, though interested in sedition and conflict even where there was no actual bloodshed, did not know or care for the *arcana imperii*. A philosopher by training, with no political experience, he saw political conflicts entirely in moral terms and knew little about the working of Roman politics. His interest centres in crises and characters, not in causes, motives, and developments. This is clear not only from the surviving books, but particularly from his treatment of the nineties of the first century. While the Social War appears to fill the greater part of five books, and even the year 100 has nearly a book, one book (lxx) contained all the events of the years 98 to 92, including even the beginning of M. Drusus' tribunate; and a large part of this was taken up with foreign wars, in Celtiberia, Cappadocia and Thrace, and even (it seems) with the misfortunes of the Seleucid *epigoni*. Not much space, clearly, remained for the causes of the great convulsions at the end of the decade—the trial of P. Rutilius Rufus; the tribunate of M. Drusus; the revolt of the Allies. Yet information was available in plenty: 2000 years later, with almost the whole of the literature of the period lost, historians have been able to do far better than, apparently, Livy did. Why, then, this sudden interest in the eighties? The tendency of the *Periocha* is clear and consistent, at least down to late 84: Sulla reasonable and ready to compromise; the Senate working hard for peace; citizens and Italians unwilling to fight Sulla; and only Cinna, Carbo, and their *factio*, 'cui bellum uidebatur utilius', working for war and wrecking all negotiations. So far the *Periocha*. Eutropius (v 7) and Orosius (v 20, *init.*) provide one sentence— basically the same in each: the remnant of the Senate—all those (Orosius specifies) who had escaped the murderous fury of Cinna, Marius, Fimbria and Sertorius—crossed to Greece and implored Sulla to come to the aid of his suffering country. There can be no question that this is also from Livy; yet it plainly contradicts the account in the *Periocha*. As so often in the surviving books, Livy, even in the case of this more recent period, seems to vary with the sources he transcribes—clearly still without much effort to eliminate their contradictions. Readers of his early books will hardly be surprised.

Here, then, he seems to have used two main sources, each pro-Sullan, yet each with its own case to make out: one, that Sulla invaded Italy in the company and at the request of all that mattered of the Senate; the other, that only a small clique had wanted civil war and that the Senate as a whole, opposing them, had worked for *concordia* as long as possible. (In this version, the *nobilitas* joins Sulla only in Italy.) Perhaps it would be presumptuous to aim at more: to try to give *names* to those two sources used by

Livy in a lost portion of his work. Yet it is worth attempting: the difference in breadth of treatment between the nineties and the period here discussed should assist explanation.

Plutarch (*Sulla* 22, *init.*) tells us that, to escape the persecutions of Cinna and Carbo, so many senators joined Sulla in Greece that he had 'a kind of Senate' (σχῆμα βουλῆς) with him; there came also his wife Metella and their children, after barely escaping with their lives; and Metella begged him to come to the aid of those at home. Sulla, sadly rejecting this appeal, considered it his duty to defeat the foreign enemy first [i.e. the scene takes place in 86]. At this point, providentially, an envoy from Mithridates arrived to initiate the negotiations that led to the peace of Dardanus. (The chapter continues with Sulla's indignant refusal of an offer by Mithridates to help him against his enemies in Rome.) It is generally agreed that this chapter and the story of the negotiations is based on Sulla's *Commentarii* (see Calabi, *I Commentari di Silla*, *MAL* 1950, 291 f.). Indeed, they are cited at the beginning of the next chapter. The apologia is too crude, the protest against the obvious charge of having allied himself with Mithridates against Rome is overdone, the exodus of senators to Greece clearly over-emphasized to gain a shadow of legality for his conduct: at the time, as we shall see, he did not dream of denying the authority of the Roman government, with which he continued to negotiate. Much of the actual language, moreover, recurs in a letter to the Senate reported by Appian, to which we shall return (below, p. 226). There probably never was any ultimate detailed source other than the *Commentarii* for the Eastern War (despite Calabi, *op. cit.*)—just as no participant ever wrote another set of *Commentarii de bello Gallico*. The *motiv* of Sulla's being begged to invade Italy for patriotic reasons clearly goes back to Sulla himself, as does that other one of a large part of the Senate being with him in Greece by 86. But these two are the main features of that part of Livy's narrative reproduced by Orosius and Eutropius. The differences are unimportant; the odd assortment of murderers' names was surely supplied by Orosius himself from his knowledge of Marian leaders; the fact that he ascribes the request for help to the senators and not to Metella is satisfactorily accounted for by compression in both Plutarch and Orosius-Eutropius. Nor does it matter whether Plutarch used Sulla's

Commentarii directly or through an intermediate source: we may be content to have noted that they are what we may for convenience call the 'Sullan' source in Livy.

Can we identify the other source (let us call it the 'senatorial' source)? The tendency it shows can be paralleled. Young M. Tullius Cicero, defending his own conduct against possible imputations in the *pro Rosc. Am.* (136), claims that everyone knows how he worked for *concordia* as long as possible, and then for Sulla's victory: 'sciunt ii qui me norunt me . . . posteaquam id quod maxime uolui fieri non potuit, ut componeretur, id maxime defendisse ut ii uincerent qui uicerunt'. This, clearly, was the accepted and acceptable interpretation of the conduct of those who stayed in Rome in Sulla's absence. Sulla was not eager to treat those who had not been with him as being against him—especially if they belonged to the senatorial class. The first proscription list contained only forty senatorial names (App., *b.c.* i 95; see Gabba, *ad. loc.*)—hardly enough to account for the officers opposing him—and we know most of them. And though Appian says that more were added (l.c., accepted by Gabba), no other number is given anywhere; this, in view of the delight of our sources in painting the monstrous massacre, is significant. There cannot have been *many* more.

We now know in what circles to look for our source. Who did write on the period? There are no great Memoirs, like those of M. Scaurus and P. Rutilius Rufus for the age immediately preceding. There are not even many contemporary historians. In fact, only three seem to matter.[4] L. Lucceius, Cicero's friend, had almost finished a history of the Social and Civil Wars in 56, when Cicero thought him ready to sing his own praises (*fam.* v 12). There is no evidence that anyone apart from Cicero and Atticus ever read it: Peter could not find a single fragment (or, outside Cicero, even *testimonium*). Claudius Quadrigarius is a more serious candidate. We know that he dealt with the period in his nineteenth book and that he was used by Livy: but that was for the battle of Sacriportus (Oros. v 20, 6). It seems that he did not devote much space to our period. Book xix certainly contained the siege of Piraeus, and much of it must have been devoted to the Eastern war. Peter assigned the Sacriportus fragment (fr. 84: 82 B.C.) to this book, for fair reasons. At any rate, it is clear enough that

book xxi contained post-Sullan matter (probably Lepidus), and
that thus there was not much space for our period apart from the
Mithridatic War. Moreover, Claudius Quadrigarius was not a
likely person to compose the apologia of the Roman upper class—
or, even if he did, he is not likely to have made it up. In view of
his station, he is probably not a real 'primary source', even for
his own age. He would base his *Annales* on other men's work, as
Valerius Antias and Livy did. Just as his account of the Mithridatic War will have been based on Sulla, so we may take it that
his account of Roman politics will have followed the interpretation of a participant: he himself had not been an actor in important
events, and *historia* was a pursuit for *honestissimus quisque*—men
who had helped to *make* history or, at least, moved in the same
circles as those who had. Cornelius Nepos notes (*ap*. Suet. *rhet*. 27)
that a client of Pompey, a schoolmaster, was the first freedman
to write *historia* in Rome.

Inevitably, we come to L. Cornelius Sisenna. This man—of
good praetorian (and probably Patrician) family—was recognized
as the greatest historian of his age. Sallust—not given to eulogy—
singles him out for praise in the *b.J.* (95, 2), though he disapproves
of his partiality for Sulla. Cicero thought him the best Roman
historian to date, though deficient by ideal standards (*Br*. 228;
leg. i 7). Varro, writing a *logistoricus* on history, gave it Sisenna's
name (Gell. xvi 9, 5). Here, clearly, is our distinguished senatorial
historian. Moreover, we know that he was used by Livy: the
story (in Livy, *per*. lxxix) of the soldier who killed his own brother
in the battle of the Janiculum (87 B.C.) comes from Sisenna.
Tacitus cites him for it (*hist*. iii 51), ignoring Livy.

What can we gather about Sisenna, apart from the fact that he
was *praetor* (*urbanus et peregrinus*) in 78 and then governed Sicily
(see *RE*, s.v. 'Cornelius', no. 374)? Henry Bardon (*Litt. latine
inconnue* i (1952) 255) has tried the psychological approach.
Noting his fondness for battle scenes, he concludes: 'Homme de
guerre, il se plaisait à ses évocations'. We note that Cicero, amid
many complimentary references, never calls him 'uir fortis' (as he
does A. Gabinius and others); and we think of that master painter
of battle scenes, the formidable warrior Titus Livius of Patavium.
It might be better to look at the evidence.

For we know a little about him (see *RE*, l.c.). He was well off and of good family, an Epicurean (Cic. *div.* i 99), a promising orator and writer in various fields. Given to adapting strict law to please his friends (Cic. *ap.* Asc. 74 Clark), he had many friends. As early as 88 we meet him in a circle that includes Q. Hortensius the orator and L. Lucullus, both of about the same age (Plut. *Luc.* 1). Later he appears, still with Hortensius, in that most respectable *causa*, the defence of Verres (2 *Verr.* iv 43). Another friend of his—no doubt to the surprise of those who view Roman politics in terms of 'parties' of Optimates and Populares—was C. Licinius Macer (the 'Popular' tribune and historian), whose ultimate presence on the winning side in the *bellum Sullanum* thus appears to be revealed (Cic. *leg.* i 7). With another friend, A. Gabinius, relations were particularly close: he seems to have given Gabinius a son for adoption (see *Philologus* 103 (1959) 97). It is not surprising that we meet this well-connected man in the Pirate War as a legate of Pompey in a not very strenuous theatre—and as the man chosen (Dio xxxvi 1) to mediate between Pompey and Q. Metellus Creticus (though he died without accomplishing this task).

Sisenna's work *ab urbe condita* (fr. 3 P) in fact gave only a brief *archaeologia* in part of the first book and then proceeded to its main subject, the Social and Civil Wars (fragments in Peter, *HRR*). It probably went down to 79 B.C. The first book already mentions Aesernia; Sulla's appointment to the dictatorship was treated in book xxiii (fr. 132)—so we are told in the MSS of Nonius. Even if that figure should be corrected to xiii (which the scale of the earlier books makes extremely likely), more than a book per year ensures ample treatment. We remember that Claudius had got from the siege of Grumentum to a date beyond Sulla in less than four (frr. 80–88 (Lepidus)). Sisenna affected unusual and poetic words (cf. Cic. *Br.* 259)—fortunately for us: we have over 130 fragments, since he was the delight of lexicographers. The fragments illustrate a perverse, though often effective, attention to colour in style, interest in character and continuity (he refuses to write 'uellicatim aut saltuatim' (fr. 127)); above all, they show that breadth of treatment which the number of books suggests and which made Fronto (whom one might have expected to admire that recherché style) condemn him as writing 'longinque' (*ep.* i 1). Cicero tells us that Sisenna aimed at a *readable* history, after the manner of Clitarchus (*leg.* i 7). We know that Sisenna's history lacked the *grauitas* of a Sallust. Yet Sallust himself admired Sisenna so much that he saw no need to do the task again. Nor did his views fundamentally change between the *b.J.* and the mature *Histories*. In Maurenbrecher's edition of the latter (a rough but fair guide), eighteen fragments ($= 5\frac{1}{2}$ pages) are from the *prooemium*; five ($= 1$ page) deal with the Social War; thirty ($= 7$ pages) with the period 88–79 (including the First Mithridatic War); and no fewer than 100 fragments ($= c.$ 28 pages) of book i deal with events already within the period that Sallust, probably with explicit reference to Sisenna, defined as his own. Thus it is clear that an introduction briefly discounted Sisenna's bias, but that the task of writing the definitive history of the years 90 to 79 had already been done.

We may accept the consensus of Cicero and Sallust: surely there were not many things, in life or literature, on which those two agreed. Sisenna's was the standard history of his period. It would be astonishing if it had *not* been one of Livy's main sources. Since we can see from the *Periocha* that the 'senatorial' interpretation forms the backbone of Livy's account, we may surely now conclude that what we have called the 'senatorial' interpretation is in fact Sisenna's. Nor does Bardon seem to be right even in assuming that Sisenna served under Sulla in the East, like, e.g., his friend A. Gabinius. Cicero (*Br.* 228) mentions him as an orator, apparently a younger rival of P. Antistius, who flourished only between 89 and 82. It thus appears almost certain that Sisenna, like his other friend Q. Hortensius, spent those years in Rome. One might even suspect a quaestorship—but men preferred not to mention such things later. It is thus quite natural that it was he who, in his *History*, presented the case of those who had stayed at home. A source of acknowledged excellence and known breadth of treatment, he chiefly accounts for Livy's greater interest in Roman politics during this period.

Livy, then, drew on two sources and, as in his earlier books, did not always succeed in reconciling them. This is one of the levers we can use for removing the screen of prejudice and propaganda. But chiefly we must rely on methods that will by-pass it entirely. Fortunately, we have enough information—at least in many instances —to adopt prosopographical methods that will enable us to do so.

Let us begin by asking: who were the men on whose behalf Sisenna's case was presented? Can we judge how much truth there is in Sulla's claim that as early as 86 he had 'a kind of Senate' with him? That he represented the *causa nobilitatis* against every kind of riffraff was bound to be said by everyone after his victory. As we know, it was—and at that time it was true, since the *nobilitas* had, on the whole, seen in good time who was going to win. But what was the position during the preceding years?

In any crisis, as Syme has taught us, we must begin by observing the attitude of the consulars—the *auctores publici consilii* and interpreters of *mos maiorum*. War and natural mortality had decimated them. By the time of Cinna's bloody return in 87, only a handful were alive. Four were killed in the terror of those days: Q. Catulus (*cos.* 102), M. Antonius (*cos.* 99). P. Crassus (*cos.* 97), L. Caesar (*cos.* 90).[5] One or two were away on provincial commands: C. Valerius Flaccus (*cos.* 93); probably C. Coelius Caldus (*cos.* 94). P. Rutilius Rufus (*cos.* 105) was in exile. These men play no further part in our story and may be ignored for our purpose; though it will soon become obvious that at least one of them, C. Flaccus, can safely be presumed (if we may judge by all his known relatives) to have recognized the Roman government. Four consulars, apart from Marius and Cinna themselves, remained alive in the city: L. Valerius Flaccus (*cos.* 100), Q. Mucius Scaevola (*cos.* 95), M. Perperna (*cos.* 92), L. Philippus (*cos.* 91). Three of these more than passively accepted the authority of the government. Philippus and Perperna were elected to the censorship of 86, and L. Flaccus became *princeps Senatus*. Moreover, Philippus recognized the validity of the government's action against his mother's brother, the absent Ap. Claudius, by omitting him from the Senate list (Cic. *dom.* 84). The crisis of 87 was the culmination of a deep split within the oligarchy. Yet it is clear that, even after the massacre of 87 and the violent acts that followed at the beginning of 86 (see Bennett, *Cinna* 25 f.), responsible opinion in Rome had no doubt as to the constitutional position. Perhaps the fourth of our consulars is the most interesting. We must not be deceived by the fact that Q. Mucius Scaevola did not compete for the censorship (the only office he could have reasonably been expected to hold): it seems to have been a tradition in his family—perhaps a form of that inverted snobbery not uncommon in some great noble families—not to hold the office (Cic. *Br.* 161). By the very fact that he stayed in Rome and attended the Senate—a fact that Cicero, in a somewhat similar position, later tried to explain and to claim as a precedent (*Att.* viii 3, 6)—the eminent lawyer and *Pontifex Maximus*, the one man whose *auctoritas* in such matters even his peers would probably have accepted as superior to anyone else's, made the constitutional position clear beyond doubt both to contemporaries and to posterity. That L. Sulla—the man who had marched on Rome to the disgust of his own officers (App. *b.c.* i 57) and had ruled there by naked force to the disgust of the Senate (Plut. *Sulla* 10, 4), murdering a tribune from the heart of the *nobilitas*; who had, on the expiry of his consulship, ignored a summons by a tribune to stand a fair trial (*MRR* ii 47); and who, before many months had passed, was treating as a private dynast with the chief enemy of Rome and murderer of many of her citizens—that this man was defending law, justice and the cause of the nobles was a pretence so ludicrous that even Sulla himself does not seem to have bluntly advanced it—at the time. It is clear that it never occurred to anyone who mattered.

We have seen that the surviving consulars stayed in Rome and co-operated. It is interesting, in the next place, to observe the behaviour of the relatives of the consulars killed in 87. They, if anyone, might be thought *Sullani* 'by nature'. As usual, there is not enough evidence; but, as usual, there is some. Q. Catulus and the younger M. Antonius (the later Creticus) are not attested anywhere. Creticus' son (the Triumvir) was born, it seems, in 83. Not only was his paternal grandfather one of the consular victims; his mother, a Julia, was closely related to two others. (See *RE*, s.v. 'Iulius', no. 543.) Was he born in exile? There is no mention of it. Surely his biographer Plutarch, surely Cicero, scraping together the most outrageous charges about his life and associates, would have recorded it. Nor is there any evidence that his father—a mild-natured gentleman, rather in awe of his formidable wife (Plut. *Ant.* 1)—took part in the Eastern or in the Italian war of Sulla: his later performance in Crete hardly suggests such an apprenticeship. Other Caesares survived in peace and honour. C. Caesar the praetorian died a natural death at Pisa in 85 (Pliny *n.h.* vii 181); his son, the future Dictator, was actually appointed *flamen Dialis* and, for the purpose, married a daughter of the Patrician L. Cinna (cf. *Gnomon* 33 (1961) 598). The husband and son of a Julia need not have much to fear.

Q. Catulus, briefly recorded as escaping the massacre, only reappears as *cos.* 78. What had he been doing? It is very difficult to believe that a noble of his prominence could escape mention, had he been active in the wars in the East and in Italy. *MRR* lists fourteen promagistrates (in addition to Sulla), thirteen legates and two prefects for the year 82 alone, and several can be added from earlier lists. And this argument does not stand alone: even more than in the case of M. Antonius, it can be shown that there was no need for him to go into exile. His sister Lutatia was married—by 91, it seems (Cic. *de or.* iii 228)—to the orator Q. Hortensius. Hortensius was one of the most active and most prominent orators in Rome during this period (Cic. *Br.* 308); there is no reason to assume (without evidence) that his wife's brother was in exile. We may also profitably look at Catulus' colleague in the consulship of 78: where was M. Aemilius Lepidus during *Cinnae dominatio*? Again there is no mention of him in the East, probably no mention in the Italian War. A legate named Lepidus captured Norba for Sulla (App. *b.c.* i 94). He is often identified with the *cos.* 78. But Broughton is rightly doubtful. Mam. Lepidus (*cos.* 77) appears as early as 88 as a successful officer: he seems to be the man who defeated Poppaedius Silo in the latter's last fight (Livy, *per.* lxxvi; Diod. xxxvii 2, 10). Surely *he* is the conqueror of Norba. There is more than negative evidence. Sallust (*hist.* i 78 M) mentions a leader superior in numbers, but inexperienced in war. Maurenbrecher rightly saw that this must be M. Lepidus. Nor does his military service, such as we know it, contradict this. His name is plausibly restored by Cichorius in Cn. Pompeius Strabo's *consilium* at Asculum (*Röm. Stud.* 147).[6] Cicero, though not present on that occasion, also served under Strabo: would he be called experienced in war? Sallust's comment merely implies lack of experience of command. It could not be said of a man who had taken Norba—perhaps not of a man who had fought, even as a legate, under Sulla in the East. Ready for a praetorship by 81—even if we do not suspect an earlier one— men like Catulus and Lepidus would necessarily have held positions of high responsibility in Sulla's army, had they been present;

P

all the more so, if they had served with him for many years. M. Lepidus, *priuos militiae*, clearly had not. His connections make it apparent. He had married an Appuleia, of the family of Saturninus, and he had been one of a band of young Patricians who attached themselves to the rising star of Marius (see my *Foreign Clientelae*, 200 f.). His eldest son, as Münzer has convincingly shown (*RA*, 307 f.), was given to another Patrician to adopt— L. Scipio Asiagenus, *cos.* 83 and one of the most prominent supporters of the government against Sulla. Lepidus would have no trouble in Rome.

We have seen that it is almost certain that Q. Catulus did not join Sulla after his father's death and that he had connections that might enable him to stay in Rome. And we have noticed that his colleague in the consulship of 78 is in the same position, but with his connections so close, and his own political attachment so unambiguous, that his staying in Rome may be regarded as certain—indeed, we may well suspect political advancement (i.e., the praetorship). The two cases reinforce each other; and that for Catulus can be further strengthened. Cn. Domitius Ahenobarbus (*cos.* 96, censor 92) was his *auunculus*: i.e., he was the son of a Domitia,[7] who would be his father's first wife. The Domitii were among the most loyal of aristocratic families: Catulus' cousin Cn. Ahenobarbus, a son-in-law of Cinna, fell for the cause in Africa, fighting against Pompey (*MRR* ii 69). But (it might be said) his mother was probably dead; what of his step-mother? Servilia, widow of the elder Q. Catulus and mother of Lutatia, was well connected. We have seen the prominence and fame that came during these years to her son-in-law Q. Hortensius. She was also a close relative—probably a sister—of that Q. Caepio who had opposed M. Livius Drusus. (On these connections, see *Historia* 6 (1957) 318 f. [= pp. 42 ff., above].) A daughter of that same Q. Caepio (i.e., Servilia's niece, it seems) was married to M. Junius Brutus, father of the tyrannicide—and the Bruti, again, were among the few noble families that remained stubbornly loyal to the losing cause against Sulla. Catulus' step-mother would be as useful to him as his relatives on his own mother's side. He too had nothing to fear in Rome.

Q. Catulus, son of Marius' hated enemy; M. Antonius; those Caesares about whom we have any positive information at all—

the relatives of the consular victims seem to have stayed in Rome, unmolested and in some cases honoured. So, probably, did others: we have noticed M. Lepidus. We should like to have the lists of magistrates for these years. But it is doubtful whether even Livy gave lists of praetors. It is noticeable how little these things were later talked about, except to malign an enemy. However, some men—relatives of victims, or intended victims themselves—did leave Rome. Did they flock to Sulla? On one son of a murdered consular we are well informed: M. Crassus escaped—to Spain, where he went into hiding, well provided with civilized amenities by a faithful client of the family (Plut. *Cr.* 4). It was only when Sulla was preparing to invade Italy, long after the disintegration of government in Rome and the provinces (see below, p. 229), that Crassus joined him—and it is worth noting (in view of the absence of evidence for so many others) that his movements are amply attested (*MRR* ii 71). Similarly a praetorian, M. Caecilius Cornutus: hidden, in a macabre fashion, by faithful slaves, he escaped—to Gaul (App. *b.c.* i 73). As for Q. Metellus Pius, Sulla's *adfinis* and head of a renowned family, he conspicuously refused to join Sulla: he went to Africa (*MRR Suppl.* 11; cf. below).

Detailed enquiry has been necessary to avoid facile generalization. It could be further extended: there is more information than might appear at first sight. The evidence is scattered and incomplete; yet it is cumulative, establishing increasing probability by geometric progression. It is clear, at the very least, that no one doubted the constitutional position in 86: not the closest relatives of the victims of Marius' rage, nor a praetorian who barely escaped assassination. No one for a moment thought of Sulla as the protector of the nobility: not even the head of the great family that had supported him in 88 and was to do so again in later years. When Caesar crossed the Rubicon, over half the consulars (as Syme has shown: *Rom. Rev.* 61 f.) either supported him or at least remained in Rome without opposing: the great men on Pompey's side were 'a rash and factious minority'. What words could describe Sulla's followers?

Mature statesmen might be guided by *mos maiorum* and, relying on family connections, prove willing to compromise. Did Sulla attract the young, the ardent, the adventurous, like that other rebellious proconsul a generation later? We have already seen that there is reason to doubt it. Our information here is not as good as we should like; but two examples may suffice. M. Crassus must certainly be put in this category: his achievement in collecting a private army as soon as the administration disintegrated proves it. As we have seen, he had no thought of joining Sulla for years. The other undoubted case is Pompey: he stayed in Rome and even joined Cinna's expedition (see below, p. 229). Nor, to balance these, is there any record of men of their type who did rally to Sulla. Quaestors, of course, continued to be elected from among ambitious men. We know the names of some of them, and they include men of all classes: a Verres, whose name shrieks the *nouitas* of the family; men of good senatorial rank like Cicero's later client M. Fonteius; young *nobiles* like M. Terentius Varro and Cicero's friend M. Pupius Piso. (On all these, see *MRR*.) Ambitious men had no need to leave Rome.

Who, then, were the *Sullani*? The answer is so simple that the erudite historian has tended to overlook it. They were Sulla's officers. No other link among them is to be discovered. A. Gabinius, L. Minucius Basilus, and one or two other young men, distinguish or disgrace themselves as junior officers. No doubt there were some we do not know about: each legion had six tribunes, and there will have been men of senatorial family among them. But one comment on their quality must be made: remarkably few of the men prominent in the next generation can boast service in the Mithridatic War. And—most important—there is a dearth of senior officers. L. Lucullus, Sulla's *adfinis* and quaestor, had been loyal in 88: there can be little doubt that he was the one officer (simply described as 'one quaestor' in App. *b.c.* i 57) who remained with him during the march on Rome. (Oddly enough, modern works do not usually recognize this.) He stayed with Sulla throughout and was sent to carry out missions demanding tact, skill and standing: Sulla entirely lacked consular legates. L. Licinius Murena, praetorian of praetorian family; C. Scribonius Curio, of praetorian descent; L. Hortensius, a relative of the orator; a Sulpicius Galba, the only man of really distinguished family; we may add a praetorian Gabinius. (See *MRR*, with *Supplement*.) They are not a glorious lot: hardly any to represent the very best families, and no more who attained real distinction later. And we can trace no additions to their ranks, despite ample reports on the war in the East, until 84: we have seen where the best men were. Sulla's faction, during the crucial three years, was his personal creation. In 88, when he marched on Rome, his officers (all but one) deserted him. The effect of this must be appreciated. Restive under Sulla's methods, the governing class refused to follow him; and we have seen that his behaviour in Rome did nothing to change their minds. But Sulla now had an unusual opportunity. Having to appoint a new military hierarchy, he naturally picked men whom he knew and trusted. Nothing in their background links them for us, beyond Sulla's choice. L. Lucullus was his wife's cousin, the son of a Metella (*RE*, s.v. 'Licinius', no. 104). He is the only one of that far-flung and powerful clan who is with him. Q. Metellus Pius, head of the family, was in Africa, refraining from any action against the lawful government. C. Scribonius Curio, we may note, had prosecuted a Metellus, and the family were his sworn *inimici* (*RE*, s.v. 'Scribonius', col. 864). None of these men (except Galba) are known in senior positions before; not one of the numerous *legati* of the Social War is among them (except that same Galba—and his identification is conjectural, with alternatives offering: see *RE*, s.v. 'Sulpicius', no. 60).

Sulla's army—troops bound to their *imperator* in the Social War and tested in the march on Rome; officers hand-picked for personal loyalty above constitutional scruples—this is a new and alarming phenomenon. It lies outside the framework of Roman politics as it had been known. In a truer sense (perhaps) than even Caesar or Octavian, Sulla stood against the Republic. For three years Rome was puzzled.

The first decade of the century had seen bitter struggles within the oligarchy, with Marius—enigmatically—at their centre (see *Historia* 6 (1957), 318 f. [= pp. 34–70 ff., above]). The *nouus homo* who had saved the Republic for his aristocratic friends in 100 was gradually deserted by them. In 87, returning after exile and humiliation, he took terrible vengeance. It is a remarkable fact that all those victims of 87 about whose past we know anything at all (except for the consuls Octavius and Merula, clearly guilty of high treason) were former friends of Marius whom he had reason to hate for betraying him. The sources on the massacre of 87 divide the blame between Cinna and Marius, according to the

point they wish to make (see Carney, *Hermes* 88 (1960) 382 f.);
and modern writers, according to the point *they* wish to make,
have often followed them to exculpate one of the two. Yet the facts
are clear and suggestive. Cinna could use legal methods to deal
with those who had used force against a consul of the Roman
People: he had no need for murder (see Bennett's careful discussion of the massacre—which he perhaps excessively disbelieves
—in his *Cinna*, 25 f.). The consul Octavius might have been
tried; he was killed in the fury of the first occupation, perhaps by a
personal enemy (App. *b.c.* i 71). Apart from him, none of those
assassinated are known to have done Cinna any harm. The prosecutions of those guilty of treason contrast with the fate of those
whom Marius had reason to hate. As is known, Cinna did his
best to stop the slaughter; and the terror did not last beyond
Marius' providential death. Cinna had been an uneasy accom-
plice. He had not relished Marius as an ally. Even before the capture of Rome, he had privately negotiated with Cn. Pompeius
Strabo, to the exclusion of Marius (see *Foreign Clientelae*, 239).
With Marius dead, the new government, universally recognized,
could breathe a sigh of relief and embark upon a policy of conciliation. It was the only possible policy. Q. Catulus, horrified at
Sulla's methods at the height of the proscriptions, is reported to
have flung at him the question: 'Cum quibus tandem uicturi
sumus?' (Oros. v 21). Perhaps even Sulla did not need the
reminder. Cinna certainly did not. He intended to go on living in
Rome, and governing it.

As far as is known, Cinna had taken no part in the struggles of
the nineties. This is not conclusive; but the lack of any disreput-
able details about his early life is significant, in the case of a figure
so much hated and denigrated in retrospect. There was no
reason, it seems, why he should not succeed in healing the rift.
As we have seen, the consulars thought so. Nor were they all
Mariani. Q. Scaevola had been neutral in politics, as far as one
could be. Of the others, who collaborated actively, L. Flaccus, of
course, was an old Marian—more Marius' slave than his colleague
(in 100), as P. Rutilius Rufus had said (Plut. *Mar.* 28, 8). The
Flacci were given to taking up new men and families: inscriptions
(*Inschr. v. Magn.* 144 f.) reveal a policy of low-class connections.
They had taken up Marius, as they previously had the elder Cato.

The Perpernae may have been another discovery of theirs. Yet the Perpernae show a link with the Claudii (see *RE*, s.v. 'Perperna'). And L. Philippus, last of the four consulars, was— despite violent things said in the heat of 91—the son of a Claudia and had (it seems) had the support of the *factio* when standing for the consulship (see Münzer, *RA*, 95 f.). He had earlier been defeated by a Herennius (Cic. *Br.* 166; *Mur.* 36)—a Marian family, if ever there was one (see Carney, *Acta Iuridica* i (1959) 232 f.). The consulars, few as they were, were not a *paucorum factio*.

On Marius' death, L. Valerius Flaccus, related to the *cos.* 100, was made consul suffect and passed a law to deal with the crushing burden of debt—*uolentibus omnibus bonis* (Sall. *b.C.* 33, 3), as a man reminding the ruling class of its traditional compassion was to say. The claim would be pointless if untrue. At least, this measure obviously was not meant to attract the Equites. Another measure, stabilizing the currency, was of benefit to everyone (see *MRR* ii 53 f.). And the government made no move to rally the Italians. Censors were appointed to enrol the new citizens—and one of them was L. Philippus, the chief opponent of Italian enfranchisement in 91. (See *MRR* ii 54. Cf. L. R. Taylor, *Voting Districts*, 105, n. 12, noting this and puzzled at it.) Nothing was done to redeem Cinna's promise to effect the redistribution of the new citizens through all the tribes.[8] L. Flaccus was sent against Mithridates. He was the obvious choice: he had been in Asia before, and a popular governor (see *RE*, s.v. 'Valerius', coll. 26 f.). C. Flavius Fimbria was assigned to him as a legate. He was a man of proved military skill — and one better removed from the city. He had embarrassed the régime by a violent attack on Q. Scaevola and had proclaimed an intention of prosecuting him (Cic. *Rosc. Am.* 33). Presumably there were private *inimicitiae*: the elder Fimbria (*cos.* 104) had had many enemies, in a hard climb to the top (Cic. 2 *Verr.* v 181), one of them apparently M. Scaurus (Cic. *Font.* 24), with whom Q. Scaevola was sometimes associated. In any case, Fimbria was sent away and nothing further is heard of the intended prosecution. Sulla, of course, was to claim that the army was sent against *him*.[9] The 'stab at Sulla's back' recurs in more recent accounts. Luckily we know better, having (for once) a source not tainted by Sullan propaganda. Memnon gives us the Senate's instructions, and they show that the contumacious fugitive from justice was given another chance, for the sake of Rome: let him co-operate if he would submit to the Senate; or, if not, at any rate fight the enemy first (Memnon (*F. Gr. Hist.* 434), F 24). The facts confirm this version. Asia was Flaccus' province and he made straight for it along the *Via Egnatia*. It could, of course, be claimed that this was due to fear that the troops might desert to Sulla (App. *Mith.* 51, *fin.*). In fact, Sulla, stationed in Thessaly, not many miles from Flaccus' route, made no move to stop him. Perhaps fears of desertion were not all on one side. The consul of the Senate and People of Rome might still impress the supporters of the fugitive. In any case, Sulla *de facto* accepted—while it suited him—the Senate's alternative. *Concordia* was still possible. He did not intend to fight both Rome and Mithridates (Plut. *Sulla* 24, *fin.*).

Nor, on this question of *concordia*, is there good evidence of division between Cinna and the Senate. No measures against Sulla were taken in 86 or early 85: no troops collected against him in Italy, no attempt made to interfere with him in Greece, illegal though his tenure was. When L. Scipio Asiagenus went out to govern Macedonia in 85, he fought various barbarian tribes, claiming some success. Sulla fought some of the same tribes, claiming greater success. (See *PACA* 1 (1958) 6 f. [= pp. 80 f., above].) We need not search for the truth. What matters is what did *not* happen: fighting the same tribes in the same year, Scipio and Sulla did not clash. In Africa, Q. Metellus Pius remained quiet and unharmed: there is no evidence of fighting until 84 (*MRR* ii 60). That he had been legally banished, like Ap. Claudius (see above) and Sulla himself, is very likely. In none of those cases was anything done to persecute the exiles. Even M. Crassus might well have been found by determined efforts. None were made.

By 85, Fimbria had murdered Flaccus (*MRR* ii 56, 59). That made no essential difference in Rome. Cinna was re-elected consul for 85. That was natural and excusable. The *boni* themselves had agreed to Marius' repeated consulships (see especially Dio, fr. 94, 1) in the face of the German danger. Surely Mithridates was as great a threat as the German hordes. Sulla need not even have been mentioned. What was important was the colleague he would choose. It was Cn. Papirius Carbo. Cicero later proclaimed no love for the Carbones (*fam.* ix 21, 3). In fact, neither he nor anyone else knows anything to the discredit of Cn. Carbo in his youth, except a moderately demagogic tribunate and *inimicitiae* with L. Crassus (Cic. *leg.* iii 42). The former was quite respectable in an ambitious *nobilis*—and both were shared by that later pillar of the Sullan settlement, L. Philippus. (See *RE*, s.v. 'Marcius', coll. 1562 f.). Not everyone, in the best circles, was as fond of the slippery orator as Cicero, in pious memory, would have us believe: we know that P. Rutilius Rufus disapproved (*de or.* i 227, with blunt invective). Support for Cinna in 87 was a necessary qualification: no one could object to that. Another connection is worth noting, particularly as it again obtrudes the name of L. Philippus: Carbo had joined him and the young Q. Hortensius in defending Pompey after the establishment of the new régime (Cic. *Br.* 230; Val. Max. vi 2, 8). It is not difficult to see that Philippus, censor in the very year of Carbo's election, had something to do with recommending him. As for young Hortensius, we have seen something of his background. We may be certain that Carbo's election was applauded in the best circles. There was no promotion, under Cinna's administration, for unworthy *noui homines*, no neglect of the *leges annales*. *Mos* and *ius* conspicuously flourished.

Suddenly, late in 85, came the first serious shock. Hitherto Sulla, as we have seen, had been contumacious, but not rebellious: he might claim to be acting in the best interests of his country. But in 86 Mithridates had been twice defeated in Greece, and during 85 Asia was falling to a skilful offensive by Fimbria. He shut Mithridates up at Pitane and called on Lucullus, in charge of Sulla's fleet, to support him. But Lucullus had other instructions. For Sulla, having raised his price by victory, had begun negotiations with the King. He had nothing to gain by eliminating the King: that would leave Fimbria in possession of Asia—and L. Scipio was still in Macedonia. And it was clear that, outside his army, Sulla could expect little support. Lucullus let Mithridates escape, and by late summer Sulla had become his ally. The King gave up all his gains (Sulla's troops insisted on that) and undertook to furnish Sulla with ships, money and other supplies. In return, Sulla promised to secure him recognition as a friend and ally of Rome and, it seems, made certain promises about his friends in Asia. (References *MRR* ii 55, 58 f.) With overwhelming superiority Sulla now faced Fimbria. The story of the spontaneous enthusiasm of Fimbria's men for Sulla (Plut. *Sulla* 25, *init.*) is belied by his treatment of the *Fimbriani* (or *Valeriani*): they simply refused to fight against impossible odds and received nothing but their lives (see Smith, *Phoenix* 14 (1960) 12 f.). With all the resources of the East at his disposal, Sulla now cautiously proceeded towards rebellion. The victorious proconsul sent a letter to the Senate.

The letter, as summarized by Appian (*b.c.* i 77), contains a striking verbal similarity to Plutarch's passage about Metella's escape, and the rush of exiles to join Sulla (Plut. *Sulla* 22, 1). It ends with a threat and a promise: he would come to punish his enemies; but no one else (old citizens or new) need fear him. Appian's letter must come from Sulla's *Commentarii* and is suspect in detail: the promise to new citizens is patently anachronistic. It took Sulla a long time and much bitter experience before he bound himself to leave their rights untouched.[10] We may be certain that the original letter was more diplomatic; in any case, while stressing Sulla's claims, it *ipso facto* recognized the Senate's authority. (See Gabba, *ad loc.*) The *princeps Senatus* responded with a great speech on *concordia*,[11] and envoys were sent to offer Sulla an amnesty in return for his services. This, of course, was simply a continuation of Cinna's conciliatory policy. Yet the consuls now had to prepare for war. Naturally, they had themselves re-elected: the emergency was now graver than ever. But no attempt was made to 'pack' the other magistracies. It was soon to become apparent that the tribunician college of 84 was hostile and the quaestors none too reliable.[12] There is no sign of *dominatio*. Sulla had moved towards rebellion; but nothing else had changed.

The consuls had to prepare for war. (Sources for what follows in *MRR*.) They sent for ships and toured Italy, where (it seems) *Cinnae dominatio* had allowed more local freedom than had been known for generations. While Carbo collected troops, Cinna embarked on a bold plan. At the beginning of 84, too early to avoid the seasonal storms, he began to send men across from Ancona to Liburnia. The men were unwilling to go, and the consul was killed in a riot. So far the facts. Naturally, the sources stress unwillingness to fight against Sulla. This is not at all obvious after Sulla's landing in Italy. A Pompeian biographer picked up by

Plutarch (*Pomp.* 5, 1 f.) added that the men were worried about Pompey's fate. While this has rightly caused nothing but amusement, another tale (App. *b.c.* i 77, *fin.*) has had undeserved success. The *CAH*, a few lines after informing us that Cinna had 'lost his nerve', tells us (ix 269) that he now planned to fight Sulla in Greece. Broughton (*MRR* ii 60) states that he wanted to cross to Epirus. Yet Appian (*b.c.* i 77 f.) knew perfectly well where Liburnia was—roughly, the stretch of coast centred on Iader (Zadar) and going as far as Scardona, where Dalmatia began. That, in fact, is the only stretch of coast to which anyone in his senses would cross from Ancona (*vir. ill.* 69, 4). Nor would a reasonable man choose to march down the Dalmatian coast to invade Epirus and fight in Greece. A glance at a map is enough to dispose of this story. Not that Cinna was *unable* to cross to Epirus: Sulla was in Asia, squeezing money out of the cities and letting his men (who had shown some unrest after the cynical alliance with Mithridates) live on the fat of the land (Plut. *Sulla* 24, 5; 25, 3 f.); Scipio, probably, was still in Macedonia (see p. 224, above).

There is only one explanation for the expedition to Liburnia. The country, at the time, had hardly been touched by the Romans. In neighbouring Dalmatia, odd triumphs had been obtained (best known that of Metellus Delmaticus: *MRR* i 529); and it is interesting that in 78 we find a Roman commander fighting a war there and (in 77) capturing Salonae (*MRR* ii 88). 78 B.C. was the first year in which the restored Republic proceeded to deal with barbarians on the frontiers—all frontiers at once, we are told (Oros. v 23, 1; Eutr. vi 1). It is not impossible that the Dalmatians were clamouring to be fought in 84. In any case, if Roman troops appear in Liburnia, there was only one thing they could do there —fight. Thus the whole affair becomes intelligible.

Cinna, who was an experienced commander (he had fought in the Social War (*MRR* ii 26, 28, 30, 36, 39, 43) as well as in 87), knew quite well that his new levies would stand no chance against the veterans of the Asian war: Pompey was equally aware of such an elementary fact, thirty-five years later. But, unlike Pompey in 49, Cinna had plenty of time: Sulla could not be in Italy before the very end of the year, if then. He therefore prepared to train his men in a short campaign in Illyria, to give them confidence, cohesion and experience. Fifty years later another man facing a great *imperator* based in the East reasoned similarly. It is not impossible that Octavian knew of Cinna's plan: Cinna's grandson became *cos. suff.* in 32 (*MRR* ii 417; *PIR*², C 1338). The soldiers' objection to the war also becomes intelligible (though, on a long-term view, unjustified): quite apart from the rough crossing, they did not see why they should be taken overseas to fight an unnecessary war, when their homes might be threatened. Carbo drew the inevitable conclusion and called off the whole enterprise. The result, equally inevitable, followed in the Sullan War.

Cinna's death was the turning-point. Legally, of course, nothing had changed. But that ceased to matter. Carbo, recalled by the tribunes to elect a consul suffect (see p. 233, n. 12), was prevented by dire omens.[13] When the Senate's envoys returned from Sulla with a temporizing answer (he only asked for restoration for himself and the other exiles and in other respects submitted to the Senate), it proved fruitless. Livy (*per.* lxxxiv) says that the Senate accepted the terms, but that Carbo's faction prevented agreement. It is difficult to see why Carbo should reject such an offer—though easy enough to understand why Sisenna (here undoubtedly Livy's source) should paint this picture of a peaceable Senate opposed by the wicked faction. A little later, Livy apparently reported that a decree of the Senate disbanding all armies was 'brought about by the faction of Carbo and [the younger] Marius'! This, clearly, is Sulla, with a different axe to grind: Livy's sources—fortunately for us—are still unreconciled. However, in the absence of Livy's full text, it is Appian to whom we must turn for the crucial detail: though the Senate's envoys returned to Rome with Sulla's moderate offer, Sulla's own envoys who had gone with them, hearing at Brundisium of the breakdown of government following Cinna's death,[14] went back to Sulla. He at once gave embarkation orders. We may ask where Appian's report comes from. The answer should be clear: Sulla, unlike Sisenna, had no need to stress the Senate's work for conciliation against bellicose tyrants; *his* point was the anarchy from which he saved his country. As we have seen, the decree to disband all armies was, in his version, a plot by his enemies. Like so much else in Appian, this is from the *Commentarii*. Sulla, in this instance, had nothing to gain by disguising the true facts, whatever we may think of his motives. In fact, he now knew he could win.

Indeed, this sudden disintegration of government is as dramatic as anything in history. With Appian to point it out to us, the fact that the standard modern works ignore it is a forceful illustration of the lack of serious interest in this period. Yet the evidence is there, for all to see. In Picenum, only a few miles from Rome, Pompey, who had witnessed Cinna's death, knew that the régime was doomed. Using his inherited connections, he successfully prevented the government from levying soldiers. Before long, he was doing so himself (Plut. *Pomp.* 5). In Africa, Q. Metellus Pius, after keeping the peace for years, rose in arms. He had miscalculated: the governor was strong enough to drive him out (*MRR* ii 60 f.), and he now joined Sulla, giving him—at last— the seal of approval by the *boni* (see especially Dio, fr. 106 B). In Further Spain, M. Crassus, with no more authority than young Pompey, emerged from hiding, began to recruit men, and indeed succeeded in raising a large force (Plut. *Cr.* 6). There is no mention of opposition, nor even of a legitimate governor. The authorities now had difficulty in finding reliable men. For some time C. Valerius Flaccus seems to have been looking after Citerior as well as Transalpine Gaul (see *PACA* I (1958) 11 f. [= pp. 95 f., above]). If he was intended to keep an eye on Ulterior as well— and, certainly, no one nearer appears in our record—the task was clearly impossible. Sertorius, assigned—despite what some modern works report—the whole of Spain in 83 (so it seems: Plut. *Sert.* 6; App. *b.c.* i 86, giving his *prouincia*), was unable to go out for some time (cf. Exup. 7 f.). Macedonia saw no successor to L. Scipio.

In Italy and the provinces, the machinery of government had slipped out of Carbo's grasp. Sulla and Pompey, Metellus and Crassus, were not the only men to see it. The *nobilitas* began to flock to Sulla's camp (Livy, *per.* lxxxv). A few men are named for us: P. Cornelius Cethegus (App. *b.c.* i 80), Q. Lucretius Ofella (*MRR* ii 72), L. Sergius Catilina (*RE*, s.v. 'Sergius', coll. 1694 f.). The selection is significant: they are all ruffians and intriguers. We may add the quaestor C. Verres, who left his allotted consul with the *fiscus* (Cic. 2 *Verr.* i 34 f.). But better men—we may gather incidentally—did the same. L. Flaccus passed the law that made Sulla dictator (*MRR* ii 68). Late in 83 or early in 82, L. Philippus himself conquered Sardinia for Sulla (Livy, *per.* lxxxvi). By then he was a legate of Sulla. It was not long since he had been censor and Carbo's friend. M. Pupius Piso, friend of Cicero's youth, forms a striking contrast to the villainous Verres: allotted as quaestor to the consul L. Scipio, he did not join him—thus violating neither his own *fides* nor *mos maiorum* nor the obligation of the lot (Cic. 2 *Verr.* i 37). This virtuous young man, slower than some to see the full effect of Cinna's death, had married Cinna's widow (Vell. ii 41, 2) and thus, no doubt, gained his quaestorship for 83. On Sulla's victory, he at once divorced her. M. Aemilius Lepidus, who also divorced his Appuleia, became one of the great profiteers of the proscriptions (Sall. *hist.* i 55, 18). But he was to die of a broken heart, in Sardinia (Pliny, *n.h.* vii 122, 186; App. *b.c.* i 107). Many names can be added. Some cannot. We should like to know who divorced the Valeria who was soon to conquer the conqueror Sulla. The Valerii Messallae had had Marian connections.[15] One other name is of sufficient intrinsic interest to be worth a mention *honoris causa*. M. Terentius Varro, the anti-quarian, quaestor (as is known) not later than 85, saw service in Liburnia in his youth. Cichorius, in his fascinating discussion of Varro's life and work, thought that he must have been there as a legate in 78–7 (*Röm. Stud.* 191 f.). This leads to certain difficulties, which cannot be very successfully overcome. It is surely obvious enough that he was there on the one occasion, during his youth, when Liburnia is actually mentioned in our records—in Cinna's army, and (since the date fits) probably as his quaestor. We may hazard the conjecture that it was he who crossed with the advance party to organize the landing. (We know that he actually reached Liburnia, whenever it was.) An officer would be needed for this, and Cinna himself stayed behind. Yet between 84 and 82 (see Cichorius, l.c.) we find Varro studying philosophy in Athens. He avoided an awkward time. But he at least did not join the victor in war against the government under which he had served.

I have, on another occasion (*Foreign Clientelae*, 243 f.), devoted some attention to the government's last measures: the move to rally the Italians and freedmen and thus at last fulfil the promise of so many years' standing (late 84: see p. 233, n. 8); the election of that significant pair, a L. Scipio and the new man (perhaps new citizen) C. Norbanus as consuls for 83; finally, the youth C. Marius made consul, in a desperate attempt to collect the loyalty owed to an honoured name. It all proved vain. In any case, it is beyond our immediate purview here. But we must close with a glance at the final atrocity of those years of tyranny and persecution, the massacre (in 82) of 'omnis quae in urbe erat nobilitas' (Livy, *per.* lxxvi)—a fitting end to the period of *non mos, non ius*. Only four names are mentioned (App. *b.c.* i 88), and not (we may take it) for want of searching. They are P. Antistius (Pompey's father-in-law), L. Domitius (closely related to the Cn. Ahenobarbus who was killed by Pompey in Africa), C. Carbo Arvina (cousin of the tyrant); worst of all, Q. Mucius Scaevola (an *adfinis* of the consul C. Marius). In the light of what so many others *succeeded* in doing, it is not hard to see what these men were *prevented* from doing, and to blame the government rather less effusively than the sources do. At any rate, it is significant that three of the four were related to loyalist leaders, and that these leaders neither objected nor complained, nor showed the slightest sign of turning against the murderers of their kinsmen.

But it was fitting that the period that began with the massacre of 87—already much exaggerated—should end with the massacre of 82; and it was a godsend to many, looking for *ex post facto* justification. In the final crisis—as in any final test—loyalty was again not entirely a matter of family or connections; though it was firmer among those—especially stalwart Etruscans—who had not forgotten Marius, much firmer among new men than among the inheritors of ancestral *uirtus*. Yet even among the *nobilitas* some names stand out and deserve a mention: thus, in addition to those already listed, the Junii Bruti. Above all, we should not forget the name of L. Scipio Asiagenus, blackened by the tradition of those who could not bear the contrast: twice offered pardon by Sulla, who would not lightly harm a fellow-Patrician, this man, of no known Marian connections, preferred exile and the obloquy of *ex parte* history.

Yet on the whole Sulla's victory, as all agree, was that of the *nobilitas*. In 80, with the Republic reconstituted, politics could begin again according to the old rules, with Sulla no longer the feared Dictator, but the noble consul of outstanding *auctoritas*, loyally supporting the candidacy of his *adfines*.[16] By the time of the elections for 78, Sulla could support a good man not particularly connected with him (Q. Catulus—see pp. 217 f., above) and permit the election of a man he distrusted (M. Lepidus) against the other candidate of his choice.[17] The game could go on.

The shattering effects of Sulla's rebellion were nevertheless to become obvious before long. This is—rightly—a commonplace of modern scholarship. But perhaps a detailed study of that rebellion can give us a better insight into the character and morale of the men who claimed the divine right to govern the Roman world. As we have seen, the lawful government of Rome during those years has been compared to 'mice at play'. Perhaps the victorious nobility invites comparison with a species of larger rodent. In the end, they had all been waiting for Sulla.

NOTES

[1] This is an expanded version of a paper first read to the Society for the Promotion of Roman Studies in London on November 1st, 1960, and since, in adapted form, at Bryn Mawr College and to the Oxford branch of the Classical Association. I should like to thank those who contributed to the discussion on those various occasions, and to record my pleasure that Professors T. R. S. Broughton and Sir Ronald Syme, to whom the approach here adopted perhaps owes more than to any other living scholar, were kind enough to take the chair at two of the meetings. The views expressed, of course, are entirely my own.

[2] For a survey of recent work in some parts of this field, see *Historia* 11 (1962) 197 f. (unfortunately only up to 1959).

[3] In this as in so much else Scullard's is markedly superior even to other quite recent general works. Thus, e.g., Heuss's *Röm. Geschichte* (1960) 168 f., still moves within the bias of the sources. Among specialist works, Gabba's edition of App. *b.c.* i shows that scholar's usual balance and learning (e.g. p. 205). One must also recall H. Bennett, *Cinna and his Times* (1923)—a whole generation in advance of its day, and therefore ignored until recently. It is still by far the best book on this period.

[4] Valerius Antias, in view of his omission in Cic. *leg.* i, *init.*, may belong to a later period.

[5] It is no longer necessary to give full documentation for these and similar generally known facts: this can be found, admirably collected and briefly discussed, in *MRR* (with the 1960 *Supplement*).

[6] Cichorius has shown (*ibid.* 167 f.) that that interesting body is not conspicuous for attachment to Sulla—except for those who, like Pompey and Catiline, joined him in the hour of victory. Several of its members (where we can trace them) later appear as *Cinnani*, some later still as *Sertoriani*.

[7] This caused Münzer needless difficulty (*RE*, s.v. 'Lutatius', no. 7, col. 2073). We have seen that the elder Catulus married a Servilia, who was Hortensius' mother-in-law; she was a *femina primaria* at the time of the Verres trial (Cic. 2 *Verr.* ii 24). Münzer needlessly assumed that she must also be the mother of the younger Catulus. He, in 70 B.C., would be at least fifty-one years old—very probably some years older, since his consulship is likely to have been retarded by the civil troubles. Was Servilia, then,

necessarily seventy? It would be *possible*, of course. But since the younger Catulus is attested as (*prima facie*) the son of a Domitia, why assume it? There seems to have been a considerable difference in age between the two children of the elder Catulus: the younger Catulus, *cos*. 78, was born, at the latest, in 121 (probably earlier); his sister's husband Q. Hortensius was born in 116 (Cic. *Br.* 229), and we know that girls of noble family usually married much earlier than the men. We may safely follow the evidence, on its simplest interpretation, and hold that the elder Catulus married twice, first a Domitia and then a Servilia: the latter, at the time of the Verres trial, need have been only in her fifties.

8 Livy, *per.* lxxxiv: 'nouis ciuibus senatus consulto suffragium datum est' (84 B.C., after Cinna's death, reported in the previous book). No other plausible interpretation has ever been (or apparently can be) suggested for this statement: there is no record of *ciuitas sine suffragio* for new citizens. L. R. Taylor (*Voting Districts* 105) finds it inconceivable that Cinna should not have rewarded his loyal allies the Italians; yet even modern governments are often less quick to reward proved loyalty than reason and justice would seem to demand—and more given to aiming at placating opponents and neutrals. [One might perhaps compare a letter written by Bonaparte to Kléber in Egypt (Herold, *Bonaparte in Egypt* (1963) 145): 'No matter what you do to the Christians, they will always be our friends. You must prevent them from becoming too insolent.'] Miss Taylor, naturally, is also puzzled by the election of L. Philippus to a censorship, to enrol the Italians whose enfranchisement he had so violently opposed a few years before. The connection and the policy behind it are far from puzzling. The full enfranchisement of the freedmen (Livy, *ibid.*) was a similar redemption of an old promise.

9 λόγῳ μὲν ἐπὶ Μιθριδάτην, ἔργῳ δὲ ἐπ' ἐκεῖνον αὐτόν (Plut. *Sulla* 20, 1).

10 Arrival in Italy: Livy, *per.* lxxxv, *init.*; *foedus* with the Italians: half-way through Livy, *per.* lxxxvi. A great deal intervenes.

11 Livy, *per.* lxxxiii. Since this is one of the few speeches noted by the epitomator, it must have been a showpiece of Livian oratory. Cicero (*Att.* viii 3, 6) mentions Flaccus, together with Philippus and Scaevola, as a precedent for his own guidance in 49; but he neither there nor anywhere else refers to Flaccus as an orator. Livy, finding the scene described by Sisenna, would be free to invent a worthy piece of oratory.

12 The tribunes later opposed Carbo after Cinna's death (App. *b.c.* i 78). Of the quaestors, we need only mention Verres (*MRR* ii 61); in the following year there was M. Piso, on whom see below. Much has been written about the statement that 'L. Cinna et Cn. Papirius Carbo a se ipsis consules per biennium creati' (Livy, *per.* lxxxiii). But the truth is not all that dramatic. (Greenidge-Clay² here as so often—e.g. on the matter of the redistribution of the new citizens—has the right interpretation.) There is no warrant for assuming that elections were not held: no source, however hostile, states this, and 'magistratum creare' does not, in normal usage, imply the absence of elections (contrast *per.* lxxx, on the *coss.* 86). The only irregularity was that both the consuls had themselves re-elected (apparently earlier in the year than usual: App. *b.c.* i 77), which had not happened before—not even at the height of the Hannibalic War—and was worse than the re-election of one consul under his own presidency. But such innovations proliferate from precedent to precedent in grave emergencies: had the consuls been successful, no one would have remembered it against them, any more than Marius' *continuatio* was later held against him. The election of a hostile college of tribunes (and the tribunes' action against Carbo must have been unanimous to be effective) speaks for itself, answering the question of *dominatio*.

13 Which Sisenna apparently reported in detail (fr. 130 P).

14 Κίνναν τε πυθόμενοι τεθνάναι καὶ τὴν πόλιν ἀδιοίκητον εἶναι (*b.c.* i 79). This is followed immediately by Sulla's invasion of Italy. Sulla did not disguise these facts, and Appian understood them.

Q

[15] See *Historia* 6 (1957) 338 [=p. 53, above]. On the Messallae, see especially Syme, *JRS* 45 (1955) 158.

[16] On this, see my discussion, *Historia* 11 (1962) 230.

[17] Sulla seems to have supported Mam. Lepidus, who—as we have seen—had probably rendered him good service. Sall. *hist.* i 86 M shows that Mam. Lepidus had suffered a *repulsa*. No other year is plausible for this; and Sulla's opposition to M. Lepidus is recorded by many sources.

The *Lex Thoria*: A Reconsideration

Cɪc. *Brutus* 136 'Sp. Thorius satis ualuit in populari genere dicendi, is qui agrum publicum uitiosa et inutili lege uectigali leuauit'.

Id. *de oratore* ii 284 (an example of *quod est praeter exspectationem*) ' ... Appi maioris illius [read 'illud'?], qui in senatu, cum ageretur de agris publicis et de lege Thoria et peteretur [?] Lucilius ab iis qui a pecore eius depasci agros publicos dicerent, "non est", inquit, "Lucili pecus illud: erratis." (defendere Lucilium uidebatur.) "ego liberum puto esse: qua libet pascitur."' (The name 'Lucilius' is uncertain.)

Appian, *b.c.* i 27 ' ... μέχρι Σπούριος Θόριος [Βο(υ)ριος MSS] δημαρχῶν εἰσηγήσατο νόμον· τὴν μὲν γῆν μηκέτι διανέμειν, ἀλλ' εἶναι τῶν ἐχόντων, καὶ φόρους ὑπὲρ αὐτῆς τῷ δήμῳ κατατίθεσθαι, καὶ τάδε τὰ χρήματα χωρεῖν ἐς διανομάς.'

Discussion about Thorius and his law shows no sign of abating.[1] Not that the matter is of really outstanding historical importance: the final outcome of the post-Gracchan agrarian legislation is well known and clearly summed up by Appian a few lines later ('ὁ δῆμος ἀθρόως ἁπάντων ἐξεπεπτώκει'). But for the interpretation of the obscure period between the time of the Gracchi and the age of Marius—a period that is still, at present, as dark an age for us as the age of Marius itself was until recently—the matter is of considerable interest. Our view of the dating and the political aims of the three agrarian laws listed in the chapter of Appian cited must have a profound effect on our interpretation of the political struggles of the period—if we ever succeed in forming such an interpretation. Thus the matter is, at any rate, of more than merely antiquarian interest.

Moreover, to stimulate us further, there is the humiliating nature of the situation in which we find ourselves. Scholars working on this period of history all consider themselves tolerably familiar with Latin: some of us have been teaching and writing it for years, and all of us might feel deeply offended if charged with

235

inability to understand a simple Latin sentence. Yet here most of us must of necessity plead guilty to the charge. For consider the first of these Ciceronian passages: Cicero here makes what, to him, was undoubtedly a perfectly plain statement about Thorius, in line with the simple statements about the other rather obscure orators in the context of the passage. His readers (and, in the work, his imaginary audience) were expected to take it in with that immediate comprehension characteristic of one's reaction to a simple statement in a language one knows well. There is no question or explanation in the dialogue, and clearly none was needed. Although Cicero and his contemporaries were not excessively familiar with the detailed history of the late second century B.C. (and Cicero nowhere in the *Brutus* assumes any such familiarity), there could clearly be no ambiguity about this. To modern scholars, however, several interpretations of this passage have seemed equally plausible, or very nearly so; and there is no unanimity as to which is the real meaning. Yet, of all the opinions advanced by distinguished scholars, only one can be the right one—the one intended by Cicero and understood by his audience. The situation is therefore embarrassing. Our right to claim understanding of *any* Latin text is challenged.

Part of the trouble is that scholars have tended to investigate the legal and historical background and then to translate Cicero's sentence in accordance with the theory they thus formed. Since the background is anything but clear, this has inevitably deepened confusion.

In fact, the interpretation of Cicero's statement here is purely a matter of Latinity, to be investigated by linguistic methods; and the consequent understanding of Cicero's meaning (which should not be impossible to reach) is the only firm base for legal and historical interpretation.[2]

Four translations theoretically possible appear to result from the following facts: that *uectigali* can be (or, at least, has been) taken as either noun or adjective; and that the ablative can have either instrumental or separative meaning. We thus get the following possibilities:[3]

A. *uectigali* a noun:

(I) first ablative (*lege*) instrumental, second (*uectigali*) separative: 'Thorius relieved the public land of a rent by means of a ... law';

(II) first ablative (*lege*) separative, second (*uectigali*) instru-mental: 'Thorius relieved the public land of a ... law by means of a rent';

B. *uectigali* an adjective (going with *lege*):

(I) ablative instrumental: 'Thorius relieved the public land by means of a faulty and useless rent law';

(II) ablative separative: 'Thorius relieved the public land of a faulty and useless rent law'.

Each of these—perhaps even B (I), arrant nonsense though it is —seems to have had its defenders. (As translations are not always explicitly given, it is sometimes not certain which has been adopted.)

Let us proceed by elimination. B seems to be a measure of despair, invented (probably) to circumvent the difficulties of A. It would produce an easy and (on almost any interpretation) manœuvrable meaning (B II), and the only point against it is that it is unfortunately not Latin. Mommsen long ago pointed out that *lex uectigalis*, meaning 'a law about a rent', is linguistically impossible: not that the word 'uectigalis' cannot be an adjective (it is)—but it has a known meaning, and this meaning is simply quite different. Vagueness and evasion cannot overcome this.[4] We are therefore thrown back upon having to grapple with the 'ambiguity' of A. That it cannot be a genuine ambiguity we have seen: Cicero did not see one, nor (apparently) did his readers: and he was far too good a stylist anyway to let such a major blemish slip through unobserved. Purely formal ambiguity, on the other hand, where the real meaning is obvious, is (as is well known) never a cause for concern to writers of Latin prose. We shall see one or two examples of this presently.

We might begin by asking the question: if two ablatives, one instrumental and one separative, go together, in what order does Cicero normally arrange them? This is clearly the first line of approach, and it has not been altogether ignored. Intuition will not help—as the differences of opinion among eminent Latinists show. For what it is worth, the majority of those whom I asked and who replied without analysis or argument favoured A (I).

Among those who have written about this, no less an authority than Niccolini[5] maintained that 'quello strumentale suole essere, grammaticalmente, più vicino al verbo'.

Unfortunately, Schmalz-Hofmann has nothing to say about this, and I have not been able to find statistics on the point. Such evidence as I have is inconclusive and seems to show that this approach will not help.

In the only other passage where both these ablatives are used with *leuare*, the order is indeed as Niccolini claims.[6] But it would be rash to assert that the meaning is due to the order—that the two ablatives could not be interchanged without change of meaning. As soon as we turn to *liberare* (akin in meaning and more frequently used in this construction), it appears clear that no rule of strict order is observed.[7] Nevertheless, it is equally clear that in none of these examples is there genuine ambiguity: whatever the order, the 'ambiguity' is merely formal, such as we must believe it to be in the case under discussion.

It also at once becomes clear why this is so. In fact, an entirely different approach is necessary, by way of meaning and usual combinations. It has, of course, often been observed[8] that a *uitiosa et inutilis lex* is a most improbable instrument of relief, but a very probable evil from which relief may be sought and given. Those who, for reasons extraneous to the passage or through 'intuition', opt for A (I) must gloss over this or depreciate its importance. Yet the evidence suggests that, where there are two ablatives in this construction, this is the *sole* criterion, and an infallible one: as we have seen, there is no real ambiguity in other passages of this sort, and no reason to think that there was in this one. Let us collect (from Merguet's *Lexikon zu den philos. Schriften Ciceros*) the ablatives found, in a separative meaning, with *leuare*: we have *aegritudine, cruciatu, erroribus, molestiis, onere, opinione* (= *false* opinion), *prauitate, superstitione, uinclis, uitiis*. It is clear that the *uitiosa et inutilis lex* will fit splendidly into this series. It might be argued that a *uectigal* also would: no one likes death and taxes. However, this first of all assumes that Cicero would have disapproved of a rent on public land. There is no reason to think that he would, and good reason to think that he would not. We know how concerned he was, over a period of years, about preserving the revenue from the *ager Campanus*. And he shows frequent concern for the *aerarium*, even charging C. Gracchus with having defended it in words while exhausting it in fact.[9] Above all, if Cicero would not necessarily think a rent on public land an evil from which the land should be relieved, it is *impossible* (as such a rendering forces us to do) to believe that he would think a 'faulty and useless law' a fit means of giving this relief. I have not found a single instance in which the means of giving relief is thus spoken of in an emphatically derogatory way.[10]

I hope that the distinguished scholar whom we are honouring will not think this attention given to a single Latin sentence a waste of time, since what emerges is merely the obvious. My excuse must be that the obvious, in this case, has been obscured by much prejudice; it has been ignored for the sake of *a priori* interpretations of what Cicero *ought* to mean, or recognized and evaded, or legislated out of existence without evidence. It should now take more than such methods to upset the plain fact that, in a construction of this sort, it is *only* the meaning and the usual connotations of the words used that will enable a clear meaning for the phrase as a whole to emerge; and that in this case they furnish a meaning not one whit less obvious than in the other cases where Cicero uses this construction. What 'ambiguity' there is has been imported by scholars who have either failed to recognize or deliberately rejected the way in which phrases of this sort acquire an immediate and unmistakable meaning. It is not surprising that Cicero's audience can have had no such difficulty.

It is now time to take a further step. Once it is clear that Thorius imposed a *uectigal* (in order to rid the public land of a reprehensible law—whichever law it was: a matter too complicated for treatment here), we can confidently accept the outline of his law as given in Appian. There is no longer any reason to reject the easy emendation in Appian's text or the identification of his second law with Cicero's *lex Thoria*;[11] since one need not—indeed, should not —use Appian to arrive at the meaning of the *Brutus* passage, the latter is independent evidence strongly supporting the emendation in Appian—a point of method worth making. But it merely clinches what is already a very strong probability. That out of a very small number of agrarian laws (three, according to Appian) passed over a short period of years (fifteen, according to Appian) one should have been passed, as Cicero tells us, by a Sp. Thorius,

and one of the others by a Sp. Borius (?) would be sufficiently hard
to believe; and the argument approaches Cloudcuckooland when
its proponents have to admit that the very name of this hypothetical tribune is unknown to the extensive record of Latin nomenclature.[12] Nor should the *praenomen* be forgotten, as it all too often
is in such discussions. 'Spurius' is one of the rarest of *praenomina*:
in the *index nominum* to *CIL* vi (206 large pages of names) it occurs
five times (and one of them is the *cos.* 466—two of the others, not
unexpectedly, are Carvilii); in the Index to Broughton's *Magistrates of the Roman Republic* it occurs (apart from one very doubtful
case) only eight times after 200 B.C. (in addition to Thorius there
are 4 Postumii, 2 Carvilii and a Lucretius). On every count, the
hypothetical 'Spurius Borius' is a bastard begotten by a copyist.[13]

Only a few words remain to be added on the second Cicero
passage—the anecdote about the consul of 130 B.C.[14] *Prima facie*, it
does not reveal much. Cicero's point is the joke, not the historical
background, and he does not even directly tell us whether *Appius
maior* favoured or opposed the *lex Thoria*. However, it takes an
elaborate paradox to deny that the discussion referred to is the
usual one held in the Senate before the vote on a tribunician law.[15]
Even the bill of Ti. Gracchus, as is known,[16] was ultimately thus
discussed. And the point of the joke is that Appius Claudius
favoured some restriction on unlimited grazing on public land.
(This concern with the public land links him, as Münzer and
others have pointed out, with his relative, the *cos.* 143, father-in-
law and most distinguished friend and adviser of Ti. Gracchus.)
Such a restriction cannot have existed at the time (whether *de jure*
or *de facto*). Now, although Cicero does not actually say so in so
many words, it is surely the most straightforward interpretation
of the passage that the *lex Thoria* proposed (at least *inter alia*) to
deal with this abuse—which, perhaps, was due to the *uitiosa et
inutilis lex* that it superseded. Nor is it difficult to conjecture *how*
it proposed to deal with it: since we know that Thorius imposed a
uectigal, it was surely precisely this that he did to surplus grazing
lands: he will have imposed a *uectigal* on (at least *inter alia*) grazing
land *ultra modum*.

It would lead us too far to take the next step and attack that
other vexed problem, the relation of the *lex Thoria* to the *Lex
Agraria* of the great bronze tablets. It is a problem on which much

has been written—not all of it keeping within the limits imposed by the evidence (the very fragmentary nature of the *Lex Agraria*), and not all of it avoiding the concealed traps that threaten the merely diligent.[17] I do not think that any firm conclusion can be reached in the state of our evidence; but what I have written will perhaps show (what, in fairness, I must openly state) that I lean towards the conclusion so ably argued by Niccolini: that the two laws can be identified. But this needs very extensive investigation, for which—particularly as it must be rather inconclusive—this is not the place.[18]

NOTES

[1] Recent bibliography in Gabba's edition of Appian, *b.c.* i (1958) 93 f. The principal earlier views are summarized by Niccolini, *Fasti dei tribuni della plebe* (1934) 179 f.

[2] In view of this, I asked several eminent Latinists with no axe to grind for their views on the interpretation of the *Brutus* passage. Most of them produced an intuitive translation, without argument; but their views were far from unanimous. Both meanings in A were suggested, and B (II) got one vote as a 'possible'. (For the classification of meanings, see below.) I owe particular thanks to my Durham colleagues, Professor E. C. Woodcock and Mr N. E. Collinge, and to Dr W. F. Jackson Knight of Exeter, for detailed discussion of the passage. Needless to say, though I have profited greatly by their views, they are not responsible for mine.

[3] As it does not matter for our present purpose, I shall not detail who has held which view. (For a bibliography, see the works cited in n. 1.) The *tour de force* of taking *both* ablatives as instrumental—proposed in despair by some eminent scholars—had best be covered with a charitable veil.

[4] See, e.g., Douglas, *AJP* 1956, 388, n. 32: 'adjectives attached to *lex* often have vague or unusual meanings'. No parallels are given, since none can be. The meaning of an adjective attached to *lex*, however vague or unusual, must be explicable according to the known rules of Latin.

[5] *Op. cit.* 183—but also without evidence.

[6] '*ut animus molestiis hac potissimum re leuaretur*' (*div.* ii 7).

[7] A few examples: '*cum se maximo aere alieno Faberii manu liberarit*' (*Att.* xiv 18, 1); '*domum meam iudicio pontificum religione liberatam uideri*' (*har. resp.* 13); '*quam (urbem) L. Lucullus uirtute assiduitate consilio summis obsidionis periculis liberauit*' (*l. Man.* 20).

[8] Most clearly, again, by Niccolini (l.c.), but again without examples.

[9] *off.* ii 72; *Tusc. disp.* iii 48. On *uectigalia*, see also *leg. agr.* i 21; ii 80 f.

[10] As we have seen, our sentence is a plain statement from a mere list of orators: no obscure rhetorical trick is possible.

[11] Rightly accepted recently by Gabba, l.c. (Cf. Broughton, *MRR Suppl.* (1960) 62.) Broughton (*MRR* i 542) unfortunately had followed D'Arms (*AJP* 1935, 232 f.) in rejecting it. D'Arms tried to reduce the sequence of orators in Cicero's *Brutus* to a strict chronological sequence, with the result that he ended up with a whole crop of agrarian laws and the impossibility of accepting the emendation in Appian. Douglas (*AJP* 1956, 376 f.; corrections *ibid.* 1957, 89) recognized that D'Arms's strict chronological order is quite untenable: Cicero too obviously jumps about and, e.g., treats many an important man more than once. But Douglas tried to save an adapted form

of the theory and could do so only by introducing exceptions and *ad hoc* assumptions at every point, until one has the impression of reading a defence of pre-Copernican astronomy. That there *is* a vague chronological pattern in the *Brutus* is obvious: on the whole, it moves from the beginnings to Cicero's own day. But there are so many cross-currents (grouping by subject-matter and by association other than chronological) that the order in the *Brutus* will not help in fixing the chronology of a man or an event not otherwise chronologically anchored.

[12] Broughton, still under the spell of D'Arms, was reduced to looking round for vaguely similar names. But see my comment on the *praenomen*.

[13] The form of the *praenomen* varies slightly in the MSS, perhaps by partial confusion with the similar *nomen*, which also led to the form 'Βούριος' for the latter.

[14] The identification is almost certain. See Cichorius, *Unt. zu Luc.* 61 f.; Münzer, *RE*, s.v. '*Claudius*', no. 11; Niccolini, *op. cit.* 182—none of them, unfortunately, noticed by Broughton (l.c.). In the *Supplement* (62) he gives the credit for the identification to Douglas.

[15] Rightly, e.g., Cichorius, l.c.

[16] Plut., *Ti. Gr.* 11.

[17] An example that has led to the downfall of many elaborate arguments is noted by Gabba (*op. cit.* 94). There are other subtle traps that will have to be detailed some day.

[18] I should like to thank the University of California at Los Angeles for its hospitality.

Oratorum Romanorum Fragmenta[*]

THE practice of oratory is bound up with Roman life at the height
of Roman greatness in a way that no art, nor even Science, can
equal in our own day. No loss in the field of Roman letters is
therefore more grievous to all those trying to understand and
interpret Roman life and Roman history than the all but total
disappearance of oratorical literature, which has not only deprived
us of irreplaceable sources for Roman history, but, by leaving the
sole survivor—Cicero—in an unnatural position, has falsified
and distorted the picture presented by standard accounts down
to our own day. Accordingly, there are few living scholars who
more deserve the thanks of readers of this *Journal* than Professor
Malcovati, whose care and acumen have salvaged far more from
the wreck than would have seemed possible. The first edition of
her work (three volumes, 1930) has long been impossible to buy
(and difficult to borrow) in this country. What is presented here is
practically a new work—the tally of orators raised to 176, the
references of modern works brought up to date, the arrangement
completely revised (a convenient treatment by individual orators
supersedes the earlier imitation of Peter), and the whole produced
in a single volume of the typographical excellence and reasonable
price that we have come to expect from the house of Paravia.
The orators are numbered consecutively. Under each entry there
is first a general discussion with modern references, then a collection or copious selection of general *testimonia,* and finally the
testimonia and fragments collected for each individual speech.
Under the head of each orator, all extracts (*testimonia* and fragments) are numbered consecutively for convenience of reference,
as are the titles of individual speeches. Typographical aids (use of
different sizes, of Roman and Italic, of Arabic and Roman numer-

[*] Henrica Malcovati, *Oratorum Romanorum Fragmenta Liberae Rei Publicae iteratis curis
recensuit collegit* (Corpus Scriptorum Latinorum Paravianum). Aug. Taurinorum:
Paravia, 1955.

als) are employed with skill and care, except that, under each speech, it was not considered possible to distinguish actual fragments of it from *testimonia* concerning it: this is at times misleading, as fragments are thus concealed within apparent *testimonia* (e.g., 44–7, pp. 254–7); and it should have been possible to avoid it. The text is accompanied by notes (including, most usefully, the context in which the fragments are quoted) and by a short *apparatus*. The language of presentation and discussion is, as it should be, Latin. At the end there is an alphabetical *Index Oratorum* (which might be even more helpful if it gave the page numbers and not only the entry numbers), a concordance for Cato the Elder between this edition and the first, and finally a full table of contents.

An immense amount of knowledge, skill, and labour has gone into the making of this book, and few other living scholars would have been qualified to attempt it. The section on Cato alone is a major work of scholarship. Yet errors will go unnoticed and room for legitimate disagreement will remain. First, perhaps, some general points. One cannot help feeling that there is unnecessary duplication. Thus—to quote by page number, number of orator, and number of speech or fragment—260, 67, 1, is repeated in *ibid.*, 4; 493, 165, 3, in 496, 165, 20; and so quite often. Sometimes the same fragment is quoted twice (as a whole or in part), within a few pages, for different speeches by the same man (e.g., 226, 65, 17 = 233, 65, 3; or, more strikingly, 314, 92, 13 = 14). Yet this is not set policy; often a cross-reference is given, and much space could have been saved if this had been done consistently. More serious is the problem of whom and what to include or exclude. Clearly Professor Malcovati's ideas on this have changed considerably between the two editions, and she must often have faced the question, which soon obtrudes itself on the reader: 'Who is an orator?' (And, no less disturbing: 'What is a fragment of an orator?') On these matters a statement of editorial policy would have been welcome; as it is, this policy is difficult to disengage. The *de oratore* and other works are full of quoted snippets: how many of these come from speeches, and how many that do not are still worth including? Sometimes the editor has included what are obviously impromptu sallies (e.g., 129, 21, 21–2; 236, 65, 35–6 (with an apology); 269, 70, 15–17); others seem to get in by the back door as *testimonia* on speeches (e.g., Memmius' 'uide, Scaure, mortuus rapitur, si potes esse possessor'—217, 60, 5); yet some quotations both familiar and important have not gained entry. Thus we miss Glaucia's splendid iambic line on Q. Metellus: 'uillam in Tiburti habes, cortem in Palatio' (*de or.* ii 263); yet surely it must actually be part of a speech—we can hardly imagine it in an *altercatio*. We might also plead for Ap. Claudius' comment on the sheep of Lucilius (*de or.* ii 284) which has some historical importance. Greater generosity might at times have been an advantage. After all, even parts of *altercationes* are entitled to rank as *fragmenta oratorum* (though not *orationum*)—for it is precisely thus that Cicero uses them, to show the orator in action and demonstrate his sureness of touch and of taste. Yet in other matters the editor has often been over-generous: unexpected entries include M. Antonius' rhetorical treatise; the edicts of Bibulus, which that watcher of the heavens did not deliver as speeches; and Brutus' *laudatio* of Cato.

More important than *what* to include is *whom* to include. Who, after all, is an orator? Anyone who ever proposed a law must have spoken in its favour; yet this is not our test, as practically no one before the second century is included and many later legislators are omitted. Is our minimum qualification to be surviving reference to at least one speech? No; for twenty-four men are included, of whose speeches not even a title or occasion of delivery has survived. Can our criterion be the arbitrary, but intelligible, one of survival in Cicero's day? No; for that would exclude many second-century orators (beginning with M. Cethegus, 'Suadai medulla'— 11, 7, 1), and might imperil the status of M. Antonius, who left no speeches extant in writing (Cic. *Clu.* 140). Few speeches survived in Cicero's day and fewer were read: 'iam euanerunt', or its equivalent, is his frequent comment. These questions are bound to be asked, and one feels that they should have been answered for us by the editor, who must surely have answered them for herself. As it is, we are often left puzzled. Admittedly, we do not enjoy *de faece haurire* any more than Atticus does in the *Brutus*. But Atticus had to put up with it for the sake of completeness, and the modern reader, trying to recreate history and *la littérature inconnue*, would often be more appreciative. C. Sicinius, who died as a *quaestorius* of promise, is included, though no reference to an actual speech survives (438, 141); but Cn. Octavius (*cos.* 87), whose *contiones* made history and were much applauded (*Br.* 176), is omitted. Consuls naturally had to be able to speak, both to attain their rank and to occupy it worthily. Many appear in Cicero and at least some might have been admitted, e.g. C. Coelius Caldus (*Br.* 165; *de or.* i 117; and elsewhere); especially as M. Aurelius Scaurus (*cos.* 108) is put in and, rather oddly, assigned a speech 'in consilio Cimbrorum' (214, 59, 1). The praetorian L. Cotta ought to be there, if only as a warning example (*Br.* 137 and 259; *de or.*, *passim*). But perhaps the most serious gaps are in the ranks of those tribunes who wrote their names on the pages of history. L. Quinctius has a good run (349, 107), largely through his connection with Cicero's early forensic career; but Sp. Thorius, a good popular orator (*Br.* 136) and author of a notorious law, is absent; and so, to our amazement, are L. Appuleius Saturninus and C. Servilius Glaucia, the former 'seditiosorum omnium post Gracchos eloquentissimus' (surely high praise, whether 'post' refers to chronology or to merit), the latter 'peracutus et callidus cum primisque ridiculus' (*Br.* 224). Of this last quality we have instances: one, which ought alone to have secured him a place, has already been pointed out; and his admonition to the People to look at the opening words of a bill to see whether it concerned them (*Rab. Post.* 14) ought to be worth salvaging as a *fragmentum incertae sedis*. Others worth considering for admission—though their claims are less compelling—are Cn. Pomponius, who at one time 'habitabat in rostris' (*Br.* 305— there are numerous other references); T. Junius, a successful prosecutor (*Br.* 180); and the M. Octavius whose eloquence persuaded the People to abrogate the *Lex Sempronia frumentaria* (*Br.* 222).

The historical and biographical commentaries provided show the editor's wide reading. References to modern authors naturally stress Italian work; and Rotondi's *Leges Publicae* is perhaps cited more often than—for this period—it nowadays deserves. The amount of information given varies greatly: sometimes there might have been more, as when (to take a random example) L. Munatius Plancus' triumph and career under the Triumvirate are ignored (446, 149). There are some errors that should be corrected: M. Aemilius Scaurus (the *Princeps Senatus*) is given a suffect consulship in 107 (p. 163); Caesar is said to have triumphed after his Spanish governorship (p. 383); M. Crassus and Pompey are given the office of Triumvir (pp. 342, 358, and Index), though Caesar escapes it. That M. Fulvius Flaccus in 125 'leges *tulit* de civitate, etc,' is misleading; that Ti. Gracchus 'potestatem intercedendi [of Octavius] per seditionem abrogavit' is false; that P. Cornelius Lentulus, *ille princeps*, was killed in a Gracchan riot (103, 15) is disproved by Val. Max. v 3, 2, which cannot be ignored. As these few examples show, this part of the work is in need of revision.

Names and identities, in a work of this kind, are of particular importance. The editor sets a very high standard by learned discussion of points of spelling, e.g. in the case of the Sulpicii Gali (102, 14, and elsewhere), and of the Popillii (184, 48, viii); thus the reader is made more critical. Why 'Aquilius' (pp. 103, 227, etc.) and 'Callaecus' (131 and *passim*)? The correct spelling of the former's name is given in the *Fasti* (*Inscr. It.* xiii 1, 82) and in *ILS* 27. The latter name, like that of the tribe from which it is derived, is variously written in the MSS; but the *Fasti* again give the correct form 'Callaicus' (*op. cit.* 52), and Martial, who ought to know, confirms it by invariably—where metre enables us to check—making the name quadrisyllabic (iv 39, 10; x 37, 4 and 20; xiv 95, 1). Cicero's client should not be called Archia, though slaves and freedmen often are. It is misleading to say that P. Crassus Mucianus 'Dives cognominatus est': his adoptive father's father already bears the name. The portmanteau name, 'M. Tullius Albinovanus' (326, xix) was thrown out of court long ago by Hübner's researches (*Eph. ep.* ii 31 f.). The censor of 115 B.C. was probably Diadematus (see *MRR* 531–3), not Baliaricus (thus 194, 48, xviii); and the correct spelling of the latter's name is given by the *Fasti* (*op. cit.* 82). Sometimes our texts pose problems. The man whom L. Caesulenus accused appears (209, 57), without discussion, as Saufeius; but the OCT reads 'Sabellius' (*Br.* 131), and this is almost certainly at the back of our MS tradition: the name, though rare, is plausible and does occur (e.g., *CIL* ix 396). One might even wonder whether we are really entitled to emend the name of Caesar's Samnite client to 'Decidius' (396, 121, xiii), despite high modern authority: there must have been many Samnites called Decius. The Cominii of Spoletium (439, 143–4) provide a nice puzzle in *praenomina*. Münzer (in *RE*) builds up Gaius as the chief figure: yet the text leaves no doubt that Publius was the elder brother and far more important (e.g., *Br.* 271; *Clu.* 100). 'Gaius' is a very doubtful character: he seems to be mentioned once, by initial only, in Asconius (p. 59 Clark). Cicero calls the second brother Lucius (*Clu.* 100), which Malcovati rejects. But could Cicero have made this slip in front of an audience that knew the men? On the other hand, Asconius (unfortunately for the trust that is sometimes put in him) undoubtedly could: for he confuses the two L. Manlii Torquati, father and son —a point on which Cicero decisively convicts him of error. Malcovati (356, 109), following many other scholars, here also seems to prefer the scholiast to the contemporary speaking to an audience that knew the men. Yet it seems advisable to believe Cicero both on the Torquati and on the Cominii, whose names should thus be left as Publius and Lucius. T. Annius Luscus is dissected (as also by Broughton) into father and son; but Fraccaro (cited by Malcovati), as usual, long ago recognized the truth: the new man who first appears in junior offices in 172 and 169 duly becomes consul in 153—not by any means an unreasonable interval: we need only recall how long Metellus Numidicus expected Marius to wait for the consulate, and compare the career of M. Cornelius Cethegus. For this son of a great Patrician (*cos.* 204) was Annius' colleague as *IIIuir* in 169 and reached the consulship in 160. Annius was fortunate in waiting only seven years longer.

In textual matters the editor is at her best. Her attitude is one of sound, but not unreasoning, conservatism; she prefers admitting defeat to other editors' wild guesswork; and characteristically sensible comments abound (e.g., 185, 48, x; 245, 66, 27). Misprints are not numerous. The following are worth noting: 'vi' for 'iv' (110, near end); 'exulis' for 'exules' (282, 76, 16, l. 4); 'Gallo' for 'Gallio' (435, 140, 3, l. 2); 'amantissime' for 'amentissime' (475, 159, 16, l. 49); 'domi' for 'domui' (533, 176, 20, l. 1). Occasionally gibberish is left unobelized: e.g., 'ursici' (181, 48, 25), and the text of 532, 176, 15. Judgments are bound to differ on points of detail, but these are hardly worth quoting; for in many cases we cannot hope to have anything like the original text. It would be self-delusion to pretend the opposite. Grammarians quote for their limited purposes, without bothering to give the precise words, except for the few that illustrate their point. As everyone knows, even Quintilian misquotes—not to mention Cicero. The conventions of scholarship were different from ours. Some well-known fragments provide interesting examples, as they are variously quoted; e.g., 497, 165, 25 (probably the best-known fragment of Calvus). Most illuminating, perhaps, is Cicero's quotation from the jurist Brutus' *de iure ciuili*—the phrases reported as quoted by Crassus in the famous battle of wits with the jurist's son (254, 66, xii). What purport to be the same words are quoted in the *de oratore* and in the *pro Cluentio*, and each of the three passages in fact reads differently in the two works. In the circumstances it hardly matters whether we read 'inspectabilem' (8, 4, 3, l. 10—rightly, it seems) or something else, or whether we can improve on conjectures like 'nos diuinitus' (108, 18, 7, l. 3) in a *locus desperatus*. One fragment, however, deserves mention because of its historical importance. It is interesting to puzzle out what Laelius said about Scipio Aemilianus' death; for the story that he was murdered was soon assiduously circulated, with various people cast for the role of murderer. Did Laelius, at the time, speak of natural death? Unfortunately the passage is corrupt (121, 20, 22) and everything depends on emendation. Malcovati has abandoned the reading she accepted in the first edition and obelized the passage ('cumeo morborumtemouit'). But there may be a much simpler remedy than the violent interventions of Carcopino, Bardon, and others: could we not read 'cum eum morbus tum remouit', thus establishing natural death in simple words? (In the same fragment we should probably read 'hace ciuitate' in l. 3 (cf. *Lex rep.*, 41, 58, *al.*) and perhaps 'eo dem<um>tempore' in l. 5.)

If the reviewer has naturally often been concerned with disagreeing, it is only in the hope that this important work may thereby be made even more helpful. The classics of scholarship may be defined as those works which are cited by initials. Among them, *ORF* has long had its place assured. But those classics (like Peter's *HRR*) are often left to become venerable rather than useful. Malcovati, in this edition, has shown that she will not leave her work to such a fate. May we, therefore, hope for a third edition?

R

The Lost Histories of Alexander the Great[*]

No man, in antiquity, had so many books written about him as Alexander the Great. Fragments of dozens survive, many more are nothing but names to us, and there must be scores of which we have not even heard. It is a devastating comment on our knowledge of the ancient world that the earliest narrative substantially surviving is that of Diodorus Siculus, and that we turn to a writer of the age of Hadrian for our most trustworthy information. Needless to say, this state of affairs has stimulated *Quellenforschung* more than in most fields of ancient history. And in the sad state of our evidence we can take some comfort in the fact that scholars of the calibre of Schwartz and Jacoby have laboured to sift the débris and reconstruct the edifice of the tradition. Pearson has bravely joined them; and inevitably he owes a great deal to them.[1]

After an Introduction giving some general characteristics of the known writers on Alexander, P. proceeds roughly in chronological order. He claims to write as a student of literature and 'to attempt a new chapter in the history of Greek literature' by investigating, in particular, the Alexander historians of the first generation. It is hard to see much novelty in this; but it is true that no book of precisely this scope and shape had yet been written. It is useful to have it in this form, especially to the student and teacher in an English-speaking university. That this audience has been considered is clear throughout: practically no untranslated Greek defaces the text, no knowledge of previous literature is assumed, and long passages (up to over two pages) of fragments are cited in full, in very accurate translation. One who has already used this book with a class ignorant of Greek (a state of affairs not unparalleled nowadays) can vouch for its didactic excellence. It is enhanced by the fact that P. has worked over the whole of the

[*] Lionel Pearson, *The Lost Histories of Alexander the Great*. New York: American Philological Association; Oxford: Blackwell 1960.

evidence himself (the book took nearly ten years to complete) and that, at least up to 1955 or so, there is little in the modern literature that has escaped him.

The approach is very orthodox. P. asks the usual questions and gives sound common-sense answers. He knows the limitations imposed by the evidence and tries to keep within them. That this is salutary and far from obvious, anyone familiar with the vagaries of Kornemann, Tarn and the early Robinson (not to mention the thesis-writers) will attest. P.'s method consists in going over the fragments in detail and discussing each problem as it arises.

The first main chapter deals with Callisthenes. The circumstances of his invitation are duly appreciated, but no reason is given for the odd statement that he perhaps did not understand that he was meant to kindle Greek enthusiasm for Alexander. P.'s own later discussion (e.g., 33) makes it clear that he understood only too well. It is curious to find a scholar of P.'s habitual caution apparently accepting (24) the tale of Callisthenes' two declamations (Plut. *Alex.* 54), including even the quotation threatening Alexander's life. The reason given is that 'Plutarch says that Stroebus ... recounted this incident to Aristotle'. In fact he says that Hermippus reports that Stroebus did so; and he does not even make it clear whether the final quotation is still supposed to be Stroebus or Hermippus pure and simple. Callisthenes' *Periplus* is rightly accepted as genuine: it must surely be related to the work on Alexander (thus Westermann). Our fragments are confined to Asia Minor, and so (probably) was the *Periplus*, perhaps inserted in the history. (At a higher level, we might compare Polybius—not to mention Herodotus.)

P. falsely states (28) that nothing is known of Theophrastus' *Callisthenes* except the title; yet this is preferable to the fantastic interpretations often put upon the work (cf. *CQ* N.S. 8 (1958) 154 f.).[1a] P. however seems to accept the consequence of those interpretations—the 'Peripatetic' view of Alexander, as elaborated by Stroux and Tarn (thus, e.g., 88). This lack of clarity and consistency is repeated with regard to Callisthenes' attitude to Alexander's deification. In his discussion of the '*proskynesis* of the sea' (37), P. rightly notices that the wording of this notorious 'fragment' may be the scholiast's and that nothing can be built on it; also that whatever Callisthenes did write may be 'courtly reminiscence of Homer'. But he follows modern authority in *rejecting* this, chiefly on the strength of Alexander's visit to Ammon, where 'Alexander's godhead is formally announced'.[2] However, nothing in Strabo's account gives the slightest justification for holding that Callisthenes proclaimed Alexander's 'godhead': he merely spread the story (no doubt with the King's consent) that the King was *the son* of a god. The difference is crucial: see Arrian iv 11, not genuine (of course), but probably (like much in Arrian's speeches) based on good tradition, in this case perhaps really Peripatetic. At any rate, the distinction between hero and god, which it asserts, is known to be central to Greek religious thought; and it alone makes sense of Callisthenes' behaviour. Far from being an unprincipled fool, as he appears in most of our literature from Timaeus to Tarn,[3] he faced death for his principles —which few Greeks were ready to do. Alexander's divine sonship was the noble lie (clearly not meant literally for educated men) that embodied a sincere belief in Alexander's mission; for heroization was permissible, and divine sonship an expression of it as a myth. But deification was blasphemy. Nor, if Antipater knew this (*ap.* Suidas), can it be claimed that Alexander did not. The King's deification was a milestone: within a few years we have sunk to the *Hymn to Demetrius*. Yet the whole tradition shows that in Alexander's case it was new and, to many, unthinkable.[4]

The excessively literary approach has here led to serious error, and P. has not quite had the courage of his insight. Yet historians have usually done no better. It is difficult to believe (for the sceptic as for the Christian) that the Greeks could take their religion seriously. But Callisthenes' courage confirms the implications of the events of 324, and Arrian gives us the theoretical background; and after all, it is no more incredible than the vitality of modern religions, when the logical observer of daily life might conclude that they were stone dead.

P. ingeniously and convincingly relates the 'discovery' of many Homeric peoples and places along Alexander's route to Callisthenes' courtly efforts (40 f.). Less convincing is his attempt to disprove Callisthenes' bias against Parmenio; but this is a matter that each student must weigh up for himself.

Chapter 3 discusses an assortment of minor writers, most important of them Chares. P.'s general attitude to him is, on the whole, that of Jacoby: the fragments make it hard to picture his work as serious history. P. corrects the common description of it as a *History of Alexander* (thus, e.g., C. A. Robinson): the title is well-attested and must mean *Stories of Alexander*. P. is not immune to the temptation of pushing 'internal evidence' too far in trying to identify fragments. That Chares described a feast in Macedon just before the Susa marriages (51 f.) cannot be argued from some verbal similarities (only one at all striking) between his account of the latter and Diodorus' account of the former (xvii 16): Chares' work was there for all to read, and it is far more likely that some-one (Clitarchus, or even Diodorus himself) adapted a description he found in it to a similar occasion than that Chares in fact verbally repeated himself within a few sentences. More seriously misleading is P.'s conjecture that Chares (as chamberlain) will be behind all accounts of 'introductions' to the King. P. mentions Plutarch's account of the fall of Philotas, where, after Philotas has refused to take the informer to the King, 'another person' finally does so; and he thinks that the account may be from Chares and the other person Chares himself. Unfortunately, much as we should like to know the author of this account, there are no good grounds for identifying him; and the 'other person' was the page Metron (Curt. vi 7, 22). The fuller version in Curtius reads very unlike what little we have of Chares. (See P.'s comments—61—on these fragments.)[5]

Of the other minor authors in this chapter, Ephippus is worth noting. It is customary to describe his work on the deaths of Hephaestion and Alexander (the title is not known) as a vicious lampoon. Athenaeus is the only source for fragments, and P. shrewdly notes that he naturally would quote the work for drink-ing habits. P. stresses the serious reasons that may underlie the publication of a hostile pamphlet not long after the King's death. But his portrait of Ephippus as a disgraced official, a refugee in Athens, who wrote in the Athenian interest about the time of the Lamian War, is more ingenious than acceptable. The identification with Ephippus son of Chalcideus (see Jacoby, *FGrHist* ii D, p. 438), an official in Egypt, is pure guesswork, and Ephippus' story of Gorgus the hoplophylax (F 5) surely shows his presence at the court late in 324. P. seems determined to discredit a source that gives an unflattering portrait of Alexander (an attitude that may derive from Tarn): the fact that the Gorgus story fits in well with our epigraphical evidence is said to be proof, not of its presumptive truth, but of 'how skilfully Ephippus has built up his stories on the basis of certain well-attested facts'; and 'the motivation of the story is also clear', viz. Athenian propaganda. The unprejudiced reader, finding an author supported by chance epigraphical finds, prefers simply to *believe* him: if he did not, history could hardly be written. And Ephippus nowhere says that Alexander threatened to attack Athens—clearly the chief point that a propagandist such as P. imagines would have made. Similarly Ephippus' account of the King's divine costumes. According to P. there is no need to believe that it is accurate or trustworthy (65). But is there any reason to believe that it is not? As far as our slender evidence goes, the account is confirmed; why, therefore, should we believe that Ephippus, writing shortly after the King's death about matters known to tens of thousands, made himself a laughing-stock by silly invention? Strange devices are necessary to circumvent the evidence: thus the odd statement that, in 323, most people in Greece had had no eye-witness account of Alexander's appearance. And if the idea of his sitting for his portrait wielding a thunderbolt (cf. Plut. *Alex.* 4) 'strains the imagination too far', P. should look at the evidence on the last months of Alexander's life as a whole (see, e.g., Hamilton, *CQ* N.S. 3 (1953) 151 f.—not known to P.). It is a pity that P. cannot escape the reluctance—common among English-speaking scholars—to accept any evidence that conflicts with an idealized *a priori* image of Alexander. He rightly rejects the division of the sources into 'favourable' and 'unfavourable' (241); but he refuses to discard the attitude of which it is symptomatic.

Chapter 4 deals with Onesicritus, who (P. thinks) was probably born at Astypalaea and published his work by 310. P. wants to amend the title (as recorded by Diog. Laert.) to Πῶς Ἀλέξανδρος ⟨ἀν⟩ήχθη, which he takes to mean *The Anabasis of Alexander* (but can it?); Diogenes' comparison of it to the Παιδείαν Κύρου then has to be corrected to Ἀνάβασιν Κύρου. This arbitrary procedure is supported by weak arguments, such as the attempt to assign the whole of Plut. *Alex.* 14 (meeting with Diogenes and the Pythia) to Onesicritus, on the strength of a supposed similarity with Xenophon's consultation of Socrates and Apollo (*anab.* iii 1). The main point of the Diogenes story is said to be that he at least did not tell the King to stay at home! It takes much faith to believe all this. Not much that is new or exciting can really be said about Onesicritus, and it is best not attempted. More reference to excellent previous treatments (in this case by Strasburger in *RE* and by T. S. Brown in his University of California Monograph, 1949) would, as so often, have saved a good deal of space.

Next comes a useful account of Nearchus; though again, 37 pages (with long extracts) seems more than he deserves. P. skilfully brings out the influence of the *Odyssey* and the standard form of the *Periplus* (as well as that of Herodotus) and rightly concludes that the work was a mixture of art and science, not above sacrificing the latter to the former. Nearchus' portrait of the King is well analysed (147–8); though at times P. again follows modern orthodoxy against the evidence (e.g., on πόθος, and on the supposed 'policy of hellenization'). On one of the more puzzling questions (Nearchus' account of the march through Gedrosia) P. has nothing to say in its place: Strasburger's reconstruction in *Hermes* 80 (1952) 456 f. seems to have reached him later and is mentioned (and rejected, perhaps a little hastily) only in n. 171 (p. 178).

We now come to the most important authors: Aristobulus, Ptolemy and Clitarchus have a chapter each, in that order (which P. regards as chronological). P. goes over the usual indecisive data on Aristobulus' life and rightly accepts a late date (after 285) for the composition of the work. The history of the long dispute on the order of the three authors is briefly surveyed (152 f.); but P. does not know Strasburger's decisive refutation of Tarn in *BO* 9 (1952) 202 f. (after which it is hard to take Tarn seriously).

P. goes through the fragments of Aristobulus in detail, citing and summarizing at length. Few will find much to quarrel with here. He sensibly rejects the frequent attempts to ascribe too much of Arrian to Aristobulus. Then he fully presents the overwhelming evidence that justifies the ancient view of this author as a κόλαξ (i.e., panegyrist): thus the attack on Thebes is redeemed by the tale of Timoclea; the Gordian knot is duly untied; worst of all, Alexander attended drunken orgies merely because he enjoyed the conversation (158—this was gratefully believed by Tarn; but see, e.g., Strasburger, *Ptol. u. Alex.* 13 f.). After this, the adulterated versions of the deaths of Clitus and Callisthenes cause no surprise. It was this element in Aristobulus that endeared him to Tarn, whose purpose was similarly panegyric and apologetic; but P., while showing full knowledge of the evidence, ends by joining Tarn in concluding that Aristobulus merely 'did not show the hostility ... that philosophers were supposed to feel for tyrants': again he shies away from the consequences of his own analysis.

The chapter on Ptolemy is less purely narrative than most. As P. points out, the named fragments are few and not all trustworthy: C. A. Robinson is probably the only one who has printed Synesius' story of why the Macedonian warriors had to shave as a genuine fragment. (He may yet change his mind in his *Commentary*.) Our view of Ptolemy must be based on Arrian. P. shows restraint and good judgment. He admits (193 f.) that we do not really know when Ptolemy wrote or for what purpose, or even what manner of work it was. He rejects Kornemann's fantastic *tour de force* and he rightly questions the common assumption (which was unfortunately shared even by Strasburger) that Ptolemy worked largely from documents. In this respect, Ptolemy was almost certainly less well off than Lord Montgomery—far from being a second Thucydides (a view that P. tears to pieces). But he thinks that 'we are on firmer ground' with the belief that the history was largely military. Why are we? Arrian cites Aristobulus rather more often than Ptolemy; yet, had it not been for Strabo, who could have guessed Aristobulus' interest in geography? Pliny cites Ptolemy twice: in his bibliography (book i) as a source for books xii and xiii, on foreign trees. We need not conclude that the King's interests were chiefly arboricultural; but it should make us wonder about the modern image of the stern soldier—a picture belied by what we know of Ptolemy's career after Alexander's death. Strasburger has surely killed this scholarly abstraction. Though Ptolemy drew the line at the story of the Amazon (F 28a), he liked a good story (F 2—characteristically, he is not named for it by Arrian, which again should give the source-tracker pause), particularly if it helped to glorify Alexander (F 7 and 12; and we must not forget the snakes on the way to Ammon (F 8)). Even his military narrative shows traces of this (F 6), as of lack of *akribeia* (F 19: he failed to say how the Indus was crossed).

P. very properly warns against indiscriminate enthusiasm for his military descriptions. Yet he still falls into some exaggeration of his merits, at least in the later battle scenes. There is the battle with Porus' son, of which we have three accounts (171 f., 198). Ptolemy is Arrian's main authority, and he must take the blame for the battle order (see 199 for comments on this) and for the statement that Alexander hoped he could easily defeat the *whole* of Porus' forces with his cavalry (Arr. v 14, 2). By contrast, the alleged letter of Alexander (*ap*. Plut. *Alex*. 60) makes good sense, since the King could certainly hope to defeat the enemy's *cavalry* with his own.[6]

The battle with Porus' son is crucial in any discussion of the dates of Ptolemy and Aristobulus. P. translates Arr. v 14, 5 in such a way as to make the reflection on Aristobulus' story Ptolemy's and not Arrian's own, even though he notes that this is the only time that Ptolemy stoops to argue.[7] In fact neither language nor logic demands this translation: it can be held that the return to the Ptolemy quotation is clearly indicated by Arrian (ἀλλὰ ... γὰρ λέγει ... ἀφικέσθαι), after an excursion into direct speech. If so (and the matter is, at the least, uncertain), this passage has no bearing on the problem of the relative dates of the two authors. (On the substantive question, see Strasburger, *Ptol. u. Alex.* 15 f., which P. ought to have considered: Ptolemy's priority is more likely than not.)

P. rightly asks (208) whether Ptolemy's 'accounts of incidents he did not himself witness are noticeably different in quality', and he finds shortcomings in them (city of the Malli and defeat in Bactria). The shortcomings are undeniable (and, in the Bactrian affair, worse than P. paints them); but we have seen that Ptolemy's military narrative is not always satisfactory: his memory and powers of interpretation, though good in outline, were far from perfect. No real difference on these lines can be established.

P. sums up (210–11) by saying that Ptolemy threw no new light on Alexander's character or on the main problems of interpretation; that he withheld judgment on them; and that Arrian did not necessarily regard him as a great historian. In so far as this is a reaction against conventional enthusiasm for Ptolemy, it is to be welcomed. But as a complete view of Ptolemy it is untenable. Strasburger, while going too far in enthusiasm, certainly made this clear long ago. Nothing justifies us in confining Ptolemy's interest to military affairs: at the most, we can say that Arrian used him in this way (and F 2 should make us cautious about this too). Pliny obviously did not. And we have little idea of how (e.g.) Curtius used him.[8]

It is commonly said that Ptolemy wrote his history in extreme old age, when he had nothing better to do. P. makes it clear that there is no real evidence, and it is perhaps hardly worth arguing about. Yet what we know of Ptolemy's old age suggests that his faculties were not unimpaired (as those of Seleucus were); while it is worth recalling that it was he who snatched Alexander's body and buried it in his capital: at least for a while, he clearly tried to create the image of himself as the true Successor. Can it have been in this phase that he composed the History? Ptolemy the author and Ptolemy the King have perhaps been too much dissociated. On this hypothesis, much would fall into place: the snakes in the desert; the fantastic figures of enemy losses; finally the mixture of *suppressio ueri* and *suggestio falsi* that makes up what P. thinks his 'apparent reserve' in his treatment of characters and politics. A writer who reports that Philotas was 'convicted by clear proofs' (and cites a miserable and irrelevant specimen); who reports Callisthenes' guilt as a fact, without proof (not that there was any —except perhaps the word of a boy under torture); who ignores the *proskynesis* affair and the well-attested court intrigues (such as the influence of the unsavoury Bagoas: see *CQ* N.S. 8 (1958) 149 f.)—such a writer is, at least, practising a highly selective and purposeful reserve (see Strasburger, *op. cit.* 50 f.). And we have seen that he is fond enough of stories when they suit his purpose. Being a king, he could not afford to be caught out in a lie. That is probably the meaning of Arrian's notorious remark about his reason for trusting Ptolemy (*prooem.* 2), which has so often been used to convict Arrian of a *naïveté* that he never in fact shows, either in this sensible context or elsewhere in his work. What Arrian did not sufficiently consider (and in this many moderns, not gifted with the lucid historical sense of a Strasburger, have followed him) is that kings are perhaps more tempted than most others to indulge in lies in which they *cannot* be caught out.

The last substantial chapter deals with Clitarchus: the evidence is re-examined to show the solid basis for the orthodox conclusion that his work underlies Diodorus and much of Curtius. On his date, P. is inclined to follow Tarn, though he admits that some of

Tarn's arguments are poor and that there is no decisive evidence. He duly comes to grips with the two crucial pieces of 'direct evidence': Diodorus' reference (ii 7, 3) contrasting Ctesias with 'Clitarchus and some of those who later crossed to Asia with Alexander', and Pliny's list (*n.h.* iii 57 f.) of early Greek references to Rome, putting him (it seems) between Theopompus and Theophrastus. On the first point, P. suggests (229) that Diodorus thoughtlessly copied the phrase contrasting Ctesias with 'those who later crossed ... ' from Clitarchus, inserting Clitarchus' own name in the wrong place. This is artificial, unconvincing and unnecessary. It is simplest to take the passage *as it stands* to mean that Clitarchus and those who later (i.e. later than Ctesias, just mentioned) crossed ... disagreed with Ctesias. This implies, *prima facie*, that Diodorus did not include Clitarchus among those who were in Asia with Alexander; and he mentioned him first because he was such an important author. The passage implies nothing on Clitarchus' date. The Pliny passage is difficult to interpret, and I do not agree with P. that *hic iam plus quam ex fama* refers to Theophrastus: he has been named as the principal subject, and an inserted pronoun would dislocate the whole structure of the sentence.[9] The phrase must apply to Clitarchus, and it seems to mean that he wrote from his own knowledge and not from hearsay—i.e. that he saw the Roman envoys. But, of course, as P. says, Pliny's opinion on this is not worth much. P. advances some arguments (indecisive, as he rightly makes clear) for agreeing with Tarn's date. For the contrary view, see (e.g.) Strasburger, *BO* 9 (1952) 202 f., especially 208. No decision seems possible on any evidence yet advanced.

A chapter on minor writers of the Hellenistic period concludes the book. P. reiterates his rejection of the 'Ephemerides' (argued by him in *Historia* 4 (1955) 429 f.). This is his greatest contribution to scholarship on Alexander. The incubus of this supposed original source has weighed on students of the period too long. Even scholars of the calibre of Jacoby and Strasburger have suffered from the consequences, and C. A. Robinson's early 'biography' of this source is a monument of misdirected effort. P. is less categorical now (258 f.) than he was in his article just cited in rejecting all of Alexander's correspondence as fictitious; rightly so, since the fact that some letters are obvious forgeries does not support the conclusion that those that look all right must be forged: each case must be examined on its merits, and in some cases forgery can almost be ruled out. (See, e.g., Hamilton's remarks—not known to P.—on the letter to Craterus, Attalus and Alcetas, *CQ* N.S. 5 (1955) 219 f.)

Altogether this is a sound book and a useful one, especially to the teacher. P.'s common sense is salutary, and it is a pity that he was at times restrained by the pervasive influence of orthodoxy from following it through to a logical conclusion. Perhaps there is not much more than can be done in this much-tilled field: perhaps it would be better to direct more effort towards using the sources we have to full effect, relying on the achievement of the great *Quellenforscher* as not indeed a satisfactory basis, but the best we can hope to have. However, if any real progress can still be made in refining this instrument, it will have to start from careful work on the surviving sources (Curtius seems to offer the best prospects) rather than from a re-examination of the ultimate origins. Tarn attempted this, and the example may seem discouraging; but it was not the method that was necessarily at fault, but the arbitrary and prejudiced approach (see Strasburger's review, cited above). Perhaps P., some of whose best work is along these lines, will be able to turn to this.

NOTES

[1] Like the ancient writers whom he censures on this score, he should perhaps have made his general obligations more explicit. The only references to Jacoby in the Preface (there are none to Schwartz) are as to a collector of fragments. The greatest living (as he then was) expert on Greek historical writing should have rated a mention as an exception to the dubious statement that P.'s task 'has been attempted more frequently by students of history than by students of ancient literature'.

[1a] [See now E. Mensching, *Historia* 12 (1963) 274 ff.—lacking precision and consistency, but generally confirming my conclusions on Theophrastus and the 'Peripatetic tradition'.]

[2] The argument from Alexander's defying the weather merely shows the danger of the purely literary approach: far from being a peculiarity of Callisthenes' writing, this was a peculiarity of Alexander's character: the Indian monsoons, the heat of Gedrosia and the snows of the Cossaeans bear witness to it long after Callisthenes' death.

[3] Tarn, unlike P., clearly recognizes that Callisthenes never wanted to make Alexander a god (*Alexander* ii 362 *et al.*); yet in the *proskynesis* affair he speaks of Callisthenes' 'amazing volte-face'.

[4] Ch. Habicht, in his classic treatment of the subject (*Gottmenschentum und griech. Städte*), finds a few possible cases before Alexander, of which I can accept at most one (Lysander at Samos) as proven. (It is isolated and peculiar.) Alexander's importance

emerges from the fact that, in that exhaustive survey, 14 pages cover all these cases, 20 Alexander himself, while 90 pages collect later instances.

[5] Aristobulus and Chares are *thrice* cited as joint authorities (once by Plutarch: F 12); more important, they agree in substance on Callisthenes' death (F 15).

[6] See J. R. Hamilton, *PACA* 4 (1961) 8 f.

[7] We might add the story of the Amazon, if Plutarch has got it right; but Arrian's version is different and mentions no explicit denial by Ptolemy.

[8] That he did so is very likely, even though he only cites Ptolemy once (as he cites Clitarchus twice, this is indecisive). Strasburger (*op cit.* 6 f.) collected an array of parallels with Arrian, though he preferred to leave the explanation open. P. admits that Curtius is sometimes clearly based on Ptolemy (198). Once (190) he even goes so far as to suggest that Curtius must have quoted from Arrian—a view in which few will follow him nowadays. (On the date of Curtius, see now D. Korzeniewski, *Die Zeit des Q. Curtius Rufus*—unanswerable, at least, in its arguments against a post-Hadrianic date; [and cf. p. 263, below].) Curtius' sources need more careful investigation; though we cannot be sure that anything would come of it!

[9] [Pearson has reaffirmed his view in *Mnemosyne* S. 4, 15 (1962) 46 f.; but as he has not succeeded in finding parallel passages or in making the construction logically plausible, no further discussion is possible at this point.]

The Struggle for the Succession to Alexander the Great[*]

THE first and decisive stage in the disintegration of Alexander's empire was a favourite subject of discussion a generation ago: Beloch (balanced, as so often, between the brilliant and the eccentric), Schachermeyr, Ensslin, Schwahn, De Sanctis, Bengtson—even a selective roll-call demonstrates (if demonstration be needed) the importance and interest of those truly historic years. Yet since Bengtson's summing-up, 25 years ago (in vol. i of his *Strategie*), interest has faded and there has been no large-scale work on the period. We must be grateful to F. for producing one; and it is not surprising that it should be done by a pupil of Manni, whose school of research in early Hellenistic history is undoubtedly the most vigorous that is at present to be found.

After a brief introduction on Alexander's generals, three chapters are devoted to the arrangements at Babylon. The next two chapters take us to Triparadisus and Antipater's supremacy. Three more trace the decline, from Antipater's death to that of Eumenes. After a short Conclusion there follows a long Appendix on the sources, and a rather fussy Corrigenda. As in too many Italian works, there is no Bibliography or Index. The latter can perhaps be spared, in this case; the absence of the former is a major annoyance, particularly as the author uses 'op. cit.' to refer, for ever after, to any work once cited. Surely scholars and publishers should at last agree to stop this waste of the reader's time and strain on his patience!

The situation at Babylon was uncertain and dangerous. Alexander had refused to designate a successor; but, by giving his ring to Perdiccas (a detail we have no right to question), he had shown whom he meant to leave in charge. Perdiccas had *de facto* been *chiliarchus* since Hephaestion's death and thus controlled the apparatus of empire. Any other choice by the King would have

[*] Maria José Fontana, *Le lotte per la successione di Alessandro Magno dal 323 al 315.* Palermo 1960.

meant instant civil war. As it was, with the dying King's blessing to bolster possession of power, Perdiccas was impregnable. No one could think of attacking him. Curtius (x 6, 18) gives us a great scene in which Perdiccas pretends to refuse the task:

'haerebat inter cupiditatem pudoremque et, quo modestius quod spectabat adpeteret, peruicacius oblaturos esse credebat.'

The picture of the dynast eager for power, but pretending hesitancy, is prepared by the author's own reflection:

'sed maior moles erat quam ut unus subire eam posset' (x 5, 37).

That picture is not painted for us by any other source. It should surely be obvious that its inspiration is to be sought in Roman history. G. V. Sumner[1] has recently revived, with persuasive arguments, the view that the historian Curtius is identical with the *nouus homo* of Tacitus *ann.* xi 20 f. and Pliny *ep.* vii 27, and with the rhetorician of Suetonius *de rhet.* (Index): his *History of Alexander* would be written under Gaius and Claudius. Sumner would put his quaestorship about A.D. 15, but one may safely suggest a date of birth about 15 B.C. and a quaestorship before Augustus' death. Present in the Senate on a historic occasion, he later could not help seeing the succession to Alexander in terms of that to Augustus, with Perdiccas cast for the part of Tiberius: with his eye for political reality, Curtius saw real similarity through constitutional differences.

All this, involving (as it does) questions that range from Alexander to Tacitus, cannot be developed here. But it is clear that Curtius, like Tacitus, tends to overstress alternative candidates for power: the other sources show us that Perdiccas, like Tiberius, was in fact unchallenged and unchallengeable. It is possible that the ill-advised Meleager tried—unsuccessfully—to turn the soldiers' dissatisfaction against the *chiliarchus*; but the actual point of the dissatisfaction was quite different: it was the danger of a vacant throne. F. believes (23), following indications in Curtius, that 'the principal cause was opposition to Perdiccas, thought guilty of aiming at the throne'. This mistakes the whole character of the situation: we have no good reason to believe that such fears were a prominent factor.

F. next proceeds to disbelieve the feeble-mindedness of Arrhidaeus. This is said to be misrepresentation due to Hieronymus of Cardia; in fact the prince was merely 'weak or perhaps ill' (33).

From this it follows that a guardianship was unnecessary. F. is right in stressing that there was no legal guardianship dispensing the King from signing documents (or, perhaps more accurately, sealing them): Polyperchon's 'freedom of the Greeks' and (of epigraphical documents) the Eresus decree (*OGIS* 8, lines 95 f.) were issued in Philip's name. But this was legal fiction. Not only was Arrhidaeus the only male Argead left alive by Alexander (which is strong evidence), but we always find him, in his brief reign, in someone else's power. He never acts independently of a noble or his own ambitious wife; in fact, someone is always in charge of him. F. has difficulty in explaining away, e.g., the '*epimeletae* of the Kings' appointed after Perdiccas' death ('soltanto un modo di dire geronimiano') and has to mistranslate *epimeletes* as 'ministro'.

F. rightly notes that Philip III alone was regarded as King and believes that Alexander IV was his designated successor. This may well be true. But it is rash actually to deny that the infant had a royal title or to accuse Hieronymus of merely inventing this. In view of the state of our sources, we cannot be sure either that he consistently spoke of 'the Kings' or that no one else did. Perhaps the legal position after the compromise of Babylon was less clear and satisfactory than scholars would wish. It was, as has recently been said (by R. H. Simpson, *Historia* 6 (1957) 372), a time of 'political make-believe and pretence, where legality is obscure'.

This brings us to the central problem of the Babylon settlement: the position of Craterus. Beloch was the first to read into the sources the view that Craterus was appointed to a position (perhaps called *prostasia*) superior to that of Perdiccas: only after the Cappadocian campaign did Perdiccas assume the highest office, thereby forcing Craterus into defensive action. This view (often basically accepted since) leads to some odd consequences. As Schwahn succinctly put it (*Klio* 23 (1930) 212), it means 'dass ... zum Regenten ein Abwesender bestellt wird, der voraussichtlich das Amt noch auf längere Zeit nicht ausüben kann und tatsächlich nie ausgeübt hat'. Nor is Perdiccas' 'arrogation' as such attested. Diodorus (xviii 23) tells us that, when still insecure, Perdiccas had wooed Nicaea in order to gain the favour of her father Antipater; but after gaining control of the royal forces, he began (at first secretly) to aim higher and to consider marriage to

Cleopatra, Alexander's sister. This comment follows the Cappadocian campaign—the time when the two princesses first appear on the scene. But Diodorus mentions no constitutional change, no arrogation of *prostasia*, then or at any other time. In fact, according to him (xviii 2, 4) Perdiccas was given the highest post at Babylon, where Craterus is not mentioned. Though secure at Babylon itself, Perdiccas was still insecure as long as the attitude of the absent generals was undeclared. It was clearly then that he sought Antipater's support—chiefly, we may surmise, against Craterus. When it became clear that Craterus would not move, he began to think of Cleopatra. The point when he gained secure control of the royal forces, incidentally, is mentioned at the end of xviii 4. Perhaps it was as early as this that he approached Cleopatra, if indeed (as Diodorus implies) he was responsible for her arrival in Asia at the time of the Cappadocian campaign.

At Babylon, Perdiccas was, for the moment, impregnable. His chief enemy Meleager looked for a pretext to attack the man who had Alexander's ring and the reins of power. He had an excellent one ready-made: the proposal to leave the kingdom temporarily without a king, though quite probably made in good faith (since no one had much to fear from Arrhidaeus), was constitutionally absurd and exacerbated the mutual suspicions that Alexander had taken care to sow. It was not insisted on. With the acceptance of the compromise, the turbulent could be eliminated. What, then, of Craterus? He had been sent to supersede Antipater, but, for obvious reasons (see *JHS* 81 (1961) 34 f.), had preferred to wait in Cilicia. There, at Alexander's death, he was stranded. F. insists (48 f.) on the ferocity and nationalism of the 10,000 Macedonians whom Craterus was leading home: had Craterus been dissatisfied, he could have marched on Babylon with them. But we may wonder whether most of them would have followed him. Long eager to return home, they had already had to wait (with their rich gifts) for months, owing to political developments that must have been unintelligible to them. Would they have marched right back, against the man who had Alexander's ring? F., while eager to expose Hieronymus' bias, does not notice the sources' patent exaggeration of Craterus' popularity, for the greater glory of his conqueror Eumenes.[2] We know how difficult it was, for a long time, to make Macedonians fight against their brothers. Craterus

S

had to take the consequences of his unfortunate absence. Perdiccas, whom Curtius saw (albeit with exaggeration) as the true successor to Alexander's empire, would never have accepted subordination to him.

It is Beloch's excessive ingenuity that has created this problem. The sources (tabulated by F. 38) say nothing of the kind, with one exception. Indeed, Diodorus, Curtius and Appian agree in omitting Craterus; Justin puts him (we do not know why) in charge of the royal exchequer. Only Arrian and Dexippus (based on him), both in Photius' summary, mention the notorious *prostasia*. Dexippus alone calls it the highest Macedonian honour. F. attributes the definition to Hieronymus (completely contradicting the later analysis of the sources of the extant writers—on which, see below). On this view, the omission of Craterus in the other accounts becomes inexplicable. Unfortunately scholars of the third century A.D. were no less given to embroidery of what they did not know than some of our own age; and we do not even possess Dexippus' own text.

It is doubtful whether a certain interpretation can ever be found, where an odd statement has seen contraction and expansion by several hands before reaching us. Clearly a post of sorts was found for Craterus: he could not be ignored. But there is little point in following F. in an elaborate search for the meanings of *prostasia*. The silence of most of the sources is supported by the logic of the situation. In fact, F. ends up by making it 'a dignity devoid of power'—for the simple reason that there are no powers left that can be assigned to Craterus or that he in fact exercised. This definition of the (imagined) highest dignity in the empire is the *reductio ad absurdum* of Beloch's view and should suffice to kill it. Giving the Macedonians a figure-head president *as well as* two kings and a prime minister, it beautifully illustrates Schwahn's dictum that this whole line of argument 'lässt sich wohl im Studierzimmer theoretisch ausdenken, praktisch aber nicht durchführen'. Schwahn's own suggestion is still the most attractive (*Klio* 24 (1931) 324 f.): Arrian's context makes it likely that Craterus' assignment was to Macedonia, where (of course) Alexander had sent him. There were few of the men of Babylon who would dislike the prospect of his arguing it out with Antipater: being absent, neither of these two could speak up for himself.

F. ascribes the break-up of the empire chiefly to Antigonus' ambitious machinations. This is surely a little naïve. The insecure position of Craterus and, in consequence, perhaps of Antipater is as well attested as (e.g.) Craterus' failure to accede to Antipater's urgent request for much-needed aid in the Lamian War or, for that matter, the early ambitions of Leonnatus (Plut. *Eum.* 3—not negligible, even if exaggerated). F. carries the fashionable denigration of Hieronymus to extremes. Yet he, though writing at Antigonus' court, did not hesitate to expose Antigonus' ambitions. The facts make it clear that we need not distrust his indictment of the others. Loyalty—to one another or the throne—had never been a characteristic of Macedonian nobles, and Alexander had done little to encourage it. With the terror of his presence removed, the law of the jungle could resume its sway.

It would take too long to do what F. essentially fails to do: to follow the early relations among the great dynasts from Babylon to Triparadisus as far as the sources permit. Much work still remains to be done here, by someone less concerned with the legal cloak than with the naked political reality. After Triparadisus things become a little easier. F. (76 f.) has less difficulty with this settlement, though the *prostasia* still spooks about the scene; and there is still too much of the foredoomed attempt to form a legally tidy picture, in the light of incompetent third-hand literary accounts, of a situation based on pure power-politics. But the facts now become plain. F. recognizes (following Schachermeyr) that, by entrusting the Kings to Antigonus, Antipater intended to give up supreme authority, but that he changed his mind when Cassander aroused his suspicions of Antigonus. Antipater never showed any interest in Asia and clearly held on to the Kings' persons merely to be safe in Macedon. With this secured, it did not matter if Antigonus called himself 'general of Asia'.

The remaining years are less encumbered with modern speculation, and here, more often alone with the sources, F. is much more at ease and has a great deal of interest to say. Of particular value is the application of a chronological grid—in the manner of F.'s teacher—to the events of Polyperchon's regency. An interesting study of the development of Polyperchon's plans emerges: the 'freedom of the Greeks' comes soon after Antipater's death, the invitation to Olympias several months later. And this is correlated with the fortunes of the war in Asia. The result seems an advance on the most recent of F.'s predecessors, Lenschau in *RE*, s.v. 'Polyperchon', coll. 1800 f., where the sequence of events is ignored. But F. still fails to explain the mysterious turning-point of the period: Cassander's success in stealing the army away from Alexander's mother and son. Polyperchon's failure to prevent this *tour de force*, even more than his inglorious later career, defeats any attempt to credit him with real political or military skill (against Beloch and Lenschau) or to see him as the 'leader' (92) of a traditionally minded Macedonian party. Of course, the form of the famous proclamation shows him *trying* to gain their support by appealing to Philip II and Alexander. But we do not know of any garrison commanders who went home as a result, and it is clear that Cassander's 'tough' policy towards the Greeks had the support of his compatriots: even Philip V was to get into trouble with his nobles for phil-Hellenism. The policy that failed to gain Greece for Polyperchon must have helped to lose him Macedon; but F. is debarred from seeing it.

The last substantive chapter traces the struggle of Eumenes and Antigonus. This is correlated with events in Europe. Again there is much of interest here: such correlation, not attempted in our sources, is essential for a proper understanding. But not all of F.'s arguments can be accepted. Thus, it is true (133) that the death of Philip III (October 317, according to F—but the precision is a little artificial, and we do not really know the date of the actual execution or of its public announcement) was not officially known in Babylon on the 1st Nisan (March–April) following: the year 316/15 begins as the eighth of Philip III. Whatever the reason for this, it seems impossible to believe that Eumenes did not hear of it until the *late summer* of 316, when, to encourage his army, he composed the 'false letter' of Diodorus xix 23. This document, despite F.'s elaborate argument, in fact presupposes that both Eumenes and his men were well informed of what had been happening in Macedon up to a recent past: knowing of Cassander's invasion, it *a fortiori* implies knowledge of Philip's death; and indeed, he is not mentioned in it. Its starting-point is clearly the state of affairs after Cassander's attack on the victorious Olympias and Polyperchon, and before the outcome of that action was known.

All this part of F.'s system will have to be given up. However, the method itself, properly applied, should help to overcome the usual tendency to treat the movements of Antigonus and Eumenes as a self-contained story.

After a Conclusion summarizing the results, an Appendix almost as long as the whole text discusses the sources. A diagram (237) summarizes F.'s views: all our main immediate sources are derived, in varying proportions, from both Hieronymus of Cardia and Duris, who himself uses both Hieronymus and others. The sole exception is Curtius, who uses Duris only. Schwahn, in what was hitherto the fullest discussion (*Klio* 23 (1930)), thought Diodorus pure Hieronymus and therefore best; Curtius and Justin pure Duris and therefore worst; and the others mixed and in between. His investigation was not sufficiently detailed to give firm support to his thesis. But it is remarkable how close F.'s conclusions, based on a thorough survey worthy of a pupil of Manni, turn out to be to the intuitions of a fine scholar working by mere sampling. F.'s most important contribution is the rehabilitation of the *Einquellenprinzip* (recently shaken for other parts of his work) for books xviii–xx of Diodorus: after xviii 1–4 (probably Duris), he reproduces Hieronymus as best he can. Though one could argue about points of detail, F. seems to be right in that Diodorus has nothing that cannot be from Hieronymus and much that must be. This is surely as near real proof as we can hope to get. On Arrian and Plutarch, F.'s conclusions are, in general, the same as Schwahn's; though the latter made more adequate allowance for the unfortunate roles of Dexippus and Photius in producing our version of Arrian. On the other hand, F. duly notes the part of Justin in creating our version of Trogus; but whoever is to blame for it, there is not much of use in this account, and F. perhaps lays too much stress on what has, somehow or other, come from Hieronymus—not all of it certain. Finally Curtius: here there is much more to be done. This was the weakest part of Schwahn's work: he almost equated him with Justin. F. takes no notice of this (rightly), but still postulates an *Einquellenprinzip* (Duris). This is ill-advised and embodies the abuses that have made this principle suspect nowadays. It is based (210 f.) on nothing better than the fact that Curtius has some elements of Hieronymus and some of various other authors (not all can be identified), all of it welded into a highly personal and sophisticated interpretation. It is an advance on previous work that the fact has at last been recognized. But F. then follows the textbook vice of ascribing this interpretation to a (to us) shadowy predecessor whose work is lost, rather than to the Roman senator whose life and work we know.

In this, as in the main part of the work, F. has suffered from excess of learning and immaturity of judgment. Scholars a generation ago—even the greatest of them—often tended to construct elaborate legal edifices to house relatively simple historical situations—or so it often seems to us now. In many fields the history of scholarship in the last few decades has been that of a sharp reaction. If this has at times gone too far, that must be corrected. But the return from the study to real life has surely been healthy. Unfortunately F., reopening a discussion that was vigorously pursued a generation ago and has since been dormant, and knowing the literature with enviable thoroughness, has been unable to get away from the old idiom and the old categories. It is worth mentioning that those whom F. follows have not stood still: Schachermeyr's *Alexander*, for instance, shows a very different approach from that of his early work on this period—which F. now imitates. Yet this is a welcome book: the thorough discussion of the sources supersedes much vague talk and much partial and distorted presentation, and will provide a firm basis for future work. Manni's chronological methods have been put to good use and will yield further results. It is a pity that F., overwhelmed by much learning, was unable to arrive at a significant historical interpretation of a crucial period in world history.

NOTES

[1] In an important but inaccessible article: *AUMLA* 15 (May 1961) 30 f. The view had not been popular lately. (See, however, Syme, *Tacitus* ii 563, n. 1, *obiter*.)

[2] Schubert long ago noticed this fantastic exaggeration (in his *Quellen z. Gesch. d. Diadochenzeit* (1914)), ascribing it to Duris.

The Political Thought of Sallust[*]

A MAJOR work on Sallust has long been almost an annual event. This one differs from most in being short, unencumbered by long summaries of predecessors, and in English. The aim is 'the eluci- dation of the main ideas which Sallust adopted as a foundation for his work'; style, historical accuracy and biography are treated only where relevant.

Chapter 1 shows that the prooemia to the two monographs define Sallust's principal ideas and vocabulary in the field dis- cussed. They also state his theory of the decline of Rome after the destruction of Carthage. The ideas are not original, and their sources cannot be clearly determined; but they are more closely related to the Roman aristocratic tradition than to Greek thought.

The next two chapters discuss the aristocratic ideal of *uirtus* and compare Sallust's with it. *Virtus* was traditionally displayed by public service, but also denoted a certain standard in performing this, as well as the qualities that would make such service possible. The Roman ethical vocabulary is centred on public life, and *uirtus* is cumulatively hereditary in a family. For Sallust, *ingenium* (good or bad) is the criterion as between *uirtus* and various vices (notably *ambitio*, which is closest to it.) His *uirtus* is not limited to public service by Romans; yet in practice such service is still its most important aspect. However, he refuses (like his Marius) to accept hereditary as opposed to personal distinction as a merit. This is essentially the view of the *nouus homo* of his age. It is also one (but only one) ingredient of Cicero's thought.

Chapter 4 investigates Sallust's view of the moral crisis at Rome. 146 B.C. is, for him, the starting-point of the decline; his prede- cessors, on the whole, had put it earlier. The oversimplified view of the monographs (with full *concordia* down to 146) is slightly modified in the *Histories*, where *maxima concordia* is claimed only for the half-century preceding that date. His idealized view forces him to postdate the appearance of *luxuria* (only with the return of

* D. C. Earl, *The Political Thought of Sallust*. Cambridge: University Press 1961.

Sulla!) and to ignore some other relevant facts of history, which were common knowledge. Scipio Nasica's well-known argument against the elder Cato provided Sallust with his convenient turning-point: the end of *metus hostilis*. The crisis of the late Republic is seen entirely in moral terms: *ambitio* leads the nobles to oppress the people, who then over-assert their *libertas* when they have the chance.

The next three chapters discuss the *Jugurtha*, the *Catiline* and the *Histories*. E. shows in detail how Sallust's ideas are worked out in the monographs. The *Catiline* describes the fully-developed moral degeneration; the *Jugurtha* is intended to show an earlier (pre-Sullan) stage of it: hence the stress on *auaritia* (70). Metellus and Marius illustrate the imperfection, in that age, of even the best of *nobiles* and *noui homines*: Metellus, after restoring *concordia* for a short time by his *uirtus*, shows himself guilty of *superbia*; Marius, after a perfect start, lapses into *ambitio* (71 f.). Once guilty of these vices, neither gets fair treatment from Sallust. This explains, *inter alia*, his stress on supernatural assistance for Marius. As for the *Catiline*, the view that it was meant as a defence of Caesar deservedly gets short shrift. Catiline typifies the fully corrupt noble of the post-Sullan age. Sallust knows that, with Pompey's victorious army in the East, the conspiracy had no chance of lasting success. But to him it illustrates the naked and unprincipled struggle for power—a 'disorderly scramble' (103)— and the perversion of moral and political terms into mere catch-words (93 f.). The speeches and *syncrisis* of Caesar and Cato are discussed at length, and E. shows that Cato emerges as the victor —indeed, he is 'a man out of his time' (101), consciously depicted as recalling his great ancestor. Of the *Histories* too little is known for serious analysis; but what we have shows that Sallust had not changed his mind on essentials.

A Conclusion sums up the chief results. E. argues that the view of 'the failure of the Roman Republic in terms of the degeneration of *virtus* has a certain validity' (113). But, in the *Jugurtha* much more than in the *Catiline*, Sallust's theory leads him into over-simplification and distortion. It seems that, after isolating the presence of *concordia* before 146 as the chief difference between that age and his own, and believing *concordia* necessarily connected with *uirtus*, he was driven into artificially arranging convenient intermediate stages of degeneration. Finally, Sallust's own position is one of disillusionment: it is not mere chance that his favourite authors appear to be Thucydides and the elder Cato.

There is a Bibliography and an Index. The latter is the chief blemish on the book: its quality is summed up in the fact that it has no entry for Cicero. The Preface is dated January 1st, 1959. This kind of delay (*experto credite!*) appears to be the rule rather than the exception in British publishing and deserves public execration.

Perhaps attention should be drawn to something that is not there: the *Letters to Caesar* are not discussed. A footnote (4) states the author's belief that *ep.* 2 is certainly and *ep.* 1 probably spurious. This will arouse outraged protests, even though the solid acceptance of those compositions in Germany and Italy has recently shown signs of cracking. (La Penna and Drexler have suspended judgment.) However, there is no real need for excitement. The intensity of discussion has tended to obscure the unimportance of its subject, and 50 pages of Büchner did not extract much from the *Letters* that cannot be got out of the historical works.

Not much, in details of interpretation, will strike the reader as new: not much that is new can by now be said about Sallust, and there is no point in tracing every idea to predecessors. Basically, E. accepts (but does not argue) the view of Pöschl and others, that political thought in Rome was confined to belief in simple ethical values. There is little doubt that this is essentially true. But E.'s Sallust is not a mere mouthpiece for *mos maiorum*. We are familiar with a Sallust who is a Pure Artist or a Party Politician; a Sallust who is a Greek Philosopher (of various schools) or a Romantic *Geschichtsphilosoph*; we have just had—within a few months, and presented with equally magistral vituperation for the non-believer— a Sallust who is practically an epic poet and a Sallust who is a bourgeois democrat, the product of social-economic forces. It is refreshing to find, presented without fuss or rhetoric, a Sallust who is a Roman *nouus homo* of his age (with a few simple, but sincerely held, ideas), yet an individual and not a type or puppet. Of the terrifying array of writers on Sallust, few have thus placed him against his social background, without making him a product of mechanical forces.

What emerges is clearly not tidy or consistent. If Sallust saw *concordia* as the chief distinguishing mark of his idealized early second century (a view close to that of R. E. Smith in our own day, and—as E. notes—up to a point a useful one), why should this make him ignore the evidence for *ambitio, auaritia* and *luxuria*, evidence which his age knew better than we do? E. can only suggest that Sallust thought *concordia* necessarily connected with *uirtus*. But this crucial connection is nowhere made explicit. Sallust (as E. helps to remind us) was not a deep thinker: he operated with commonplaces which (however sincerely felt) act as a *substitute* for thought, and he cared for consistency no more than for accuracy. Though his Greek philosophical reading can be traced easily enough, it is clear that Sallust profited little by it, and E. is right to ignore this much-debated subject. Again, if E. is anything but clear on *ingenium* (is it, e.g., innate or moulded, *hexis* or *energeia*?), the muddle is surely Sallust's: he never thinks about the meanings of his basic terms. Perhaps this pervasive philosophical incompetence should have been more explicitly recognized. As it is, E. seems to saddle himself with some of the blame. Within his sensible framework, he still leans towards the myth of 'Sallust the thinker': hence, e.g., the strange attempt (10) to distinguish between *animus* and *anima* (in fact mere stylistic variants: most clearly seen *b.J.* 2, 1); hence the rare instance of apologetic scholasticism. Thus *b.C.* 10–11, self-contradictory on whether *auaritia* or *ambitio* came first in Rome's decline, cannot be saved by playing with words (14: 'although *avaritia* came first, it was *ambitio* which first tormented men's minds'). Sallust's 'time-table' of the decline, so clearly expounded by E., is a fraud. The *Jugurtha* shows that he knew quite well how both *auaritia* and *ambitio* were there all the time. For that matter, *luxuria* is rampant long before Sulla's return: Marius attacks (*b.J.* 85, 40 f.) the nobles' *munditiae, supellex* and sexual licence.

Sallust's general treatment of the crisis is naïvely schematic— a warning to all those who want to fit history 'scientifically' into simple *a priori* generalizations. It is quite likely (as E. argues) that the subjects of the two monographs were chosen to illustrate two 'stages' of the decline. But, except for the trite observation that things are worse in the *Catiline* than in the *Jugurtha*, there is no sign of any consistent attempt to illustrate a graduated deterioration. In fact, the later 'stage' has, what the earlier lacks, two examples (Cato and Caesar) of real *uirtus*! Nor, alas, is this due to Sallust's being so great a historian that the truth bursts through the strait-jacket of theory. Neither distortion nor factual errors can be denied, any more than his philosophical incompetence. But, just as Schur's glorious failure did not suffice to discourage the systematizers, so there will no doubt continue to be apologists who will explain away, or at least make light of, the summary of Marius's early career[1] or the meeting at the house of Laeca,[2] and perhaps even the treatment of M. Scaurus—if on no other grounds, then by invoking a 'bohrende Wahrheitssuche' (Büchner) beyond caring for mere facts. Yet it can be shown (see, e.g., La Penna's treatment—though he would not put it in these terms) both that Sallust is not above distortion when it suits his purpose, and that there are many errors not thus explicable. He is no Toynbee or Mashkin, and we are now far from the days when scholars like Schwartz, De Sanctis and von Fritz gave him credit for malignant and purposeful consistency.

Great stylist he undoubtedly was; yet even here, as in qualities we might regard as more important in a historian, his merits have probably been exaggerated through the accident of survival. His chief claim is perhaps that he created a (for Rome) new kind of historical writing. This, after being responsible for some of the worse as for some of the better elements in Livy (let us not forget that Livy agreed with him in the idealization of *concordia*, with —in part—similar consequences), ultimately gave us Tacitus. E.'s little book, pleasant to read and (without boring paraphrase) in constant touch with Sallust's actual writings, will be beneficial in enabling the reader daunted by modern Sallustian mythography to penetrate behind the smoke-screen and make up his mind on the facts.

NOTES

[1] Even La Penna (*Giug.* 52) partly excuses this as due to Sallust's mere 'failure to inform himself'. Yet all his sources must have had the facts; and had he really not read the *pro Plancio* (§ 51)?

[2] See La Penna's excellent discussion (*Cat.* 20 f.).

Index

This index lists all names of persons mentioned more than once, and of those mentioned once if anything of interest is said about them, as well as a generous selection of geographical names; though, for obvious reasons, there is no entry for 'Rome'. In the case of geographical names, the name of a country or city is meant to include that of its inhabitants—e.g., for 'Aetolia' read (where required by the sense) 'Aetolians' or 'Aetolian League'. Roman personal names are listed under *nomina*, arranged as in *The Magistrates of the Roman Republic*, with women and families in their alphabetical places; Greek names are Latinized. Writers discussed as such are listed under their familiar English names (e.g. 'Sallust'); but M. Tullius Cicero, being also an actor in the story, has had to go under his *nomen*. The fact that footnotes have become end-notes naturally causes a little difficulty. In general, where the name concerned is mentioned in the note, only the page reference is given and the reader will be able to find the note for himself. Where the name is not mentioned in the note, a precise reference to the note has been given; but these cases have been listed only where the note contains some discussion. All dates, unless otherwise marked, are B.C. It is hoped that the indexing, particularly of the prosopographical articles, will increase their usefulness to the reader and help to connect the different studies. The essay on Ancient Alexandria, which was intended for light reading, has not been indexed.

T